Contents

Mazda 626 1600 LX

Mazda 626 Owners Workshop Manual

by Larry Warren and John H Haynes

Member of the Guild of Motoring Writers

Models covered:

Mazda 626 front-wheel-drive
1600 LX Saloon & Hatchback; 1587 cc
2000 GLX Saloon, Hatchback & Coupe; 1998 cc

Does not cover fuel injection or Turbo conversions

ABCDE
FGHIJ
KLMNO
PQRST

Haynes Publishing Group
Sparkford Nr Yeovil
Somerset BA22 7JJ England

Haynes Publications, Inc
861 Lawrence Drive
Newbury Park
California 91320 USA

Acknowledgements

We are grateful for the help and cooperation of the Mazda Motor Company for their assistance with technical information, certain illustrations and vehicle photos, and the Champion Sparking Plug Company who supplied the illustrations of various spark plug conditions.

A book in the **Haynes Owners Workshop Manual Series**

Printed by J. H. Haynes & Co., Ltd, Sparkford, Nr. Yeovil, Somerset BA22 7JJ, England

ISBN 0 85696 929 X

British Library Cataloguing in Publication Data
Warren, Larry
  Mazda 626 (Front-wheel-drive) owner's workshop manual.–
  (Owner's Workshop Manuals)
  1. Mazda automobile
  I. Title   II. Series
  629.28'722   TL215.M39
  ISBN 0 85696 929 X

About this manual

Its purpose

The purpose of this manual is to help you get the best value from your vehicle. It can do so in several ways. It can help you decide what work must be done, even if you choose to have it done by a dealer service department or a repair shop; it provides information and procedures for routine maintenance and servicing; and it offers diagnostic and repair procedures to follow when trouble occurs.

It is hoped that you will use the manual to tackle the work yourself. For many simpler jobs, doing it yourself may be quicker than arranging an appointment to get the vehicle into a shop and making the trips to leave it and pick it up. More importantly, a lot of money can be saved by avoiding the expense the shop must pass on to you to cover its labor and overhead costs. An added benefit is the sense of satisfaction and accomplishment that you feel after having done the job yourself.

Using the manual

The manual is divided into Chapters. Each Chapter is divided into numbered Sections, which are headed in bold type between horizontal lines. Each Section consists of consecutively numbered paragraphs (sometimes called Steps).

The two types of illustrations used (figures and photographs), are referenced by a number preceding their caption. Figure reference numbers denote Chapter and numerical sequence within the Chapter; (i.e. Fig. 3.4 means Chapter 3, figure number 4). Figure captions are followed by a Section number which ties the figure to a specific portion of the text. All photographs apply to the Chapter in which they appear and the reference number pinpoints the pertinent Section and paragraph; i.e., 3.2 means Section 3, paragraph 2.

Procedures, once described in the text, are not normally repeated. When it is necessary to refer to another Chapter, the reference will be given as Chapter and Section number i.e. Chapter 1/16). Cross references given without use of the word "Chapter" apply to Sections and/or paragraphs in the same Chapter. For example, "see Section 8" means in the same Chapter.

Reference to the left or right side of the vehicle is based on the assumption that one is sitting in the driver's seat, facing forward.

References to the front and rear of the engine usually mean the pulley and flywheel ends respectively, rather than vehicle front and rear.

Even though extreme care has been taken during the preparation of this manual, neither the publisher nor the author can accept responsibility for any errors in, or omissions from, the information given.

Note for UK readers

This book was written in the USA. Due allowance must be made for differences in terminology — see the Glossary — and in some working practices. There are also some differences between UK and USA specification vehicles, and where known these have been pointed out.

NOTE

A **Note** provides information necessary to properly complete a procedure or information which will make the steps to be followed easier to understand.

CAUTION

A **Caution** indicates a special procedure or special steps which must be taken in the course of completing the procedure in which the **Caution** is found which are necessary to avoid damage to the assembly being worked on.

WARNING

A **Warning** indicates a special procedure or special steps which must be taken in the course of completing the procedure in which the **Warning** is found which are necessary to avoid injury to the person performing the procedure.

Introduction to the Mazda 626

These models are available in 2-door coupe, 4-door sedan and 4-door liftback body styles and feature four coil suspension and front wheel drive.

The cross-mounted four cylinder engine is equipped with a conventional carburetor. The engine drives the front wheels through a choice of either a 4-speed or 5-speed manual transaxle or a 3-speed automatic transaxle. The rack and pinion steering gear is mounted behind the engine.

The brakes are disc at the front and drum-type at the rear, with vacuum servo assist as standard equipment.

1985 Mazda 626 coupe

General dimensions

Overall dimensions (approx)

Length	174.4 in (4.430 m)
Width	66.5 in (1.690 m)
Height	
2-door models, 1.6 litre	53.1 in (1.350 m)
2-door models, 2.0 litre	53.7 in (1.365 m)
4-door models, 1.6 litre	54.9 in (1.395 m)
4-door models, 2.0 litre	55.5 in (1.410 m)

Vehicle identification numbers

Modifications are a continuing and unpublicized process in vehicle manufacturing. Since spare parts manuals and lists are compiled on a numerical basis, the individual vehicle numbers are essential to correctly identify the component required.

Vehicle identification number (VIN)

This very important identification number is located on a plate attached to the top left corner of the dashboard of all US vehicles. The VIN is also stamped on the firewall in the engine compartment and on the adjacent body identification tag. The VIN also appears on the Vehicle Certificate of Title and Registration. It contains valuable information such as where and when the vehicle was manufactured, the model year and the body style.

Engine identification numbers

The engine identification numbers are stamped on the cylinder block below the number one spark plug, adjacent to the alternator.

Transaxle numbers

The transaxle ID numbers are stamped on a label affixed to the bellhousing, below the rear of the cylinder head.

Alternator numbers

The alternator numbers are located on a tag affixed to the housing.

Vehicle Emissions Control Information label (not UK models)

The Emissions Control Information label is attached to the underside of the hood.

Engine information labels (not UK models)

The vacuum hose routing, recommended lubricant and drivebelt checking adjustment procedure diagram labels are all located on the underside of the hood (photo).

Body identification

The body identification tag is attached to the engine compartment firewall.

Tire pressures (UK models)

Recommended tire pressures will be found on a label attached to the driver's door jamb.

On US models the Vehicle Identification Number (VIN) is located on the driver's side of the dashboard and is visible through the windshield

The VIN number can also be found stamped on the engine compartment firewall (A) and the body identification plate (B)

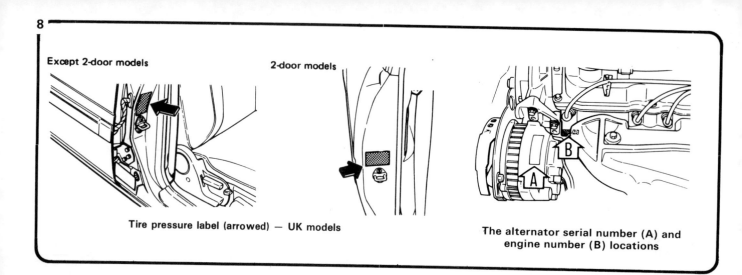

Except 2-door models

2-door models

Tire pressure label (arrowed) — UK models

The alternator serial number (A) and engine number (B) locations

The Vehicle Emissions Control Information label (US models only) is located on the hood near the latch hook

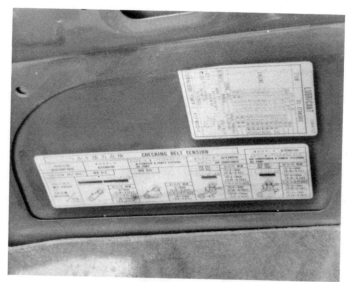

The recommended lubricant and engine drivebelt information labels can be found on the underside of the hood (US models only)

Buying parts

Replacement parts are available from many sources, which generally fall into one of two categories — authorized dealer parts departments and independent retail auto parts stores. Our advice concerning these parts is as follows:

Authorized dealer parts department: This is the best source for parts which are unique to your vehicle and not generally available elsewhere such as major engine parts, transaxle parts, trim pieces, etc. It is also the only place you should buy parts if your vehicle is still under warranty, as non-factory parts may invalidate the warranty. To be sure of obtaining the correct parts, have your engine and chassis numbers available and, if possible, take the old parts along for positive identification.

Retail auto parts stores: Good auto parts stores will stock frequently needed components which wear out relatively fast such as clutch components, exhaust systems, brake parts, tune-up parts, etc. These stores often supply new or reconditioned parts on an exchange basis, which can save a considerable amount of money. Discount auto parts stores are often very good places to buy materials and parts needed for general vehicle maintenance such as oil, grease, filters, spark plugs, belts, touch up paint, bulbs, etc. They also usually sell tools and general accessories, have convenient hours, charge lower prices, and can often be found not far from your home.

Maintenance techniques, tools and working facilities

Maintenance techniques

There are a number of techniques involved in maintenance and repair that will be referred to throughout this manual. Application of these techniques will enable the home mechanic to be more efficient, better organized and capable of performing the various tasks properly, which will ensure that the repair job is thorough and complete.

Fasteners

Fasteners are nuts, bolts, studs and screws used to hold two or more parts together. There are a few things to keep in mind when working with fasteners. Almost all of them use a locking device of some type, either a lockwasher, locknut, locking tab or thread adhesive. All threaded fasteners should be clean and straight, with undamaged threads and undamaged corners on the hex head where the wrench fits. Develop the habit of replacing all damaged nuts and bolts with new ones. Special locknuts with nylon or fiber inserts can only be used once. If they are removed, they lose their locking ability and must be replaced with new ones.

Rusted nuts and bolts should be treated with a penetrating fluid to ease removal and prevent breakage. Some mechanics use turpentine in a spout-type oil can, which works quite well. After applying the rust penetrant, let it work for a few minutes before trying to loosen the nut or bolt. Badly rusted fasteners may have to be chiseled or sawed off or removed with a special nut breaker, available at tool stores.

If a bolt or stud breaks off in an assembly, it can be drilled and removed with a special tool commonly available for this purpose. Most automotive machine shops can perform this task, as well as other repair procedures, such as the repair of threaded holes that have been stripped out.

Flat washers and lockwashers, when removed from an assembly, should always be replaced exactly as removed. Replace any damaged washers with new ones. Never use a lockwasher on any soft metal surface (such as aluminum), thin sheet metal or plastic.

Fastener sizes

For a number of reasons, automobile manufacturers are making wider and wider use of metric fasteners. Therefore, it is important to be able to tell the difference between standard (sometimes called USS or SAE) and metric hardware, since they cannot be interchanged.

All bolts, whether standard or metric, are sized according to diameter, thread pitch and length. For example, a standard 1/2 — 13 x 1 bolt is 1/2 inch in diameter, has 13 threads per inch and is 1 inch long. An M12 — 1.75 x 25 metric bolt is 12 mm in diameter, has a thread pitch of 1.75 mm (the distance between threads) and is 25 mm long. The two bolts are nearly identical, and easily confused, but they are not interchangeable.

In addition to the differences in diameter, thread pitch and length, metric and standard bolts can also be distinguished by examining the bolt heads. To begin with, the distance across the flats on a standard bolt head is measured in inches, while the same dimension on a metric bolt is sized in millimeters (the same is true for nuts). As a result, a standard wrench should not be used on a metric bolt and a metric wrench should not be used on a standard bolt. Also, most standard bolts have slashes radiating out from the center of the head to denote the grade or strength of the bolt, which is an indication of the amount of torque that can be applied to it. The greater the number of slashes, the greater the strength of the bolt. Grades 0 through 5 are commonly used on automobiles. Metric bolts have a property class (grade) number, rather than a slash, molded into their heads to indicate bolt strength. In this case, the higher the number, the stronger the bolt. Property class numbers 8.8, 9.8 and 10.9 are commonly used on automobiles.

Strength markings can also be used to distinguish standard hex nuts from metric hex nuts. Many standard nuts have dots stamped into one side, while metric nuts are marked with a number. The greater the number of dots, or the higher the number, the greater the strength of the nut.

Metric studs are also marked on their ends according to property class (grade). Larger studs are numbered (the same as metric bolts),

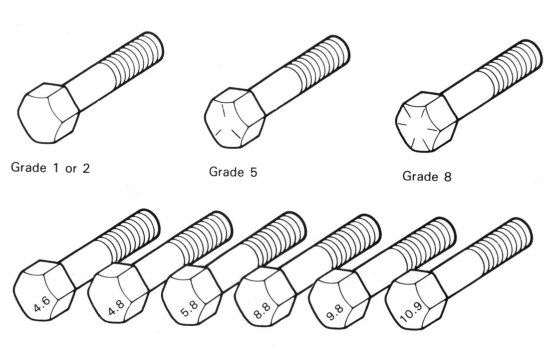

Grade 1 or 2   Grade 5   Grade 8

Bolt strength markings (top – standard/SAE/USS; bottom – metric)

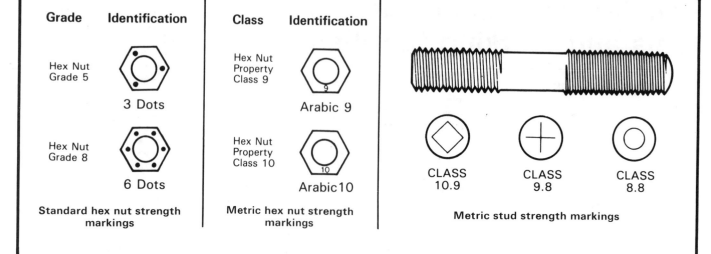

Grade	Identification
Hex Nut Grade 5	3 Dots
Hex Nut Grade 8	6 Dots

Standard hex nut strength markings

Class	Identification
Hex Nut Property Class 9	Arabic 9
Hex Nut Property Class 10	Arabic 10

Metric hex nut strength markings

CLASS 10.9   CLASS 9.8   CLASS 8.8

Metric stud strength markings

while smaller studs carry a geometric code to denote grade.

It should be noted that many fasteners, especially Grades 0 through 2, have no distinguishing marks on them. When such is the case, the only way to determine whether it is standard or metric is to measure the thread pitch or compare it to a known fastener of the same size.

Standard fasteners are often referred to as SAE, as opposed to metric. However, it should be noted that SAE technically refers to a non-metric *fine thread* fastener only. Coarse thread non-metric fasteners are referred to as USS sizes.

Since fasteners of the same size (both standard and metric) may have different strength ratings, be sure to reinstall any bolts, studs or nuts removed from your vehicle in their original locations. Also, when replacing a fastener with a new one, make sure that the new one has a strength rating equal to or greater than the original.

Tightening sequences and procedures

Most threaded fasteners should be tightened to a specific torque value (torque is the twisting force applied to a threaded component such as a nut or bolt). Overtightening the fastener can weaken it and cause it to break, while undertightening can cause it to eventually come loose. Bolts, screws and studs, depending on the material they are made of and their thread diameters, have specific torque values, many of which are noted in the Specifications at the beginning of each Chapter. Be sure to follow the torque recommendations closely. For fasteners not assigned a specific torque, a general torque value chart is presented here as a guide. As was previously mentioned, the size and grade of a fastener determine the amount of torque that can safely be applied to it. The figures listed here are approximate for Grade 2 and Grade 3 fasteners. Higher grades can tolerate higher torque values.

Metric thread sizes	Ft-lb	Nm
M-6	6 to 9	9 to 12
M-8	14 to 21	19 to 28
M-10	28 to 40	38 to 54
M-12	50 to 71	68 to 96
M-14	80 to 140	109 to 154

Pipe thread sizes		
1/8	5 to 8	7 to 10
1/4	12 to 18	17 to 24
3/8	22 to 33	30 to 44
1/2	25 to 35	34 to 47

U.S. thread sizes		
1/4 — 20	6 to 9	9 to 12
5/16 — 18	12 to 18	17 to 24
5/16 — 24	14 to 20	19 to 27
3/8 — 16	22 to 32	30 to 43
3/8 — 24	27 to 38	37 to 51
7/16 — 14	40 to 55	55 to 74
7/16 — 20	40 to 60	55 to 81
1/2 — 13	55 to 80	75 to 108

Fasteners laid out in a pattern, such as cylinder head bolts, oil pan bolts, differential cover bolts, etc., must be loosened or tightened in sequence to avoid warping the component. This sequence will normally be shown in the appropriate Chapter. If a specific pattern is not given, the following procedures can be used to prevent warping.

Initially, the bolts or nuts should be assembled finger-tight only. Next, they should be tightened one full turn each, in a criss-cross or diagonal pattern. After each one has been tightened one full turn, return to the first one and tighten them all one-half turn, following the same pattern. Finally, tighten each of them one-quarter turn at a time until each fastener has been tightened to the proper torque. To loosen and remove the fasteners, the procedure would be reversed.

Component disassembly

Component disassembly should be done with care and purpose to help ensure that the parts go back together properly. Always keep track of the sequence in which parts are removed. Make note of special characteristics or marks on parts that can be installed more than one

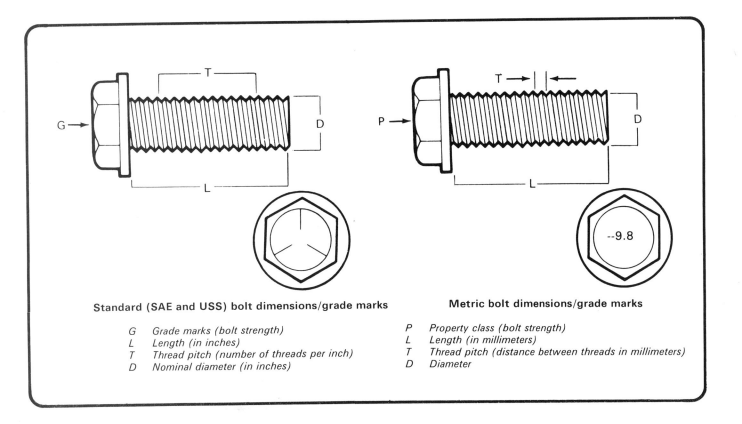

Standard (SAE and USS) bolt dimensions/grade marks

G	Grade marks (bolt strength)
L	Length (in inches)
T	Thread pitch (number of threads per inch)
D	Nominal diameter (in inches)

Metric bolt dimensions/grade marks

P	Property class (bolt strength)
L	Length (in millimeters)
T	Thread pitch (distance between threads in millimeters)
D	Diameter

way, such as a grooved thrust washer on a shaft. It is a good idea to lay the disassembled parts out on a clean surface in the order that they were removed. It may also be helpful to make sketches or take instant photos of components before removal.

When removing fasteners from a component, keep track of their locations. Sometimes threading a bolt back in a part, or putting the washers and nut back on a stud, can prevent mix-ups later. If nuts and bolts cannot be returned to their original locations, they should be kept in a compartmented box or a series of small boxes. A cupcake or muffin tin is ideal for this purpose, since each cavity can hold the bolts and nuts from a particular area (i.e. oil pan bolts, valve cover bolts, engine mount bolts, etc.). A pan of this type is especially helpful when working on assemblies with very small parts, such as the carburetor, alternator, valve train or interior dash and trim pieces. The cavities can be marked with paint or tape to identify the contents.

Whenever wiring looms, harnesses or connectors are separated, it is a good idea to identify the two halves with numbered pieces of masking tape so they can be easily reconnected.

Gasket sealing surfaces

Throughout any vehicle, gaskets are used to seal the mating surfaces between two parts and keep lubricants, fluids, vacuum or pressure contained in an assembly.

Many times these gaskets are coated with a liquid or paste-type gasket sealing compound before assembly. Age, heat and pressure can sometimes cause the two parts to stick together so tightly that they are very difficult to separate. Often, the assembly can be loosened by striking it with a soft-face hammer near the mating surfaces. A regular hammer can be used if a block of wood is placed between the hammer and the part. Do not hammer on cast parts or parts that could be easily damaged. With any particularly stubborn part, always recheck to make sure that every fastener has been removed.

Avoid using a screwdriver or bar to pry apart an assembly, as they can easily mar the gasket sealing surfaces of the parts, which must remain smooth. If prying is absolutely necessary, use an old broom handle, but keep in mind that extra clean up will be necessary if the wood splinters.

After the parts are separated, the old gasket must be carefully scraped off and the gasket surfaces cleaned. Stubborn gasket material can be soaked with rust penetrant or treated with a special chemical to soften it so it can be easily scraped off. A scraper can be fashioned from a piece of copper tubing by flattening and sharpening one end. Copper is recommended because it is usually softer than the surfaces to be scraped, which reduces the chance of gouging the part. Some gaskets can be removed with a wire brush, but regardless of the method used, the mating surfaces must be left clean and smooth. If for some reason the gasket surface is gouged, then a gasket sealer thick enough to fill scratches will have to be used during reassembly of the components. For most applications, a non-drying (or semi-drying) gasket sealer should be used.

Hose removal tips

Warning: *If the vehicle is equipped with air conditioning, do not disconnect any of the A/C hoses without first having the system depressurized by a dealer service department or an air conditioning specialist.*

Hose removal precautions closely parallel gasket removal precautions. Avoid scratching or gouging the surface that the hose mates against or the connection may leak. This is especially true for radiator hoses. Because of various chemical reactions, the rubber in hoses can bond itself to the metal spigot that the hose fits over. To remove a hose, first loosen the hose clamps that secure it to the spigot. Then, with slip-joint pliers, grab the hose at the clamp and rotate it around the spigot. Work it back and forth until it is completely free, then pull it off. Silicone or other lubricants will ease removal if they can be applied between the hose and the outside of the spigot. Apply the same lubricant to the inside of the hose and the outside of the spigot to simplify installation.

As a last resort (and if the hose is to be replaced with a new one anyway), the rubber can be slit with a knife and the hose peeled from the spigot. If this must be done, be careful that the metal connection is not damaged.

If a hose clamp is broken or damaged, do not reuse it. Wire-type clamps usually weaken with age, so it is a good idea to replace them with screw-type clamps whenever a hose is removed.

Tools

A selection of good tools is a basic requirement for anyone who plans to maintain and repair his or her own vehicle. For the owner who has few tools, the initial investment might seem high, but when compared to the spiraling costs of professional auto maintenance and repair, it is a wise one.

To help the owner decide which tools are needed to perform the tasks detailed in this manual, the following tool lists are offered: *Maintenance and minor repair, Repair/overhaul* and *Special.*

The newcomer to practical mechanics should start off with the maintenance and minor repair tool kit, which is adequate for the simpler jobs performed on a vehicle. Then, as confidence and experience grow, the owner can tackle more difficult tasks, buying additional tools as they are needed. Eventually the basic kit will be expanded into the repair and overhaul tool set. Over a period of time, the experienced do-it-yourselfer will assemble a tool set complete enough for most repair and overhaul procedures and will add tools from the special category when it is felt that the expense is justified by the frequency of use.

Maintenance and minor repair tool kit

The tools in this list should be considered the minimum required for performance of routine maintenance, servicing and minor repair work. We recommend the purchase of combination wrenches (box-end and

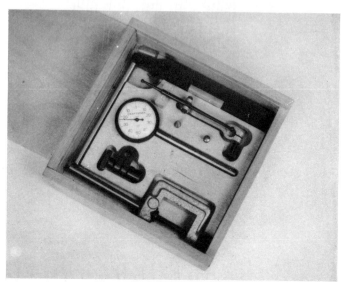

Micrometer set   Dial indicator set

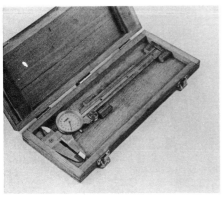

Dial caliper

Hand-operated vacuum pump

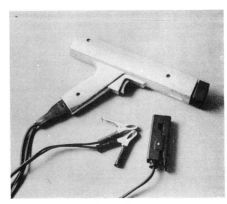

Timing light

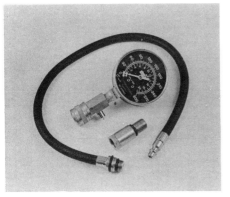

Compression gauge with spark plug
hole adapter

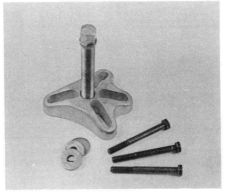

Damper/steering wheel puller

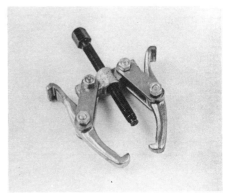

General purpose puller

Valve spring compressor

Valve spring compressor

Ridge reamer

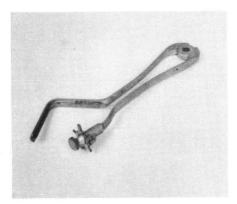

Piston ring groove cleaning tool

Ring removal/installation tool

Ring compressor

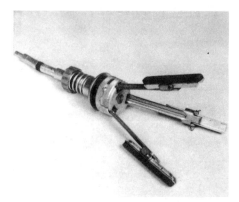

Cylinder hone

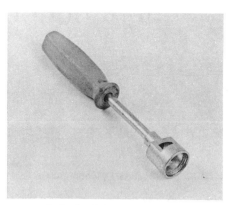

Brake hold-down spring tool

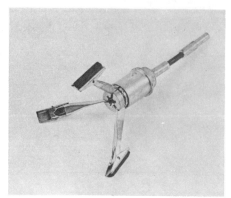

Brake cylinder hone

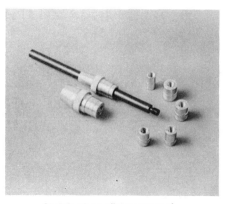

Clutch plate alignment tool

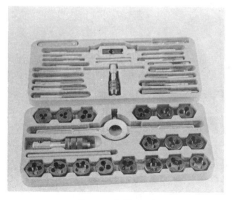

Tap and die set

open-end combined in one wrench). While more expensive than open end wrenches, they offer the advantages of both types of wrench.

Combination wrench set (6 mm to 19 mm)
Adjustable wrench, 8 inch
Spark plug wrench with rubber insert
Spark plug gap adjusting tool
Feeler gauge set
Brake bleeder wrench
Standard screwdriver (5/16-inch x 6 inch)
Phillips screwdriver (No. 2 x 6 inch)
Combination pliers — 6 inch
Hacksaw and assortment of blades
Tire pressure gauge
Oil can
Fine emery cloth
Wire brush
Oil filter wrench
Funnel (medium size)
Safety goggles
Jackstands (2)
Drain pan

Note: *If basic tune-ups are going to be part of routine maintenance, it will be necessary to purchase a good quality stroboscopic timing light and tachometer. Although they are included in the list of special tools, it is mentioned here because they are absolutely necessary for tuning most vehicles properly.*

Repair and overhaul tool set

These tools are essential for anyone who plans to perform major repairs and are in addition to those in the maintenance and minor repair tool kit. Included is a comprehensive set of sockets which, though expensive, are invaluable because of their versatility, especially when

various extensions and drives are available. We recommend the 1/2-inch drive over the 3/8-inch drive. Although the larger drive is bulky and more expensive, it has the capacity of accepting a very wide range of large sockets. Ideally, however, the mechanic should have a 3/8-inch drive set and a 1/2-inch drive set.

Socket set(s)
Reversible ratchet
Extension — 10 inch
Universal joint
Torque wrench (same size drive as sockets)
Ball peen hammer — 8 ounce
Soft-face hammer (plastic/rubber)
Standard screwdriver (1/4-inch x 6 inch)
Standard screwdriver (stubby — 5/16-inch)
Phillips screwdriver (No. 3 x 8 inch)
Phillips screwdriver (stubby — No. 2)
Pliers — vise grip
Pliers — lineman's
Pliers — needle nose
Pliers — snap-ring (internal and external)
Cold chisel — 1/2-inch
Scriber
Scraper (made from flattened copper tubing)
Centerpunch
Pin punches (1/16, 1/8, 3/16-inch)
Steel rule/straightedge — 12 inch
Allen wrench set (4 mm to 10 mm)
A selection of files
Wire brush (large)
Jackstands (second set)
Jack (scissor or hydraulic type)

Note: *Another tool which is often useful is an electric drill motor with a chuck capacity of 3/8-inch and a set of good quality drill bits.*

Special tools

The tools in this list include those which are not used regularly, are expensive to buy, or which need to be used in accordance with their manufacturer's instructions. Unless these tools will be used frequently, it is not very economical to purchase many of them. A consideration would be to split the cost and use between yourself and a friend or friends. In addition, most of these tools can be obtained from a tool rental shop on a temporary basis.

This list primarily contains only those tools and instruments widely available to the public, and not those special tools produced by the vehicle manufacturer for distribution to dealer service departments. Occasionally, references to the manufacturer's special tools are included in the text of this manual. Generally, an alternative method of doing the job without the special tool is offered. However, sometimes there is no alternative to their use. Where this is the case, and the tool cannot be purchased or borrowed, the work should be turned over to the dealer service department or an automotive repair shop.

Valve spring compressor
Piston ring groove cleaning tool
Piston ring compressor
Piston ring installation tool
Cylinder compression gauge
Cylinder ridge reamer
Cylinder surfacing hone
Cylinder bore gauge
Micrometers and/or dial calipers
Balljoint separator
Universal-type puller
Impact screwdriver
Dial indicator set
Stroboscopic timing light (inductive pick-up)
Hand operated vacuum/pressure pump
Tachometer
Universal electrical multimeter
Cable hoist
Brake spring removal and installation tools
Floor jack

Buying tools

For the do-it-yourselfer who is just starting to get involved in vehicle maintenance and repair, there are a number of options available when purchasing tools. If maintenance and minor repair is the extent of the work to be done, the purchase of individual tools is satisfactory. If, on the other hand, extensive work is planned, it would be a good idea to purchase a modest tool set from one of the large retail chain stores. A set can usually be bought at a substantial savings over the individual tool prices, and they often come with a tool box. As additional tools are needed, add-on sets, individual tools and a larger tool box can be purchased to expand the tool selection. Building a tool set gradually allows the cost of the tools to be spread over a longer period of time and gives the mechanic the freedom to choose only those tools that will actually be used.

Tool stores will often be the only source of some of the special tools that are needed, but regardless of where tools are bought, try to avoid cheap ones, especially when buying screwdrivers and sockets, because they won't last very long. The expense involved in replacing cheap tools will eventually be greater than the initial cost of quality tools.

Care and maintenance of tools

Good tools are expensive, so it makes sense to treat them with respect. Keep them clean and in usable condition and store them properly when not in use. Always wipe off any dirt, grease or metal chips before putting them away. Never leave tools lying around in the work area. Upon completion of a job, always check closely under the hood for tools that may have been left there so they won't get lost during a test drive.

Some tools, such as screwdrivers, pliers, wrenches and sockets, can be hung on a panel mounted on the garage or workshop wall, while others should be kept in a tool box or tray. Measuring instruments, gauges, meters, etc. must be carefully stored where they cannot be damaged by weather or impact from other tools.

When tools are used with care and stored properly, they will last a very long time. Even with the best of care, though, tools will wear out if used frequently. When a tool is damaged or worn out, replace it. Subsequent jobs will be safer and more enjoyable if you do.

Working facilities

Not to be overlooked when discussing tools is the workshop. If anything more than routine maintenance is to be carried out, some sort of suitable work area is essential.

It is understood, and appreciated, that many home mechanics do not have a good workshop or garage available, and end up removing an engine or doing major repairs outside. It is recommended, however, that the overhaul or repair be completed under the cover of a roof.

A clean, flat workbench or table of comfortable working height is an absolute necessity. The workbench should be equipped with a vise that has a jaw opening of at least four inches.

As mentioned previously, some clean, dry storage space is also required for tools, as well as the lubricants, fluids, cleaning solvents, etc. which soon become necessary.

Sometimes waste oil and fluids, drained from the engine or cooling system during normal maintenance or repairs, present a disposal problem. To avoid pouring them on the ground or into a sewage system, pour the used fluids into large containers, seal them with caps and take them to an authorized disposal site or recycling center. Plastic jugs, such as old antifreeze containers, are ideal for this purpose.

Always keep a supply of old newspapers and clean rags available. Old towels are excellent for mopping up spills. Many mechanics use rolls of paper towels for most work because they are readily available and disposable. To help keep the area under the vehicle clean, a large cardboard box can be cut open and flattened to protect the garage or shop floor.

Whenever working over a painted surface, such as when leaning over a fender to service something under the hood, always cover it with an old blanket or bedspread to protect the finish. Vinyl covered pads, made especially for this purpose, are available at auto parts stores.

Booster battery (jump) starting

Certain precautions must be observed when using a booster battery to jump start a vehicle.

   a) Before connecting the booster battery, make sure that the ignition switch is in the Off position.
   b) Turn off the lights, heater and other electrical loads.
   c) The eyes should be shielded. Safety goggles are a good idea.
   d) Make sure the booster battery is the same voltage as the dead one in the vehicle.
   e) The two vehicles must not touch each other.
   f) Make sure the transaxle is in Neutral (manual transaxle) or Park (automatic transaxle).
   g) If the booster battery is not a maintenance-free type, remove the vent caps and lay a cloth over the vent holes.

Connect the red jumper cable to the *positive* (+) terminals of each battery.

Connect one end of the black jumper cable to the *negative* (–) terminal of the booster battery. The other end of this cable should be connected to a good ground on the vehicle to be started, such as a bolt or bracket on the engine block. Use caution to insure that the cable will not come into contact with the fan, drivebelts or other moving parts of the engine.

Start the engine using the booster battery, then, with the engine running at idle speed, disconnect the jumper cables in the reverse order of connection.

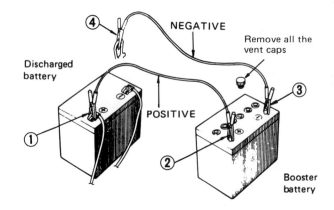

Booster battery (jump starting) cable connections should be made in the numbered order

Jacking and towing

Jacking

The jack supplied with the vehicle should only be used for raising the vehicle when changing a tire or placing jackstands under the frame. **Warning:** *Never work under the vehicle or start the engine while this jack is being used as the only means of support.*

The vehicle should be on level ground with the wheels blocked and the transaxle in Park (automatic) or Reverse (manual). If the tire is to be changed, pry off the hub cap (if equipped) using the tapered end of the lug wrench. If the wheel is being replaced, loosen the wheel nuts one-half turn and leave them in place until the wheel is raised off the ground. Refer to Chapter 10 for the tire changing procedure.

Place the jack under the side of the vehicle in the indicated position and raise it until the jack head groove fits into the rocker flange notch. Operate the jack with a slow, smooth motion until the wheel is raised off the ground.

Lower the vehicle, remove the jack and tighten the nuts (if loosened or removed) in a criss-cross sequence by turning the wrench clockwise. Replace the hub cap (if equipped) by placing it in position and using the heel of your hand or a rubber mallet to seat it.

Towing

The vehicle can be towed with all four wheels on the ground, provided that speeds do not exceed 30 mph and the distance is not over 50 miles, otherwise transaxle damage can result. For greater speeds or distances the vehicle can be towed with the rear wheels only on the ground and the front wheels suspended. **Do not** allow the vehicle to be towed with the front wheels only on the ground.

Towing equipment specifically designed for this purpose should be used and should be attached to the main structural members of the vehicle and not the bumper or brackets.

Safety is a major consideration when towing and all applicable state and local laws must be obeyed. A safety chain system must be used for all towing.

While towing, the parking brake should be released and the transaxle should be in Neutral. The steering must be unlocked (ignition switch in the Acc position). Remember that power steering and power brakes will not work with the engine off.

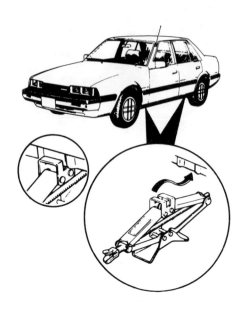

The jack should be placed at the specified lifting points

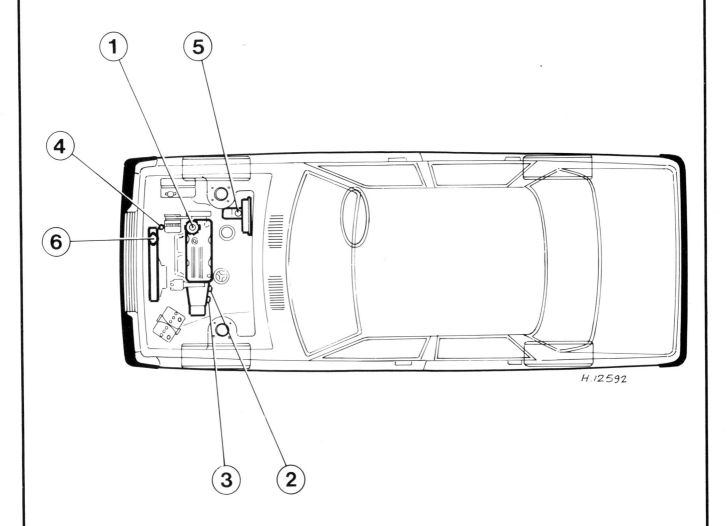

H.12592

Recommended lubricants and fluids

Component or system	Lubricant type or specification
1 Engine	Multigrade engine oil, viscosity range 10W-30 to 20W-50, to API SD or SE
2 Manual transaxle	Gear oil, SAE 80W-90 or 90, to API GL-4 or GL-5
3 Automatic transaxle	ATF Type F
4 Power steering	ATF type F
5 Brake hydraulic system	Hydraulic fluid to FMVSS 116, DOT 3 or DOT 4, or SAE J1703a
6 Cooling system	Ethylene glycol based antifreeze and soft water

These are general recommendations for temperate climates. If in doubt consult a Mazda dealer or other specialist.

Safety first!

Regardless of how enthusiastic you may be about getting on with the job at hand, take the time to ensure that your safety is not jeopardized. A moment's lack of attention can result in an accident, as can failure to observe certain simple safety precautions. The possibility of an accident will always exist, and the following points should not be considered a comprehensive list of all dangers. Rather, they are intended to make you aware of the risks and to encourage a safety conscious approach to all work you carry out on your vehicle.

Essential DOs and DON'Ts

DON'T rely on a jack when working under the vehicle. Always use approved jackstands to support the weight of the vehicle and place them under the recommended lift or support points.

DON'T attempt to loosen extremely tight fasteners (i.e. wheel lug nuts) while the vehicle is on a jack — it may fall.

DON'T start the engine without first making sure that the transmission is in Neutral (or Park where applicable) and the parking brake is set.

DON'T remove the radiator cap from a hot cooling system — let it cool or cover it with a cloth and release the pressure gradually.

DON'T attempt to drain the engine oil until you are sure it has cooled to the point that it will not burn you.

DON'T touch any part of the engine or exhaust system until it has cooled sufficiently to avoid burns.

DON'T siphon toxic liquids such as gasoline, antifreeze and brake fluid by mouth, or allow them to remain on your skin.

DON'T inhale brake lining dust — it is potentially hazardous (see *Asbestos* below)

DON'T allow spilled oil or grease to remain on the floor — wipe it up before someone slips on it.

DON'T use loose fitting wrenches or other tools which may slip and cause injury.

DON'T push on wrenches when loosening or tightening nuts or bolts. Always try to pull the wrench toward you. If the situation calls for pushing the wrench away, push with an open hand to avoid scraped knuckles if the wrench should slip.

DON'T attempt to lift a heavy component alone — get someone to help you.

DON'T rush or take unsafe shortcuts to finish a job.

DON'T allow children or animals in or around the vehicle while you are working on it.

DO wear eye protection when using power tools such as a drill, sander, bench grinder, etc. and when working under a vehicle.

DO keep loose clothing and long hair well out of the way of moving parts.

DO make sure that any hoist used has a safe working load rating adequate for the job.

DO get someone to check on you periodically when working alone on a vehicle.

DO carry out work in a logical sequence and make sure that everything is correctly assembled and tightened.

DO keep chemicals and fluids tightly capped and out of the reach of children and pets.

DO remember that your vehicle's safety affects that of yourself and others. If in doubt on any point, get professional advice.

Asbestos

Certain friction, insulating, sealing, and other products — such as brake linings, brake bands, clutch linings, torque converters, gaskets, etc. — contain asbestos. *Extreme care must be taken to avoid inhalation of dust from such products since it is hazardous to health.* If in doubt, assume that they *do* contain asbestos.

Fire

Remember at all times that gasoline is highly flammable. Never smoke or have any kind of open flame around when working on a vehicle. But the risk does not end there. A spark caused by an electrical short circuit, by two metal surfaces contacting each other, or even by static electricity built up in your body under certain conditions, can ignite gasoline vapors, which in a confined space are highly explosive. Do not, under any circumstances, use gasoline for cleaning parts. Use an approved safety solvent.

Always disconnect the battery ground (−) cable *at the battery* before working on any part of the fuel system or electrical system. Never risk spilling fuel on a hot engine or exhaust component.

It is strongly recommended that a fire extinguisher suitable for use on fuel and electrical fires be kept handy in the garage or workshop at all times. Never try to extinguish a fuel or electrical fire with water.

Fumes

Certain fumes are highly toxic and can quickly cause unconsciousness and even death if inhaled to any extent. Gasoline vapor falls into this category, as do the vapors from some cleaning solvents. Any draining or pouring of such volatile fluids should be done in a well ventilated area.

When using cleaning fluids and solvents, read the instructions on the container carefully. Never use materials from unmarked containers.

Never run the engine in an enclosed space, such as a garage. Exhaust fumes contain carbon monoxide, which is extremely poisonous. If you need to run the engine, always do so in the open air, or at least have the rear of the vehicle outside the work area.

If you are fortunate enough to have the use of an inspection pit, never drain or pour gasoline and never run the engine while the vehicle is over the pit. The fumes, being heavier than air, will concentrate in the pit with possibly lethal results.

The battery

Never create a spark or allow a bare light bulb near the battery. The battery normally gives off a certain amount of hydrogen gas, which is highly explosive.

Always disconnect the battery ground (−) cable *at the battery* before working on the fuel or electrical systems.

If possible, loosen the filler caps or cover when charging the battery from an external source. Do not charge at an excessive rate or the battery may burst.

Take care when adding water and when carrying a battery. The electrolyte, even when diluted, is very corrosive and should not be allowed to contact clothing or skin.

Always wear eye protection when cleaning the battery to prevent the caustic deposits from entering your eyes.

Household current

When using an electric power tool, inspection light, etc., which operates on household current, always make sure that the tool is correctly connected to its plug and that, where necessary, it is properly grounded. Do not use such items in damp conditions and, again, do not create a spark or apply excessive heat in the vicinity of fuel or fuel vapor.

Secondary ignition system voltage

A severe electric shock can result from touching certain parts of the ignition system (such as the spark plug wires) when the engine is running or being cranked, particularly if components are damp or the insulation is defective. In the case of an electronic ignition system, the secondary system voltage is much higher and could prove fatal.

Conversion factors

Length (distance)
Inches (in)	X	25.4	= Millimetres (mm)	X 0.0394	= Inches (in)
Feet (ft)	X	0.305	= Metres (m)	X 3.281	= Feet (ft)
Miles	X	1.609	= Kilometres (km)	X 0.621	= Miles

Volume (capacity)
Cubic inches (cu in; in^3)	X 16.387 = Cubic centimetres (cc; cm^3)	X 0.061	= Cubic inches (cu in; in^3)
Imperial pints (Imp pt)	X 0.568 = Litres (l)	X 1.76	= Imperial pints (Imp pt)
Imperial quarts (Imp qt)	X 1.137 = Litres (l)	X 0.88	= Imperial quarts (Imp qt)
Imperial quarts (Imp qt)	X 1.201 = US quarts (US qt)	X 0.833	= Imperial quarts (Imp qt)
US quarts (US qt)	X 0.946 = Litres (l)	X 1.057	= US quarts (US qt)
Imperial gallons (Imp gal)	X 4.546 = Litres (l)	X 0.22	= Imperial gallons (Imp gal)
Imperial gallons (Imp gal)	X 1.201 = US gallons (US gal)	X 0.833	= Imperial gallons (Imp gal)
US gallons (US gal)	X 3.785 = Litres (l)	X 0.264	= US gallons (US gal)

Mass (weight)
Ounces (oz)	X 28.35 = Grams (g)	X 0.035	= Ounces (oz)
Pounds (lb)	X 0.454 = Kilograms (kg)	X 2.205	= Pounds (lb)

Force
Ounces-force (ozf; oz)	X 0.278 = Newtons (N)	X 3.6	= Ounces-force (ozf; oz)
Pounds-force (lbf; lb)	X 4.448 = Newtons (N)	X 0.225	= Pounds-force (lbf; lb)
Newtons (N)	X 0.1 = Kilograms-force (kgf; kg)	X 9.81	= Newtons (N)

Pressure
Pounds-force per square inch (psi; lbf/in^2; lb/in^2)	X 0.070 = Kilograms-force per square centimetre (kgf/cm^2; kg/cm^2)	X 14.223	= Pounds-force per square inch (psi; lbf/in^2; lb/in^2)
Pounds-force per square inch (psi; lbf/in^2; lb/in^2)	X 0.068 = Atmospheres (atm)	X 14.696	= Pounds-force per square inch (psi; lbf/in^2; lb/in^2)
Pounds-force per square inch (psi; lbf/in^2; lb/in^2)	X 0.069 = Bars	X 14.5	= Pounds-force per square inch (psi; lbf/in^2; lb/in^2)
Pounds-force per square inch (psi; lbf/in^2; lb/in^2)	X 6.895 = Kilopascals (kPa)	X 0.145	= Pounds-force per square inch (psi; lbf/in^2; lb/in^2)
Kilopascals (kPa)	X 0.01 = Kilograms-force per square centimetre (kgf/cm^2; kg/cm^2)	X 98.1	= Kilopascals (kPa)

Torque (moment of force)
Pounds-force inches (lbf in; lb in)	X 1.152 = Kilograms-force centimetre (kgf cm; kg cm)	X 0.868	= Pounds-force inches (lbf in; lb in)
Pounds-force inches (lbf in; lb in)	X 0.113 = Newton metres (Nm)	X 8.85	= Pounds-force inches (lbf in; lb in)
Pounds-force inches (lbf in; lb in)	X 0.083 = Pounds-force feet (lbf ft; lb ft)	X 12	= Pounds-force inches (lbf in; lb in)
Pounds-force feet (lbf ft; lb ft)	X 0.138 = Kilograms-force metres (kgf m; kg m)	X 7.233	= Pounds-force feet (lbf ft; lb ft)
Pounds-force feet (lbf ft; lb ft)	X 1.356 = Newton metres (Nm)	X 0.738	= Pounds-force feet (lbf ft; lb ft)
Newton metres (Nm)	X 0.102 = Kilograms-force metres (kgf m; kg m)	X 9.804	= Newton metres (Nm)

Power
Horsepower (hp)	X 745.7 = Watts (W)	X 0.0013	= Horsepower (hp)

Velocity (speed)
Miles per hour (miles/hr; mph)	X 1.609 = Kilometres per hour (km/hr; kph)	X 0.621	= Miles per hour (miles/hr; mph)

Fuel consumption*
Miles per gallon, Imperial (mpg)	X 0.354 = Kilometres per litre (km/l)	X 2.825	= Miles per gallon, Imperial (mpg)
Miles per gallon, US (mpg)	X 0.425 = Kilometres per litre (km/l)	X 2.352	= Miles per gallon, US (mpg)

Temperature
Degrees Fahrenheit = ($°C \times 1.8$) + 32

Degrees Celsius (Degrees Centigrade; $°C$) = ($°F$ - 32) x 0.56

*It is common practice to convert from miles per gallon (mpg) to litres/100 kilometres (l/100km),
where mpg (Imperial) x l/100 km — 282 and mpg (US) x l/100 km = 235

Troubleshooting

Contents

This section provides an easy reference guide to the more common problems which may occur during the operation of your vehicle. These problems and possible causes are grouped under various components or systems; i.e. Engine, Cooling system, etc., and also refer to the Chapter and/or Section which deals with the problem.

Remember that successful troubleshooting is not a mysterious *black art* practiced only by professional mechanics. It is simply the result of a bit of knowledge combined with an intelligent, systematic approach to the problem. Always work by a process of elimination, starting with the simplest solution and working through to the most complex — and never overlook the obvious. Anyone can forget to fill the gas tank or leave the lights on overnight, so don't assume that you are above such oversights.

Finally, always get clear in your mind why a problem has occurred and take steps to ensure that it doesn't happen again. If the electrical system fails because of a poor connection, check all other connections in the system to make sure that they don't fail as well. If a particular fuse continues to blow, find out why — don't just go on replacing fuses. Remember, failure of a small component can often be indicative of potential failure or incorrect functioning of a more important component or system.

Engine

1 Engine will not rotate when attempting to start

1 Battery terminal connections loose or corroded. Check the cable terminals at the battery. Tighten the cable or remove corrosion as necessary.
2 Battery discharged or faulty. If the cable connections are clean and tight on the battery posts, turn the key to the On position and switch on the headlights and/or windshield wipers. If they fail to function, the battery is discharged.
3 Automatic transmission not completely engaged in Park.
4 Broken, loose or disconnected wiring in the starting circuit. Inspect all wiring and connectors at the battery, starter solenoid and ignition switch.
5 Starter motor pinion jammed in flywheel ring gear. If manual transmission, place transmission in gear and rock the vehicle to manually turn the engine. Remove starter and inspect pinion and flywheel at earliest convenience.
6 Starter solenoid faulty (Chapter 5).
7 Starter motor faulty (Chapter 5).
8 Ignition switch faulty (Chapter 12).

2 Engine rotates but will not start

1 Fuel tank empty.
2 Battery discharged (engine rotates slowly). Check the operation of electrical components as described in previous Section.
3 Battery terminal connections loose or corroded. See previous Section.
4 Carburetor flooded and/or fuel level in carburetor incorrect. This will usually be accompanied by a strong fuel odor from under the hood. Wait a few minutes, depress the accelerator pedal all the way to the floor and attempt to start the engine.
5 Choke control inoperative (Chapter 4).
6 Fuel not reaching carburetor. With ignition switch in Off position, open hood, remove the top plate of air cleaner assembly and observe the top of the carburetor (manually move the choke plate back if necessary). Have an assistant depress the accelerator pedal and check that fuel spurts into the carburetor. If not, check the fuel filter (Chapter 1), fuel lines and fuel pump (Chapter 4).
7 Excessive moisture on, or damage to, ignition components (Chapter 5).
8 Worn, faulty or incorrectly gapped spark plugs (Chapter 1).
9 Broken, loose or disconnected wiring in the starting circuit (see previous Section).
10 Distributor loose, causing ignition timing to change. Turn the distributor as necessary to start engine, then set ignition timing as soon as possible (Chapter 1).
11 Broken, loose or disconnected wires at the ignition coil or faulty coil (Chapter 5).

3 Starter motor operates without rotating engine

1 Starter pinion sticking. Remove the starter (Chapter 5) and inspect.
2 Starter pinion or flywheel teeth worn or broken. Remove the cover at the rear of the engine and inspect.

4 Engine hard to start when cold

1 Battery discharged or low. Check as described in Section 1.
2 Choke control inoperative or out of adjustment (Chapter 4).
3 Carburetor flooded (see Section 2).
4 Fuel supply not reaching the carburetor (see Section 2).
5 Carburetor in need of overhaul (Chapter 4).
6 Distributor rotor carbon tracked and/or mechanical advance mechanism rusted (Chapter 5).

5 Engine hard to start when hot

1 Choke sticking in the closed position (Chapter 1).
2 Carburetor flooded (see Section 2).
3 Air filter clogged (Chapter 1).
4 Fuel not reaching the carburetor (see Section 2).

6 Starter motor noisy or excessively rough in engagement

1 Pinion or flywheel gear teeth worn or broken. Remove the cover at the rear of the engine (if so equipped) and inspect.
2 Starter motor mounting bolts loose or missing.

7 Engine starts but stops immediately

1 Loose or faulty electrical connections at distributor, coil or alternator.
2 Insufficient fuel reaching the carburetor. Disconnect the fuel line at the carburetor and place a container under the disconnected fuel line. Turn the engine over with the starter and observe the flow of fuel from the line. If little or none at all, check for blockage in the lines or filter (Chapter 1) and/or replace the fuel pump (Chapter 4).
3 Vacuum leak at the gasket surfaces of the intake manifold and/or carburetor. Make sure that all mounting bolts/nuts are tightened securely and that all vacuum hoses connected to the carburetor and manifold are positioned properly and in good condition.

8 Engine lopes while idling or idles erratically.

1 Vacuum leakage. Check mounting bolts/nuts at the carburetor and intake manifold for tightness. Make sure that all vacuum hoses are connected and in good condition. Use a stethoscope or a length of fuel hose held against your ear to listen for vacuum leaks while the engine is running. A hissing sound will be heard. A soapy water solution will also detect leaks. Check the carburetor and intake manifold gasket surfaces.
2 Leaking EGR valve or plugged PCV valve (see Chapters 1 and 6).
3 Air filter clogged (Chapter 1).
4 Fuel pump not delivering sufficient fuel to the carburetor (see Section 7).
5 Carburetor out of adjustment (Chapter 4).
6 Leaking head gasket. If this is suspected, take the vehicle to a repair shop or dealer where the engine can be pressure checked.
7 Timing belt slipped or incorrectly installed (Chapter 2).
8 Camshaft lobes worn (Chapter 2).

9   Engine misses at idle speed

1   Spark plugs worn or not gapped properly (Chapter 1).
2   Faulty spark plug wires (Chapter 1).
3   Choke not operating properly (Chapter 1).

10   Engine misses throughout driving speed range

1   Fuel filter clogged and/or impurities in the fuel system (Chapter 1). Also check fuel pump output at the carburetor (see Section 7).
2   Faulty or incorrectly gapped spark plugs (Chapter 1).
3   Incorrect ignition timing (Chapter 1).
4   Check for cracked distributor cap, disconnected distributor wires and damaged distributor components (Chapter 1).
5   Leaking spark plug wires (Chapter 1).
6   Faulty emissions system components (Chapter 6).
7   Low or uneven cylinder compression pressures. Remove spark plugs and test compression with gauge (Chapter 1).
8   Weak or faulty ignition system (Chapter 5).
9   Vacuum leaks at carburetor, intake manifold or vacuum hoses (see Section 8).

11   Engine stalls

1   Idle speed incorrect (Chapter 1).
2   Fuel filter clogged and/or water and impurities in the fuel system (Chapter 1).
3   Choke improperly adjusted or sticking (Chapter 1).
4   Distributor components damp or damaged (Chapter 5).
5   Faulty emissions system components (Chapter 6).
6   Faulty or incorrectly gapped spark plugs (Chapter 1). Also check spark plug wires (Chapter 1).
7   Vacuum leak at the carburetor, intake manifold or vacuum hoses. Check as described in Section 8.
8   Valve clearances incorrectly set (Chapter 1).

12   Engine lacks power

1   Incorrect ignition timing (Chapter 1).
2   Excessive play in distributor shaft. At the same time, check for worn rotor, faulty distributor cap, wires, etc. (Chapters 1 and 5).
3   Faulty or incorrectly gapped spark plugs (Chapter 1).
4   Carburetor not adjusted properly or excessively worn (Chapter 4).
5   Faulty coil (Chapter 5).
6   Brakes binding (Chapter 1).
7   Automatic transaxle fluid level incorrect (Chapter 1).
8   Clutch slipping (Chapter 8).
9   Fuel filter clogged and/or impurities in the fuel system (Chapter 1).
10   Emissions control system not functioning properly (Chapter 6).
11   Use of substandard fuel. Fill tank with proper octane fuel.
12   Low or uneven cylinder compression pressures. Test with compression tester, which will detect leaking valves and/or blown head gasket (Chapter 1).

13   Engine backfires

1   Emissions system not functioning properly (Chapter 6).
2   Ignition timing incorrect (Chapter 1).
3   Faulty secondary ignition system (cracked spark plug insulator, faulty plug wires, distributor cap and/or rotor) (Chapters 1 and 5).
4   Carburetor in need of adjustment or worn excessively (Chapter 4).
5   Vacuum leak at carburetor, intake manifold or vacuum hoses. Check as described in Section 8.
6   Valve clearances incorrectly set, and/or valves sticking (Chapter 1).

14   Pinging or knocking engine sounds during acceleration or uphill

1   Incorrect grade of fuel. Fill tank with fuel of the proper octane rating.
2   Ignition timing incorrect (Chapter 1).
3   Carburetor in need of adjustment (Chapter 4).
4   Improper spark plugs. Check plug type against Emissions Control Information label located in engine compartment (US models only). Also check plugs and wires for damage (Chapter 1).
5   Worn or damaged distributor components (Chapter 5).
6   Faulty emissions system (Chapter 6).
7   Vacuum leak. Check as described in Section 8.

15   Engine diesels (continues to run) after switching off

1   Idle speed too high (Chapter 1).
2   Idle system malfunction (Chapter 4).
3   Ignition timing incorrectly adjusted (Chapter 1).
4   Thermo-controlled air cleaner heat valve not operating properly (Chapter 1).
5   Excessive engine operating temperature. Probable causes of this are malfunctioning thermostat, clogged radiator, faulty water pump (Chapter 3).

Engine electrical system

16   Battery will not hold a charge

1   Alternator drivebelt defective or not adjusted properly (Chapter 1).
2   Electrolyte level low (Chapter 1).
3   Battery terminals loose or corroded (Chapter 1).
4   Alternator not charging properly (Chapter 5).
5   Loose, broken or faulty wiring in the charging circuit (Chapter 5).
6   Short in vehicle wiring causing a continual drain on battery.
7   Battery defective internally.

17   Ignition light fails to go out

1   Fault in alternator or charging circuit (Chapter 5).
2   Alternator drivebelt defective or not properly adjusted (Chapter 1).

18   Ignition light fails to come on when key is turned on

1   Warning light bulb defective (Chapter 12).
2   Alternator faulty (Chapter 5).
3   Fault in the printed circuit, dash wiring or bulb holder (Chapter 12).

Fuel system

19   Excessive fuel consumption

1   Dirty or clogged air filter element (Chapter 1).
2   Incorrectly set ignition timing (Chapter 1).
3   Choke sticking or improperly adjusted (Chapter 1).
4   Emissions system not functioning properly (not all vehicles, see Chapter 6).
5   Carburetor idle speed and/or mixture not adjusted properly (Chapter 1).
6   Carburetor internal parts excessively worn or damaged (Chapter 4).
7   Low tire pressure or incorrect tire size.
8   Inappropriate driving habits, or persistently unfavourable conditions.

20 Fuel leakage and/or fuel odor

1   Leak in a fuel feed or vent line (Chapter 4).
2   Tank overfilled. Fill only to automatic shut-off.
3   Evaporative emission control system fault (not UK models).
4   Vapor leaks from system lines (Chapter 4).
5   Carburetor internal parts excessively worn or out of adjustment (Chapter 4).

Cooling system

21 Overheating

1   Insufficient coolant in system (Chapter 1).
2   Radiator core blocked or radiator grille dirty and restricted (Chapter 3).
3   Thermostat faulty (Chapter 3).
4   Fan not operating correctly (Chapter 3).
5   Radiator cap not maintaining proper pressure. Have cap pressure tested by gas station or repair shop.
6   Ignition timing incorrect (Chapter 1).
7   Inaccurate temperature gauge (Chapter 12).

22 Overcooling

1   Thermostat faulty (Chapter 3).
2   Inaccurate temperature gauge (Chapter 12)

23 External coolant leakage

1   Deteriorated or damaged hoses or loose clamps. Replace hoses and/or tighten clamps at hose connections (Chapter 1).
2   Water pump seals defective. If this is the case, water will drip from the weep hole in the water pump body (Chapter 3).
3   Leakage from radiator core or header tank. This will require the radiator to be professionally repaired (see Chapter 3 for removal procedures).
4   Engine drain plugs or water jacket core plugs leaking (see Chapter 2).

24 Internal coolant leakage

Note: *Internal coolant leaks can usually be detected by examining the oil. Check the dipstick and inside of the camshaft cover for water deposits and an oil consistency like that of a milkshake.*

1   Leaking cylinder head gasket. Have the cooling system pressure tested.
2   Cracked cylinder bore or cylinder head. Dismantle engine and inspect (Chapter 2).

25 Coolant loss

1   Too much coolant in system (Chapter 1).
2   Coolant boiling away due to overheating (see Section 21).
3   Internal or external leakage (see Sections 23 and 24).
4   Faulty radiator cap. Have the cap pressure tested.

26 Poor coolant circulation

1   Inoperative water pump. A quick test is to pinch the top radiator hose closed with your hand while the engine is idling, then let it loose. You should feel the surge of coolant if the pump is working properly.
2   Restriction in cooling system. Drain, flush and refill the system

(Chapter 1). If necessary, remove the radiator (Chapter 3) and have it reverse flushed.
3   Thermostat sticking (Chapter 3).

Clutch

27 Fails to release (pedal pressed to the floor — shift lever does not move freely in and out of Reverse)

1   Improper linkage free play adjustment (Chapter 1).
2   Clutch plate warped or damaged (Chapter 8).

28 Clutch slips (engine speed increases with no increase in vehicle speed)

1   Linkage out of adjustment (Chapter 1).
2   Clutch plate oil soaked or lining worn. Remove clutch (Chapter 1) and inspect.
3   Clutch plate not seated. It may take 30 or 40 normal starts for a new one to seat.
4   Weak or damaged diaphragm spring.

29 Grabbing (chattering) as clutch is engaged

1   Oil on clutch plate lining. Remove (Chapter 8) and inspect. Correct any leakage source.
2   Worn or loose engine or transaxle mounts. These units move slightly when clutch is released. Inspect mounts and bolts.
3   Worn splines on clutch plate hub. Remove clutch components (Chapter 8) and inspect.
4   Warped pressure plate or flywheel. Remove clutch components and inspect.

30 Squeal or rumble with clutch fully engaged (pedal released)

1   Improper adjustment; no free play (Chapter 1).
2   Release bearing binding on transmission bearing retainer. Remove clutch components (Chapter 8) and check bearing. Remove any burrs or nicks, clean and relubricate before reinstallation.
3   Weak linkage return spring. Replace the spring.

31 Squeal or rumble with clutch fully disengaged (pedal depressed)

1   Worn, defective or broken release bearing (Chapter 8).
2   Worn or broken pressure plate springs (or diaphragm fingers) (Chapter 8).

32 Clutch pedal stays on floor when disengaged

1   Bind in linkage or release bearing. Inspect linkage or remove clutch components as necessary.
2   Linkage springs being over-extended. Adjust linkage for proper free play.

Manual transaxle

33 Noisy in neutral with engine running

1   Excessive gear backlash.
2   Damaged main drive gear bearing.
3   Worn bearings.

34 Noisy in all gears

1   Any of the above causes, and/or:
2   Insufficient lubricant (see checking procedures in Chapter 1).

35 Noisy in one particular gear

1   Worn, damaged or chipped gear teeth for that particular gear.
2   Worn or damaged synchronizer for that particular gear.

36 Slips out of high gear

1   Transaxle loose on clutch housing (Chapter 7).
2   Improperly installed engine mount (Chapter 2).
3   Shift rods not working freely (Chapter 7).
4   Worn shift fork.
5   Dirt between transaxle case and engine or misalignment of transaxle (Chapter 7).
6   Worn or damaged shift linkage (Chapter 7).

37 Difficulty in engaging gears

1   Clutch not releasing completely (see clutch adjustment in Chapter 1).
2   Loose or damaged shift linkage. Make a thorough inspection, replacing parts as necessary (Chapter 7).

38 Oil leakage

1   Excessive amount of lubricant in transaxle (see Chapter 1 for correct checking procedures). Drain lubricant as required.
2   Oil seal in need of replacement (Chapter 7).

Automatic transaxle

Note: *Due to the complexity of the automatic transaxle, it is difficult for the home mechanic to properly diagnose and service this component. For problems other than the following, the vehicle should be taken to a dealer or reputable mechanic.*

39 General shift mechanism problems

1   Chapter 7 deals with checking and adjusting the shift linkage on automatic transaxles. Common problems which may be attributed to poorly adjusted linkage are:
   Engine starting in gears other than Park or Neutral.
   Indicator on shifter pointing to a gear other than the one actually being used.
   Vehicle moves when in Park.
2   Refer to Chapter 7 to adjust the linkage.

40 Transaxle will not downshift with accelerator pedal pressed to the floor

   Chapter 7 deals with adjusting the kickdown switch cable to enable the transaxle to downshift properly.

41 Transaxle slips, shifts rough, is noisy or has no drive in forward or reverse gears

1   There are many probable causes for the above problems, but the home mechanic should be concerned with only one possibility — fluid level.

2   Before taking the vehicle to a repair shop, check the level and condition of the fluid as described in Chapter 1. Correct fluid level as necessary or change the fluid if needed. If the problem persists, have a professional diagnose the probable cause.

42 Fluid leakage

1   Automatic transmission fluid is a deep red color. Fluid leaks should not be confused with engine oil, which can easily be blown by air flow to the transaxle.
2   To pinpoint a leak, first remove all built-up dirt and grime from around the transaxle. Degreasing agents and/or steam cleaning will achieve this. With the underside clean, drive the vehicle at low speeds so air flow will not blow the leak far from its source. Raise the vehicle and determine where the leak is coming from. Common areas of leakage are:
   a) Pan: Tighten mounting bolts and/or replace pan gasket as necessary (see Chapter 7).
   b) Filler pipe: Replace the rubber seal where pipe enters transaxle case.
   c) Transaxle oil lines: Tighten connectors where lines enter transaxle case and/or replace lines.
   d) Vent pipe: Transaxle overfilled and/or water in fluid (see checking procedures, Chapter 1).
   e) Speedometer connector: Replace the O-ring where speedometer cable enters transaxle case.

Driveaxles

43 Clicking noise in turns

   Worn or damaged outboard joint. Check for cut or damaged seals. Repair as necessary (Chapter 8).

44 Knock or clunk when accelerating from a coast

   Worn or damaged inboard joint. Check for cut or damaged seals. Repair as necessary (Chapter 8).

45 Shudder or vibration during acceleration

1   Worn or damaged inboard or outboard joints. Repair or replace as necessary (Chapter 8).
2   Sticking inboard joint assembly. Correct or replace as necessary (Chapter 8).

Rear axle

46 Noise

1   Road noise. No corrective procedures available.
2   Tire noise. Inspect tires and check tire pressures (Chapter 1).
3   Rear wheel bearings loose, worn or damaged (Chapters 1 and 10).

Brakes

   Note: *Before assuming that a brake problem exists, make sure that the tires are in good condition and inflated properly (see Chapter 1), that the front end alignment is correct and that the vehicle is not loaded with weight in an unequal manner.*

47 Vehicle pulls to one side during braking

1   Defective, damaged or oil contaminated disc brake pads on one side. Inspect as described in Chapter 1.

2   Excessive wear of brake pad material or disc on one side. Inspect and correct as necessary.
3   Loose or disconnected front suspension components. Inspect and tighten all bolts to the specified torque (Chapter 10).
4   Defective caliper assembly. Remove caliper and inspect for stuck piston or other damage (Chapter 9).
5   Defective, damaged or contaminated rear brake shoes. Inspect as described in Chapter 1.
6   Defective rear wheel cylinder (Chapter 9).

48   Noise (high-pitched squeal without the brakes applied)

Disc brake pads worn out. The noise comes from the wear sensor rubbing against the disc (does not apply to all vehicles). Replace pads with new ones immediately (Chapter 9).

49   Excessive brake pedal travel

1   Partial brake system failure. Inspect entire system (Chapter 9) and correct as required.
2   Insufficient fluid in master cylinder. Check (Chapter 1), add fluid and bleed system if necessary (Chapter 9).
3   Rear brakes not adjusting properly. Make a series of starts and stops. If this does not correct the situation, remove drums and inspect self-adjusters (Chapter 9).
4   Rear brake linings worn. Inspect as described in Chapter 1.

50   Brake pedal feels spongy when depressed

1   Air in hydraulic lines. Bleed the brake system (Chapter 9).
2   Faulty flexible hoses. Inspect all system hoses and lines. Replace parts as necessary.
3   Master cylinder mounting bolts/nuts loose.
4   Master cylinder defective (Chapter 9).

51   Excessive effort required to stop vehicle

1   Power brake booster not operating properly (Chapter 1).
2   Excessively worn linings or pads. Inspect and replace if necessary (Chapters 1 and 9).
3   One or more caliper pistons or wheel cylinders seized or sticking. Inspect and rebuild as required (Chapter 9).
4   Brake linings or pads contaminated with oil or grease. Inspect and replace as required (Chapters 1 and 9).
5   New pads or shoes installed and not yet seated. It will take a while for the new material to seat against the drum (or rotor).

52   Pedal travels to the floor with little resistance

Little or no fluid in the master cylinder reservoir caused by leaking wheel cylinder(s), leaking caliper piston(s), loose, damaged or disconnected brake lines. Inspect entire system and correct as necessary.

53   Brake pedal pulsates during brake application

1   Wheel bearings not adjusted properly or in need of replacement (Chapter 1).
2   Caliper not sliding properly due to improper installation or obstructions. Remove and inspect (Chapter 9).
3   Rotor defective. Check for excessive lateral runout and parallelism (Chapter 9). Have the rotor resurfaced or replace it with a new one.

Suspension and steering systems

54   Vehicle pulls to one side

1   Tire pressures uneven (Chapter 1).
2   Defective tire (Chapter 1).
3   Excessive wear in suspension or steering components (Chapter 10).
4   Front end in need of alignment.
5   Braking system fault (Section 47).

55   Shimmy, shake or vibration

1   Tire or wheel out-of-balance or out-of-round. Have professionally balanced.
2   Loose, worn or out-of-adjustment wheel bearings (Chapters 1 and 10).
3   Shock absorbers and/or suspension components worn or damaged (Chapter 10).

56   Excessive pitching and/or rolling around corners or during braking

1   Defective shock absorbers. Replace as a set (Chapter 10).
2   Broken or weak springs and/or suspension components. Inspect as described in Chapter 10.

57   Excessively stiff steering

1   Lack of fluid in power steering fluid reservoir (Chapter 1).
2   Incorrect tire pressures (Chapter 1).
3   Lack of lubrication at steering joints.
4   Front end out of alignment.
5   See also Section 59.

58   Excessive play in steering

1   Loose front wheel bearings.
2   Excessive wear in suspension or steering components (Chapter 10).
3   Steering gearbox out of adjustment.

59   Lack of power assistance

1   Steering pump drivebelt faulty or not adjusted properly (Chapter 1).
2   Fluid level low (Chapter 1).
3   Hoses or lines restricted. Inspect and replace parts as necessary.
4   Air in power steering system. Bleed system (Chapter 10).

60   Excessive tire wear (not specific to one area)

1   Incorrect tire pressures (Chapter 1).
2   Tires out of balance. Have professionally balanced.
3   Wheels damaged. Inspect and replace as necessary.
4   Suspension or steering components excessively worn (Chapter 10).
5   Poor road surfaces and/or unsympathetic driving style.

61   Excessive tire wear on outside edge

1   Inflation pressures incorrect (Chapter 1).
2   Excessive speed in turns.
3   Front end alignment incorrect (excessive toe-in). Have professionally aligned.
4   Suspension arm bent or twisted (Chapter 10).

62   Excessive tire wear on inside edge

1   Inflation pressures incorrect (Chapter 1).
2   Front end alignment incorrect (toe-out). Have professionally aligned.
3   Loose or damaged steering components (Chapter 10).

63   Tire tread worn in one place

1   Tires out of balance.
2   Damaged or buckled wheel. Inspect and replace if necessary.
3   Defective tire (Chapter 1).
4   Brake rotor or drum out-of-true or out-of-round (Chapter 9).

Chapter 1 Tune-up and Routine maintenance

Contents

Specifications

Fluid capacities (approx)

Engine oil (including filter)	6.3 Imp pints (3.8 US quarts, 3.6 litres) drain and refill
Cooling system (including heater)	
1.6 litre	12.1 Imp pints (7.3 US quarts, 6.9 litres)
2.0 litre	12.7 Imp pints (7.6 US quarts, 7.2 litres)
Fuel tank	13.2 Imp gallons (15.9 US gallons, 60 litres)
Manual transaxle	6.0 Imp pints (3.6 US quarts, 3.4 litres)
Automatic transaxle	10.0 Imp pints (6.0 US quarts, 5.7 litres)

General engine

Radiator cap opening pressure . . . . 13 ± 2 psi

Thermostat

   Starts to open . . . . 188° to 193°F (88° to 90°C)
   Fully open . . . . 212°F (100°C)

	US	UK (2.0 litre)	UK (1.6 litre)
Engine idle speed*			
Automatic transaxle	700 rpm	900 rpm	
Manual tranaxle	750 rpm	800 rpm	800 rpm

CO level at idle (UK models) . . . . 2.0 ± 0.5%
Valve clearance (engine warm), intake and exhaust . . . . 0.012 in (0.30 mm)
Engine compression pressure . . . . Lowest reading should not be less than 70% of the highest cylinder reading with no cylinder below 115 psi

	New belt	Used belt
Drivebelt deflection		
Without air conditioning	0.24 to 0.32 in (6 to 8 mm)	0.39 to 0.47 in (10 to 12 mm)
With air conditioning		
Alternator drivebelt	0.16 to 0.20 in (4 to 5 mm)	0.24 to 0.28 in (6 to 7 mm)
Compressor-only drivebelt	0.24 to 0.32 in (6 to 8 mm)	0.39 to 0.47 in (10 to 12 mm)
Compressor and power steering pump drivebelt	0.16 to 0.20 in (4 to 5 mm)	0.24 to 0.28 in (6 to 7 mm)

*Refer to the Emission Control label in the engine compartment (US models) and follow the information on the label if it differs from that shown here.

Ignition system

Distributor direction of rotation	Clockwise
Firing order	1-3-4-2
Location of No. 1 cylinder	Pulley end
Spark plug type*	
Champion	RN9Y or RN9YC
NGK	BPR-5ES, BPR-6ES
Nippon Denso	W16EXR-U, W20EXR-U
Spark plug gap*	0.030 to 0.033 in (0.76 to 0.84 mm)
Ignition timing (BTDC)*	6°

*Refer to the Emission Control Label in the engine compartment (US models) and follow the information on the label if it differs from that shown here.

Brakes

Pad and shoe lining minimum thickness	0.04 in (1.0 mm)
Parking brake engagement	7 to 9 notches at 22 lbs (10 kg)

Clutch

Clutch pedal	
Free play at pedal	0.43 to 0.67 in (10 to 16 mm)
Release lever clearance	0.08 to 0.12 in (2 to 3 mm)
Engaged height	8.5 in (212 mm)
Disengaged height	3.2 in (83 mm)

Tire pressures (cold)*

	Front	Rear
Normal load	29 psi (2.0 kg/cm²)	26 psi (1.8 kg/cm²)
Maximum load (165 SR 13 tires)	30 psi (2.1 kg/cm²)	27 psi (1.9 kg/cm²)
Maximum load (other tire sizes)	Same as normal load	

*Refer to vehicle handbook, or to sticker on driver's door jamb, for details specific to vehicle

Torque specifications

	Ft-lbs	M-kg
Cylinder head bolts		
Warm	69 to 80	9.5 to 11.0
Cold	59 to 64	8.2 to 8.8
Spark plugs	11 to 17	1.5 to 2.3
Wheel lug nuts	65 to 87	9.0 to 12.0
Rocker arm cover bolts	2 to 3	0.28 to 0.41
Rear wheel bearing spindle nut initial preload . .	18 to 22	2.48 to 3.0
Automatic transaxle drain plug	12	1.6
Brake caliper mounting bolts		
Upper	11 to 18	1.5 to 2.48
Lower	14 to 22	1.9 to 3.0

1 Introduction and routine maintenance schedule

This Chapter is designed to help the home mechanic maintain his or her vehicle for peak performance, economy, safety and long life.

On the following pages you will find a maintenance schedule along with Sections which deal specifically with each item on the schedule. Included are visual checks, adjustments and item replacements.

Servicing your vehicle using the time/mileage maintenance schedule and the sequenced Sections will give you a planned program of maintenance. Keep in mind that it is a full plan, and maintaining only a few items at the specified intervals will not give you the same results.

You will find as you service your vehicle that many of the procedures can, and should, be grouped together, due to the nature of the job at hand. Examples of this are as follows:

If the vehicle is raised for a chassis lubrication, for example, it is an ideal time for the following checks: exhaust system, suspension, steering and fuel system.

If the tires and wheels are removed, as during a routine tire rotation, check the brakes and wheel bearings at the same time.

If you must borrow or rent a torque wrench, service the spark plugs and check the wheel bearings all in the same day to save time and money.

The first step of the maintenance plan is to prepare yourself before the actual work begins. Read through the appropriate Sections for all work that is to be performed before you begin. Gather together all the necessary parts and tools. If it appears that you could have a problem during a particular job, don't hesitate to seek advice from your local parts man or dealer service department.

Routine maintenance intervals

The following recommendations are given with the assumption that the vehicle owner will be doing the maintenance or service work, as opposed to having a dealer service department do the work. The following are factory maintenance recommendations. However, the owner, interested in keeping his or her vehicle in peak condition at all times and with the vehicle's ultimate resale in mind, may want to perform many of these operations more often. We encourage such owner initiative.

When the vehicle is new it should be serviced initially by a factory authorized dealer service department to protect the factory warranty. In many cases the initial maintenance check is done at no cost to the owner. **Note:** *The following maintenance intervals are recommended by the manufacturer. In the interest of vehicle longevity, we recommend shorter intervals on certain operations, such as fluid and filter replacement.*

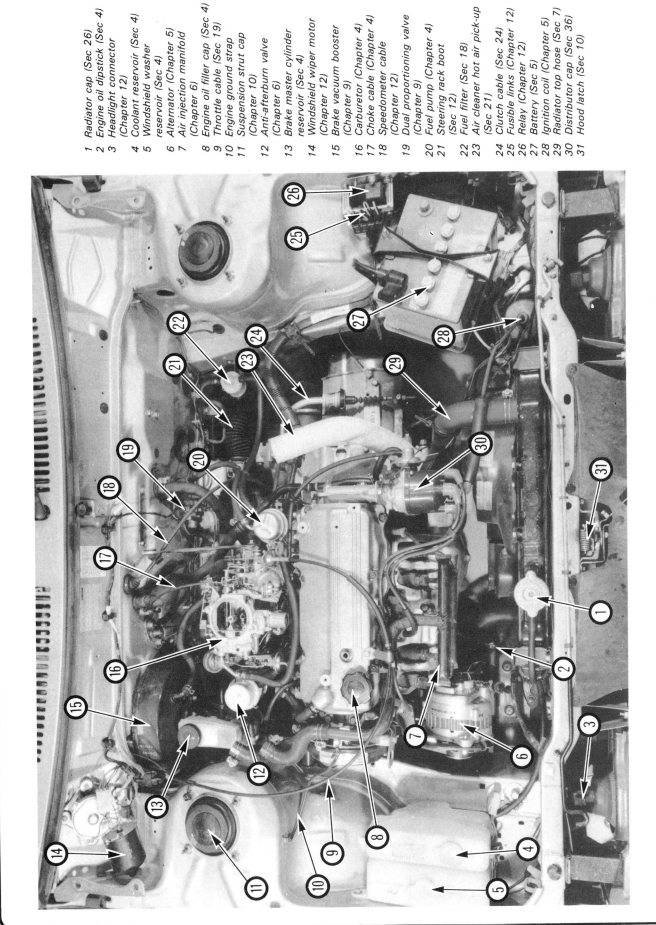

1 Radiator cap (Sec 26)
2 Engine oil dipstick (Sec 4)
3 Headlight connector (Chapter 12)
4 Coolant reservoir (Sec 4)
5 Windshield washer reservoir (Sec 4)
6 Alternator (Chapter 5)
7 Air injection manifold (Chapter 6)
8 Engine oil filler cap (Sec 4)
9 Throttle cable (Sec 19)
10 Engine ground strap
11 Suspension strut cap (Chapter 10)
12 Anti-afterburn valve (Chapter 6)
13 Brake master cylinder reservoir (Sec 4)
14 Windshield wiper motor (Chapter 12)
15 Brake vacuum booster (Chapter 9)
16 Carburetor (Chapter 4)
17 Choke cable (Chapter 4)
18 Speedometer cable (Chapter 12)
19 Dual proportioning valve (Chapter 9)
20 Fuel pump (Chapter 4)
21 Steering rack boot (Sec 12)
22 Fuel filter (Sec 18)
23 Air cleaner hot air pick-up (Sec 21)
24 Clutch cable (Sec 24)
25 Fusible links (Chapter 12)
26 Relay (Chapter 12)
27 Battery (Sec 5)
28 Ignition coil (Chapter 5)
29 Radiator top hose (Sec 7)
30 Distributor cap (Sec 36)
31 Hood latch (Sec 10)

Fig. 1.1 Engine compartment component layout (typical UK model) with air cleaner removed

Fig. 1.2 Typical view of the underside of the front of the vehicle

1 Driveaxle boot (Sec 22)
2 Fuel and vapor lines (Sec 17)
3 Automatic transaxle drain plug (Sec 28)

4 Exhaust system heat shield (Sec 11)
5 Exhaust system hanger (Sec 11)
6 Steering gear boot (Sec 12)

7 Engine oil drain plug (Sec 16)
8 Front disc brake (Sec 13)
9 Tire tread (Sec 3 and 23)

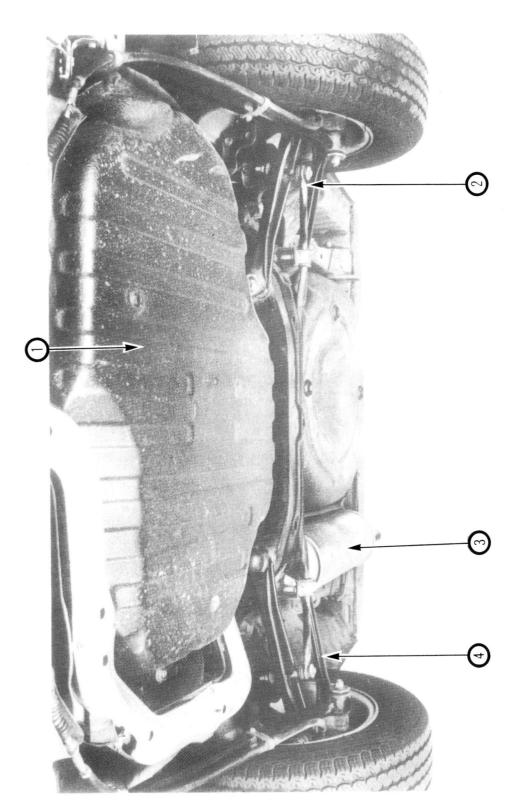

Fig. 1.3 Typical view of the underside of the rear of the vehicle

1 Fuel tank (Sec 17)
2 Sway bar link (Sec 12)
3 Muffler (Sec 11)
4 Lower suspension arm (Sec 12)

Every 250 miles or weekly, whichever comes first

Check the engine oil level (Sec 4)
Check the engine coolant level (Sec 4)
Check brake fluid level (Sec 4)
Check battery electrolyte level (if possible — see Sec 5)
Check the windshield washer fluid level (Sec 4)
Check the tires and tire pressures (Sec 3)
Check the operation of all lights
Check the horn operation

Every 6000 miles or 6 months, whichever comes first

Check the power steering fluid level (Sec 4)
Change the engine oil and oil filter (Sec 16)
Check the tightness of the carburetor mounting bolts (Sec 20)
Check and lubricate the chassis components (Sec 10)
Check the cooling system (Sec 7)
Check and replace (if necessary) the underhood hoses (Sec 8)
Check the exhaust system (Sec 11)
Check and adjust (if necessary) the engine valve clearances (Sec 37)
Check and adjust (if necessary) the engine drivebelts (Sec 6)
Check and adjust (if necessary) ignition timing (Sec 34)
Check and adjust (if necessary) idle speed and mixture (Sec 15)
Check clutch pedal free play (Sec 24)
Inspect spark plugs, clean and regap or replace (Sec 35)
Check 'coasting leaner' system (UK only — Sec 39)
Rotate tires if wished (Sec 23)
Check the steering and suspension components (Sec 12)
Check the transaxle oil level (Sec 4)
Check the driveaxle boots (Sec 22)
Check the disc brake pads (Sec 13)
Check the brake system (Sec 13)
Check and service the battery (Sec 5)
Check and replace (if necessary) the windshield wiper blades (Sec 9)

Every 12,000 miles or 12 months, whichever comes first

In addition to the items in the previous schedule
Check the drum brake linings (Sec 13)
Check the operation of the choke (Sec 14)
Check the parking brake (Sec 13)
Check the thermostatically controlled air cleaner for proper operation (Sec 21)
Check the fuel system components (Sec 17)
Check the throttle linkage (Sec 19)
Replace fuel filter (Sec 18)
Check tightness of front suspension strut mountings and driveaxle nuts (see Chapter 10 Specifications)

Every 18,000 miles or 18 months, whichever comes first

In addition to the items in the 6000-mile/6-month schedule
Check the EGR system (not UK) (Sec 32)
Check the evaporative emissions system (not UK) (Sec 33)
Check the engine compression (Sec 38)

Every 24,000 miles or 24 months, whichever comes first

In addition to the items in the 6000-mile and 12,000-mile schedules
Check tightness of cylinder head bolts (Contained in Sec 37)
Check tightness of inlet and exhaust manifold nuts
Drain, flush and refill the cooling system (Sec 26)
Drain and refill the manual transaxle oil (Sec 25)
Lubricate and adjust the rear wheel bearings (Sec 27)
Inspect and replace, if necessary, the PCV valve (Sec 31)
Replace the air filter and PCV filter (Sec 29)

Inspect and replace, if necessary, the spark plug wires, distributor cap and rotor (Sec 36)
Check the oxygen sensor (Chapter 6) and replace if necessary (Sec 30) (not UK)
Replace the brake fluid by bleeding (Chapter 9)

Every 48,000 miles or 48 months, whichever comes first

In addition to the items previously specified
Drain and refill the automatic transaxle (Sec 28)

Every 60,000 miles or 60 months, whichever comes first

Replace the engine timing belt (Chapter 2)

Severe operating conditions

Severe operating conditions are defined as:
Frequent short trips or long periods of idling
Driving at sustained high speeds during hot weather (over 90°F, 32°C)
Driving in severe dust conditions
Driving in temperatures below 10°F (−12°C) for 60 or more days
Driving in extremely humid conditions
Mountain driving or where the brakes are used extensively
If the vehicle has been operated under severe conditions, follow these maintenance intervals:
Change the air and fuel filters more frequently
Change the engine oil and oil filter every 2000 miles or two months
Drain and refill the automatic transaxle every 22,500 miles

2   Tune-up sequence

The term *tune-up* is used for any general operation that puts the engine back in its proper running condition. A tune-up is not a specific operation, but rather a combination of individual operations, such as replacing the spark plugs, adjusting the idle speed, setting the ignition timing, etc.

If, from the time the vehicle is new, the routine maintenance schedule (Section 1) is followed closely and frequent checks are made of fluid levels and high wear items, as suggested throughout this manual, the engine will be kept in relatively good running condition and the need for additional tune-ups will be minimized.

More likely than not, however, there will be times when the engine is running poorly due to lack of regular maintenance. This is even more likely if a used vehicle, which has not received regular and frequent maintenance checks, is purchased. In such cases, an engine tune-up will be needed outside of the regular routine maintenance intervals.

The following series of operations are those most often needed to bring a generally poor running engine back into a proper state of tune.

Minor tune-up
Clean, inspect and test battery (Sec 5)
Check all engine related fluids (Sec 4)
Check engine compression (Sec 38)
Check and adjust drivebelts (Sec 6)
Replace spark plugs (Sec 35)
Inspect distributor cap and rotor (Sec 36)
Inspect spark plug and coil wires (Sec 36)
Check and adjust idle speed and mixture (Sec 15)
Check and adjust timing (Sec 34)
Replace fuel filter (Sec 18)
Check PCV valve (Sec 31)
Check cooling system (Sec 7)

Major tune-up
(the above operations and those listed below)
Check EGR system (not UK) (Chapter 6)
Check ignition system (Chapter 5)

Check charging system (Chapter 5)
Check fuel system (Sec 17)

3 Tire and tire pressure checks

1   Periodically inspecting the tires may not only prevent you from being stranded with a flat tire, but can also give you clues as to possible problems with the steering and suspension systems before major damage occurs.
2   Proper tire inflation adds miles to the lifespan of the tires, allows the vehicle to achieve maximum miles per gallon figures and contributes to the overall quality of the ride.
3   When inspecting the tires, first check the wear of the tread. Irregularities in the tread pattern (cupping, flat spots, more wear on one side than the other) are indications of front end alignment and/or balance problems. If any of these conditions are noted, take the vehicle to a repair shop to correct the problem.
4   Check the tread area for cuts and punctures. Many times a nail or tack will embed itself into the tire tread and yet the tire will hold its air pressure for a short time. In most cases, a repair shop or gas station can repair the punctured tire.
5   It is important to check the sidewalls of the tires, both inside and outside. Check for deteriorated rubber, cuts, and punctures. Inspect the inboard side of the tire for signs of brake fluid leakage, indicating that a thorough brake inspection is needed immediately.
6   Incorrect tire pressure cannot be determined merely by looking at the tire. This is especially true for radial tires. A tire pressure gauge must be used. If you do not already have a reliable gauge, it is a good idea to purchase one and keep it in the glovebox. Built-in pressure gauges at gas stations are often unreliable.
7   Always check tire inflation when the tires are cold. Cold, in this case, means the vehicle has not been driven more than one mile after sitting for three hours or more. It is normal for the pressure to increase four to eight pounds when the tires are hot.
8   Unscrew the valve cap protruding from the wheel or hubcap and press the gauge firmly onto the valve. Observe the reading on the gauge and compare the figure to the recommended tire pressure listed on the tire placard. The tire placard is usually attached to the driver's door jamb.
9   Check all tires and add air as necessary to bring them up to the recommended pressure levels. Do not forget the spare tire. Be sure to reinstall the valve caps, which will keep dirt and moisture out of the valve stem mechanism.
10 For further information see Chapter 10, Section 1.

4 Fluid level checks

1   There are a number of components on a vehicle which rely on the use of fluids to perform their job. During normal operation of the vehicle, these fluids are used up and must be replenished before damage occurs. See *Recommended lubricants and fluids* at the front of this manual for the specific fluid to be used when addition is required. When checking fluid levels, it is important to have the vehicle on a level surface.

Engine oil

2   The engine oil level is checked with a dipstick. The dipstick travels through a tube and into the oil pan to the bottom of the engine.
3   The oil level should be checked before the vehicle has been driven, or about 15 minutes after the engine has been shut off. If the oil is checked immediately after driving the vehicle, some of the oil will remain in the upper engine components, producing an inaccurate reading on the dipstick.
4   Pull the dipstick from the tube (photo) and wipe all the oil from the end with a clean rag or paper towel. Insert the clean dipstick all the way back into the oil pan and pull it out again. Observe the oil at the end of the dipstick. At its highest point, the level should be between the L and F marks (photo).
5   It takes one litre of oil to raise the level from the L mark to the F mark on the dipstick. Do not allow the level to drop below the L mark as engine damage due to oil starvation may occur. On the other hand, do not overfill the engine by adding oil above the F mark since it may result in oil fouled spark plugs, oil leaks or oil seal failures.
6   Oil is added to the engine after removing a twist off cap located on the rocker arm cover. An oil can spout or funnel will reduce spills.
7   Checking the oil level can be an important preventative maintenance step. If you find the oil level dropping abnormally, it is an indication of oil leakage or internal engine wear which should be corrected. If there are water droplets in the oil, or if it is milky looking, component failure is indicated and the engine should be checked immediately. The condition of the oil can also be checked along with the level. With the dipstick removed from the engine, take your thumb and index finger and wipe the oil up the dipstick, looking for small dirt or metal particles which will cling to the dipstick. This is an indication that the oil should be drained and fresh oil added (Section 16).

Engine coolant

8   All vehicles covered by this manual are equipped with a pressurized coolant recovery system. A white coolant reservoir attached to the

4.4a   The engine oil dipstick is located on the front (radiator side) of the engine

4.4b   The oil level should appear between the F and L marks — do not overfill the crankcase

inner fender panel is connected by a hose to the radiator cap. As the engine heats up during operation, coolant is forced from the radiator, through the connecting tube and into the reservoir. As the engine cools, the coolant is automatically drawn back into the radiator to keep the level correct.

9   The coolant level should be checked when the engine is hot. Observe the level of fluid in the reservoir, which should be at or near the Full mark on the side of the reservoir (photo). If the system is completely cool, also check the level in the radiator by removing the cap.

10   **Warning:** *Under no circumstances should the radiator cap or the coolant recovery reservoir cap be removed when the system is hot, because escaping steam and scalding liquid could cause serious personal injury. In the case of the radiator, wait until the system has cooled completely, then wrap a thick cloth around the cap and turn it to the first stop. If any steam escapes, wait until the system has cooled further, then remove the cap. The coolant recovery cap may be removed carefully after it is apparent that no further boiling is occurring in the recovery tank.*

11   If only a small amount of coolant is required to bring the system up to the proper level, regular water can be used. However, to maintain the proper antifreeze/water mixture in the system, both should be mixed together to replenish a low level. High quality antifreeze offering protection to −20 °F should be mixed with water in the proportion specified on the container. Do not allow antifreeze to come in contact with your skin or painted surfaces of the vehicle. Flush contacted areas immediately with plenty of water.

12   Coolant should be added to the reservoir until it reaches the Full mark. If the radiator cap has been removed, add coolant until the radiator is brim full, then install the cap.

13   As the coolant level is checked, note the condition of the coolant. It should be relatively clear. If it is brown or a rust color, the system should be drained, flushed and refilled (Section 26).

14   If the cooling system requires repeated additions to maintain the proper level, have the radiator cap checked for proper sealing ability. Also check for leaks in the system from cracked hoses, loose hose connections, leaking gaskets, etc.

Windshield washer fluid

15   Fluid for the windshield washer system is located in a plastic reservoir located next to the coolant reservoir. The reservoir should be kept no more than 2/3 full to allow for expansion should the fluid freeze. The use of an additive such as windshield washer fluid, available at auto parts stores, will help lower the freezing point of the fluid and will result in better cleaning of the windshield surface. Do not use antifreeze because it will cause damage to the vehicle's paint.

16   To help prevent icing in cold weather, warm the windshield with the defroster before using the washer.

Rear window washer

17   On models equipped with rear window washers, the reservoir is accessible behind a panel in the rear compartment and should also be kept at the 2/3 full level using the same fluid as in the windshield washer.

Headlight washer

18   Some models are equipped with headlight washers, the reservoir for which is located in the engine compartment. Because of the variety of reservoir configurations used, trace the tubes leading from the washers to the reservoir to determine its location. The reservoir should be kept at the 2/3 full level with the same fluid used in the windshield and rear window washer reservoirs.

Battery electrolyte

19   Some vehicles with which this manual is concerned are equipped with a battery which is permanently sealed (except for vent holes) and has no filler caps. Water does not have to be added to these batteries at any time (photo).

20   When a battery with detachable cell caps is fitted, remove the caps periodically and check that the cell plates are covered by 0.4 to 0.8 in (10 to 20 mm) with electrolyte. Top up if necessary using distilled or de-ionized water. Do not overfill, and mop up any spillage immediately. Install the cell caps on completion (photos).

Brake fluid

21   The brake master cylinder is mounted on the front of the power booster unit in the engine compartment. The fluid level should be maintained at the Max marking on the reservoir (photo).

22   If a low level is indicated, be sure to wipe the top of the reservoir

4.9   The coolant and windshield washer reservoirs are located next to each other but use different fluids, so don't mix them up

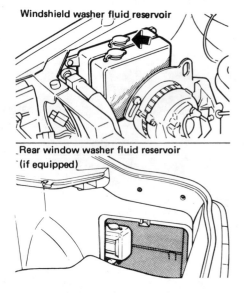

Fig. 1.4   Windshield and rear window washer reservoir locations (Sec 4)

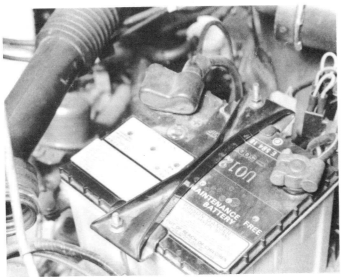

4.19   This type of battery never requires the addition of water, but normal maintenance should be performed

4.20a   Topping up battery electrolyte

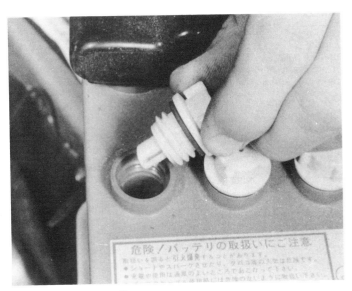

4.20b   Installing a cell cap

4.21   The brake fluid level can be checked without removing the cap

cover with a clean rag, to prevent contamination of the brake system, before lifting the cover.

23   When adding fluid, pour it carefully into the reservoir, taking care not to spill any onto surrounding painted surfaces. Be sure the specified fluid is used, since mixing different types of brake fluid can cause damage to the system. See *Recommended lubricants and fluids* or your owner's manual.

24   At this time the fluid and cylinder can be inspected for contamination. The manufacturer recommends that the fluid be renewed by bleeding at the specified intervals (Chapter 9). The fluid should also be renewed if deposits, dirt particles or water droplets are seen in it.

25   After filling the reservoir to the proper level, make sure the lid is properly seated to prevent fluid leakage and/or system pressure loss.

26   The brake fluid in the master cylinder will drop slightly as the brake shoes or pads at each wheel wear down during normal operation. If the master cylinder requires repeated replenishing to keep it at the proper level, this is an indication of leakage in the brake system, which should be corrected immediately. Check all brake lines and connections, along with the wheel cylinders and booster (see Section 13 for more information).

27   If, upon checking the master cylinder fluid level, you discover one

or both reservoirs empty or nearly empty, the brake system should be bled (Chapter 9).

Manual transaxle oil

28   Manual transaxles do not have a dipstick. The fluid level is checked by removing the speedometer driven gear.

29   Remove the retaining bolt, withdraw the gear, wipe the driven gear clean and reinsert it. Pull the gear out again and check that the oil level is between the F and L level as shown in the accompanying illustration.

30   If the transaxle needs more oil, use a syringe to squeeze the appropriate lubricant into the speedometer gear hole.

31   Install the gear, thread the attaching bolt into the transaxle and tighten it securely. Drive the vehicle a short distance, then check for leaks.

Automatic transaxle fluid

32   The level of the automatic transaxle fluid should be carefully maintained. Low fluid level can lead to slipping or loss of drive, while overfilling can cause foaming and loss of fluid.

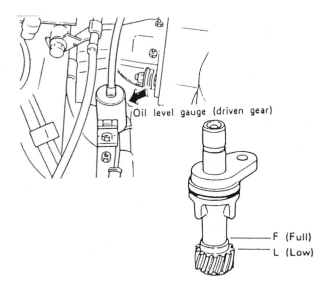

Fig. 1.5   Manual transaxle driven gear and oil level gauge
(Sec 4)

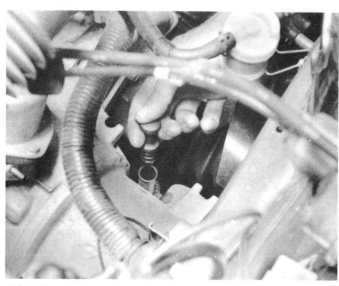

4.34 The automatic transaxle dipstick is located at the rear of
the transaxle

33 With the parking brake set, start the engine, then move the shift
lever through all the gear ranges, ending in Park. The fluid level must
be checked with the vehicle level and the engine running at idle. **Note:**
*Incorrect fluid level readings will result if the vehicle has just been driven
at high speeds for an extended period, in hot weather in city traffic,
or if it has been pulling a trailer. If any of these conditions apply, wait
until the fluid has cooled (about 30 minutes).*
34 With the transaxle at normal operating temperature, remove the
dipstick from the filler tube (photo).
35 Wipe the fluid from the dipstick with a clean rag and push it back
into the filler tube until the cap seats.
36 Pull the dipstick out again and note the fluid level.
37 The level should be in the area between the L and F mark (photo).
38 Add just enough of the recommended fluid to fill the transmission
to the proper level. It takes about one pint to raise the level from the
L mark to the F mark with a hot transaxle, so add the fluid a little at
a time and keep checking the level until it is correct. Take great care
not to introduce any dirt or foreign matter into the transaxle.

39 The condition of the fluid should also be checked along with the
level. If the fluid at the end of the dipstick is a dark reddish-brown color,
or if the fluid has a burned smell, the transaxle fluid should be changed.
If you are in doubt about the condition of the fluid, purchase some
new fluid and compare the two for color and smell.

Power steering fluid

40 Unlike manual steering, the power steering system relies on fluid
which may, over a period of time, require replenishing.
41 The fluid reservoir for the power steering pump is located behind
the radiator near the front of the engine (photo).
42 For the check, the front wheels should be pointed straight ahead
and the engine should be off.
43 Use a clean rag to wipe off the reservoir cap and the area around
the cap. This will help prevent any foreign matter from entering the
reservoir during the check.
44 Run the engine until it is at normal operating temperature.
45 Remove the dipstick, wipe it off with a clean rag, reinsert it, then

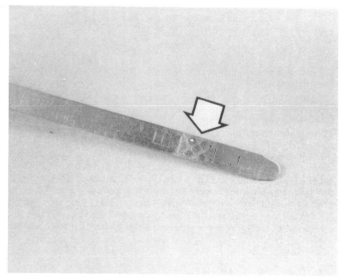

4.37 The automatic transaxle fluid level should be kept within
the hatched area on the dipstick (arrow) — do not overfill

4.41 The power steering reservoir is located near the engine oil
dipstick

withdraw it and read the fluid level. The level should be between the Add and Full Hot marks.

46 If additional fluid is required, pour the specified type directly into the reservoir, using a funnel to prevent spills.

47 The dipstick must be reinstalled with the arrow on the cap pointing forward, toward the radiator.

48 If the reservoir requires frequent fluid additions, all power steering hoses, hose connections, the power steering pump and the rack and pinion assembly should be carefully checked for leaks.

5 Battery check and maintenance

1 Tools and materials required for battery maintenance include eye and hand protection, baking soda, petroleum jelly, a battery cable puller and a cable/terminal post cleaning tool (photo). If the battery has detachable cell caps, a hydrometer will also be required.

2 A sealed battery is standard equipment on some vehicles with which this manual is concerned. Although this type of battery has many advantages over the older, capped cell type, and never requires the addition of water, it should nevertheless be routinely maintained according to the procedures which follow. **Warning:** *Hydrogen gas in small quantities is present in the area of the side vents on sealed batteries, so keep lighted tobacco and open flames or sparks away from them.*

3 The external condition of the battery should be monitored periodically for damage such as a cracked case or cover.

4 Check the tightness of the battery cable clamps to ensure good electrical connections and check the entire length of each cable for cracks and frayed conductors.

5 If corrosion (visible as white, fluffy deposits) is evident, remove the cables from the terminals, clean them with a battery brush and reinstall the cables. Corrosion can be kept to a minimum by applying a layer of petroleum jelly or grease to the terminals and cable clamps after they are assembled.

6 Make sure that the rubber protector (if so equipped) over the positive terminal is not torn or missing. It should completely cover the terminal.

7 Make sure that the battery carrier is in good condition and that the hold-down clamp bolts are tight. If the battery is removed from the carrier, make sure that no parts remain in the bottom of the carrier when the battery is reinstalled. When reinstalling the hold-down clamp bolts, do not overtighten them.

8 Corrosion on the hold-down components, battery case and surrounding areas may be removed with a solution of water and baking soda, but take care to prevent any solution from coming in contact with your eyes, skin or clothes. Protective gloves should be worn. Thoroughly wash all cleaned areas with plain water.

9 Any metal parts of the vehicle damaged by corrosion should be covered with a zinc-based primer then painted.

10 If the battery has detachable cell caps, check the specific gravity of the electrolyte using a battery hydrometer (photo). Draw electrolyte from one cell into the hydrometer and note the specific gravity, shown by the position of the hydrometer float. Return the electrolyte to the same cell, then repeat the process for the remaining cells. Typical readings (at 68°F/20°C electrolyte temperature) are as follows:

Fully charged — 1.260
Half charged — 1.160
Discharged — 1.060

11 If one cell persistently gives a lower hydrometer reading than the others, it may be that the battery is nearing the end of its life. Alternatively, electrolyte may have been lost from that cell and the deficiency made up with water. Consult a battery specialist if electrolyte replenishment is necessary.

12 Further information on the battery, charging and jumpstarting can be found in Chapter 5 and at the front of this manual.

6 Drivebelt check, adjustment and replacement

1 The drivebelts, or V-belts as they are more often called, are located at the front of the engine and play an important role in the overall operation of the vehicle and its components. Due to their function and material make up, the belts are prone to failure after a period of time and should be inspected and adjusted periodically to prevent major engine damage.

2 These vehicles use ribbed belts of a special design which must always be replaced with belts of the same design.

3 The number of belts used on a particular vehicle depends on the accessories installed. Drivebelts are used to turn the generator/alternator, power steering pump and air conditioning compressor. Depending on the pulley arrangement, a single belt may be used to drive more than one of these components.

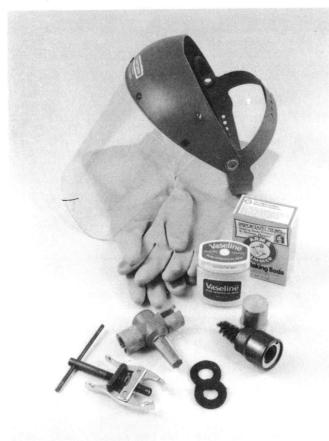

5.1 Eye and hand protection, baking soda, petroleum jelly and tools required for battery maintenance

5.10 Using a hydrometer to check the battery electrolyte specific gravity

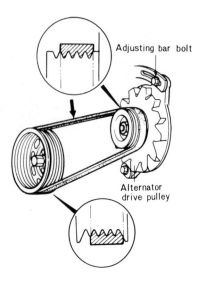

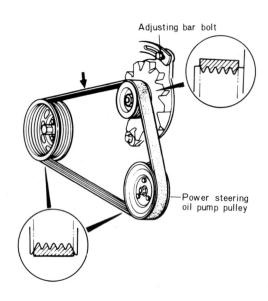

Fig. 1.6   Drivebelt arrangement — alternator only. Tension checking point arrowed (Sec 6)

Fig. 1.7   Drivebelt arrangement — alternator and power steering pump. Tension checking point arrowed (Sec 6)

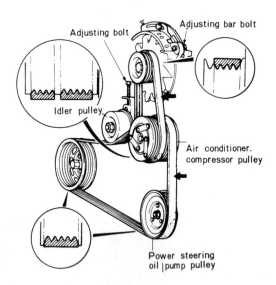

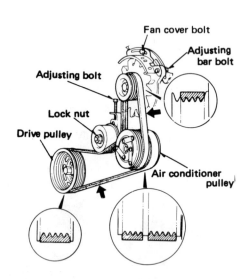

Fig. 1.8   Drivebelt arrangements with air conditioning. Tension checking points arrowed (Sec 6)

4   The various belt configurations are shown in the accompanying illustrations.

5   With the engine off, open the hood and locate the various belts at the front of the engine. Using your fingers (and a flashlight, if necessary), move along the belts checking for cracks and separation of the belt plies. Also check for fraying and glazing, which gives the belt a shiny appearance. Both sides of the belt should be inspected, which means you will have to twist the belt to check the underside.

6   The tension of each belt is checked by pushing on the belt at a distance halfway between the pulleys (at the points indicated by arrows in the illustrations). Push firmly with your thumb and see how much the belt moves (deflects). Measure the deflection with a ruler and compare the amount of deflection with Specifications (photo).

7   If it is necessary to adjust the belt tension, either to make the belt tighter or looser, it is done by moving the belt-driven accessory on the bracket.

8   For each component there will be an adjusting bolt and a pivot bolt. Both bolts must be loosened slightly to enable you to move the component. On the serpentine power steering and air conditioning compressor belt, tension is adjusted by turning only the idler pulley adjusting bolt (photo). The idler pulley locknut must be slackened before making adjustments, and tightened when adjustment is correct.

9   After the two bolts have been loosened, move the component away from the engine to tighten the belt or toward the engine to loosen the belt. Hold the accessory in position and check the belt tension. If it is correct, tighten the two bolts until just snug, then recheck the tension. If the tension is correct, tighten the bolts.

10   It will often be necessary to use some sort of pry bar to move the accessory while the belt is adjusted. If this must be done to gain the proper leverage, be very careful not to damage the component being moved or the part being pried against.

11   To replace a drivebelt, slacken the old belt as just described until

6.6   Measuring the drivebelt deflection (arrow)

6.8   The serpentine belt adjustment bolt location (arrow)

it can be slipped off the pulleys. (When two belts are fitted, the one furthest from the engine must be removed first, even if it is not to be replaced.)
12   Install the new belt(s) and adjust the tension as just described. Remember that the deflection is different for a new belt — see Specifications.
13   Recheck the tension of a new belt after a few hundred miles.

7   Cooling system check

1   Many major engine failures can be attributed to a faulty cooling system. If the vehicle is equipped with an automatic transmission, the cooling system also plays an important role in prolonging transmission life.
2   The cooling system should be checked with the engine cold. Do this before the vehicle is driven for the day or after it has been shut off for at least three hours.

3   Remove the radiator cap and thoroughly clean the cap, inside and out, with clean water. Also clean the filler neck on the radiator. All traces of corrosion should be removed (photo).
4   Carefully check the upper and lower radiator hoses along with the smaller diameter heater hoses. Inspect each hose along its entire length, replacing any hose which is cracked, swollen or shows signs of deterioration. Cracks may become more apparent if the hose is squeezed (photo).
5   Make sure that all hose connections are tight. A leak in the cooling system will usually show up as white or rust colored deposits on the areas adjoining the leak.
6   Use compressed air or a soft brush to remove bugs, leaves, etc. from the front of the radiator or air conditioning condenser. Be careful not to damage the delicate cooling fins or cut yourself on them.
7   Finally, have the cap and system pressure tested. If you do not have a pressure tester, most gas stations and repair shops will do this for a minimal charge.

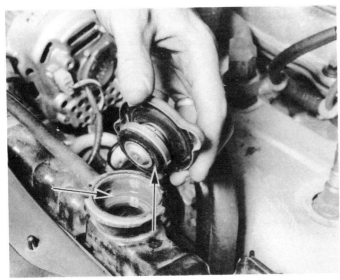

7.3   Never remove the radiator cap while the engine is hot. Inspect the gasket sealing surfaces (arrows) for corrosion and damage

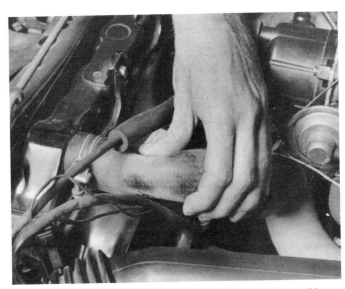

7.4   Although this radiator hose appears to be in good condition, it should be periodically checked for cracks, which are more easily revealed when squeezed

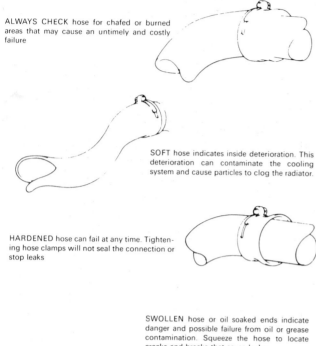

ALWAYS CHECK hose for chafed or burned areas that may cause an untimely and costly failure

SOFT hose indicates inside deterioration. This deterioration can contaminate the cooling system and cause particles to clog the radiator.

HARDENED hose can fail at any time. Tightening hose clamps will not seal the connection or stop leaks

SWOLLEN hose or oil soaked ends indicate danger and possible failure from oil or grease contamination. Squeeze the hose to locate cracks and breaks that cause leaks.

Fig. 1.9   Simple checks can detect radiator hose defects (Sec 7)

8   Underhood hose check and replacement

Warning: *Replacement of air conditioning hoses must be left to a dealer or air conditioning specialist who has the proper equipment to depressurize the system safely. Never remove air conditioning components or hoses until the system has been depressurized.*

Vacuum hoses

1   High temperatures under the hood can cause the deterioration of the rubber and plastic hoses used for engine, accessory and emission systems operation.
2   Periodic inspection should be made for cracks, loose clamps, material hardening and leaks.
3   Some, but not all, vacuum hoses use clamps to secure the hoses to fittings. Where clamps are used, check to be sure they haven't lost their tension, allowing the hose to leak. Where clamps are not used, make sure the hose has not expanded and/or hardened where it slips over the fitting, allowing it to leak.
4   It is quite common for vacuum hoses, especially those in the emissions system, to be color coded or identified by colored stripes molded into the hose. Various systems require hoses with different wall thicknesses, collapse resistance and temperature resistance. When replacing hoses be sure to use the same hose material on the new hose.
5   Often the only effective way to check a hose is to remove it completely from the vehicle. Where more than one hose is removed, be sure to label the hoses and their attaching points to insure proper reattachment.
6   When checking vacuum hoses, be sure to include any plastic T-fittings in the check. Check the fittings for cracks and the hose where it fits over the fitting for enlargement, which could cause leakage.
7   A small piece of vacuum hose (1/4-inch inside diameter) can be used as a stethoscope to detect vacuum leaks. Hold one end of the

hose to your ear and probe around vacuum hoses and fittings, listening for the "hissing" sound characteristic of a vacuum leak. **Warning:** *When probing with the vacuum hose stethoscope, be careful not to allow your body or the hose to come into contact with moving engine components such as drivebelts, the cooling fan, etc.*

Fuel hose

8   **Warning:** *There are certain precautions which must be taken when inspecting or servicing fuel system components. Work in a well ventilated area and do not allow open flames (cigarettes, appliance pilot lights, etc.) or bare light bulbs near the work area. Mop up any spills immediately and do not store fuel soaked rags where they could ignite.*
9   The fuel lines are usually under a small amount of pressure, so if any fuel lines are to be disconnected be prepared to catch fuel spillage.
10   Check all rubber fuel lines for deterioration and chafing. Check especially for cracking in areas where the hose bends and just before clamping points, such as where a hose attaches to the fuel pump, fuel filter and carburetor.
11   High quality fuel line, usually identified by the word *Fluroelastomer* printed on the hose, should be used for fuel line replacement. Under no circumstances should unreinforced vacuum line, clear plastic tubing or water hose be used for fuel line replacement.
12   Spring-type clamps are commonly used on fuel lines. These clamps often lose their tension over a period of time, and can be "sprung" during the removal process. Therefore it is recommended that all spring-type clamps be replaced with screw clamps whenever a hose is replaced.

Metal lines

13   Sections of metal line are often used for fuel line between the fuel pump and carburetor. Check carefully to be sure the line has not been bent and crimped and that cracks have not started in the line in the area of bends.
14   If a section of metal fuel line must be replaced, only seamless steel tubing should be used, since copper and aluminum tubing do not have the strength necessary to withstand normal engine operating vibration.
15   Check the metal brake lines where they enter the master cylinder and brake proportioning unit (if used) for cracks in the lines or loose fittings. Any sign of brake fluid leakage calls for an immediate thorough inspection of the brake system.

9   Wiper blade inspection and replacement

1   The windshield and rear window (if equipped) wiper and blade assembly should be inspected periodically for damage, loose components and cracked or worn blade elements.
2   Road film can build up on the wiper blades and affect their efficiency, so they should be washed regularly with a mild detergent solution.
3   The action of the wiping mechanism can loosen the bolts, nuts and fasteners, so they should be checked and tightened, as necessary, at the same time the wiper blades are checked.
4   If the wiper blade elements are cracked, worn or warped, they should be replaced with new ones.
5   Lift the arm assembly away from the glass for clearance and remove the blade by lifting the release lever (photos)
6   Remove the retaining clip with needle nose pliers and slide the blade element out (photo).
7   Insert the new blade element and snap the retaining clip in place.
8   Lift the release lever and insert the blade element pin until it snaps securely in position.
9   Check the wiper arm nut to make sure it is securely tightened (photo).

10   Chassis lubrication

1   There is no provision for lubrication of chassis or steering components on these models. Only the rear wheel bearings (Section 27) require periodic lubrication.
2   Lubricate all the hinges (door, hood, hatch) with a few drops of light engine oil to keep them in proper working order.
3   Open the hood and lubricate the latch mechanism with lithium base white grease (photo).

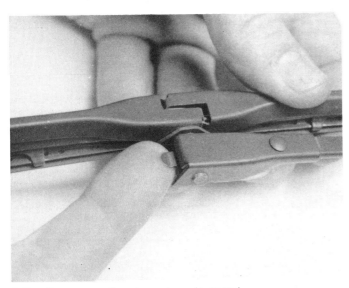

9.5a Press up on the wiper release lever and . . .

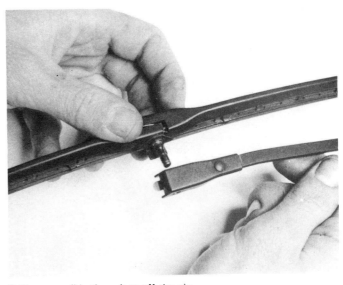

9.5b . . . slide the wiper off the pin

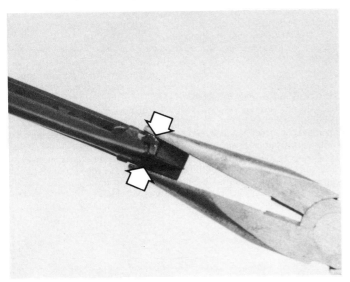

9.6 Squeeze the wiper tabs together and slide the wiper out of the arm

9.9 Rotate the trim cap up (arrow) for access to the wiper arm nut

4   Lubricate the door and trunk or liftgate weatherstripping with silicone spray. This will reduce chafing and retard wear.
5   The key lock cylinders can be lubricated with spray-on graphite, which is available at auto parts stores.

11 Exhaust system check

1   With the engine cold (at least three hours after the vehicle has been driven), check the complete exhaust system from its starting point at the engine to the end of the tailpipe. This should be done on a hoist where unrestricted access is available.
2   Check the pipes and connections for signs of leakage and/or corrosion indicating a potential failure. Make sure that all brackets and hangers are in good condition and tight.
3   At the same time, inspect the underside of the body for holes, corrosion, open seams, etc. which may allow exhaust gases to enter the passenger compartment. Seal all body openings with silicone or body putty.
4   Rattles and other noises can often be traced to the exhaust system, especially the mounts and hangers. Try to move the pipes, muffler and (when fitted) the catalytic converter. If the components can come in

10.3 Multi-purpose grease is used to lubricate the hood latch mechanism

11.4 Check the exhaust system rubber hangers for cracks and (when fitted) the heat shield bolts for looseness

contact with the body or suspension parts, secure the exhaust system with new mounts (photo).
5   Check the running condition of the engine by inspecting inside the end of the tailpipe. The exhaust deposits here are an indication of engine state-of-tune. If the pipe is black and sooty or coated with white deposits, the engine is in need of a tune-up, including a thorough carburetor inspection and adjustment.

12 Suspension and steering check

1   Raise the front of the vehicle periodically and visually check the suspension and steering components for wear.
2   Indications of a fault in these systems are excessive play in the steering wheel before the front wheels react, excessive sway around corners, body movement over rough roads or binding at some point as the steering wheel is turned.
3   Before the vehicle is raised for inspection, test the shock absorbers by pushing down to rock the vehicle at each corner. If you push down and the vehicle does not come back to a level position within one or two bounces, the shocks/struts are worn and must be replaced. As this is done, check for squeaks and noises coming from the suspension components. Information on suspension components can be found in Chapter 10.
4   Raise the front end of the vehicle and support it securely on jackstands placed under the frame rails. Because of the work to be done, make sure the vehicle cannot fall from the stands.
5   Check the wheel bearings (see Section 27).
6   From under the vehicle check for loose bolts, broken or discon-nected parts and deteriorated rubber bushings on all suspension and steering components. Look for grease or fluid leaking from the rack and pinion steering assembly. Check the power steering hoses and con-nections for leaks. Check the balljoints for wear.
7   Have an assistant turn the steering wheel from side-to-side and check the steering components for free movement, chafing and binding. If the steering does not react with the movement of the steering wheel, try to determine where the slack is located.

13 Brake check

Note: *For detailed photographs of the brake system, refer to Chapter 9.*
1   The brakes should be inspected every time the wheels are removed or whenever a defect is suspected. Indications of a potential brake system defect are: the vehicle pulls to one side when the brake pedal

is depressed; noises coming from the brakes when they are applied; excessive brake pedal travel; pulsating pedal; leakage of fluid, usually seen on the inside of the tire or wheel.

Disc brakes

2   The front disc brakes can be visually checked without removing any parts except the wheels.
3   Raise the vehicle and place it securely on jackstands. Remove the wheels (see *Jacking and towing* at the front of the manual, if necessary).
4   The disc brake calipers, which contain the pads, are now visible. There is an outer pad and an inner pad in each caliper. All pads should be inspected.
5   Check the pad thickness by looking at each end of the caliper and through the inspection hole in the caliper body (photo). If the lining material is 0.04 in (1mm) or less, the pads should be replaced. Keep in mind that the lining material is riveted or bonded to a metal backing shoe and the metal portion is not included in this measurement.
6   If it is difficult to measure the exact thickness of the remaining lining material, remove the pads for further inspection or replacement if you are in doubt as to the quality of the pad.
7   Before installing the wheels, check for leakage around the brake hose connections leading to the caliper and damage (cracking, splitting, etc.) to the brake hose. Replace the hose or fittings as necessary, referring to Chapter 9.
8   Check the condition of the rotor. Look for scoring, gouging and burned spots. If these conditions exist, the hub/rotor assembly should be removed for servicing (Chapter 9).

Drum brakes — rear

9   Remove the brake drum/hub assembly (Section 27). If this proves difficult, make sure the parking brake is released. See also Chapter 9 Section 6, paragraph 4.
10   With the drum removed, carefully brush away any accumulations of dirt and dust. **Warning:** *Do not blow the dust out with compressed air. Make an effort not to inhale the dust, as it contains asbestos and is harmful to your health.*
11   Note the thickness of the lining material on the rear brake shoes (photo). If the material is within 0.04 in (1 mm) of the recessed rivets or metal backing, the shoes should be replaced. If the linings look worn, but you are unable to determine their exact thickness, compare them with a new set at an auto parts store. The shoes should also be replaced if they are cracked, glazed (shiny surface) or contaminated with brake fluid.
12   Check to see that all the brake assembly springs are connected and in good condition.
13   Check the brake components for signs of fluid leakage. With your finger, carefully pry back the rubber cups on the wheel cylinder located at the top of the brake shoes. Any leakage is an indication that the

13.5 The amount of disc pad material (arrows) remaining can be checked by looking through the hole in the caliper

13.11   After removing the brake drum, the remaining shoe lining can be measured

wheel cylinders should be overhauled immediately (Chapter 9). Also check the hoses and connections for signs of leakage.
14   Wipe the inside of the drum with a clean rag and denatured alcohol. Again, be careful not to breathe the dangerous asbestos dust.
15   Check the inside of the drum for cracks, scores, deep scratches and hard spots, which will appear as small discolored areas. If imperfections cannot be removed with fine emery cloth, the drum must be taken to a machine shop for resurfacing. Also check the condition of the hub bearing oil seal and replace it if necessary (Section 27).
16   After the inspection process, if all parts are found to be in good condition, reinstall the hub/brake drum (see Section 27). Install the wheel and lower the vehicle to the ground.

Parking brake

17   Pull up on the parking brake handle with a force of approximately 22 lbs to check that the handle moves the specified number of clicks. If it does not, adjust the parking brake (Chapter 9).

18   The easiest way to check the operation of the parking brake is to park the vehicle on a steep hill with the parking brake set and the transmission in Neutral. If the parking brake cannot prevent the vehicle from rolling, it is in need of adjustment (see Chapter 9).

Power brake booster

19   With the engine stopped, press the brake pedal several times to destroy any residual vacuum in the booster.
20   Hold the brake pedal depressed with firm foot pressure and start the engine. If the booster is working correctly, the brake pedal will be felt to move downwards as manifold vacuum is applied.
21   If the booster seems not to be working, check the vacuum hose and non-return valve before replacing the booster itself (Chapter 9).

14   Carburetor choke check

Note: *This Section applies to vehicles with an automatic choke. For manual choke adjustment see Chapter 4.*

1   The choke only operates when the engine is cold, so this check should be performed before the engine has been started for the day.
2   Open the hood and remove the top plate of the air cleaner assembly. It is held in place by a wing nut and three clips. Place the top plate and nut aside, out of the way of moving engine components.
3   Look at the top of the carburetor at the center of the air cleaner housing. You will notice a flat plate at the carburetor opening (photo).
4   Have an assistant press the accelerator pedal to the floor. The plate should close completely. Start the engine while you observe the plate at the carburetor. **Warning:** *Do not position your face directly over the carburetor, because the engine could backfire and cause serious burns.* When the engine starts, the choke plate should open slightly.
5   Allow the engine to continue running at an idle speed. As the engine warms up to operating temperature, the plate should slowly open, allowing more air to enter through the top of the carburetor.
6   After a few minutes, the choke plate should be all the way open to the vertical position.
7   With the engine off, inspect the contact areas of the choke plate shaft for deposits which could cause binding. Use a spray choke cleaner, available at auto parts stores, to clean the choke shaft in the areas shown in the accompanying illustration while working the choke linkage by hand.
8   Use a spray lubricant, also available at parts stores, on the contact surfaces while working the linkage to make sure the choke works freely.

14.3   With the air cleaner removed, the choke plate can be checked

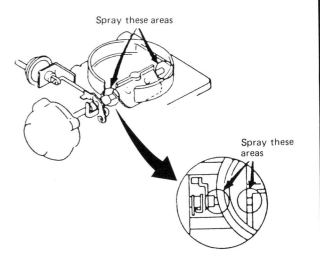

Spray these areas

Spray these areas

Fig. 1.10   Details of carburetor choke shaft cleaning (Sec 14)

9   If a malfunction is detected during the above checks, refer to Chapter 4 for specific information related to adjusting and servicing choke components.

15 Engine idle speed and mixture check and adjustment

1   Engine idle speed is the speed at which the engine operates when no accelerator pedal pressure is applied. This speed is critical to the performance of the engine itself, as well as many engine subsystems.
2   A hand held tachometer must be used when adjusting idle speed to get an accurate reading. The exact hook-up for these meters varies with the the manufacturer, so follow the particular directions included.
3   Before attempting to adjust the idle speed, valve clearances must be correct and the ignition system (timing, spark plugs) must be in good order. See Sections 34 thru 37.
4   Warm up the engine to operating temperature and make sure that the choke is fully off. Unplug the cooling fan motor connector and switch off all non-essential electrical equipment and (if fitted) air conditioning. On automatic transmission models, select 'N' and apply the parking brake.
5   Run the engine and compare the idle speed with that given in the Specifications. If adjustment is necessary, turn the idle speed adjustment screw (photo).
6   To adjust the idle mixture, an exhaust gas analyzer (CO meter) will be needed. If this is not available, have a Mazda dealer or other specialist adjust the mixture.
7   Connect the exhaust gas analyzer and run the engine at idle speed. Read the CO level and compare it with the value given in the Specifications. If adjustment is necessary, turn the mixture adjustment screw (photo).
8   If the mixture adjustment screw is covered by a tamperproof cap, the cap will have to be pried out to gain access to the screw. Satisfy yourself that you are not in breach of local or national anti-pollution laws by removing the cap, and fit a new cap on completion where this is required by law.
9   When the idle mixture is correct, recheck the idle speed and correct it if necessary.
10 Stop the engine, disconnect the test gear and reconnect the cooling fan motor.

16 Engine oil and filter change

1   Frequent oil changes may be the best form of preventative maintenance available to the home mechanic. When engine oil ages, it becomes diluted and contaminated, which leads to premature engine wear.
2   Although some sources recommend oil filter changes every other oil change, we feel that the minimal cost of an oil filter and the relative ease with which it is installed dictate that a new filter be used whenever the oil is changed.
3   The tools necessary for a normal oil and filter change are a wrench to fit the drain plug at the bottom of the oil pan, an oil filter wrench to remove the old filter, a container with at least a six-quart capacity to drain the old oil into and a funnel or oil can spout to help pour fresh oil into the engine (photo).
4   In addition, you should have plenty of clean rags and newspapers handy to mop up any spills. Access to the underside of the vehicle is greatly improved if the vehicle can be lifted on a hoist, driven onto ramps or supported by jackstands. **Warning:** *Do not work under a vehicle which is supported only a bumper, hydraulic or scissors-type jack.*
5   If this is your first oil change, get under the vehicle and familiarize yourself with the locations of the oil drain plug and the oil filter. The engine and exhaust components will be warm during the actual work, so figure out any potential problems before the engine and accessories are hot. If an oil pan protecter plate is fitted, it may be necessary to remove it.
6   Warm the engine to normal operating temperature. If the new oil or any tools are needed, use this warm-up time to gather everything necessary for the job. The correct type of oil for your application can be found in *Recommended lubricants and fluids* at the beginning of this manual.
7   With the engine oil warm (warm engine oil will drain better and

15.5   The idle speed adjustment screw (arrow) is not easy to reach. The air cleaner has been removed here for clarity

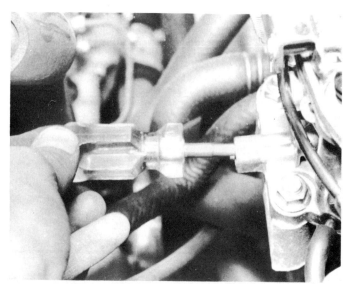

15.7   Turning the idle mixture adjustment screw

more built-up sludge will be removed with the oil), raise and support the vehicle. Make sure it is firmly supported.
8   Move all necessary tools, rags and newspapers under the vehicle. Position the drain pan under the drain plug. Keep in mind that the oil will initially flow from the pan with some force, so place the pan accordingly.
9   Being careful not to touch any of the hot exhaust components, use the wrench to remove the drain plug near the bottom of the oil pan (photo). Depending on how hot the oil has become, you may want to wear gloves while unscrewing the plug the final few turns.
10 Allow the old oil to drain into the pan. It may be necessary to move the pan farther under the engine as the oil flow slows to a trickle.
11 After all the oil has drained, wipe off the drain plug with a clean rag. Small metal particles may cling to the plug which would immediately contaminate the new oil.
12 Clean the area around the drain plug opening and reinstall the plug. Tighten the plug securely with the wrench.
13 Move the drain pan into position under the oil filter.
14 Use the filter wrench to loosen the oil filter. Chain or metal band

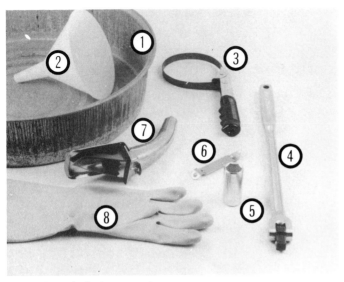

16.3   Typical oil change tools

1 Drain pan	5 Socket
2 Funnel	6 Can opener
3 Filter wrench	7 Oil can spout
4 Breaker bar	8 Rubber gloves

16.9   Oil drain plug location (arrow)

filter wrenches may distort the filter canister, but this is of no concern as the filter will be discarded anyway (photo). When an oil cooler is fitted, support it when loosening the filter so that it does not rotate.
15 Sometimes the oil filter is on so tight it cannot be loosened, or it is positioned in an area which is inaccessible with a filter wrench. As a last resort, you can punch a metal bar or long screwdriver directly through the side of the canister and use it as a T-bar to turn the filter. If so, be prepared for oil to spurt out of the canister as it is punctured.
16 Completely unscrew the old filter. Be careful, it is full of oil. Empty the oil inside the filter into the drain pan.
17 Compare the old filter with the new one to make sure they are the same type.
18 Use a clean rag to remove all oil, dirt and sludge from the area where the oil filter mounts to the engine. Check the old filter to make sure the rubber gasket is not stuck to the engine mounting surface. If the gasket is stuck to the engine (use a flashlight if necessary), remove it.
19 Apply a light coat of oil around the full circumference of the rubber gasket of the new oil filter.
20 Attach the new filter to the engine, following the tightening directions printed on the filter canister or packing box. Most filter manufacturers recommend against using a filter wrench due to the possibility of overtightening and damage to the seal. In the absence of specific directions, tighten the filter by hand through three-quarters of a turn beyond the point where the rubber gasket contacts the mounting surface.
21 Remove all tools, rags, etc. from under the vehicle, being careful not to spill the oil in the drain pan, then lower the vehicle.
22 Move to the engine compartment and locate the oil filler cap on the engine camshaft cover (photo).
23 If an oil can spout is used, push the spout into the top of the oil can and pour the fresh oil through the filler opening. A funnel may also be used.
24 Pour three quarts of fresh oil into the engine. Wait a few minutes to allow the oil to drain into the pan, then check the level on the oil dipstick (see Section 4 if necessary). If the oil level is at or near the F mark, start the engine and allow the new oil to circulate.
25 Run the engine for only about a minute and then shut it off. Immediately look under the vehicle and check for leaks at the oil pan drain plug and around the oil filter. If either is leaking, tighten with a bit more force. On models with an oil cooler, also check for leaks between the oil cooler and block. If leaks are found, remove the oil cooler (Chapter 2) and replace the oil seal.
26 With the new oil circulated and the filter now completely full, recheck the level on the dipstick and add enough oil to bring the level to the F mark on the dipstick.

16.14   A strap-type oil filter wrench works well in hard-to-reach locations

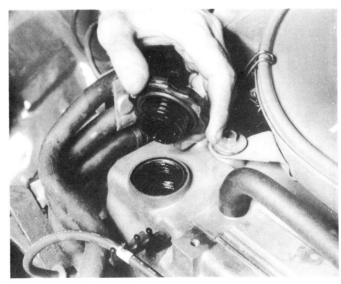

16.22   Oil is added through a filler opening in the camshaft cover

27 During the first few trips after an oil change, make it a point to check frequently for leaks and proper oil level.

28 The old oil drained from the engine cannot be reused in its present state and should be disposed of. Oil reclamation centers, auto repair shops and gas stations will normally accept the oil, which can be refined and used again. After the oil has cooled, it can be drained into a suitable container (capped plastic jugs, topped bottles, milk cartons, etc.) for transport to one of these disposal sites.

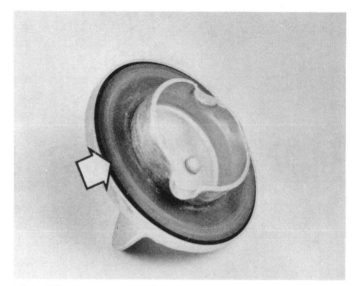

17 Fuel system check

Warning: *There are certain precautions to take when inspecting or servicing the fuel system components. Work in a well ventilated area and do not allow open flames (cigarettes, appliance pilot lights, etc.) to get near the work area. Mop up spills immediately and do not store fuel soaked rags where they could ignite.*

1 The fuel system is under a small amount of pressure, so if any fuel lines are disconnected for servicing, be prepared to catch the fuel as it spurts out. Plug all disconnected fuel lines immediately after disconnection to prevent the tank from emptying itself.

2 The fuel system is most easily checked with the vehicle raised on a hoist so the components underneath the vehicle are readily visible and accessible.

3 If the smell of gasoline is noticed while driving or after the vehicle has been in the sun, the system should be thoroughly inspected immediately.

4 Remove the gas filler cap and check for damage, corrosion and an unbroken sealing imprint on the gasket (photo). Replace the cap with a new one if necessary.

5 With the vehicle raised, inspect the gas tank and filler neck for punctures, cracks and other damage. The connection between the filler neck and the tank is especially critical. Sometimes a rubber filler neck will leak due to loose clamps or deteriorated rubber, problems a home mechanic can usually rectify. **Warning:** *Do not, under any circumstances, try to repair a fuel tank yourself (except rubber components) unless you have had considerable experience. A welding torch or any open flame can easily cause the fuel vapors to explode if the proper precautions are not taken.*

6 Carefully check all rubber hoses and metal lines leading away from the fuel tank. Check for loose connections, deteriorated hoses, crimped

17.4 With today's sophisticated emissions systems, it is essential that seals (arrow) in the gas tank cap be checked regularly

lines and other damage. Follow the lines to the front of the vehicle, carefully inspecting them all the way. Repair or replace damaged sections as necessary.

7 If a fuel odor is still evident after the inspection, refer to Section 33.

18 Fuel filter replacement

1 The fuel filter is located on the left side of the engine compartment on a spring clip mount. It is of the disposable type and should be replaced at the specified intervals.

2 Place some rags or newspapers under the fuel filter to catch spilled fuel as the hoses are disconnected.

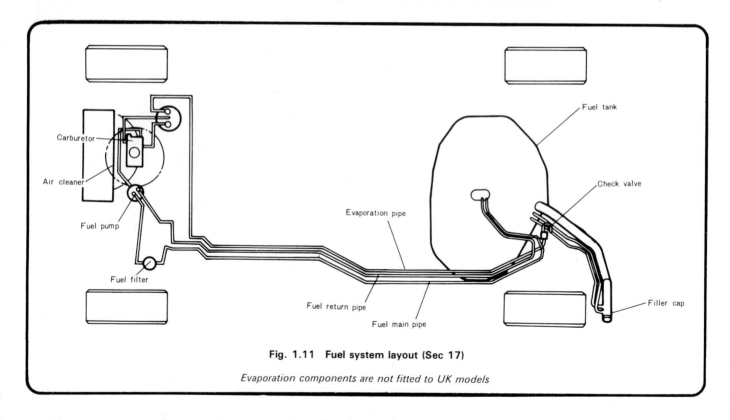

Fig. 1.11 Fuel system layout (Sec 17)

Evaporation components are not fitted to UK models

18.3 After removing the clamps with pliers, the fuel filter can be disconnected from the hoses and the clip

3 Use pliers to slide the clips back on the fuel line hoses and disconnect the hoses from the filter (photo).
4 Note the direction of flow arrow on the filter and unsnap the filter from the mounting clip.
5 Snap the new filter in place in the clip with the arrow pointing in the correct direction and connect the hoses and clamps.

19 Throttle linkage check and adjustment

1 The throttle linkage is a cable type and should be checked and adjusted periodically to assure proper function.
2 Check the entire length of the cable to make sure that it is not binding.

3 With the engine at normal operating temperature, make sure the choke plate is fully open (Section 14) and correctly adjusted (Chapter 4).
4 Measure the amount of play in the cable at the carburetor and adjust as necessary as shown in the accompanying illustration. The desired amount of play is 0.04 to 0.12 in (1 to 3 mm).

20 Carburetor mounting torque check

1 The carburetor is attached to the top of the intake manifold by four nuts. These fasteners can sometimes work loose from vibration and temperature changes during normal engine operation and cause a vacuum leak.
2 If you suspect that a vacuum leak exists at the bottom of the carburetor, obtain a length of hose about the diameter of fuel hose. Start the engine and place one end of the hose next to your ear as you probe around the base with the other end. You will hear a hissing sound if a leak exists.
3 Remove the air cleaner assembly, tagging each hose to be disconnected with a piece of numbered tape to make reassembly easier.
4 Locate the mounting nuts at the base of the carburetor. Decide what special tools or adapters will be necessary, if any, to tighten the fasteners. No torque wrench setting is specified by the manufacturers.
5 Tighten the nuts securely and evenly. Do not overtighten them, as the threads could strip.
6 If, after the nuts are properly tightened, a vacuum leak still exists, the carburetor must be removed and a new gasket installed. See Chapter 4 for more information.
7 After tightening the fasteners, reinstall the air cleaner and return all hoses to their original positions.

21 Thermostatically controlled air cleaner check

1 All engines are equipped with a thermostatically controlled air cleaner which draws air to the carburetor from different locations, depending upon engine temperature.
2 This is a simple visual check. If access is limited, however, a small mirror may have to be used.
3 Open the hood and locate the damper door inside the air cleaner assembly. It will be located inside the long snorkel of the metal air cleaner housing. Make sure that the flexible air hose(s) are securely attached and undamaged.

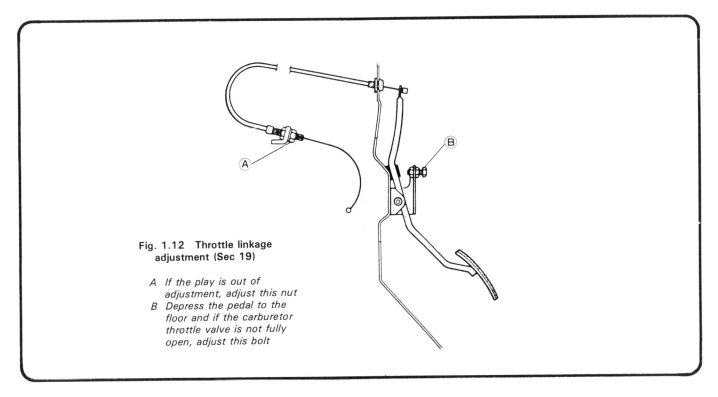

Fig. 1.12 Throttle linkage
adjustment (Sec 19)

A　If the play is out of
　adjustment, adjust this nut
B　Depress the pedal to the
　floor and if the carburetor
　throttle valve is not fully
　open, adjust this bolt

4   If there is a flexible air duct attached to the end of the snorkel, leading to an area behind the grille, disconnect it at the snorkel. This will enable you to look through the end of the snorkel and see the damper inside.

5   The check should be done when the engine and outside air are cold. Start the engine and look through the snorkel at the damper, which should move to a closed position. With the damper closed, air cannot enter through the end of the snorkel, but instead enters the air cleaner through the flexible duct attached to the exhaust manifold and the heat stove passage.

6   As the engine warms up to operating temperature, the damper should open to allow air through the snorkel end. Depending on ambient temperature, this may take 10 to 15 minutes. To speed up this check you can reconnect the snorkel air duct, drive the vehicle and then check to see if the damper is completely open (photo).

7   If the thermo-controlled air cleaner is not operating properly, see Chapter 6 for more information.

22   Transaxle output shaft seal and driveaxle boot check

1   At the recommended intervals the transaxle output shaft seals and driveaxle boots should be inspected for leaks and damage.

2   Raise the front of the vehicle and support it securely on jackstands.

3   Check the transaxle output shaft seals located at the point where the driveaxles exit from the transaxle. It may be necessary to clean this area before inspection. If there is any oil leaking from either of the driveaxle/transaxle junctions, the output shaft seals must be replaced. Refer to Chapter 7.

4   The driveaxle boots are very important because they prevent dirt, water and other foreign material from entering and damaging the constant velocity (CV) joints. Inspect the condition of all four boots (two on each axleshaft). It is a good idea to clean the boots using soap and water, as oil or grease will cause the boot material to deteriorate prematurely. If there is any damage or evidence of leaking lubricant, they must be replaced as described in Chapter 8. Check the tightness of the boot clamps. If they are loose and can't be tightened, the clamp must be replaced (photo).

23   Tire rotation

1   The tires may be rotated if wished to even out wear. Bear in mind that if this is totally successful, all four or five tires will have to be replaced at once.

2   Refer to the accompanying illustration for the preferred tire rotation pattern.

3   Refer to the information in *Jacking and towing* at the front of this manual for the proper procedures to follow when raising the vehicle and changing a tire. If the brakes are to be checked, do not apply the parking brake as stated. Make sure the tires are blocked to prevent the vehicle from rolling.

4   Preferably, the entire vehicle should be raised at the same time. This can be done on a hoist or by jacking up each corner and then lowering the vehicle onto jackstands placed under the frame rails. Always use four jackstands and make sure the vehicle is firmly supported.

5   After rotation, check and adjust the the tire pressures as necessary and be sure to check the lug nut tightness.

6   For further information on the wheels and tires, refer to Chapter 10.

24   Clutch pedal adjustment

1   If equipped with a manual shift transaxle, it is important to have the clutch pedal free play as well as engaged and disengaged heights at the proper points. Free play at the clutch pedal is the distance the pedal moves from the full-up position to where resistance is felt as the clutch begins to disengage. Clutch pedal height is the measurement from the pedal pad to the firewall when the clutch is engaged (fully up). Clutch pedal disengaged height is the distance from the pedal pad to the floor with the clutch fully disengaged so shift lever can move between first and reverse with the engine running.

2   To check the free play, depress the clutch pedal until resistance is felt. Measure the distance traveled by the pedal and compare this measurement to the Specifications.

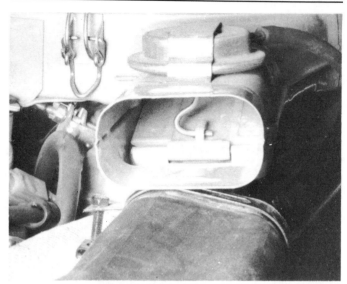

21.6   The thermostatically controlled damper door can be seen after removing the air inlet pipe

22.4   Check the driveaxle boot to make sure it is not cracked or loose

3   To check the clutch pedal height, measure from the top of the pedal to the firewall and compare this measurement to the Specifications.

4   Check the pedal fully disengaged height by measuring between the pedal pad and the floor and comparing the measurement to the Specifications.

5   To adjust the pedal height, first remove the heater air duct under the dash for clearance. Loosen the locknut (A in Fig. 1.14) and adjust the pedal height by turning the stopper bolt (B). Tighten the locknut securely after adjustment.

6   To adjust the pedal free play, press on the clutch release lever in the engine compartment while pulling on the roller and and check the clearance (A in Fig. 1.15). Loosen the locknut and adjust the clearance by turning the adjusting nut (B). Check the pedal free play and clutch lever clearance again before tightening the locknut.

25   Manual transaxle oil change

1   Raise the vehicle and support it securely on jackstands.

2   Move a drain pan, rags, newspapers and wrenches under the transaxle.

RADIAL TIRES

4 wheel rotation

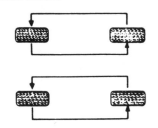

5 wheel rotation

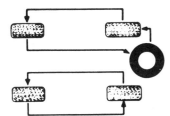

BIAS AND BIAS BELTED TIRES

4 wheel rotation

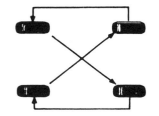

5 wheel rotation

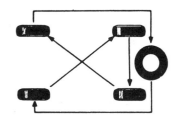

Fig. 1.13   Tire rotation diagram (Sec 23)

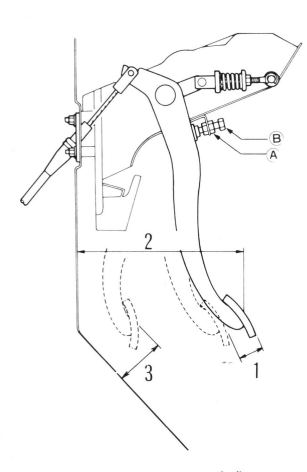

Fig. 1.14   Clutch pedal measurement and adjustment
(Sec 24)

1   Free play measurement
2   Pedal engaged height
     measurement
3   Pedal disengaged height
     measurement

A   Height adjusting locknut
B   Height adjusting stopper
     bolt

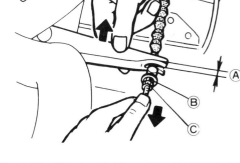

Fig. 1.15   Clutch pedal free play adjustment at the
release lever (Sec 24)

A   Clutch release lever
     clearance

B   Adjusting nut
C   Locknut

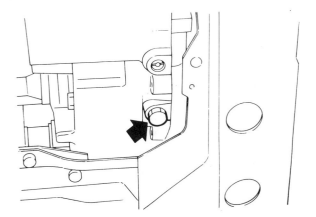

Fig. 1.16   Manual transaxle drain plug location (Sec 25)

3   Remove the transaxle drain plug at the bottom of the case and allow the oil to drain into the pan.

4   After the oil has drained completely, reinstall the plug and tighten it securely.

5   Remove the speedometer driven gear. Using a hand pump, syringe or funnel, fill the transaxle with the correct amount of the specified lubricant (Section 4). Reinstall the driven gear and tighten the bolt securely.

6   Lower the vehicle.

26 Cooling system servicing (draining, flushing and refilling)

1   Periodically, the cooling system should be drained, flushed and refilled to replenish the antifreeze mixture and prevent formation of rust and corrosion, which can impair the performance of the cooling system and cause engine damage.

2   At the same time the cooling system is serviced, all hoses and the radiator cap should be inspected and replaced if defective (see Section 7).

3   Since antifreeze is a corrosive and poisonous solution, be careful not to spill any of the coolant mixture on the vehicle's paint or your skin. If this happens, rinse immediately with plenty of clean water. Consult your local authorities about the dumping of antifreeze before draining the cooling system. In many areas, reclamation centers have been set up to collect automobile oil and drained antifreeze/water mixtures, rather than allowing them to be added to the sewage system.

4   With the engine cold, remove the radiator cap.

5   Move a large container under the radiator to catch the coolant as it is drained.

6   Drain the radiator by removing the drain plug at the bottom (photo). If this drain has excessive corrosion and cannot be turned easily, or if the radiator is not equipped with a drain, disconnect the lower radiator hose to allow the coolant to drain. Be careful that none of the solution is splashed on your skin or into your eyes.

7   Disconnect the hose from the coolant reservoir and remove the reservoir. Flush it out with clean water.

8   Place a garden hose in the radiator filler neck and flush the system until the water runs clear at all drain points.

9   In severe cases of contamination or clogging of the radiator, remove it (see Chapter 3), invert it and reverse flush it. This involves inserting the hose in the bottom radiator outlet to allow the water to run against the normal flow, draining through the top. A radiator repair shop should be consulted if further cleaning or repair is necessary.

10   When the coolant is regularly drained and the system refilled with the correct antifreeze/water mixture, there should be no need to use chemical cleaners or descalers.

11   To refill the system, reconnect the radiator hoses and install the reservoir and the overflow hose.

12   Fill the radiator to the base of the filler neck and then add more coolant to the reservoir until it reaches the lower mark.

13   Run the engine until normal operating temperature is reached and,

with the engine idling, add coolant up to the Full level. Install the radiator and reservoir caps.

14   Keep a close watch on the coolant level and the cooling system hoses during the first few miles of driving. Tighten the hose clamps and/or add more coolant as necessary.

27 Rear wheel bearing check and repack

Check

1   With the vehicle securely supported on jackstands, spin the rear wheels and check for noise, rolling resistance and free play. Now grab the top of the tire with one hand and the bottom of the tire with the other. Move the tire in-and-out. If it moves more than 0.005-inch, the bearings should be checked and adjusted, or replaced if necessary.

2   The front wheel bearings on these models require disassembly of the front hub for servicing but the rear wheel bearings can be serviced as a routine maintenance procedure.

Repack

3   Raise the rear of the vehicle and support it securely on jackstands.

4   Remove the wheels and release the parking brake.

5   Use a chisel and hammer to remove the grease cap, working around the circumference until it is dislodged and can be removed.

6   Relieve the staking and remove the hub nut. The manufacturer recommends discarding the nut. New nuts can be obtained from a dealer.

7   Pull the hub assembly out slightly and then push it back into its original position. This should force the outer bearing and washer off the spindle enough so that it can be removed with your fingers (photos). If difficulty is experienced in releasing the hub/drum assembly, refer to Chapter 9, Section 6, paragraph 4.

8   Remove the hub, place it on a suitable working surface and pry the inner bearing seal out with a screwdriver (photo).

9   Use solvent to remove all traces of the old grease from the bearings, hub and spindle. A small brush may prove useful. Make sure no bristles from the brush embed themselves inside the bearing rollers. Allow the parts to air dry.

10   Carefully inspect the bearings for cracks, scoring and uneven surfaces. If the bearing races are defective, refer to Chapter 10. Bearings and races come in matched sets, and new races require new bearings. Likewise, replacement of the bearings requires that new races be installed in the hub.

11   Use an approved high temperature wheel bearing grease to pack the bearings. Work the grease completely into the bearings, forcing it between the rollers, cone and cage (photo).

12   Apply a thin coat of grease to the spindle at the outer bearing seat, inner bearing seat, shoulder and seal seat.

13   Put a small quantity of grease inboard of each bearing race inside the hub. Using your finger, form a dam at these points to provide extra grease availability and to keep thinned grease from flowing out of the bearing.

26.6   The drain plug is located at the bottom of the radiator

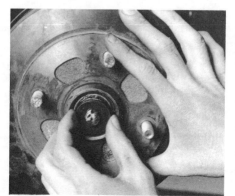

27.7a   Pull the hub out to dislodge and remove the washer . . .

27.7b   . . . and the outer bearing

27.8 Prying the bearing seal out of the hub

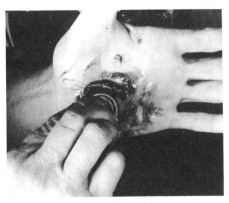

27.11 Packing a bearing with high-temperature wheel bearing grease. Work it well into the rollers

27.16 Place the hub on the spindle while holding the outer bearing and washer in place with your thumbs

27.17a Tightening the spindle nut with a torque wrench

27.17b Using a hammer and small punch to peen the nut collar into the spindle groove

14 Install the grease-packed inner bearing into the rear of the hub and put a little more grease outboard of the bearing.

15 Place a new seal over the inner bearing, with the open lip of the seal facing the bearing, and press the seal evenly into place.

16 Lubricate the lip of the seal with a light coat of grease, carefully place the hub assembly onto the spindle and push the grease-packed outer bearing and washer into position (photo).

17 Install a new spindle nut and set the bearing preload using the following procedure.
  a) Tighten the spindle nut to the initial specified torque (photo).
  b) Rotate the hub two or three times to seat the bearings, then loosen the spindle nut one turn (make sure the brakes are not dragging).
  c) Attach a spring scale to the top wheel stud and measure the torque at which the hub starts to turn (this is the oil seal resistance).
  d) Tighten the spindle nut until the resistance (point at which the hub starts to turn) is approximately 14.1 to 35.3 oz (3.9 to 9.8 Newtons) more than the oil seal resistance reading obtained in Step C.
  e) Use a hammer and punch or other suitable blunt tool to crimp the collar of the nut into the spindle groove (photo).

18 Pack the cap with grease and install it, tapping around the outer circumference with a hammer and punch to seat it.

19 Install the wheels and lower the vehicle. Tighten the lug nuts.

20 Apply the brake pedal several times to adjust the brake shoes, then check the parking brake lever stroke and adjust if necessary (Chapter 9, Section 10).

28 Automatic transaxle fluid change

1 At the specified intervals, the transaxle fluid should be drained and replaced.

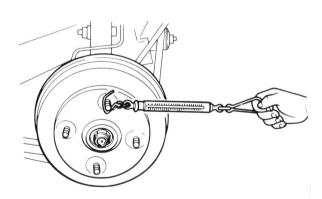

Fig. 1.17 Checking the rear wheel bearing preload with a spring scale (Sec 27)

2 Before beginning work, purchase the specified transmission fluid (see *Recommended fluids and lubricants* at the front of this manual).

3 Other tools necessary for this job include jackstands to support the vehicle in a raised position, a drain pan capable of holding at least 8 pints, newspapers and clean rags.

4 The fluid should be drained immediately after the vehicle has been driven. This will remove any built up sediment better than if the fluid were cold. Because of this, it may be wise to wear protective gloves. Fluid temperature can exceed 350°F (178°C) in a hot transaxle.

5 After the vehicle has been driven to warm up the fluid, raise it and place it on the jackstands for access underneath.

6 Move the necessary equipment under the vehicle, being careful not to touch any of the hot exhaust components.

7 Place the drain pan under the lower part of the transaxle differential

and remove the drain plug (photo). Be sure the drain pan is in position, as fluid will come out with some force.

8   After the fluid has drained completely, clean the transaxle drain plug and reinstall it. Tighten the plug securely.

9   Lower the vehicle.

10 Open the hood and remove the transaxle fluid dipstick.

11 Add the specified amount and type of fluid to the transaxle through the filler tube (use a funnel to prevent spills). It is best to add a little fluid at a time, continually checking the level with the dipstick (Section 4). Allow the fluid time to drain into the pan. Take great care not to introduce any dirt or foreign matter into the transaxle.

12 With the selector lever in Park, apply the parking brake and start the engine without depressing the accelerator pedal (if possible). Do not race the engine at high speed; run at slow idle only.

13 With the engine still idling, check the level on the dipstick. Look under the vehicle for leaks around the transaxle oil drain plug.

14 Check the fluid level to make sure it is just below the F mark on the dipstick. Do no allow the fluid level to go above this point, as the transaxle would then be overfilled, necessitating the draining of the excess fluid.

15 Push the dipstick firmly back into its tube and drive the vehicle to reach normal operating temperature. Park the vehicle on a level surface and check the fluid level on the dipstick with the engine idling and the transaxle in Park. The level should now be at the F mark on the dipstick. If not, add more fluid to bring the level up to this point. Again, do not overfill.

29 Air filter and PCV filter replacement

1   At the specified intervals, the air filter and PCV filter should be replaced with new ones. A thorough program of preventative maintenance would call for the two filters to be inspected between changes.

2   The air filter is located inside the air cleaner housing on the top of the engine. The filter is replaced by removing the wing nut at the top of the air cleaner assembly, releasing the clips and lifting off the top plate (photo).

3   While the top plate is off, be careful not to drop anything down into the carburetor.

4   Lift the air filter element out of the housing (photo).

5   Wipe out the inside of the air cleaner housing with a clean rag.

6   Place the new filter into the air cleaner housing. Make sure it seats properly in the bottom of the housing.

7   The PCV filter is also located inside the air cleaner housing. Remove the top plate and air filter as described previously, then locate the PCV filter on the side of the housing.

8   Use a screwdriver to pry the filter up an then pull it from the housing (photo).

28.7   Automatic transaxle drain plug location

29.2   Air cleaner assembly wingnut (A) and clips (B)

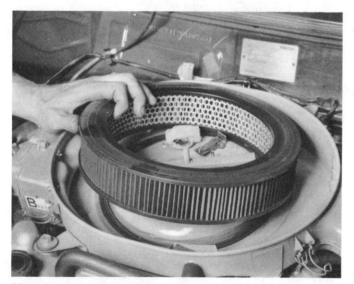
29.4   Removing the air filter element

29.8   Removing the PCV filter

9   Install a new PCV filter and the air filter.
10   Install the top plate, making sure the arrow aligns with the arrow on the air intake.

30   Oxygen sensor replacement

This Section is not applicable to UK models

Note: *Special care must be taken when handling the sensitive oxygen sensor:*

   a)   The oxygen sensor has a permanently attached pigtail and connector, which should not be removed from the sensor. Damage or removal of the pigtail or connector can adversely affect its operation.

   b)   Grease, dirt and other contaminants should be kept away from the electrical connector and the louvered end of the sensor.

   c)   Do not use cleaning solvents of any kind on the oxygen sensor.

   d)   Do not drop or roughly handle the sensor.

   e)   The silicone boot must be installed in the correct position to prevent the boot from being melted and to allow the sensor to operate properly.

1   The sensor is located in the exhaust manifold and is accessible in the engine compartment (photo).
2   Since the oxygen sensor may be difficult to remove with the engine cold, begin by operating the engine until it has warmed to at least 120°F (48°C).
3   Disconnect the electrical wire from the oxygen sensor.
4   Note the position of the silicone boot and carefully back out the oxygen sensor from the exhaust manifold. Be advised that excessive force may damage the threads. Inspect the oxygen sensor for damage.
5   A special anti-seize compound must be used on the threads of the oxygen sensor to aid in future removal. New or service sensors will have this compound already applied, but if for any reason an oxygen sensor is removed and then reinstalled, the threads must be coated before reinstallation.
6   Install the sensor and tighten it securely.
7   Connect the electrical wire.

31   Positive Crankcase Ventilation (PCV) valve check and replacement

1   The PCV valve is located in the camshaft cover.
2   With the engine idling at normal operating temperature, pull the valve (with hose attached) from the rubber grommet in the camshaft cover (photo).
3   Place your finger over the end of the valve. If the engine speed drops, the valve is working properly. If engine speed doesn't drop the valve is faulty and should be replaced with a new one.
4   To replace the valve, pull it from the end of the hose, noting its installed position and direction (photo).

30.1   The oxygen sensor (arrow) threads into the exhaust manifold

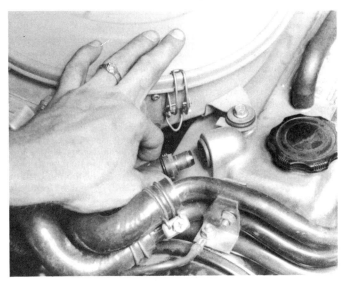

31.2   Removing the PCV valve from the camshaft cover

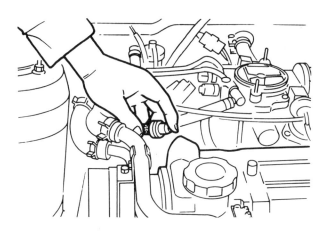

Fig. 1.18 Checking the PCV valve (Sec 31)

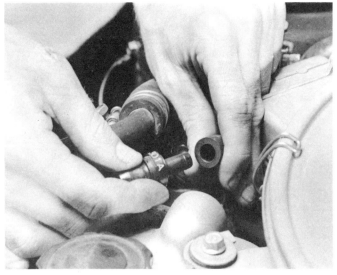

31.4   Removing the PCV valve from the hose

5   When purchasing a replacement PCV valve, make sure it is for your particular vehicle, model year and engine size. Compare the old valve with the new one to make sure they are the same.
6   Push the valve into the end of the hose until it is seated.
7   Inspect the rubber grommet for damage and replace it with a new one, if necessary.
8   Push the PCV valve and hose securely into position.
9   More information on the PCV system can be found in Chapter 6.

32   Exhaust Gas Recirculation (EGR) valve check

This Section does not apply to UK models

1   The EGR valve is located on the intake manifold, adjacent to the carburetor. Most of the time when a problem develops in this emissions system, it is due to a stuck or corroded EGR valve.
2   With the engine cold to prevent burns, reach under the EGR valve and manually push on the diaphragm. Using moderate pressure, you should be able to press the diaphragm up and down within the housing.
3   If the diaphragm does not move or moves only with much effort, replace the EGR valve with a new one. If in doubt about the condition of the valve, compare the free movement of your EGR valve with a new valve.
4   Refer to Chapter 6 for more information on the EGR system.

33   Evaporative emissions control system check

This Section does not apply to UK models

1   The function of the Evaporative Emissions Control System is to draw fuel vapors from the tank and carburetor, store them in a charcoal canister and then burn them during normal engine operation.
2   The most common symptom of a fault in the evaporative emissions system is a strong fuel odor in the engine compartment. If a fuel odor is detected, inspect the charcoal canister, located on the engine compartment firewall (photo), and system hoses.
3   A simple check of system operation is to place your hand under the canister with the engine at normal operating temperature and slowly increase engine speed. If air can be felt being sucked into the bottom of the canister the system is operating properly.
4   The evaporative emissions control system is explained in more detail in Chapter 6.

34   Ignition timing check and adjustment

Note: *On US models it is imperative that the procedures included on the Vehicle Emissions Control Information label be followed when adjusting the ignition timing. The label will include all information concerning preliminary steps to be performed before adjusting the timing, as well as the timing specifications.*

1   On US models only, locate the VECI label under the hood and read through and perform all preliminary instructions concerning ignition timing.
2   Locate the timing mark pointer plate located beside the crankshaft pulley. The *T* mark represents top dead center (TDC). The pointer plate will be marked in two degree increments, and should have the proper timing mark for your particular vehicle noted. If not, count back from the *T* mark the correct number of degrees BTDC, as noted on the VECI label, and mark the plate. In the case of the timing marks shown in Fig. 1.19, there is a timing pointer instead of a plate, and two notches on the pulley instead of one. Do not use the 'top' (TDC) notch for setting the timing.
3   Locate the notch on the crankshaft balancer or pulley and mark it with chalk or a dab of paint so it will be visible under the timing light (photo).
4   Start the engine, warm it to normal operating temperature and shut it off. Turn off all lights and other electrical loads and unplug the engine cooling fan electrical connector.

33.2   The evaporative canister is located on the firewall

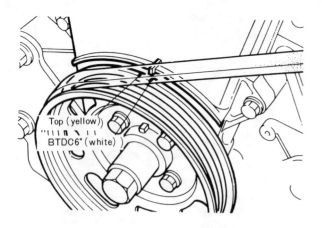

Fig. 1.19   Typical ignition timing marks (Sec 34)

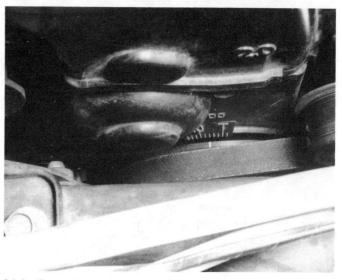

34.3   The engine timing marks are rather difficult to see so they should be marked with white paint

34.5a Connecting the timing light to the number one spark plug wire

34.5b Connecting the timing light to the battery

34.6 Aiming the timing light at the timing marks

5   With the ignition off, connect the pick up lead of the timing light to the number one spark plug. Use either a jumper lead between the wire and plug or an inductive-type pick up. Do not pierce the wire or attempt to insert a wire between the boot and wire. Connect the timing light power leads according to the manufacturer's instructions (photos).
6   Start the engine, aim the timing light at the timing mark by the crankshaft pulley and note which timing mark the notch on the pulley is lining up with (photo).
7   If the notch is not lining up with the correct mark, loosen the distributor hold-down bolt and rotate the distributor until the notch is lined up with the correct timing mark.
8   Retighten the hold-down bolt and recheck the timing.
9   Turn off the engine and disconnect the timing light. Reconnect the number one spark plug wire, if removed, and any other components which were disconnected.

35   Spark plug inspection and replacement

Note: *The makers do not specify any particular interval for replacement of the spark plugs, only that they be inspected regularly. In practice it is wise to replace the plugs at alternate inspections, even if they appear to be still in good condition.*

1   In most cases, tools necessary for a spark plug replacement include a spark plug socket, which fits onto a ratchet wrench. This socket will be insulated inside to protect the porcelain insulator and hold the plug while you direct it to the spark plug hole. Also necessary will be a wire-type feeler gauge to check and adjust the spark plug gap (photo).
2   The spark plugs are located on the front (radiator) side of the engine.
3   The best procedure to follow when replacing the spark plugs is to purchase the new spark plugs beforehand, adjust them to the proper gap, and then replace each plug one at a time.
4   When buying the new spark plugs it is important to obtain the correct plugs for your specific engine. This information can be found on the Vehicle Emissions Control Information label located under the hood (US models) or in the owner's manual. If differences exist between these sources, purchase the spark plug type specified on the Emissions Control label, because the information was printed for your specific engine.
5   With the new spark plugs at hand, allow the engine to cool completely before attempting plug removal. During this time, each of the new spark plugs can be inspected for defects and the gaps can be checked.
6   The gap is checked by inserting the proper thickness gauge between the electrodes at the tip of the plug. The gap between the electrodes should be the same as that given in the Specifications or on the Emissions Control label. The wire should just touch each of the electrodes. If the gap is incorrect, use the notched adjuster on the feeler gauge body to bend the curved side electrode slightly until the proper gap is achieved. If the side electrode is not exactly over the center electrode, use the notched adjuster to align the two. Check for cracks in the porcelain insulator, indicating the spark plug should not be used.

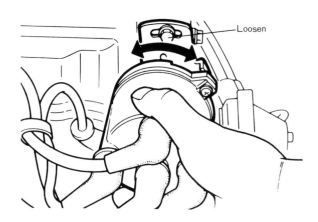

Fig. 1.20   Adjust the ignition timing by turning the distributor (Sec 34)

Loosen

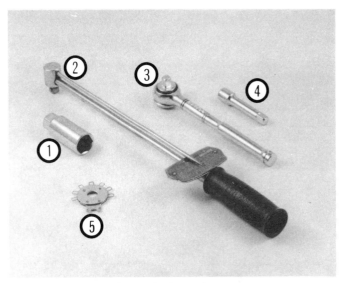

35.1   Tools required for spark plug replacement

1   *Spark plug socket*   4   *Extension*
2   *Torque wrench*   5   *Spark plug gap tool*
3   *Ratchet*

7   With the engine cool, remove the spark plug wire from one spark plug. Do this by grabbing the boot at the end of the wire, not the wire itself. Sometimes it is necessary to use a twisting motion while the boot and plug wire are pulled free.

8   If compressed air is available, use it to blow any dirt or foreign material away from the spark plug area. A common bicycle pump will also work. The idea here is to eliminate the possibility of debris falling into the cylinder as the spark plug is removed.

9   Place the spark plug socket over the plug and remove it from the engine by turning in a counterclockwise direction.

10   Compare the spark plug with those shown in the accompanying color photos to get an indication of the overall running condition of the engine. If the plug is in good condition (electrodes not burnt, insulation not damaged, thread and washer in good condition) it can be re-used after cleaning. The best method of cleaning is by abrasive blasting, which can be carried out by many service stations. Spark plug cleaners for home use can also be purchased. Reset the plug electrodes gap after cleaning.

11   Thread the plug into the head until you can no longer turn it with your fingers, then tighten it with the socket. Where there might be difficulty in inserting the spark plugs into the spark plug holes, or the possibility of cross-threading them into the head, a short piece of rubber tubing can be fitted over the end of the spark plug. The flexible tubing will act as a universal joint to help align the plug with the plug hole, and should the plug begin to cross-thread, the hose will slip on the spark plug, preventing thread damage. If one is available, use a torque wrench to tighten the plug to ensure that it is seated correctly. The correct torque figure is included in the Specifications. If a torque wrench is not available, tighten the plug no more than a quarter turn beyond the point where the washer contacts the sealing face.

12   Before pushing the spark plug wire onto the end of the plug, inspect it following the procedures outlined in Section 36.

13   Attach the plug wire to the new spark plug, again using a twisting motion on the boot until it is firmly seated on the spark plug. Make sure the wire is routed away from the exhaust manifold.

14   Follow the above procedure for the remaining spark plugs, replacing them one at a time to prevent mixing up the spark plug wires.

36   Spark plug wires, distributor cap and rotor check and replacement

1   Begin this procedure by making a visual check of the spark plug wires while the engine is running. In a darkened garage (make sure there is ventilation) start the engine and observe each plug wire. Be careful not to come into contact with any moving engine parts. If there is a break in the wire, you will see arcing or a small spark at the damaged area. If arcing is noticed, make a note to obtain new wires, then allow the engine to cool and check the distributor cap and rotor.

2   Disconnect the negative cable from the battery.

3   Loosen the distributor cap retaining screws. The screws are held in the cap with retainers. Lift off the cap (photo).

4   Inspect the cap for cracks and other damage. Closely examine the contacts on the inside of the cap for excessive corrosion (photo). Slight scoring is normal. Deposits on the contacts may be removed with a small file.

5   If the inspection reveals damage to the cap, make a note to obtain a replacement for your particular engine, then examine the rotor.

6   The rotor is visible, with the cap removed, at the top of the distributor shaft. It is held in place by two screws. Remove the screws and the rotor and inspect the rotor for cracks and other damage.

7   Carefully check the condition of the metal contact at the top of the rotor for excessive burning and pitting (photo).

8   If it is determined that a new rotor is required, make a note to that effect.

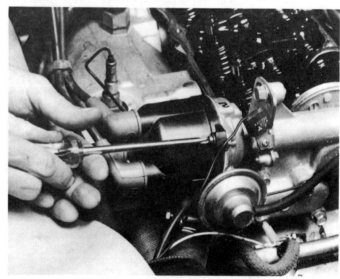

36.3   Loosen the distributor cap hold-down screws

36.4   Inspect the distributor cap contacts (arrows) for corrosion and damage

36.6   The distributor rotor screws (A) and contact (B)

Measuring plug gap. A feeler gauge of the correct size (see ignition system specifications) should have a slight 'drag' when slid between the electrodes. Adjust gap if necessary

Adjusting plug gap. The plug gap is adjusted by bending the earth electrode inwards, or outwards, as necessary until the correct clearance is obtained. Note the use of the correct tool

Normal. Grey-brown deposits, lightly coated core nose. Gap increasing by around 0.001 in (0.025 mm) per 1000 miles (1600 km). Plugs ideally suited to engine, and engine in good condition

Carbon fouling. Dry, black, sooty deposits. Will cause weak spark and eventually misfire. Fault: over-rich fuel mixture. Check: carburettor mixture settings, float level and jet sizes; choke operation and cleanliness of air filter. Plugs can be re-used after cleaning

Oil fouling. Wet, oily deposits. Will cause weak spark and eventually misfire. Fault: worn bores/piston rings or valve guides; sometimes occurs (temporarily) during running-in period. Plugs can be re-used after thorough cleaning

Overheating. Electrodes have glazed appearance, core nose very white – few deposits. Fault: plug overheating. Check: plug value, ignition timing, fuel octane rating (too low) and fuel mixture (too weak). Discard plugs and cure fault immediately

Electrode damage. Electrodes burned away; core nose has burned, glazed appearance. Fault: pre-ignition. Check: as for 'Overheating' but may be more severe. Discard plugs and remedy fault before piston or valve damage occurs

Split core nose (may appear initially as a crack). Damage is self-evident, but cracks will only show after cleaning. Fault: pre-ignition or wrong gap-setting technique. Check: ignition timing, cooling system, fuel octane rating (too low) and fuel mixture (too weak). Discard plugs, rectify fault immediately

9   Inspect the centrifugal advance assembly for damage, corrosion and broken springs. Push on the assembly to make sure it moves easily in one direction with the springs pulling it the other (photo). Lubricate the contact surfaces of the assembly with a light coat of silicone grease.

10   If the rotor and cap are in good condition, reinstall them at this time.

11   If the cap must be replaced, do not reinstall it. Leave it off the distributor with the wires still connected.

12   If the spark plug wires passed the check in Step 1, they should be checked further as follows.

13   Examine the wires one at a time to avoid mixing them up.

14   Disconnect the plug wire from the spark plug. A removal tool can be used for this, or you can grab the rubber boot, twist slightly and then pull the wire free. Do not pull on the wire itself, only on the rubber boot (photo).

15   Inspect inside the boot for corrosion, which will look like a white crusty powder. Some models use a conductive white silicone lubricant which should not be mistaken for corrosion. Scrape off corrosion with a screwdriver or knife.

16   Push the wire and boot back onto the end of the spark plug. It should be a tight fit on the plug end. If not, remove the wire and use pliers to carefully crimp the metal connector inside the wire boot until the fit is snug.

17   Using a clean rag, clean the entire length of the wire. Remove all built up dirt and grease. As this is done, check for burns, cracks and any other form of damage. Bend the wires in several places to ensure that the conductive wire inside has not hardened.

18   The wires should be checked at the distributor cap in the same manner. Remove the wire from the cap by pulling on the boot, again examining the wires one at a time, and reinstalling each one after examination.

19   If a multi-meter is available, measure the resistance of the conductor in each wire. The correct value is 4.9 k-ohms per foot (16 k-ohms per metre).

20   If the wires appear to be in good condition, make sure that all wires are secure at both ends. If the cap and rotor are also in good condition, the check is finished. Reconnect the battery cable.

21   If it was determined in Steps 14 through 19 that new wires are required, obtain them at this time, along with a new cap and rotor if so determined in the checks above.

22   If new wires are being installed, replace them one at a time. **Note:** *It is important to replace the wires one at a time, noting the routing as each wire is removed and installed, to maintain the correct firing order.*

23   Attach the cap to the distributor, then reconnect the battery cable.

---

37   Valve adjustment and cylinder head bolt torque check

1   Run the engine until normal operating temperature is reached.

2   Stop the engine and remove the air cleaner assembly from the engine. Label all the hoses and electrical wiring leading to air cleaner for ease of installation (photo).

3   Remove the PCV valve and spark plug wire mount from the camshaft cover. Use a piece of wire to hold the throttle cable out of the way.

4   Remove the camshaft cover bolts, taking care not to lose the washers (photos).

5   Use a large screwdriver with a rag wrapped around the end to carefully pry the camshaft cover free of the engine (photo). Lift the cover from the engine and remove the gasket.

6   Position the number 1 piston at top dead center (TDC) on the compression stroke. To do this, first number each the spark plug wires, then remove all of the spark plugs from the engine. Locate the number 1 cylinder spark plug wire and trace it back to the distributor. Write a number 1 on the distributor body directly under the terminal where the number one spark plug wire attaches to the distributor cap. Do this for the other cylinders (using numbers 2, 3, 4) as well, then remove the cap and wires from the distributor (photos).

7   Slowly turn the engine over in a clockwise direction by slipping a wrench or socket over the large bolt at the front of the crankshaft or (if the drivebelt is tight enough) the alternator, until the notch on the crankshaft pulley is aligned with the pointer (photos). The rotor should be pointing directly at the number 1 you made on the distributor body (photo). If it is not, turn the crankshaft one more complete revolution (360°) in a clockwise direction. If the rotor is now pointing at the 1

36.9   Push on the centrifugal advance weights to make sure the springs offer resistance

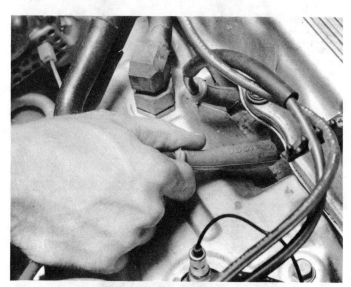

36.14   Pull on the spark plug boot, not the wire

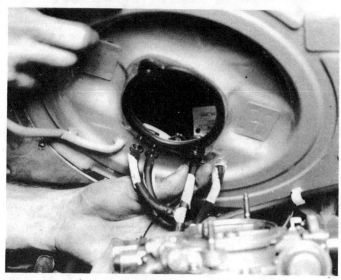

37.2   Mark the vacuum hoses which connect to the air cleaner with tape so they can be reinstalled in their original positions

37.4a   Removing the camshaft cover bolts

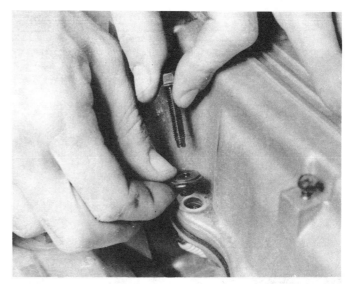

37.4b   Be sure to keep the washers with the camshaft cover bolts

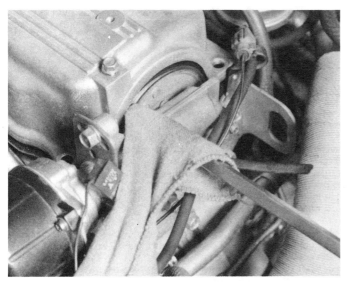

37.5   Pry the camshaft cover up to break the gasket seal, using a screwdriver and a rag so the aluminum housing won't be damaged

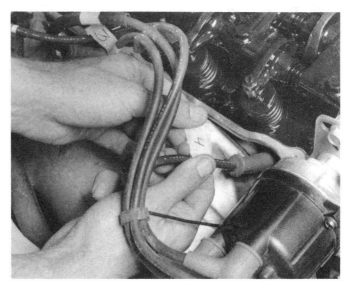

37.6a   Marking the distributor wires with tape

37.6b   Marking the distributor wire location on the housing

37.7a   With the spark plugs removed and the drivebelt tight, the engine can be rotated using a socket or wrench on the alternator nut

37.7b   The crankshaft pulley notch aligned with the Top Dead Center (TDC) mark

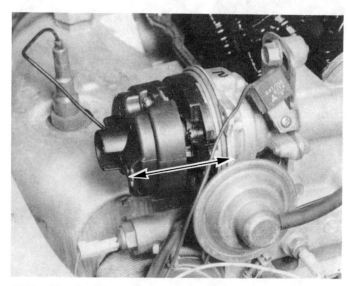

37.7c   The distributor rotor contact aligned with the number 1 spark plug wire mark (arrow) on the housing, indicating the number 1 cylinder is at TDC

on the distributor body, then the number 1 piston is at TDC on the compression stroke and the valve clearances can be checked and adjusted for the number 1 intake and exhaust valves, number 2 intake valve and number 3 exhaust valve. Intake valves are on the rear (firewall) side of the engine and exhaust valves are on the front.

8   Insert an appropriate size feeler gauge (refer to Specifications) between the valve stem and the rocker arm. If the feeler gauge fits between the valve and the rocker arm with a slight drag, then the clearance is correct and no adjustment is required.

9   If the feeler gauge will not fit between the valve and the screw, or if it is loose, loosen the adjusting screw locknut and carefully tighten or loosen the adjusting screw until you can feel a slight drag on the feeler gauge as it is withdrawn from between the valve stem and adjusting screw (photo).

10   Hold the adjusting screw with a screwdriver, to keep it from turning, and tighten the locknut securely (photo). Recheck the clearance to make sure it hasn't changed.

11   Turn the crankshaft one complete turn (360°), which will bring the number 4 piston to top dead center on the compression stroke. Verify this by checking to see that the rotor is pointing to the number 4 spark plug wire position. The valve clearance for the number 2 exhaust, number 3 intake and number 4 intake and exhaust can now be checked and adjusted.

12   With the camshaft cover removed and the engine warmed up, the cylinder head bolt torques can also be checked, using a torque wrench. Slacken one bolt by a quarter turn, then tighten it to the specified torque. Repeat for all the cylinder head bolts, following the sequence shown in the accompanying illustration.

13   Install the camshaft cover (use a new gasket) and tighten the mounting bolts evenly and securely to the specified torque (see Chapter 2A Specifications).

14   Install the spark plugs, distributor cap and spark plug wires. Install the air cleaner and hook up the various hoses, electrical connections and vacuum lines.

15   Start the engine and check for oil leakage between the camshaft cover and the cylinder head.

37.9   Adjusting the valve clearance with a feeler gauge and screwdriver

37.10   Hold the adjusting screw so that it can't move while tightening the locknut

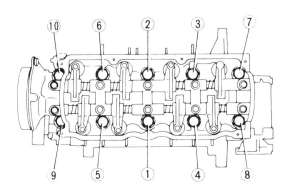

Fig. 1.21 Cylinder head bolt tightening sequence (Sec 37)

38 Compression check

1   A compression check will tell you what mechanical condition the engine is in. Specifically, it can tell you if the compression is down due to leakage caused by worn piston rings, defective valves and seats or a blown head gasket.
2   Warm the engine to normal operating temperature, shut it off and allow it to sit for ten minutes to allow the catalytic converter temperature to drop. (On models without a catalytic converter there is no need to wait ten minutes).
3   Begin by cleaning the area around the spark plugs before you remove them. This will keep dirt from falling into the cylinders while you are performing the compression test. Remove the spark plugs.
4   Disconnect the coil primary wire from the distributor. Block the throttle and choke valves open.
5   With the compression gauge in the number one spark plug hole, crank the engine over at least four compression strokes and observe the gauge. The compression should build up quickly. Low compression on the first stroke, which does not build up during successive strokes, indicates leaking valves, a blown head gasket or a cracked head. Record the highest gauge reading obtained and check this against Specifications.
6   Repeat the procedure for the remaining cylinders. The lowest compression reading should not be less than 70% of the highest reading. No reading should be less than 115 psi.

7   Pour a couple of teaspoons of engine oil (a squirt can works great for this) into each cylinder, through the spark plug hole, and repeat the test.
8   If the compression increases after the oil is added, the piston rings are definitely worn. If the compression does not increase significantly, the leakage is occurring at the valves or head gasket. Leakage past the valves may be caused by burned valve seats or faces or warped, cracked or bent valves.
9   If two adjacent cylinders have equally low compression, there is a strong possibility that the head gasket between them is blown. The appearance of coolant in the combustion chambers or the crankcase would verify this condition.
10   If the compression is higher than normal, the combustion chambers are probably coated with carbon deposits. If that is the case, the cylinder head should be removed and decarbonized.
11   If compression is way down or varies greatly between cylinders, it would be a good idea to have a leakdown test performed by an automotive repair shop. This test will pinpoint exactly where the leakage is occurring and how severe it is.

39 Coasting leaner system check

1   The coasting leaner system is fitted to UK models with a manual transaxle. Its function is to supply additional air to the intake manifold during deceleration, so reducing HC and CO emissions.
2   Run the engine until it reaches operating temperature. Stop the engine and remove the air cleaner as described in Section 37.
3   Unplug the coasting leaner valve electrical connector. Hook up a voltmeter between terminal 'B' of the connector and ground.
4   Run the engine. Increase the engine speed to above 3000 rpm, then release the throttle suddenly and observe the voltmeter. Above 2100 ± 100 rpm no voltage should be registered; below this speed the meter should read 12 volts. Stop the engine and disconnect the voltmeter.
5   Check the operation of the coasting leaner valve by applying battery voltage as shown (Fig. 1.24). A click should be heard when voltage is applied.
6   Check the idle switch as follows. Start the engine and hook up the voltmeter to the connector as shown in Fig. 1.25. At idle speed no voltage should be registered. Increase the engine speed and check that above 1200 to 1300 rpm the meter reads 12 volts. Turn the idle switch adjusting screw if necessary until the correct result is obtained.
7   Stop the engine, disconnect the voltmeter and install the air cleaner.
8   More information on the coasting leaner system will be found in Chapter 6.

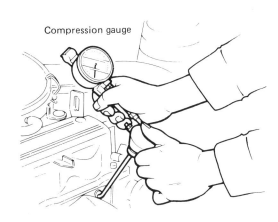

Fig. 1.22 Checking engine compression (Sec 38)

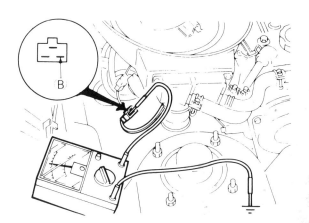

Fig. 1.23 Voltmeter connections for checking coasting leaner valve (Sec 39)

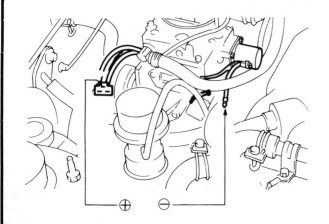

Fig. 1.24 Apply battery voltage as shown to check the function of the valve (Sec 39)

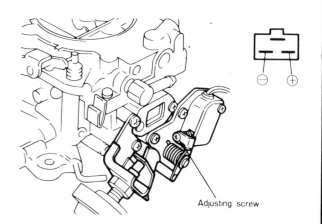

Adjusting screw

Fig. 1.25 Voltmeter connections (top right) for checking coasting leaner idle switch (Sec 39)

Chapter 2 Part A Engine

Contents

Specifications

Timing belt deflection	0.47 to 0.55 in (11.9 to 13.9 mm) under load of 22 lb (10 kg), or 0.39 to 0.47 in (10 to 12 mm) under load of 3.3 lb (1.5 kg)
Oil pump	
Outer gear tooth-to-crescent clearance limit	0.013 in (0.33 mm)
Inner gear tooth-to-crescent clearance limit	0.016 in (0.41 mm)
Outer gear-to-pump body clearance	0.008 in (0.20 mm)
Gear-to-pump cover clearance	0.004 in (0.10 mm)

Torque specifications

	Ft-lbs	M-kg
Alternator bracket to engine bolt	27 to 46	3.7 to 6.3
Alternator adjusting bolt	14 to 25	1.9 to 3.5
Cylinder head bolts		
Engine warm	69 to 80	9.5 to 11.0
Engine cold	59 to 64	8.2 to 8.8
Camshaft sprocket bolt	35 to 48	4.8 to 6.6
Camshaft cap (rocker shaft) bolts	13 to 20	1.8 to 2.8
Camshaft cover bolts	2 to 3	0.28 to 0.41
Crankshaft pulley bolts		
1.6 litre	6 to 9	0.8 to 1.2
2.0 litre	8 to 12	1.1 to 1.6
Exhaust manifold bolts/nuts	16 to 21	2.2 to 2.9
Engine mount bolts		
Number 1 engine mount-to-transaxle	27 to 38	3.7 to 5.2
Number 1 engine mount-to-body	32 to 40	4.4 to 5.5
Number 2 engine mount-to-transaxle	27 to 38	3.7 to 5.2
Number 2 engine mount-to-body	32 to 40	4.4 to 5.5
Number 3 engine mount-to-body	32 to 40	4.4 to 5.5
Number 3 engine mount-to-engine	41 to 59	5.7 to 8.1

Torque specifications (continued)

	Ft-lbs	M-kg
Flywheel/driveplate bolts	71 to 76	9.8 to 10.5
Front housing bolts	14 to 19	1.9 to 2.6
Intake manifold bolts/nuts.	14 to 19	1.9 to 2.6
Oil cooler center nut	22 to 29	3.0 to 4.0
Oil pan bolts	5 to 9	0.7 to 1.2
Oil pick-up tube flange bolts	6 to 9	0.8 to 1.2
Oil pressure switch.	9 to 13	1.2 to 1.8
Oil pump-to-block bolts.	14 to 19	1.9 to 2.6
Rear housing nuts and bolts	14 to 19	1.9 to 2.6
Timing belt cover bolt.	5 to 7	0.7 to 1.0
Timing belt sprocket bolt	80 to 87	11.0 to 12.0
Timing belt tensioner lockbolt	27.5 to 38.3	3.8 to 5.3
Torque stopper-to-engine bolt	49 to 56	6.8 to 7.7
Torque stopper-to-body bolt	40 to 50	5.5 to 6.9
Water bypass hose clamp	14 to 25	1.9 to 3.5
Water inlet pipe assembly-to-water pump bolt	14 to 19	1.9 to 2.6
Water inlet pipe bracket-to-engine bolt	28 to 38	3.9 to 5.2

1 General information

The engine block is made of cast iron and the removable head is cast aluminum. The camshaft is located in the cylinder head and actuates the valves via shaft mounted rocker arms.

The forward Sections in this Part of Chapter 2 are devoted to in-vehicle repair procedures, while the latter Sections detail engine removal and installation procedures. Information concerning engine block and cylinder head servicing can be found in Part B of this Chapter.

The repair procedures included in this part are based on the assumption that the engine is still installed in the vehicle. Therefore, if this information is being used during a complete engine overhaul, with the engine already out of the vehicle and on a stand, many of the steps included here will not apply.

The specifications included in this part of Chapter 2 apply only to the procedures found here. Part B of Chapter 2 contains the specifications necessary for engine block and cylinder head rebuilding.

2 Camshaft cover — removal and installation

Removal

1 Remove the air cleaner assembly.
2 Remove the PCV valve and hose.
3 Remove the retaining bolts and separate the cover from the engine. It may be necessary to break the gasket seal by either tapping the cover with a soft faced hammer or inserting a very thin blade scraper or screwdriver at the corner.
4 Clean all traces of gasket material from the camshaft cover gasket mating surfaces. Be careful not to nick or gouge the soft aluminum.

Installation

5 Place the cover and new gasket in position. Install the attaching bolts and tighten to the specified torque (photo).
6 Install the air cleaner and PCV assemblies.

3 Timing belt cover — removal and installation

1 Disconnect the negative cable from the battery.

Upper cover

2 Slacken the accessory drivebelt(s) (Chapter 1, Section 6). Move the drivebelt(s) out of the way.
3 Remove all of the accessible timing belt cover bolts.
4 On models with air conditioning, use the drivebelt adjuster bolt to move the adjustment pulley down and then push the adjuster out of the way for access to the remaining bolts.
5 Remove the retaining bolts and lift the cover from the engine.
6 Installation is the reverse of removal. Adjust the drivebelt tension (Chapter 1).

2.5 Use a torque wrench whenever possible, particularly when working on cylinder head components because they are made of aluminum

Lower cover

7 Remove the top retaining bolt, which is accessible from in the engine compartment.
8 Raise the front of the vehicle, support it on jackstands and remove the right front wheel and splash panel.
9 Remove the two remaining bolts and lift the cover off the engine.
10 Installation is the reverse of removal.

4 Oil pump body oil seal — replacement

Removal

1 Remove the timing belt cover (Section 3) and timing belt (Section 5).
2 Referring to the appropriate Sections, remove the crankshaft pulley and sprocket.
3 Pry the oil seal out with a screwdriver (photo).

Installation

4 Lubricate the inner diameter of the seal with engine oil and place the seal in position with the open lip facing inwards.
5 Tap the seal evenly and fully into the bore using a hammer and suitable size socket (photo).
6 Install the crankshaft sprocket and pulley.
7 Replace the timing belt and cover.

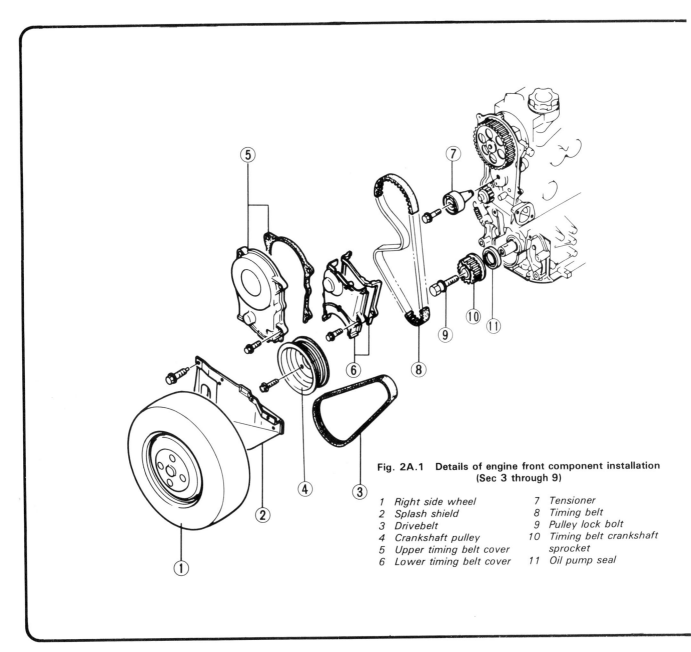

Fig. 2A.1 Details of engine front component installation
(Sec 3 through 9)

1 Right side wheel
2 Splash shield
3 Drivebelt
4 Crankshaft pulley
5 Upper timing belt cover
6 Lower timing belt cover

7 Tensioner
8 Timing belt
9 Pulley lock bolt
10 Timing belt crankshaft
sprocket
11 Oil pump seal

4.3 Pry the old seal out with a screwdriver, taking care not to nick or gouge the soft aluminum surface of the housing

4.5 A socket and hammer can be used to seat the seal evenly into the bore

5 Timing belt — removal, installation and adjustment

Removal

1 Remove the timing belt front cover (Section 3).
2 With the spark plugs removed, use a wrench on the crankshaft pulley bolt to rotate the crankshaft until the timing mark on the crankshaft pulley is aligned with the 0 degree BTDC mark on the indicator scale and the camshaft sprocket A mark (2.0 litre) or B mark (1.6 litre) lines up with the mark on the front housing as shown in the accompanying illustrations.
3 Remove the bolts and pull the crankshaft pulley off the timing belt sprocket. Because of insufficient clearance, the pulley cannot be removed from the vehicle, but for this procedure removal won't be necessary. The pulley just has to be moved clear of the sprocket. **Note:** *Mark the timing belt with an arrow indicating direction of rotation before loosening the tension if the belt is to be reused (photo).*
4 Loosen the timing belt tensioner lock bolt.
5 Work the belt off the sprockets and remove it from the engine.
6 Inspect the belt for damage, peeling, wear, cracks, hardening, crimping or signs of oil or other moisture. The belt should be replaced with a new one if any of these conditions exist or if the specified mileage has elapsed (Chapter 1).

Installation

7 Make sure the crankshaft and camshaft sprocket timing marks are aligned (photos).
8 With the spring attached to the tensioner, push on the tensioner

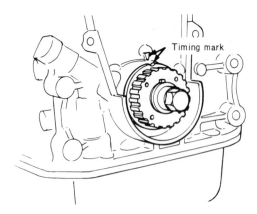

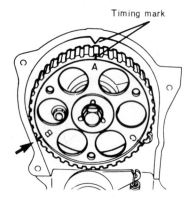

Fig. 2A.2   Proper position of the timing marks — 2.0 litre. For 1.6 litre the 'B' mark (arrowed) should be aligned with the pointer (Sec 5)

5.3   Mark the timing belt direction with an arrow if it is going to be reused

5.7a   The crankshaft sprocket marks and the . . .

5.7b   . . . camshaft sprocket marks must be aligned as indicated before installing the timing belt (2.0 litre shown)

Fig. 2A.3 Apply maximum tension to the spring in the direction shown (arrow) and then tighten the lock bolt snugly before installing the timing belt (Sec 5)

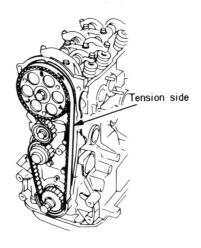

Fig. 2A.4 The timing belt must be installed from the direction of the tension side (Sec 5)

to apply maximum pressure and tighten the lock bolt to hold the tensioner in place as shown in the accompanying illustration.

9 Work the belt onto the camshaft and crankshaft sprockets from the tension side (the other side from the water pump and tensioner) so that the tension is maintained. If the old belt is being reinstalled, make sure the arrow is pointing in the proper direction.

Adjustment

10 Loosen the tensioner lock bolt so that just the spring is applying pressure.

11 Turn the crankshaft through two full turns clockwise so that equal tension is applied to both sides of the timing belt as shown in the accompanying illustration and tighten the lock bolt.

12 Check the timing marks to make sure they are still properly aligned.

13 Check the deflection of the belt midway between the crankshaft and camshaft sprockets on the tension side to make sure it is within specification. If the tension is not correct, repeat the adjustment operation described in Steps 10 thru 12.

14 Install the timing belt cover, the crankshaft pulley and the spark plugs.

6 Camshaft sprocket — removal and installation

Removal

1 Remove the timing belt front cover (Section 3)

2 Remove the timing belt (Section 5).

3 Hold the sprocket in position so it cannot turn, using an extension and socket on one of the front cover bolts. Remove the sprocket bolt, sprocket and washer.

Installation

4 Place the sprocket in position on the camshaft and align the sprocket and cover marks. The knock pin on the camshaft must engage with the hole in the sprocket.

5 Hold the camshaft sprocket and install the washer and bolt. Tighten the bolt to the specified torque.

6 Install the timing belt, cover and any other components which were removed.

7 Crankshaft pulley — removal and installation

Removal

1 Raise the front of the vehicle and support it securely on jackstands.

2 Remove the right front wheel and fender well splash shield.

3 Slacken the accessory drivebelt (Chapter 1, Section 6) and slip it off the crankshaft pulley.

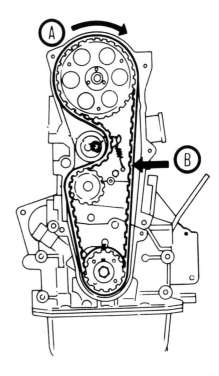

Fig. 2A.5 Rotate the timing belt to the right (A) then check the tension at point B (Sec 5)

4 Remove the pulley retaining bolts.

5 Insert a large screwdriver through the access hole in the bellhousing and into the teeth of the starter ring gear so the crankshaft cannot turn.

6 With an assistant holding the screwdriver so the crankshaft is locked, remove the timing belt sprocket bolt and washer.

7 Lift the crankshaft pulley from the engine.

Installation

8 Place the pulley in position and install the retaining bolts and the timing belt sprocket bolt finger tight.

9 With the crankshaft locked in place, tighten the sprocket bolt and pulley bolts to the specified torque.

10 Install and tension the accessory drivebelt.

11 Install the splash shield and front wheel and lower the vehicle.

8   Timing belt sprocket — removal and installation

Removal

1   Remove the timing belt (Section 5).
2   Lock the flywheel in place with a screwdriver inserted between the teeth and remove the sprocket bolt, washer and pulley.
3   Remove the sprocket from the crankshaft. Recover the Woodruff key if it is loose.

Installation

4   Install the Woodruff key (if removed). Lightly oil the key and the crankshaft nose.
5   Place the sprocket and pulley on the crankshaft and install the crankshaft sprocket bolt finger tight. Tighten the bolt to the specified torque.
6   Install and tension the timing belt (Section 5).

9   Camshaft — removal and installation

Removal

1   Remove the front timing belt cover (Section 3), timing belt (Section 5) and camshaft sprocket (Section 6).
2   Remove camshaft cover (Section 2).
3   Remove the air injection tubes (Chapter 6).
4   Remove the distributor (Chapter 5) and the rear housing (Section 10).
5   Remove the front housing bolts, carefully pry the housing away from the engine and remove it (photo).
6   Remove the rocker arm and shaft assembly from the engine (Section 11).
7   Remove the fuel pump and lift the camshaft from the engine.

Installation

8   Lubricate the journals and place the camshaft in position with the knock pin at the top.
9   Install the rocker arm and shaft assembly.
10 Install the front housing, using a new gasket.
11 Install the camshaft sprocket, making sure the sprocket and front housing marks are aligned.
12 Install the rear housing (using a new gasket) and distributor.
13 Install the fuel pump, air injection tubes, camshaft cover and timing belt and cover.
14 If a replacement camshaft has been installed, observe any break-in instructions provided by the manufacturer.

10   Rear housing — removal and installation

Removal

1   Remove the distributor (Chapter 5).
2   Remove the thermostat (Chapter 3).
3   Place newspapers or rags under the housing to catch the oil in the housing.
4   Remove the housing retaining bolts and nuts.
5   Use a screwdriver wrapped in a rag to carefully pry the housing away from the engine.

Installation

6   Carefully clean the contact surfaces of the housing and cylinder of old gasket material.
7   Coat the new gasket with sealant and place it in position on the housing.
8   Install the housing on the cylinder head, install the nuts and bolts and tighten them to the specified torque.
9   Install the thermostat and refill the cooling system.
10 Install the distributor.

11   Rocker arm assembly — removal and installation

Removal

1   Disconnect the negative battery cable.
2   Remove the camshaft cover (Section 2).
3   Loosen the rocker arm assembly retaining bolts, a little at a time, in the sequence shown in the accompanying illustration.
4   Once the bolts are loose, remove them and place them in a numbered piece of cardboard for reinstallation to the same positions.
5   Lift the rocker arm assembly from the engine.
6   If it is wished to dismantle the rocker arm assembly, make identification marks so that the components can be installed to their original positions. The rocker arms, shafts and camshaft caps are not interchangeable.

Installation

7   Carefully clean the contact areas of the rocker arm assembly and the cylinder head to remove all traces of sealant.
8   If the assembly has been disassembled, lubricate it liberally with clean engine oil prior to installation.
9   Apply sealant to the cylinder head-to-rocker arm assembly contact areas as shown in the the accompanying illustration.
10 Lower the rocker arm assembly into place and install the bolts finger tight in their original positions.
11 Tighten the bolts, a little at a time, to the specified torque in the sequence shown in the accompanying illustration.
12 Check the valve adjustment, adjusting as necessary (Chapter 1).
13 Install the camshaft cover and connect the battery cable.

9.5   A screwdriver wrapped in a rag can be used to pry off the cover without damaging the soft aluminum

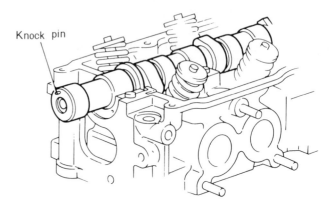

Fig. 2A.6   The camshaft knock pin must be at the top when the camshaft is installed (Sec 9)

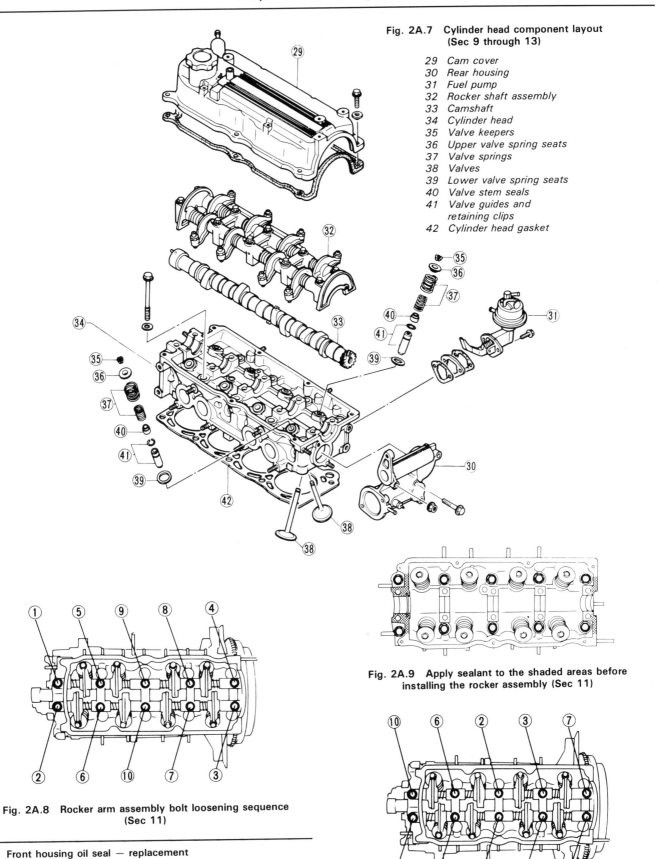

Fig. 2A.7 Cylinder head component layout (Sec 9 through 13)

29 Cam cover
30 Rear housing
31 Fuel pump
32 Rocker shaft assembly
33 Camshaft
34 Cylinder head
35 Valve keepers
36 Upper valve spring seats
37 Valve springs
38 Valves
39 Lower valve spring seats
40 Valve stem seals
41 Valve guides and retaining clips
42 Cylinder head gasket

Fig. 2A.8 Rocker arm assembly bolt loosening sequence (Sec 11)

Fig. 2A.9 Apply sealant to the shaded areas before installing the rocker assembly (Sec 11)

Fig. 2A.10 Rocker arm assembly bolt tightening sequence (Sec 11)

12 Front housing oil seal — replacement

1 Remove the timing belt (Section 5).
2 Remove the camshaft sprocket (Section 6).
3 Pry the old oil seal out with a screwdriver, taking care not to damage the sealing surface.
4 Apply a thin coat of engine oil to the lips of the new seal.

5   Place the seal squarely in position in the bore with the lips facing inwards. Use a suitable size socket to press it fully and evenly into place.
6   Install the sprocket, timing belt and cover.

13   Valves, springs and valve stem oil seals — removal and installation

Removal

1   Remove the rocker arm assembly (Section 11).
2   Remove the cylinder head (Section 16).
3   Use a compressor to compress the valve springs, one at a time, and remove the valve keepers. Release the compressor and remove the seat and springs. Use pliers to remove the valve stem oil seal.
4   Remove the valves one at a time and keep them and their keepers in order in a numbered rack or piece of cardboard so they can be reinstalled in their original locations. Refer to Chapter 2, Part B for valve component inspection procedures.

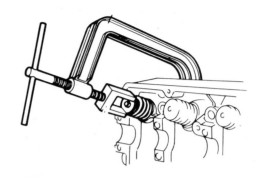

Fig. 2A.11   Removing the valve spring keepers with a compressor tool (Sec 13)

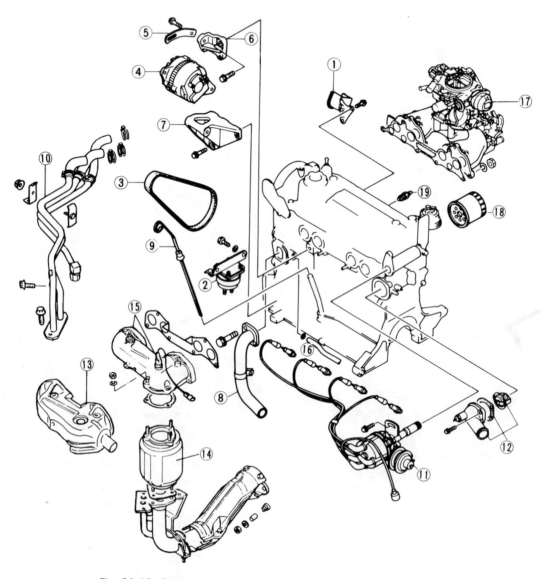

Fig. 2A.12   Engine external component layout (Sec 13 through 25)

1 Torque stopper assembly	7 Alternator bracket	11 Spark plugs, wires and distributor	15 Exhaust manifold
2 Engine mount	8 Lower water inlet pipe assembly and hose	12 Thermostat and housing	16 Bypass hose assembly
3 Drivebelt	9 Oil dipstick assembly	13 Heat shield	17 Carburetor
4 Alternator	10 Air injection pipes	14 Exhaust pipe	18 Oil filter
5 Alternator adjusting strap			19 Oil pressure switch
6 Strap bracket			

Installation

5 Insert the new valve stem oil seals into the guides and then use a suitable size socket and hammer to tap them fully into place.
6 Coat the first valve stem with clean engine oil and slide it into its original guide.
7 Install the valve springs and seats and use a valve spring compressor to install the keepers.
8 Repeat the procedure for the remaining valves.
9 Install the cylinder head and rocker arm assembly.

14 Intake manifold — removal and installation

Removal

1 Disconnect the negative cable from the battery and remove the air cleaner assembly.
2 Drain the coolant (Chapter 1).
3 Remove the air cleaner assembly.
4 Disconnect the throttle and (if equipped) choke, downshift and cruise control cables and vacuum hose from the carburetor.
5 Disconnect the heater hose at the firewall and the vacuum brake hose from the fitting on the vacuum reservoir.
6 Disconnect and plug the fuel line at the fuel pump.
7 Disconnect the charcoal canister hose from the carburetor and the purge hoses from the canister (if equipped).
8 Disconnect the four electrical connectors adjacent to the carburetor and canister.
9 Mark any remaining hoses and connections which will interfere with manifold removal with numbered pieces of tape and disconnect them.
10 Remove the manifold retaining nuts and bolts, slide the intake manifold off the studs and separate it from the cylinder head.
11 Remove the gasket.

Installation

12 Clean all traces of gasket and other foreign material from the manifold and cylinder head mating surfaces, taking care not to gouge the soft aluminum surface.
13 Install a new gasket, place the manifold in position on the studs and install the retaining nuts and bolts. Tighten the nuts and bolts to the specified torque. Work from the center of the manifold out, in a criss-cross pattern.
14 Install the components which were removed to gain access to the intake manifold.

15 Exhaust manifold — removal and installation

Removal

1 Disconnect the negative cable from the battery.
2 Remove the air injection system pipes.
3 Remove the air injection fitting, retaining bolt and oxygen sensor (if equipped) and detach the heat shroud.
4 Apply penetrating oil to the cylinder head and catalytic converter or exhaust downpipe retaining stud threads and allow it to soak for ten minutes.
5 In the engine compartment, remove the nuts retaining the exhaust manifold to the cylinder head and to the catalytic converter or exhaust downpipe.
6 Grasp the manifold, separate it from the cylinder head and the catalytic converter or exhaust downpipe and lift it from the engine.

Installation

7 Remove all traces of gasket material from the manifold and cylinder head with a gasket scraper. Take care not to nick or gouge the soft aluminum of the head.
8 Place the manifold in position on the cylinder head, using new gaskets, and install the retaining nuts to hold it in place. Install the nuts and bolts retaining the manifold to the catalytic converter or exhaust downpipe. Tighten the manifold nuts to the specified torque. Work from the center of the manifold out, in a criss-cross pattern.
9 Install the heat shroud, air injection pipes and any other components which were removed.

16 Cylinder head — removal and installation

Note: *The engine must be cold whenever the camshaft/cylinder head bolts are loosened or removed.*

Removal

1 Disconnect the negative cable from the battery and remove the air cleaner assembly and the air injection pipes.
2 Drain the cooling system and disconnect the upper radiator hose.
3 Remove the distributor (Chapter 5) and rear housing (Section 10).
4 Referring to the appropriate Sections, remove the timing belt cover and the belt.
5 Remove the fuel pump (Chapter 4).
6 Remove the intake manifold (Section 14).
7 Remove the alternator. On air conditioned models, remove the compressor through bolt and move the compressor carefully out of the way, taking care not to damage the lines (which contain high pressure) or the radiator. Remove the alternator/air conditioner bracket-to-cylinder head bolts and loosen the remaining bracket bolts.
8 Remove the camshaft cover (Section 2).
9 Remove the three bolts attaching the exhaust manifold to the catalytic converter or exhaust downpipe and separate the converter or downpipe from the manifold.
10 Loosen the cylinder head bolts, a few turns at a time, in the sequence shown in the accompanying illustration.
11 After they are all loose, remove the cylinder head bolts and place them in order in a piece of cardboard so they can be reinstalled in their original positions (photo).
12 If the cylinder head cannot be lifted off easily, break the gasket seal using a pry bar inserted between the alternator/compressor bracket and the cylinder head.
13 Separate the cylinder head from the engine and remove the gasket.

Installation

14 Remove all traces of gasket material from the engine block and cylinder head (photo). Make sure the cylinder head bolt threads and the threaded holes in the block are clean, as this could affect torque readings during installation.
15 Place the new gasket and cylinder head in position, followed by the camshaft and rocker arm assembly (if removed). Make sure that the gasket is the right way up.
16 Install the cylinder head bolts and tighten them in stages to the specified torque in the sequence shown in the accompanying illustration.
17 The remainder of the installation procedure is the reverse of removal. See Section 11 for the rocker arm bolt tightening sequence.
18 After warming up the engine, check the valve clearances and re-torque the cylinder head bolts as described in Chapter 1, Section 37.

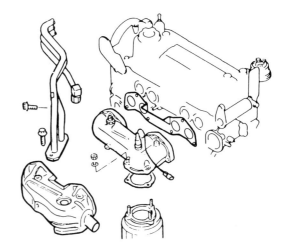

Fig. 2A.13 Exhaust manifold installation details (Sec 15)

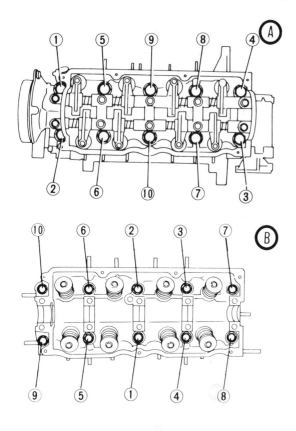

**Fig. 2A.14   Cylinder head bolt loosening (A) and
tightening (B) sequence (Sec 16)**

16.11   Use a piece of cardboard to keep the cylinder head bolts
in order

17   Front housing cover — removal and installation

Removal

1   Remove the timing cover (Section 3) and timing belt (Section 5).
2   Remove the camshaft sprocket (Section 6).
3   Remove the bolts and carefully separate the cover from the cylinder
head, using a screwdriver to break the gasket seal.

Installation

4   Carefully clean the mating surfaces of gasket material.
5   Place the housing cover in position using a new gasket and install
the retaining bolts. Tighten the bolts to the specified torque.
6   The remainder of installation is the reverse of removal.

16.14   Use a scraper to remove the gasket material

18   Oil pump — removal and installation

Removal

1   Remove the timing belt covers, timing belt and crankshaft sprocket.
2   Remove the oil pan.
3   Remove the engine mount plate/front cover bolts.
4   Unbolt and remove the pickup tube assembly.
5   Insert a screwdriver at the corner of the cover to break the gasket
seal and remove the cover.
6   Clean the oil pump mating surfaces to remove old gasket material.

Installation

7   Coat the O-ring with petroleum jelly and insert it into the pump.
Coat the pump housing with sealant as shown in the accompanying
illustration. Apply clean engine oil to the lip of the oil seal.

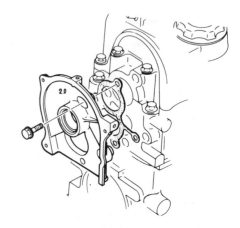

Fig. 2A.15   Front housing installation details (Sec 17)

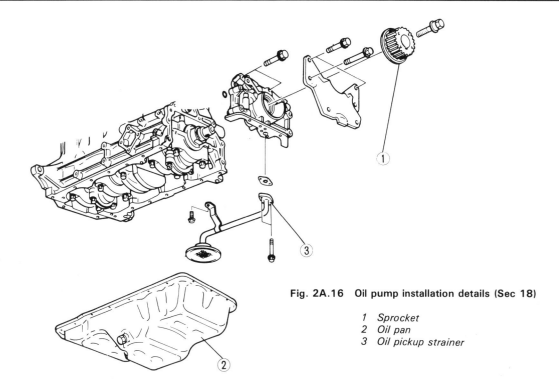

Fig. 2A.16 Oil pump installation details (Sec 18)

1 Sprocket
2 Oil pan
3 Oil pickup strainer

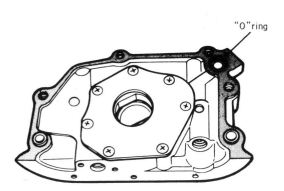

Fig. 2A.17 Apply sealant to the shaded areas of the oil pump housing (Sec 18)

8 Place the pump and new gasket in position and install the bolts. Tighten the bolts to the specified torque.
9 Using a new gasket, install the pickup tube and support assembly. Tighten the bolts to the specified torque.
10 Install the oil pan.
11 Install a new oil filter and replace the oil pressure switch harness (if removed).
12 Install the engine mount plate and tighten its bolts.
13 Install the timing belt, covers and the crankshaft sprocket.

19 Oil pump — disassembly, inspection and reassembly

Disassembly

1 Remove the retaining screws and cover from the rear of the pump (photo).
2 Remove the gears from the pump body. It may be necessary to turn the body over to remove the gears by allowing them to fall out.

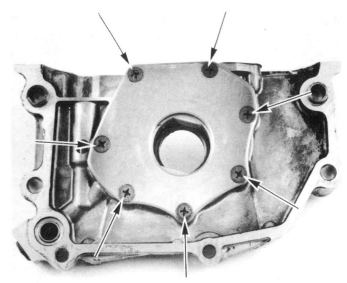

19.1 The oil pump cover screw locations (arrows)

3 Mount the pump body in a soft jawed vise and remove the snap-ring, plug, pressure regulator valve plunger and spring.

Inspection

4 Wash the oil pump parts in solvent.
5 Inspect the components for wear, cracks or other damage.
6 Check the outer (idler) gear-to-crescent clearance, inner (drive) gear-to-crescent clearance, the outer gear-to-pump body clearance and the gear-to-cover clearance, referring to the accompanying illustrations and to the Specifications.
7 Renew the oil seal as a matter of course.

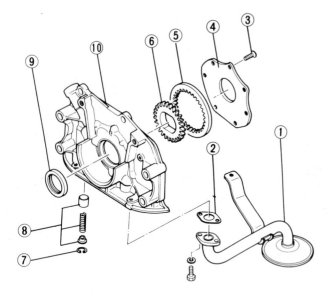

Fig. 2A.18   Oil pump components (Sec 19)

1   Oil strainer
2   Gasket
3   Bolt
4   Pump cover
5   Outer gear
6   Inner gear
7   Snap-ring
8   Plunger assembly
9   Oil seal
10 Pump body

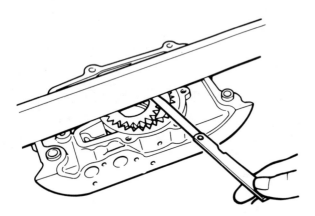

Fig. 2A.20   Measuring the oil pump gear-to-cover
clearance (Sec 19)

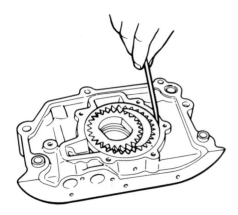

Fig. 2A.21   Checking the oil pump outer gear-to-body
clearance (Sec 19)

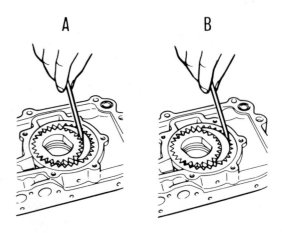

Fig. 2A.19   Checking the oil pump inner (A) and
outer (B) gear tooth tip and crescent clearance
(Sec 19)

Reassembly

8   Install the valve, plunger and spring assembly and secure with the snap-ring.
9   Lubricate and install the gears.
10 Install the pump cover and tighten the screws securely. Use thread locking agent.

20   Flywheel/driveplate and rear cover oil seal — removal and installation

Removal

1   Remove the transaxle (Chapter 7).
2   Remove the transaxle driveplate (automatic) or pressure plate, clutch disc and flywheel (manual).
3   Pry the oil seal out using a screwdriver (photo).

Installation

4   Lubricate the new seal and fit it with its lips facing inwards. Tap it into place slowly and carefully, working around the outer circumference until it bottoms in the bore (photo).
5   Install the clutch (Chapter 8) and flywheel or driveplate and torque converter assemblies. Use sealant on the bolt threads and tighten the bolts to the specified torque.
6   Install the transaxle.

21   Flywheel ring gear — replacement

1   If the flywheel ring gear teeth become damaged, the gear may be replaced as follows. (The driveplate ring gear cannot be separated from the driveplate.)
2   Remove the flywheel as described in Section 20.
3   Heat the ring gear with a blowtorch and drive it off the flywheel with a hammer and drift.
4   Heat the new ring gear to 480° to 570°F (250° to 300°C), preferably in an oven or oil bath. Place the heated gear on the flywheel. The bevelled side of the gear should face the engine when installed. Tap the gear home if necessary with the hammer and drift.
5   Install the flywheel (Section 20).

22   Oil cooler — removal and installation

1   When equipped, the oil cooler is located between the oil filter and the cylinder block. Two hoses convey coolant to and from the oil cooler.

20.3 Work from the inside of the seal when prying the seal out to lessen the chance of damaging the bore surface

20.4 Tap lightly around the seal outer circumference with a hammer and punch until the seal is fully seated in the bore

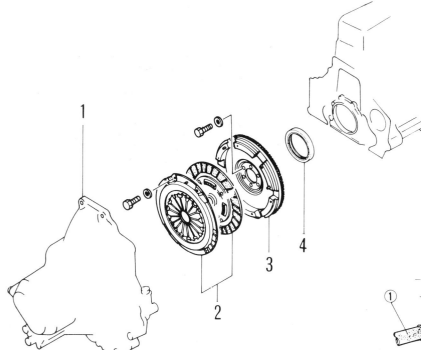

Fig. 2A.22 Details of the rear oil seal installation (Sec 20)

1 Transaxle
2 Clutch (manual transaxle)
3 Flywheel (manual transaxle) or driveplate (automatic transaxle)
4 Oil seal

2   Remove the oil filter (Chapter 1, Section 16).
3   Drain the cooling system (Chapter 1, Section 26).
4   Disconnect the coolant hoses from the oil cooler.
5   Remove the oil cooler center nut. The cooler can now be removed from the block.
6   When installing, use a new oil seal and position the cooler with the 'UP' mark facing upwards. Tighten the center nut to the specified torque.
7   Install a new oil filter and reconnect the coolant hoses.
8   Refill the cooling system. Run the engine and check for leaks of oil and coolant.
9   Stop the engine. Check the oil and coolant levels and top up if necessary.

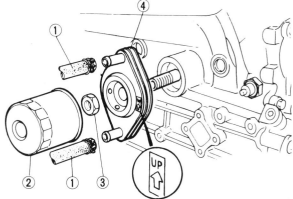

Fig. 2A.23 Oil cooler and associated components (Sec 22)

1 Coolant hoses   3 Center nut
2 Oil filter   4 Oil cooler

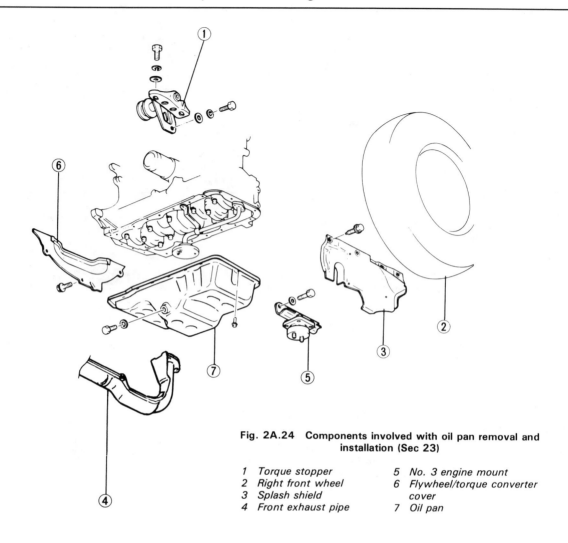

Fig. 2A.24   Components involved with oil pan removal and installation (Sec 23)

1   Torque stopper
2   Right front wheel
3   Splash shield
4   Front exhaust pipe
5   No. 3 engine mount
6   Flywheel/torque converter cover
7   Oil pan

23   Oil pan — removal and installation

Removal

1   Disconnect the battery negative cable.
2   Raise the front of the vehicle and support it securely on jackstands.
3   Drain the engine oil.
4   Remove the torque stopper assembly.
5   Remove the right front wheel and the inner fender panel.
6   Disconnect the front exhaust pipe.
7   Connect a suitable lifting device and raise the engine weight off the number 3 engine mount and unbolt and remove the mount.
8   Remove the flywheel/torque converter driveplate cover. Also remove the oil pan protector plate (when equipped).
9   Remove the oil pan bolts.
10   Raise the front of the engine and break the oil pan gasket seal by inserting a screwdriver between the pan and the block.
11   Rotate the front of the oil pan to the left and remove it from the engine.
12   Wash the oil pan thoroughly in solvent.
13   Clean the contact surfaces of the oil pan and engine block.

Installation

14   If no gasket is used, apply a 1/4-inch bead of RTV-type sealant to the contact surface of the oil pan. If a gasket is used, apply sealant to the areas shown in Fig. 2A.25.
15   Place the oil pan in position and install the retaining bolts. Tighten the bolts to the specified torque.
16   The remainder of installation is the reverse of removal.
17   After installation fill the engine with the specified amount and grade of oil, start the engine and check for leaks.

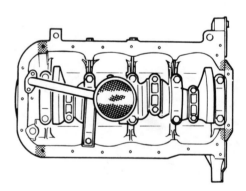

Fig. 2A.25   If a sump gasket is used, apply sealant to the shaded areas (Sec 23)

24   Engine mounts — replacement with engine in vehicle

1   The engine mounts can be replaced with the engine/transaxle still in the vehicle. Pry on the rubber mounts with a large screwdriver or bar to determine if they have become hard, split, or separated from the metal backing (photo).
2   Disconnect the negative cable from the battery.
3   Raise the front of the vehicle and support it securely on jackstands.
4   Support the engine with a jack.

24.1 Check the condition of the engine mounts by prying on them with a bar or large screwdriver

24.6a Pry out the torque stopper rubber cover with a screwdriver

24.6b The torque stopper bolt is accessible through the hole in the inner fender

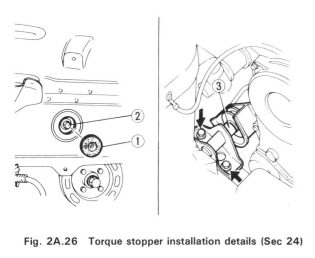

Fig. 2A.26 Torque stopper installation details (Sec 24)

1 Rubber cap
2 Bolts
3 Torque stopper

Torque stopper

5 Remove the right front wheel and the inner fender shield for access.
6 Remove the rubber access plug and bolt (photos).
7 In the engine compartment, remove the bolts and lift the stopper from the engine.

Engine mounts

8 From under the vehicle remove the retaining nuts.
9 In the engine compartment, remove the retaining bolts and then lift the mount from the engine.
10 Installation is the reverse of removal.

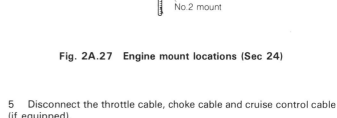

Fig. 2A.27 Engine mount locations (Sec 24)

---

25 Engine — removal and installation

See also Chapter 2B, Section 5

Removal

1 Remove the hood (Chapter 11).
2 Remove the battery and mount and drain the cooling system (Chapter 1).
3 Remove the air cleaner assembly (photos).
4 Remove the fuel inlet and return lines at the fuel pump.

5 Disconnect the throttle cable, choke cable and cruise control cable (if equipped).
6 Disconnect the speedometer cable.
7 Disconnect the clutch (manual) or shift cable (automatic) (photo).
8 Disconnect the wiring harness ground connection from the transaxle.
9 Disconnect the power brake vacuum hose (photo).
10 Unplug the vacuum switches and remove the bracket.
11 Disconnect the heater hoses.
12 Unplug the duty solenoid and vacuum sensor (when equipped) and unbolt it from the firewall.
13 Unplug the wiring harness connections to the engine.
14 Unplug any remaining electrical connectors.
15 Disconnect the distributor coil wire.

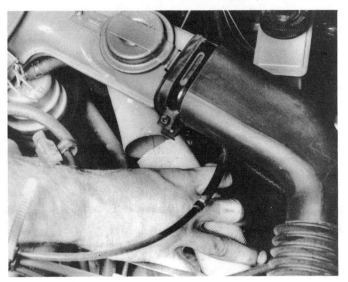

25.3a Removing the air cleaner heat hose

25.3b Removing the air cleaner air pipe

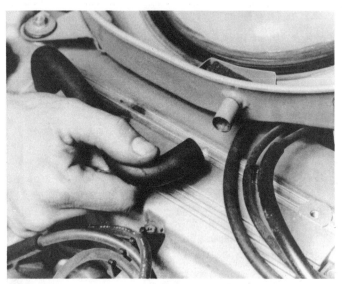

25.3c Removing the PCV hose from the air cleaner

25.3d Disconnecting the air injection hoses from the air cleaner

25.3e Removing the air cleaner-to-camshaft cover bolt

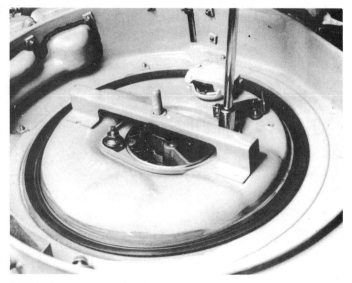

25.3f Removing the carburetor-to-air cleaner bolts

25.7 Remove the shift cable pin with needle nose pliers

25.9 Slide the clamp up the hose so it won't be lost

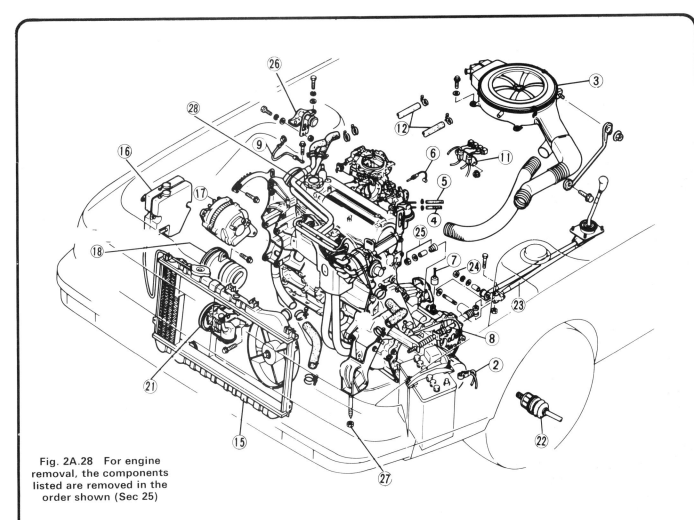

Fig. 2A.28 For engine removal, the components listed are removed in the order shown (Sec 25)

1   Hood (not shown)
2   Battery negative cable
3   Air cleaner assembly
4   Fuel hose
5   Fuel return hose
6   Throttle cable
7   Speedometer cable
8   Clutch cable
9   Engine ground cable

10 Power brake vacuum hose (not shown)
11 Power steering three-way valve and bracket
12 Heater hoses
13 Engine-to-transaxle wiring (not shown)
14 Evaporative system vacuum hoses (not shown)

15 Fan and radiator
16 Coolant and windshield washer reservoirs
17 Alternator
18 Air conditioner compressor
19 Front wheels (not shown)
20 Splash shields (not shown)
21 Power steering pump
22 Driveaxles

23 Manual transaxle change rod
24 Manual transaxle extension bar
25 Exhaust system flexible joints, bolts and nuts
26 Torque stopper
27 Engine and transaxle mounting nuts (not shown)
28 Engine and transaxle

25.24   Pry the right axleshaft out of the joint shaft housing (A) in the direction of the arrow

25.26   Exhaust pipe-to-muffler nuts (arrows)

25.30   Move the engine forward and then up to remove it from the engine compartment (arrows)

16 Disconnect the evaporative system hoses from the canister (when equipped).
17 Disconnect the radiator hoses and unplug the fan motor.
18 Remove the radiator (Chapter 3).
19 Remove the radiator coolant and windshield washer reservoirs.
20 Remove the alternator and (if equipped) air conditioning compressor from the bracket. Swing the compressor out of the way, taking care not to damage the hoses (which contain high pressure) and fasten it out of the way with a piece of wire.
21 Raise the front of the vehicle, support it securely on jackstands and remove the front wheels and inner fender splash shields.
22 Remove the power steering pump (when equipped) with the hoses still connected and fasten it out of the way in the engine compartment with a piece of wire.
23 Drain the transaxle (Chapter 1, Section 25 or 28).
24 Disconnect the front stabilizer links and front suspension balljoints, then pry or drive the axleshaft inboard ends from the transaxle or joint shaft (photo). See Chapter 8, Section 7, for more details. Leave the joint shaft inserted into the transaxle to retain the differential in position.
25 On manual transaxle models, disconnect the change control rod and extension bar from the transaxle. If necessary refer to Chapter 7, Part A, Section 4.
26 Disconnect the exhaust pipe at the muffler (photo).
27 Remove the rubber plug and inner fender shield for access and unbolt and remove the torque stopper and drive belt covers.
28 Attach a lifting device to the engine.
29 Disconnect the engine mounts.
30 Raise the engine slowly and carefully with an assistant guiding the engine forward off the muffler studs and moving the wiring harnesses out of the way (photo).
31 Raise the engine from the engine compartment and lower it onto suitable working surface. Separate the transaxle from the engine (Section 26). Block the engine in an upright position or mount it on an engine stand.

Installation

32 Reconnect the engine to the transaxle.
33 The front of the vehicle should remain raised to allow access from underneath during installation.
34 Position the engine directly over the engine compartment and lower it carefully and slowly into position.
35 Have an assistant guide the transaxle past the brake master cylinder and then guide the engine mounts and muffler studs into position while another assistant makes sure the power steering pump is moved out of the way as the engine is lowered.

36 The remainder of installation is the reverse of removal, referring to the appropriate Chapters for details of driveaxle insertion and reconnection of the front suspension.

26   Engine and transaxle — separation and reconnection

Automatic transaxle

1   Remove the starter motor.
2   Remove the joint shaft bracket bolts. The joint shaft must remain inserted into the transaxle or the differential will drop into the transaxle case.
3   Remove the transaxle torque converter cover plate.
4   Lock the starter ring gear teeth with a large screwdriver and remove the torque converter retaining bolts, rotating the crankshaft pulley with a wrench on the pulley bolt to bring each bolt into position.
5   Remove the transaxle-to-engine bolts.
6   Insert a large screwdriver between the engine and transaxle to separate them, working around the bellhousing until the transaxle can be removed. Have an assistant hold the joint shaft in the transaxle as it is moved away from the engine to make sure the differential stays in place.
7   Reconnection is a reversal of the separation procedure. Tighten the torque converter retaining bolts to the specified torque (Chapter 7, Part B, Specifications).

Manual transaxle

8   Remove the starter motor.
9   Remove the joint shaft bracket bolts.
10   Remove the transaxle-to-engine bolts.
11   Draw the transaxle off the engine. Have an assistant hold the joint shaft in the transaxle — see paragraph 6. **Do not** allow the weight of the transaxle to hang on the primary shaft, or damage may result.
12   When reconnecting, first make sure that the clutch centering is accurate (Chapter 8, Section 5). Apply a smear of grease to the primary shaft splines.
13   Offer the transaxle to the engine, again having an assistant hold the joint shaft. If the primary shaft will not enter the clutch, rock the transaxle or turn the crankshaft slightly to encourage engagement of the splines. Support the transaxle until it is located on the dowels so that the weight is not borne by the primary shaft.
14   Install the transaxle-to-engine bolts, the joint shaft bracket bolts and the starter motor.

Chapter 2 Part B
General engine overhaul procedures

Contents

Specifications

Valves and related components

Valve face angle	45°
Valve seat angle	45°
Valve head thickness (margin)	
Intake	0.020 in (0.5 mm)
Exhaust	0.039 in (1.0 mm)
Valve stem diameter	
Intake	0.3161 to 0.3167 in (8.030 to 8.045 mm)
Service limit	0.3142 in (7.980 mm)
Exhaust	0.3159 to 0.3165 in (8.025 to 8.040 mm)
Service limit	0.3140 in (7.975 mm)
Valve guide internal diameter	0.3177 to 0.3185 in (8.07 to 8.09 mm)
Stem-to-guide clearance	
Intake and exhaust	0.0010 to 0.0024 in (0.025 to 0.060 mm)
Service limit	0.0079 in (0.20 mm)
Valve seat width	0.047 to 0.063 in (1.2 to 1.6 mm)
Valve seat sinking	1.831 in (46.5 mm)
Service limit	1.890 in (48.0 mm)
Valve spring angle limit	0.071 in (1.81 mm)
Valve spring free length	
Inner	1.800 in (45.7 mm)
Service limit	1.744 in (44.3 mm)
Outer	2.063 in (52.4 mm)
Service limit	1.984 in (50.4 mm)

Rocker arm and shaft
Rocker arm bore . . . . 0.6300 to 0.6310 in (16.000 to 16.027 mm)
Shaft diameter . . . . 0.6286 to 0.6293 in (15.966 to 15.984 mm)
Clearance in rocker arm . . . . 0.0006 to 0.0024 in (0.016 to 0.061 mm)
Service limit . . . . 0.004 in (0.10 mm)

Crankshaft and connecting rods

Crankshaft end play . . . . 0.0012 to 0.0051 in (0.03 to 0.13 mm)
Service limit . . . . 0.0118 in (0.30 mm)
Connecting rod end play (side clearance) . . . . 0.004 to 0.010 in (0.110 to 0.262 mm)
Service limit . . . . 0.012 in (0.30 mm)
Main bearing journal diameter . . . . 2.359 to 2.360 in (59.937 to 59.955 mm)
Service limit . . . . 0.002 in (0.05 mm)
Grinding limit . . . . 0.03 in (0.75 mm)
Main bearing oil clearance . . . . 0.0012 to 0.0019 in (0.031 to 0.049 mm)
Service limit . . . . 0.0031 in (0.08 mm)
Connecting rod bearing journal diameter . . . . 2.005 to 2.006 in (50.940 to 50.955 mm)
Service limit . . . . 0.0020 in (0.05 mm)
Grinding limit . . . . 0.03 in (0.75 mm)
Connecting rod wrist pin bore diameter . . . . 0.8640 to 0.8646 in (21.943 to 21.961 mm)
Connecting rod bearing oil clearance . . . . 0.0010 to 0.0026 in (0.027 to 0.067 mm)
Service limit . . . . 0.0039 in (0.10 mm)
Crankshaft journal taper/out-of-round limit . . . . 0.0020 in (0.05 mm)
Crankshaft runout limit . . . . 0.0012 in (0.03 mm)

Engine block

Cylinder bore diameter
  2.0 litre . . . . 3.3859 to 3.3866 in (86.000 to 86.019 mm)
  1.6 litre . . . . 3.1890 to 3.1897 in (81.000 to 81.019 mm)
Service limit . . . . 0.006 in (0.15 mm)
Rebore sizes
  2.0 litre . . . . +0.010 and 0.020 in (0.25 and 0.50 mm)
  1.6 litre . . . . +0.010, 0.020, 0.030 and 0.040 in (0.25, 0.50, 0.75 and 1.0 mm)
Deck warpage limit . . . . 0.006 in (0.15 mm)

Pistons and rings

Piston diameter
  2.0 litre . . . . 3.3837 to 3.3845 in (85.944 to 85.964 mm)
  1.6 litre . . . . 3.1868 to 3.1876 in (80.944 to 80.964 mm)
Piston-to-bore clearance . . . . 0.0014 to 0.0030 in (0.036 to 0.075 mm)
Service limit . . . . 0.006 in (0.15 mm)
Ring groove width
  Top and second . . . . 0.059 to 0.060 in (1.52 to 1.54 mm)
  Oil . . . . 0.1583 to 0.1591 in (4.02 to 4.04 mm)
Piston ring-to-groove (side) clearance
  Top and second . . . . 0.0012 to 0.0028 in (0.03 to 0.07 mm)
  Service limit . . . . 0.006 in (0.15 mm)
Piston ring end gap
  Top . . . . 0.008 to 0.014 in (0.2 to 0.3 mm)
  Second . . . . 0.006 to 0.012 in (0.15 to 0.3 mm)
  Oil . . . . 0.012 to 0.035 in (0.3 to 0.9 mm)
  Service limit . . . . 0.039 in (1.0 mm)
Piston pin diameter . . . . 0.8651 to 0.8654 in (21.974 to 21.980 mm)
Pin-to-piston clearance . . . . Loose — 0 to 0.0009 in (0 to 0.024 mm)
Pin-to-rod clearance . . . . Press fit

Cylinder head

Height (standard) . . . . 3.620 to 3.624 in (91.95 to 92.05 mm)
Refinishing limit . . . . 0.008 in (0.20 mm)
Warpage limit . . . . 0.006 in (0.15 mm)

Camshaft

Runout . . . . 0.0012 in (0.03 mm)
Endplay . . . . 0.003 to 0.006 in (0.08 to 0.16 mm)
Service limit . . . . 0.008 in (0.20 mm)
Bearing journal diameter
  Front (number 1) . . . . 1.257 to 1.258 in (31.940 to 31.965 in
  Center (number 2, 3, 4) . . . . 1.256 to 1.257 in (31.910 to 31.935 mm)
  Rear (number 5) . . . . 1.257 to 1.258 in (31.940 to 31.965 mm)
  Service limit . . . . 0.002 in (0.05 mm)

Bearing oil clearance
- Front (number 1) . . . . 0.0014 to 0.0033 in (0.035 to 0.085 mm)
- Center (number 2, 3, 4) . . . . 0.0026 to 0.0045 in (0.065 to 0.115 mm)
- Rear (number 5) . . . . 0.0014 to 0.0033 in (0.035 to 0.085 mm)
- Service limit . . . . 0.0059 in (0.15 mm)

Lobe lift
- Intake . . . . 1.5023 in (38.157 mm)
- Service limit . . . . 1.4944 in (37.957 mm)
- Exhaust . . . . 1.5024 in (38.160 mm)
- Service limit . . . . 1.4945 in (37.960 mm)

General

Compression pressure
- Standard . . . . 164 psi at 270 rpm
- Minimum . . . . 115 psi at 270 rpm
- Cylinder numbers . . . . 1-2-3-4 (front-to-rear)
- Firing order 1-3-4-2
- Oil pressure at 3000 rpm . . . . 50 to 64 psi (3.4 to 4.5 kg/cm²)

Torque specifications

	Ft-lbs	M-kg
Alternator bracket-to-engine bolt	27 to 46	3.7 to 6.3
Alternator adjusting bolt	14 to 25	1.9 to 3.5
Cylinder head bolts		
Engine warm	69 to 80	9.5 to 11.0
Engine cold	59 to 64	8.2 to 8.8
Main bearing cap bolts	61 to 65	8.3 to 8.9
Connecting rod nuts	37 to 41	5.1 to 5.6
Camshaft sprocket bolt	35 to 48	4.8 to 6.6
Camshaft cap (rocker shaft) bolts	13 to 20	1.8 to 2.8
Camshaft cover bolts	2 to 3	0.28 to 0.41
Crankshaft pulley bolts		
1.6 litre	6 to 9	0.8 to 1.2
2.0 litre	8 to 12	1.1 to 1.6
Exhaust manifold bolts/nuts	16 to 21	2.2 to 2.9
Engine mount bolts		
Number 1 engine mount-to-transaxle	27 to 38	3.7 to 5.2
Number 1 engine mount-to-body	32 to 40	4.4 to 5.5
Number 2 engine mount-to-transaxle	27 to 38	3.7 to 5.2
Number 2 engine mount-to-body	32 to 40	4.4 to 5.5
Number 3 engine mount-to-body	32 to 40	4.4 to 5.5
Number 3 engine mount-to-engine	41 to 59	5.7 to 8.1
Flywheel/driveplate bolts	71 to 76	9.8 to 10.5
Intake manifold bolts/nuts	14 to 19	1.9 to 2.6
Oil pan bolts	5 to 9	0.7 to 1.2
Timing belt sprocket bolt	80 to 87	11.0 to 12.0
Timing belt tensioner lockbolt	27 to 38	3.9 to 5.2
Torque stopper-to-engine bolt	49 to 56	6.8 to 7.7
Torque stopper-to-body bolt	40 to 50	5.5 to 6.9
Oil pressure switch	9 to 13	1.2 to 1.8
Water bypass hose clamp	14 to 25	1.9 to 3.5
Water inlet pipe assembly-to-water pump bolt	14 to 19	1.9 to 2.6
Water inlet pipe bracket-to-engine bolt	28 to 38	3.9 to 5.2
Oil cooler center nut	22 to 29	3.0 to 4.0
Rear housing nuts and bolts	14 to 19	1.9 to 2.6
Front housing bolts	14 to 19	1.9 to 2.6
Oil pump-to-block bolts	14 to 19	1.9 to 2.6
Oil pick-up tube flange bolts	6 to 9	0.8 to 1.2
Crankshaft rear oil seal carrier (rear cover) bolts	6 to 9	0.8 to 1.2

1 General information

Included in this portion of Chapter 2 are the general overhaul procedures for the cylinder head and internal engine components. The information ranges from advice concerning preparation for an overhaul and the purchase of replacement parts to detailed, step-by-step procedures covering removal and installation of internal engine components and the inspection of parts.

The following Sections have been written based on the assumption that the engine or cylinder head has been removed from the vehicle. For information concerning in-vehicle engine repair, as well as removal and installation of the external components necessary for the overhaul, see Part A of this Chapter and Section 2 of this Part.

The Specifications included here in Part B are only those necessary for the inspection procedures which follow. Refer to Part A for additional specifications.

2 Repair operations possible with the engine in the vehicle

Many major repair operations can be accomplished without removing the engine from the vehicle.

It is a very good idea to clean the engine compartment and the exterior of the engine with some type of pressure washer before any work is begun. A clean engine will make the job easier and will prevent the possibility of getting dirt into internal areas of the engine.

Remove the hood (Chapter 11) and cover the fenders to provide as much working room as possible and to prevent damage to the painted surfaces.

If oil or coolant leaks develop, indicating a need for gasket or seal replacement, the repairs can generally be made with the engine in the vehicle. The oil pan gasket, the cylinder head gasket, intake and exhaust manifold gaskets, front and rear cover gaskets and the crankshaft oil seal are accessible with the engine in place.

Exterior engine components, such as the water pump, the starter motor, the alternator, the distributor, the fuel pump and the carburetor, as well as the intake and exhaust manifolds, are quite easily removed for repair with the engine in place.

Since the cylinder head can be removed without pulling the engine, valve component servicing can also be accomplished with the engine in the vehicle.

Replacement of, repairs to or inspection of the timing sprockets and belt and the oil pump and front cover seals are all possible with the engine in place.

In extreme cases caused by a lack of necessary equipment, repair or replacement of piston rings, pistons, connecting rods and rod bearings and reconditioning of the cylinder bores is possible with the engine in the vehicle. However, this practice is not recommended because of the cleaning and preparation work that must be done to the components involved.

Detailed removal, inspection, repair and installation procedures for the above mentioned components can be found in the appropriate Part of Chapter 2 or the other Chapters in this manual.

3 Engine overhaul — general information

It is not always easy to determine when, or if, an engine should be completely overhauled, as a number of factors must be considered.

High mileage is not necessarily an indication that an overhaul is needed, while low mileage does not preclude the need for an overhaul. Frequency of servicing is probably the most important consideration. An engine that has had regular and frequent oil and filter changes, as well as other required maintenance, will most likely give many thousands of miles of reliable service. Conversely, a neglected engine may require an overhaul very early in its life.

Excessive oil consumption is an indication that piston rings and/or valve guides are in need of attention. Make sure that oil leaks are not responsible before deciding that the rings and guides are bad. Have a cylinder compression or leakdown test performed by an experienced tune-up mechanic to determine the extent of the work required.

If the engine is making obvious knocking or rumbling noises, the connecting rod and/or main bearings are probably at fault. Check the oil pressure with a gauge installed in place of the oil pressure sending unit and compare it to the Specifications. If it is extremely low, the bearings and/or oil pump are probably worn out.

Loss of power, rough running, excessive valve train noise and high fuel consumption rates may also point to the need for an overhaul, especially if they are all present at the same time. If a complete tune-up does not remedy the situation, major mechanical work is the only solution.

An engine overhaul involves restoring the internal parts to the specifications of a new engine. During an overhaul, the piston rings are replaced and the cylinder walls are reconditioned (rebored and/or honed). If a rebore is done, new pistons are required. The main and connecting rod bearings are replaced with new ones and, if necessary, the crankshaft may be reground to restore the journals. Generally, the valves are serviced as well, since they are usually in less-than-perfect condition at this point. While the engine is being overhauled, other components, such as the carburetor, distributor, starter and alternator, can be rebuilt as well. The end result should be a like new engine that will give many trouble free miles.

Before beginning the engine overhaul, read through the entire procedure to familiarize yourself with the scope and requirements of the job. Overhauling an engine is not difficult, but it is time consuming. Plan on the vehicle being tied up for a minimum of two weeks, especially if parts must be taken to an automotive machine shop for repair or reconditioning. Check on availability of parts and make sure that any necessary special tools and equipment are obtained in advance. Most work can be done with typical hand tools, although a number of precision measuring tools are required for inspecting parts to determine if

they must be replaced. Often an automotive machine shop will handle the inspection of parts and offer advice concerning reconditioning and replacement. **Note:** *Always wait until the engine has been completely disassembled and all components, especially the engine block, have been inspected before deciding what service and repair operations must be performed by an automotive machine shop.* Since the block's condition will be the major factor to consider when determining whether to overhaul the original engine or buy a rebuilt one, never purchase parts or have machine work done on other components until the block has been thoroughly inspected. As a general rule, time is the primary cost of an overhaul, so it does not pay to install worn or substandard parts.

As a final note, to ensure maximum life and minimum trouble from a rebuilt engine, everything must be assembled with care in a spotlessly clean environment.

4 Engine rebuilding alternatives

The do-it-yourselfer is faced with a number of options when performing an engine overhaul. The decision to replace the engine block, piston/connecting rod assemblies and crankshaft depends on a number of factors, with the number one consideration being the condition of the block. Other considerations are cost, access to machine shop facilities, parts availability, time required to complete the project and experience.

Some of the rebuilding alternatives include:

Individual parts — If the inspection procedures reveal that the engine block and most engine components are in reusable condition, purchasing individual parts may be the most economical alternative. The block, crankshaft and piston/connecting rod assemblies should all be inspected carefully. Even if the block shows little wear, the cylinder bores should receive a finish hone.

Crankshaft kit — This rebuild package consists of a reground crankshaft and a matched set of pistons and connecting rods. The pistons will already be installed on the connecting rods. Piston rings and the necessary bearings will be included in the kit. These kits are commonly available for standard cylinder bores, as well as for engine blocks which have been bored to a regular oversize.

Short block — A short block consists of an engine block with a crankshaft and piston/connecting rod assemblies already installed. All new bearings are incorporated and all clearances will be correct. The existing camshaft, valve train components, cylinder head and external parts can be bolted to the short block with little or no machine shop work necessary.

Long block — A long block consists of a short block plus an oil pump, oil pan, cylinder head, rocker arm cover, camshaft and valve train components, timing sprockets and belt and timing belt cover. All components are installed with new bearings, seals and gaskets incorporated throughout. The installation of manifolds and external parts is all that is necessary.

Give careful thought to which alternative is best for you and discuss the situation with local automotive machine shops, auto parts dealers or parts store countermen before ordering or purchasing replacement parts.

5 Engine removal — methods and precautions

If it has been decided that an engine must be removed for overhaul or major repair work, certain preliminary steps should be taken.

Locating a suitable work area is extremely important. A shop is, of course, the most desirable place to work. Adequate work space, along with storage space for the vehicle, is very important. If a shop or garage is not available, at the very least a flat, level, clean work surface made of concrete or asphalt is required.

Cleaning the engine compartment and engine prior to removal will help keep tools clean and organized.

An engine hoist or A-frame will also be necessary. Make sure that the equipment is rated in excess of the combined weight of the engine and its accessories. Safety is of primary importance, considering the potential hazards involved in lifting the engine out of the vehicle.

If the engine is being removed by a novice, a helper should be available. Advice and aid from someone more experienced would also be helpful. There are many instances when one person cannot simultaneously perform all of the operations required when lifting the engine out of the vehicle.

Plan the operation ahead of time. Arrange for or obtain all of the tools and equipment you will need prior to beginning the job. Some of the equipment necessary to perform engine removal and installation safely and with relative ease are (in addition to an engine hoist) a heavy duty floor jack, complete sets of wrenches and sockets as described in the front of this manual, wooden blocks and plenty of rags and cleaning solvent for mopping up the inevitable spills. If the hoist is to be rented, make sure that you arrange for it in advance and perform beforehand all of the operations possible without it. This will save you money and time.

Plan for the vehicle to be out of use for a considerable amount of time. A machine shop will be required to perform some of the work which the do-it-yourselfer cannot accomplish due to a lack of special equipment. These shops often have a busy schedule, so it would be wise to consult them before removing the engine in order to accurately estimate the amount of time required to rebuild or repair components that may need work.

Always use extreme caution when removing and installing the engine. Serious injury can result from careless actions. Plan ahead. Take your time and a job of this nature, although major, can be accomplished successfully.

6 Engine overhaul — disassembly sequence

1   It is much easier to disassemble and work on the engine if it is mounted on a portable engine stand. These stands can often be rented for a reasonable fee from an equipment rental yard. Before the engine is mounted on a stand, the flywheel/driveplate should be removed from the engine (refer to Chapter 2, Part A, Section 20).

2   If a stand is not available, it is possible to disassemble the engine with it blocked up on a sturdy workbench or on the floor. Be extra careful not to tip or drop the engine when working without a stand.

3   If you are going to obtain a rebuilt engine, all external components must come off first in order to be transferred to the replacement engine, just as they will if you are doing a complete engine overhaul yourself. These include:

Alternator and brackets
Emissions control components
Distributor, spark plug wires and spark plugs
Thermostat and housing cover
Water pump
Carburetor
Intake/exhaust manifolds
Oil filter
Fuel pump
Engine mounts
Flywheel/driveplate

Note: *When removing the external components from the engine, pay close attention to details that may be helpful or important during installation. Note the installed position of gaskets, seals, spacers, pins, washers, bolts and other small items.*

4   If you are obtaining a short block, which consists of the engine block, crankshaft, pistons and connecting rods all assembled, then the cylinder head, oil pan and oil pump will have to be removed as well. See *Engine rebuilding alternatives* for additional information regarding the different possibilities to be considered.

5   If you are planning a complete overhaul, the engine must be disassembled and the internal components removed in the following order:

Timing belt cover
Timing belt
Camshaft cover
Front and rear housings
Cylinder head and camshaft
Oil pan
Oil pump
Piston/connecting rod assemblies
Crankshaft

6   Before beginning the disassembly and overhaul procedures, make sure the following items are available:

Common hand tools
Small cardboard boxes or plastic bags for storing parts

Gasket scraper
Ridge reamer
Vibration damper puller
Micrometers
Telescoping gauges
Dial indicator set
Valve spring compressor
Cylinder surfacing hone
Piston ring groove cleaning tool
Electric drill motor
Tap and die set
Wire brushes
Cleaning solvent

7 Cylinder head — disassembly

Note: *New and rebuilt cylinder heads are commonly available for most engines at dealerships and auto parts stores. Due to the fact that some specialized tools are necessary for the disassembly and inspection procedures, and replacement parts may not be readily available, it may be more practical and economical for the home mechanic to purchase a replacement head rather than taking the time to disassemble, inspect and recondition the original head.*

1   Cylinder head disassembly involves removal and disassembly of the intake and exhaust valves and their related components. If they are still in place, remove the camshaft and rocker arm assembly from the cylinder head. Label the parts or store them separately so they can be reinstalled in their original locations.

2   Before the valves are removed, arrange to label and store them, along with their related components, so they can be kept separate and reinstalled in the same valve guides they were removed from (photo).

3   Compress the valve spring on the first valve with a spring compressor and remove the keepers (photo). Carefully release the valve spring compressor and remove the retainer, the springs, the spring seat, the valve stem seal and the valve from the head. If the valve binds in the guide (won't pull through), push it back into the head and deburr the area around the keeper groove with a fine file or whetstone (photo).

4   Repeat the procedure for the remaining valves. Remember to keep together all the parts for each valve so they can be reinstalled in the same locations.

5   Once the valves have been removed and safely stored, the head should be thoroughly cleaned and inspected. If a complete engine overhaul is being done, finish the engine disassembly procedures before beginning the cylinder head cleaning and inspection process.

7.2   After removing the valve components, store them together in a plastic bag to keep from mixing them in with the components from other valves

7.3a   Use a valve spring compressor to compress the spring and remove the keepers from the valve stem

7.3b   If the valve stem won't pull through the guide without binding, the head of the valve is probably mushroomed slightly, which can be corrected by deburring the top of the valve stem with a small file

8   Cylinder head — cleaning and inspection

1   Thorough cleaning of the cylinder head and related valve train components, followed by a detailed inspection, will enable you to decide how much valve service work must be done during the engine overhaul.

Cleaning

2   Scrape away all traces of old gasket material and sealing compound from the head gasket, intake manifold and exhaust manifold sealing surfaces (photo). Be very careful not to gouge the soft aluminum of the cylinder head. Special gasket removal solvents are available at auto parts stores which dissolve the gasket, making removal much easier.
3   Remove any built up scale around the coolant passages.
4   Run a stiff wire brush through the oil holes to remove any deposits that may have formed in them.
5   Run an appropriate size tap into each of the threaded holes to remove any corrosion and thread sealant that may be present (photo).

If compressed air is available, use it to clear the holes of debris produced by this operation (photo).
6   Clean the exhaust and intake manifold stud threads with an appropriate size die (photo).
7   Clean the cylinder head with solvent and dry it thoroughly. Compressed air will speed the drying process and ensure that all holes and recessed areas are clean. **Note:** *Decarbonizing chemicals are available and may prove very useful when cleaning cylinder heads and valve train components. They are very caustic and should be used with caution. Be sure to follow the instructions on the container.*
8   Clean the rocker arms and shafts thoroughly. Compressed air will speed the drying process and can be used to clean out the oil passages.
9   Clean all the valve springs, keepers and retainers with solvent and dry them thoroughly. Do the components from one valve at a time to avoid mixing up the parts.
10   Scrape off any heavy deposits that may have formed on the valves, then use a motorized wire brush to remove deposits from the valve heads and stems. Again, make sure the valves do not get mixed up.

8.2   Use a gasket scraper to remove all old gasket material. Note the use of a shop towel to keep old gasket material from falling down into the engine

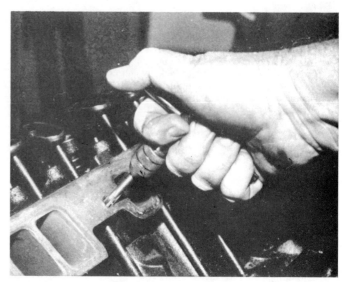

8.5a   Use a tap to remove old sealer and rust from all bolt and stud holes

8.5b After tapping out bolt and stud holes, compressed air should be used to blow out the debris left by the cleaning operation

8.6 A die can be used to clean sealant from bolt threads

Inspection

Cylinder head

11 Inspect the head very carefully for cracks, evidence of coolant leakage or other damage. If cracks are found, a new cylinder head should be obtained.

12 Using a straightedge and feeler gauge, check the head gasket mating surface for warpage. If the warpage exceeds 0.006-inch over the length of the head, it can be resurfaced at an automotive machine shop (photos).

13 Examine the valve seats in each of the combustion chambers. If they are pitted, cracked or burned, the head will require valve service that is beyond the scope of the home mechanic.

14 Check the valve stem to valve guide clearance. Use a dial indicator to measure the lateral movement of each valve stem with the valve in the guide and approximately 1/16-inch off the seat (photo). If, after this check, there is still some doubt as to the condition of the valve guides, the exact clearance and condition of the guides can be checked by an automotive machine shop, usually for a very small fee.

Rocker arm components

15 Check the rocker arm faces where they contact the camshaft and valve stems for pits, wear and rough spots. Check the rocker shaft contact areas as well.

16 Inspect the rocker shaft sliding surfaces for scuffing and excessive wear. Measure the rocker shaft and rocker arm contact surfaces to determine if the clearance is within specifications.

17 Any damaged or excessively worn parts must be replaced with new ones.

Valves

18 Carefully inspect each valve face for cracks, pits and burned spots. Check the valve stem and neck for cracks. Rotate the valve and check for any obvious indication that it is bent. Check the end of the stem for pits and excessive wear. The presence of any of these conditions indicates the need for valve service by an automotive machine shop.

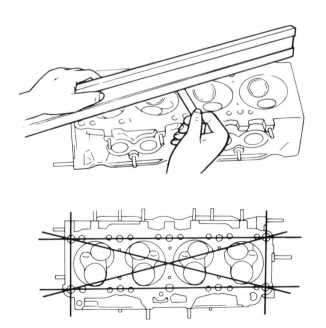

Fig. 2B.1 Check the cylinder head for warpage with a straightedge and feeler gauge on the lines shown (Sec 8)

8.12a Lay a straightedge along the head and use a feeler gauge to check for warpage

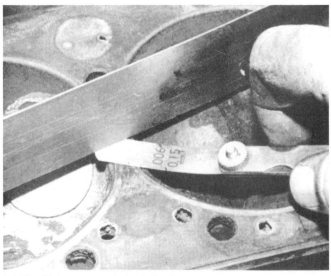

8.12b Make a second check for head straightness by laying the straightedge at an angle, from one corner of the head to the other

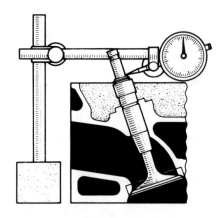

Fig. 2B.2   A dial indicator can be used to determine stem-to-guide clearance (Sec 8)

8.14 Mount a dial indicator on the head with the stem against the valve just above the valve guide, lift the valve slightly off the seat, then rock it back and forth to check for valve stem to guide clearance

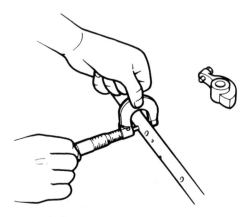

Fig. 2B.3   Measure the rocker arm shaft and rocker arm bore to determine clearance (Sec 8)

19 Measure the width of the valve margin on each valve and compare it to Specifications. Any valve with a margin narrower than specified will have to be replaced with a new one.

Valve components

20 Check each valve spring for wear (on the ends) and pits. Measure the free length and compare it to the Specifications (photo). Any springs

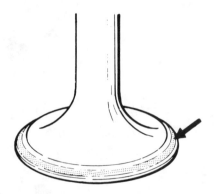

Fig. 2B.4   The margin width (arrow) on each valve must be as specified (if no margin exists, the valve must be replaced) (Sec 8)

8.20a Measure the free length of each valve spring with a dial caliper. Springs which have sagged in use should be replaced

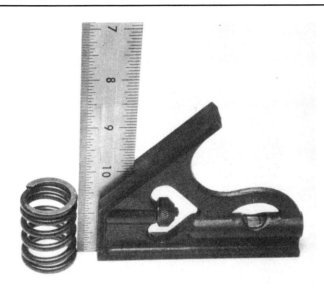

8.20b   Check each valve spring for squareness and replace any which have sagged off center

that are shorter than specified have sagged and should not be reused. Stand the spring on a flat surface and check it for squareness (photo).
21 Check the spring retainers and keepers for obvious wear and cracks. Any questionable parts should be replaced with new ones, as extensive damage will occur in the event of failure during engine operation.
22 If the inspection process indicates that the valve components are in generally poor condition and worn beyond the limits specified, which is usually the case in an engine that is being overhauled, refer to Section 9 for valve servicing recommendations.
23 If the inspection turns up no excessively worn parts, and if the valve faces and seats are in good condition, the valve train components can be reinstalled in the cylinder head without major servicing. Refer to the appropriate Section for cylinder head reassembly procedures.

9   Valves — servicing

1   Because of the complex nature of the job and the special tools and equipment needed, servicing of the valves, the valve seats and the valve guides, commonly known as a valve job, is best left to a professional.
2   The home mechanic can remove and disassemble the head, do the initial cleaning and inspection, then reassemble and deliver the head to a dealer service department or an automotive machine shop for the actual valve servicing.
3   The dealer service department, or automotive machine shop, will remove the valves and springs, recondition or replace the valves and valve seats, recondition the valve guides, check and replace the valve springs, spring retainers and keepers (as necessary), replace the valve seals with new ones, reassemble the valve components and make sure the installed spring height is correct. The cylinder head gasket surface will also be resurfaced if it is warped.
4   After the valve job has been performed by a professional, the head will be in like new condition. When the head is returned, be sure to clean it again before installation on the engine to remove any metal particles and abrasive grit that may still be present from the valve service or head resurfacing operations. Use compressed air, if available, to blow out all the oil holes and passages.

Valve grinding

5   If the valves and seats are only lightly pitted, or if new valves are being fitted to guides and seats in good condition, the valves should be ground to their seats as follows.
6   Apply a small quantity of coarse grinding paste to the sealing area of a valve head. Insert the valve into its guide and grind the head to

the seat with a to-and-fro motion. The customary tool for this operation is a rubber sucker on a stick; reciprocating attachments for electric drills are also available. Lift the valve off its seat occasionally to check progress and to redistribute the grinding paste.
7   When a smooth unbroken line of paste is present on the valve head and seat, wipe off the paste and repeat the operation with fine grinding paste.
8   When all the valves have been ground to their seats, thoroughly clean away all traces of grinding paste using kerosene, clean rags and (if available) compressed air. Any paste remaining in the cylinder head could cause rapid wear.
9   It must be noted that excessive grinding of old valves can reduce the margin to an unacceptable extent (see Section 8), or in the case of new valves and old seats can cause 'pocketing' of the valve in the seat.

10   Cylinder head — reassembly

1   Regardless of whether or not the head was sent to an automotive repair shop for valve servicing, make sure it is clean before beginning reassembly.
2   If the head was sent out for valve servicing, the valves and related components will already be in place. Begin the reassembly procedure with Step 6.
3   Install new seals on each of the valve guides. Using a hammer and a deep socket, gently tap each seal into place until it is properly seated on the guide. Do not twist or cock the seals during installation or they will not seal properly on the valve stems.
4   Install the valves, taking care not to damage the new valve stem oil seals, drop the valve spring seat around the valve guide boss and set the valve springs, cap and retainer in place.
5   Compress the springs with a valve compressor tool and install the keepers. Release the compressor, making sure the keepers are seated properly in the valve stem upper groove. If necessary, grease can be used to hold the keepers in place until the compressor is released.
6   Install the camshaft (Chapter 2, Part A).
7   Lubricate the rocker arm and shaft assembly with clean engine oil. Install the assembly and tighten the bolts in the correct sequence to the specified torque (Chapter 2, Part A, Section 11).

11   Piston/connecting rod assembly — removal

1   It is desirable to remove the ridge at the top of each cylinder. Follow the manufacturer's instructions provided with the ridge reaming tool (photo). Failure to remove the ridge before attempting to remove the

11.1   A ridge reamer can be used to remove the wear ridge at the top of each cylinder before the pistons are removed

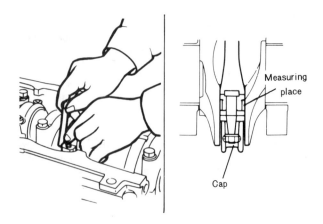

Fig. 2B.5   Checking the connecting rod end play (Sec 11)

11.4   A feeler gauge slipped between the side of the rod and the machined face of the crankshaft measures the rod side clearance

11.5a   Use a centerpunch to identify the rods before removing them from the block

piston/connecting rod assemblies may result in piston breakage. It must be added that should the ridge be big enough to break a piston, a rebore (and new pistons) will almost certainly be required.

2   Before the connecting rods are removed, check the end play. Mount a dial indicator with its stem in line with the crankshaft and touching the side of the number one connecting rod cap.

3   Push the connecting rod backward, as far as possible, and zero the dial indicator. Next, push the connecting rod all the way to the front and check the reading on the dial indicator. The distance that it moves is the end play. If the end play exceeds the service limit, a new connecting rod will be required. Repeat the procedure for the remaining connecting rods.

4   An alternative method is to slip feeler gauges between the connecting rod and the crankshaft throw until the play is removed (photo). The end play is equal to the thickness of the feeler gauge.

5   Check the connecting rods and connecting rod caps for identification marks. If they are not plainly marked, identify each rod and cap, using a small punch to make the appropriate number of indentations to indicate the cylinders they are associated with (photos).

6   Loosen each of the connecting rod cap nuts 1/2-turn. Remove the number one connecting rod cap and bearing insert. Do not drop the bearing insert out of the cap. Slip a short length of plastic or rubber hose over each connecting rod cap bolt to protect the crankshaft journal and cylinder wall when the piston is removed (photo) and push the connecting rod/piston assembly out through the top of the engine. Use a wooden tool to push on the upper bearing insert in the connecting rod. If resistance is felt, double-check to make sure that all of the ridge was removed from the cylinder.

7   Repeat the procedure for the remaining cylinders. After removal, reassemble the connecting rod caps and bearing inserts in their respective connecting rods and install the cap nuts finger tight. Leaving the old bearing inserts in place until reassembly will help prevent the connecting rod bearing surfaces from being accidentally nicked or gouged.

12   Crankshaft — removal

1   Before the crankshaft is removed, check the end play. Mount a dial indicator with the stem in line with the crankshaft and just touching the end of the crankshaft (see accompanying illustration).

2   Push the crankshaft all the way to the rear and zero the dial indicator. Next, pry the crankshaft to the front as far as possible and check the reading on the dial indicator. The distance that it moves is the end play. If it is greater than specified, check the crankshaft thrust surfaces for wear. If no wear is apparent, new main bearings should correct the end play.

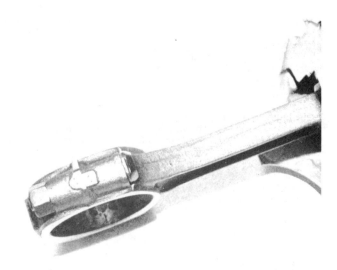

11.5b   The centerpunch marks should indicate the number of the cylinder the rod came out of, and the marks should be made on both the cap and rod to prevent mixups and to make sure the cap goes on the right way

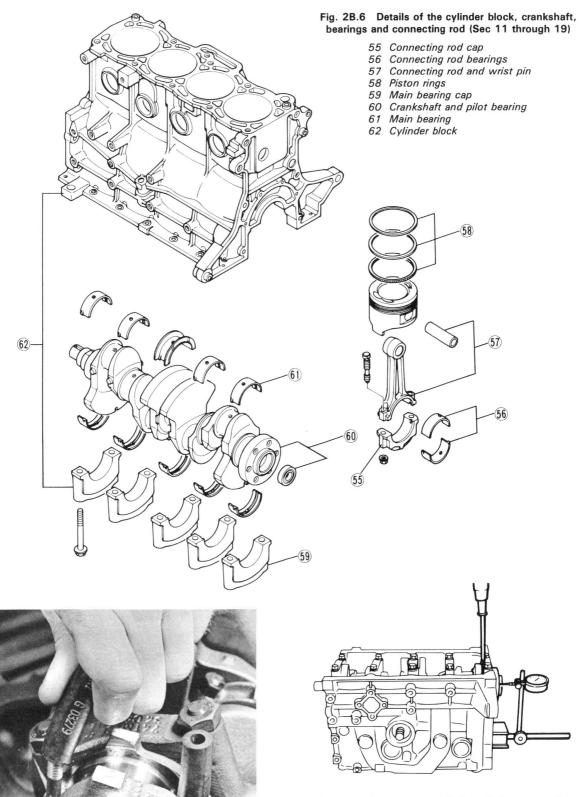

Fig. 2B.6 Details of the cylinder block, crankshaft, bearings and connecting rod (Sec 11 through 19)

55 Connecting rod cap
56 Connecting rod bearings
57 Connecting rod and wrist pin
58 Piston rings
59 Main bearing cap
60 Crankshaft and pilot bearing
61 Main bearing
62 Cylinder block

11.6 To keep the crankshaft and cylinder walls from being scratched by the rod bolt threads, slip sections of fuel line hose over the bolts before attempting to remove the rods

Fig. 2B.7 Checking crankshaft end play with a dial indicator (Sec 12)

3 If a dial indicator is not available, feeler gauges cannot easily be used because the thrust flanges on the center main bearing shell are only on the saddle side, not on the cap.

4 Loosen each of the main bearing cap bolts 1/4-turn at a time, until they can be removed by hand. Check the main bearing caps to see if they are marked as to their locations. They are usually numbered consecutively from the front of the engine to the rear. If they are not,

12.4a   Most main bearing caps are factory numbered and have a cast in arrow indicating the front of the engine

12:4b   If the main caps are not identified by numbers and arrows to indicate position and direction of installation, mark them with a centerpunch

mark them with number stamping dies or a center punch (photo). The main bearing caps have a cast-in arrow, which points to the front of the engine (photo).

5   Gently tap the caps with a soft-face hammer, then separate them from the engine block. If necessary, use the main bearing cap bolts as levers to remove the caps. Try not to drop the bearing insert if it comes out with the cap.

6   Carefully lift the crankshaft out of the engine. It is a good idea to have an assistant available, since the crankshaft is quite heavy. With the bearing inserts in place in the engine block and in the main bearing caps, return the caps to their respective locations on the engine block and tighten the bolts finger tight. On manual transaxle models, remove the pilot bearing from the end of the crankshaft, using a slide hammer (available at tool rental stores).

13   Engine block — cleaning

1   Remove the soft plugs from the engine block. To do this, knock the plugs into the block, using a hammer and punch, then grasp them with large pliers and pull them back through the holes (photos).

2   Using a gasket scraper, remove all traces of gasket material from the engine block. Be very careful not to nick or gouge the gasket sealing surfaces.

3   Remove the main bearing caps and separate the bearing inserts from the caps and the engine block. Tag the bearings according to which cylinder they were removed from and whether they were in the cap or the block and set them aside.

4   Using an Allen wrench of the appropriate size, remove any threaded oil gallery plugs from the block.

5   If the engine is extremely dirty it should be taken to an automotive machine shop to be steam cleaned or hot tanked.

6   After the block is returned, clean all oil holes and oil galleries one more time. Brushes for cleaning oil holes and galleries are available at most auto parts stores. Flush the passages with warm water until the water runs clear, dry the block thoroughly and wipe all machined surfaces with a light, rust preventative oil. If you have access to compressed air, use it to speed the drying process and to blow out all the oil holes and galleries.

7   If the block is not extremely dirty or sludged up, you can do an adequate cleaning job with warm soapy water and a stiff brush. Take plenty of time and do a thorough job. Regardless of the cleaning method used, be very sure to thoroughly clean all oil holes and galleries, dry the block completely and coat all machined surfaces with light oil.

8   The threaded holes in the block must be clean to ensure accurate torque readings during reassembly. Run the proper size tap into each of the holes to remove any rust, corrosion, thread sealant or sludge and to restore any damaged threads. If possible, use compressed air to clear the holes of debris produced by this operation. Thoroughly clean the threads on the head bolts and the main bearing cap bolts as well.

Fig. 2B.8   Removing the pilot bearing from the crankshaft (manual transaxle models) (Sec 12)

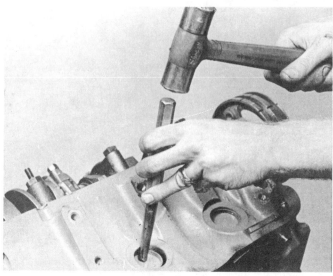

13.1a   Use a large punch to drive the soft plug into the block

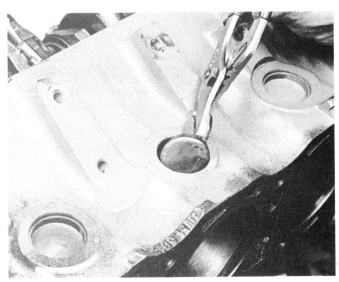

13.1b After the soft plug has been driven into the block it can be grabbed with pliers and pulled out at an angle

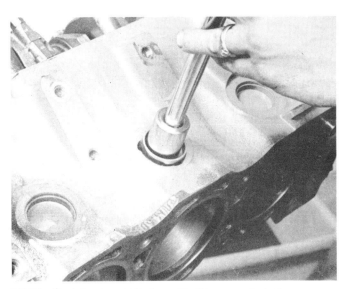

13.10 Coat the new soft plug with silicone sealant, then use a large socket to drive it into the block, being careful to keep it straight

9   Reinstall the main bearing caps and tighten the bolts finger tight.
10 After coating the sealing surfaces of the new soft plugs with a good quality gasket sealer, install them in the engine block. Make sure they are driven in straight and seated properly or leakage could result. Special tools are available for this purpose, but equally good results can be obtained using a large socket, with an outside diameter that will just slip into the soft plug, and a hammer (photo).
11 If the engine is not going to be reassembled right away, cover it with a large plastic trash bag to keep it clean.

14 Engine block — inspection

1   Thoroughly clean the engine block as described in Section 13 and double-check to make sure that the ridge at the top of each cylinder has been completely removed.
2   Visually check the block for cracks, rust and corrosion. Look for

stripped threads in the threaded holes. It is also a good idea to have the block checked for hidden cracks by an automotive machine shop that has the special equipment to do this type of work. If defects are found, have the block repaired, if possible, or replaced.
3   Check the cylinder bores for scuffing and scoring.
4   Measure each cylinder's diameter at the top (just under the ridge), center and bottom of the cylinder bore, parallel to the crankshaft axis (photos). Next, measure each cylinder's diameter at the same three locations across the crankshaft axis. Compare the results to the Specifications. If the cylinder walls are badly scuffed or scored, or if they are out of round or tapered beyond the limits given in the Specifications, have the engine block rebored and honed at an automotive machine shop. If a rebore is done, oversize pistons and rings will be required.
5   If the cylinders are in reasonably good condition and not worn to the outside of the limits, and if the piston-to-cylinder clearances can be maintained properly, then they do not have to be rebored. Honing is all that is necessary.

14.4a A telescoping gauge (snap gauge) is used to measure cylinder bore diameter

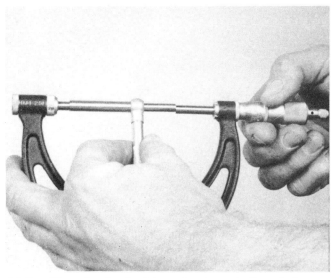

14.4b After extending the telescoping gauge to the cylinder diameter, it is removed and measured with a micrometer to determine bore size, taper and out-of-round

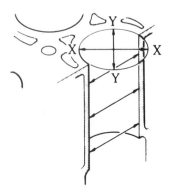

Fig. 2B.9 Measure the diameter of each cylinder just under the wear ridge (X and Y) and at the center and bottom (Sec 14)

14.7 Cylinders should always be honed before installing new rings to give the bore surface the proper finish for ring seating

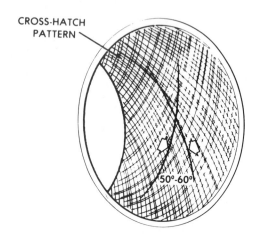

Fig. 2B.10 The cylinder hone should leave a cross-hatch pattern with the lines intersecting at approximately a 60° angle (Sec 14)

6   Before honing the cylinders, install the main bearing caps (without the bearings) and tighten the bolts to the specified torque.
7   To perform the honing operation you will need the proper size flexible hone (with fine stones), plenty of light oil or honing oil, some rags and an electric drill motor. Mount the hone in the drill motor, compress the stones and slip the hone into the first cylinder (photo). Lubricate the cylinder thoroughly, turn on the drill and move the hone up and down in the cylinder at a pace which will produce a fine crosshatch pattern on the cylinder walls with the crosshatch lines intersecting at approximately a 60° angle. Be sure to use plenty of lubricant. Do not withdraw the hone from the cylinder while it is running. Instead, shut off the drill and continue moving the hone up and down in the cylinder until it comes to a complete stop, then compress the stones and withdraw the hone. Wipe the oil out of the cylinder and repeat the procedure on the remaining cylinders. If you do not have the tools or do not desire to perform the honing operation, most automotive machine shops will do it for a reasonable fee. An acceptable result can also be produced using an abrasive flap wheel in an electric drill, or even using coarse emery paper by hand.
8   After the honing job is complete, chamfer the top edges of the cylinder bores with a small file so the rings will not catch when the pistons are installed.
9   The entire engine block must be thoroughly washed again with warm, soapy water to remove all traces of the abrasive grit produced during the honing operation. Be sure to run a brush through all oil holes and galleries and flush them with running water. After rinsing, dry the block and apply a coat of light rust preventative oil to all machined surfaces. Wrap the block in a plastic trash bag to keep it clean and set it aside until reassembly.

15 Camshaft — inspection

1   After the camshaft has been removed from the engine, cleaned with solvent and dried, inspect the bearing journals for uneven wear, pitting or evidence of seizure. If the journals are damaged, the bearing areas of the cylinder head and camshaft caps are probably damaged as well. If the damage is severe, the camshaft, caps and the cylinder head will have to be replaced.
2   Measure the camshaft lobes with a micrometer and compare the measurements to Specifications to determine if they are worn.
3   Check the camshaft lobes for heat discoloration, score marks, chipped areas, pitting or uneven wear. If the lobes are in good condition and if the lobe lift measurements are as specified, the camshaft can be reused.
4   Measure the bearing journals with a micrometer to determine if they are excessively worn or out of round (photo). If they are more than 0.020-inch out of round, the camshaft should be replaced with a new one. Measure the journals and the front oil seal surface and compare these measurements to Specifications to determine if wear is excessive.
5   With the camshaft mounted in V-blocks, check runout as shown in the accompanying illustration.
6   Place the camshaft in the cylinder head and check the end play with a dial indicator by pushing the camshaft fully rearward and then forward as shown in the accompanying illustration.

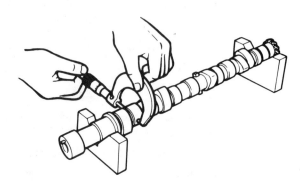

Fig. 2B.11 Measuring the camshaft lobes (Sec 15)

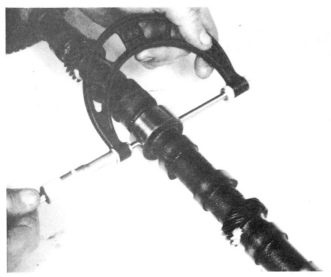

15.4 Measure the camshaft bearing journal diameter and subtract that figure from the bearing inside diameter to obtain the camshaft oil clearance

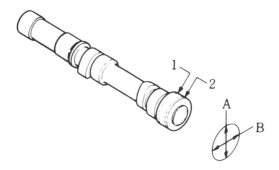

Fig. 2B.12   Camshaft journal measurement locations (Sec 15)

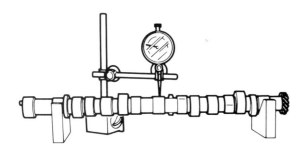

Fig. 2B.13   Checking camshaft runout with a dial indicator (Sec 22)

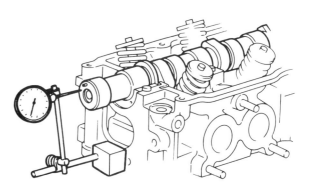

Fig. 2B.14   Checking camshaft end play with a dial indicator (Sec 15)

7   The camshaft oil clearance is checked during final assembly of the engine with the cylinder head bolted in place (Chapter 2, Part A). With the camshaft, caps and journals and completely clean and free of oil, lay a strip of Plastigage material across each journal parallel to the camshaft axis, install the caps and tighten the bolts to the specified torque. Remove the caps and measure the crushed Plastigage with the scale printed on the package to determine the oil clearance. If the clearance is out of specification, the cylinder head and camshaft caps must be replaced with new ones.

16   Piston/connecting rod assembly — inspection

1   Before the inspection process can be carried out, the piston/connecting rod assemblies must be cleaned and the original piston rings removed from the pistons. **Note:** *Always use new piston rings when the engine is reassembled.*
2   Using a piston ring installation tool, carefully remove the rings from the pistons. Do not nick or gouge the pistons in the process. If a piston ring installation tool is not available, use three old feeler blades or similar thin metal strips. Carefully spread the ends of the top ring and slide the blades between the ring and the piston, then ease the ring over the blades and remove it. Repeat with the other two rings, using the blades to prevent the lower rings falling into the upper grooves. Since the rings are to be renewed it does not matter if one or two are accidentally broken, but the experience gained in successful removal will be invaluable when it is time to install the new rings.

3   Scrape all traces of carbon from the top (or crown) of the piston. A hand-held wire brush or a piece of fine emery cloth can be used once the majority of the deposits have been scraped away. Do not, under any circumstances, use a wire brush mounted in a drill motor to remove deposits from the pistons. The piston material is soft and will be eroded away by the wire brush.
4   Use a piston ring groove cleaning tool to remove any carbon deposits from the ring grooves. If a tool is not available, a piece broken off the old ring will do the job. Be very careful to remove only the carbon deposits. Do not remove any metal and do not nick or scratch the sides of the ring grooves (photos). Protect your fingers if using a piece of broken ring — piston rings are sharp.
5   Once the deposits have been removed, clean the piston/rod assemblies with solvent and dry them thoroughly. Make sure that the oil return holes in the back sides of the ring grooves are clear (photo).
6   If the pistons are not damaged or worn excessively, and if the engine block is not rebored, new pistons will not be necessary. Normal piston wear appears as even vertical wear on the piston thrust surfaces and slight looseness of the top ring in its groove. New piston rings should always be used when an engine is rebuilt.
7   Carefully inspect each piston for cracks around the skirt, at the pin bosses and at the ring lands.
8   Look for scoring and scuffing on the thrust faces of the skirt, holes in the piston crown and burned areas at the edge of the crown. If the skirt is scored or scuffed, the engine may have been suffering from overheating and/or abnormal combustion, which caused excessively high operating temperatures. The cooling and lubrication systems should be checked thoroughly. A hole in the piston crown is an indication that abnormal combustion (preignition) was occurring. Burned areas at the edge of the piston crown are usually evidence of spark knock (detonation). If any of the above problems exist, the causes must be corrected or the damage will occur again.
9   Corrosion of the piston, evidenced by pitting, indicates that coolant is leaking into the combustion chamber and/or the crankcase. Again,

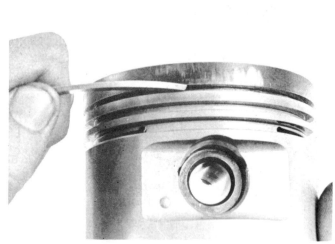

16.4a   Use a piece of broken ring to carefully remove carbon deposits from the ring grooves. Use caution not to remove any of the piston material

16.4b   If available, a ring groove cleaning tool can be used to remove carbon from the ring grooves

16.5   Make sure the oil return holes in the back of the oil ring groove are open

the cause must be corrected or the problem may persist in the rebuilt engine.

10   Measure the piston ring side clearance by laying a new piston ring in each ring groove and slipping a feeler gauge between the ring and the edge of the ring groove (photo). Check the clearance at three or four locations around each groove. Be sure to use the correct ring for each groove; they are different. If the side clearance is greater than specified, new pistons will have to be used.

11   Check the piston-to-bore clearance by measuring the bore (see Section 14) and the piston diameter. Make sure that the pistons and bores are correctly matched. Measure the piston across the skirt (photo). Subtract the piston diameter from the bore diameter to obtain the clearance. If it is greater than specified, the block will have to be rebored and new pistons and rings installed. (Piston-to-bore clearance can also be measured less accurately by installing the piston, without rings, into its bore and using feeler blades to establish the clearance.)

12   Check the piston-to-rod clearance by twisting the piston and rod in opposite directions. Any noticeable play indicates that there is excessive wear, which must be corrected. The piston/connecting rod assemblies should be taken to an automotive machine shop to have new piston pins installed and the pistons and connecting rods rebored.

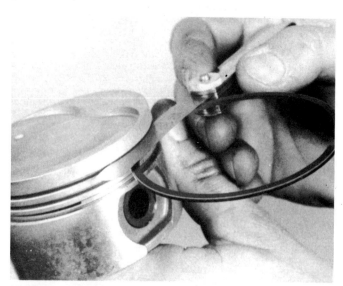

16.10   To check ring side clearance, insert the ring in the groove then use a feeler gauge to check the remaining gap

16.11   Measure the piston diameter at the thrust faces, 90° to the piston pin hole

13 If the pistons must be removed from the connecting rods, such as when new pistons must be installed, or if the piston pins have too much play in them, they should be taken to an automotive machine shop. While they are there have the connecting rods checked for bend and twist, as automotive machine shops have special equipment for this purpose. Unless new pistons or connecting rods must be installed, do not disassemble the pistons from the connecting rods.

14 Check the connecting rods for cracks and other damage. Temporarily remove the rod caps, lift out the old bearing inserts, wipe the rod and cap bearing surfaces clean and inspect them for nicks, gouges or scratches. After checking the rods, replace the old bearings, slip the caps into place and tighten the nuts finger tight.

17 Crankshaft — inspection

1 Clean the crankshaft with solvent and dry it thoroughly. Be sure to clean the oil holes with a stiff brush and flush them with solvent. Blow out all traces of solvent afterwards with compressed air. Any solvent remaining in the oilways will dilute the oil on start-up, possibly with serious results. Check the main and connecting rod bearing journals for uneven wear, scoring, pitting or cracks. Check the remainder of the crankshaft for cracks and damage.

2 Using a micrometer, measure the diameter of the main and connecting rod journals and compare the results to the Specifications. By measuring the diameter at a number of points around the journal's circumference, you will be able to determine whether or not the journal is out of round. Take the measurement at each end of the journal, near the crank counterweights, to determine whether the journal is tapered (photo). If you do not have a micrometer, a machine shop will probably measure the journals for a nominal fee.

3 If the crankshaft journals are damaged, tapered, out of round or worn beyond the limits given in the Specifications, have the crankshaft reground by a reputable automotive machine shop. Be sure to use the correct size bearing inserts if the crankshaft is reconditioned to maintain proper oil clearance.

4 Refer to Section 18 and examine the main and rod bearing inserts for unusual wear patterns.

18 Main and connecting rod bearings — inspection

1 Even though the main and connecting rod bearings should be replaced with new ones during the engine overhaul, the old bearings should be retained for close examination, as they may reveal valuable information about the condition of the engine.

2 Bearing failure occurs because of lack of lubrication, the presence of dirt or other foreign particles, overloading the engine and corrosion. Regardless of the cause of bearing failure, it must be corrected before the engine is reassembled to prevent it from happening again.

3 When examining the bearings, remove them from the engine block, the main bearing caps, the connecting rods and the rod caps and lay them out on a clean surface in the same general position as their location in the engine. This will enable you to match any bearing problems with the corresponding crankshaft journal.

4 Dirt and other foreign particles get into the engine in a variety of ways. It may be left in the engine during assembly, or it may pass through filters or breathers. It may get into the oil, and from there into the bearings. Metal chips from machining operations and normal engine wear are often present. Abrasives are sometimes left in engine components after reconditioning, especially when parts are not thoroughly cleaned using the proper cleaning methods. Whatever the source, these foreign objects often end up embedded in the soft bearing material and are easily recognized. Large particles will not embed in the bearing and will score or gouge the bearing and shaft. The best prevention for this cause of bearing failure is to clean all parts thoroughly and keep everything spotlessly clean during engine assembly. Frequent and regular engine oil and filter changes are also recommended to prevent premature bearing wear.

5 Lack of lubrication (or lubrication breakdown) has a number of inter-related causes. Excessive heat (which thins the oil), overloading (which squeezes the oil from the bearing face) and oil leakage or throw off (from excessive bearing clearances, worn oil pump or high engine speeds) all contribute to lubrication breakdown. Blocked oil passages,

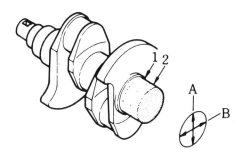

Fig. 2B.15 Measure the crankshaft at the two points (1 and 2) and the four locations (A and B) on each journal (Sec 17)

17.2 Measure the diameter of each crankshaft journal at several places to detect taper and out-of-round conditions

which usually are the result of misaligned oil holes in a bearing shell, will also oil starve a bearing and destroy it. When lack of lubrication is the cause of bearing failure, the bearing material is wiped or extruded from the steel backing of the bearing. Temperatures may increase to the point where the steel backing turns blue from overheating which can also affect the rod cap and rod bolts.

6 Driving habits can have a definite effect on bearing life. Full throttle, low speed operation, lugging the engine, puts very high loads on bearings, which tends to squeeze out the oil film. These loads cause the bearings to flex, which produces fine cracks in the bearing (fatigue failure). Eventually the bearing material will loosen in pieces and tear away from the steel backing. Short trip driving leads to corrosion of bearings because insufficient engine heat is produced to drive off the condensed water and corrosive gases. These products collect in the engine oil, forming acid and sludge. As the oil is carried to the engine bearings, the acid attacks and corrodes the bearing material, destroying it and leading to bearing failure.

7 Incorrect bearing installation during engine assembly will lead to bearing failure as well. Tight fitting bearings leave insufficient bearing oil clearance and will result in oil starvation. Dirt or foreign particles trapped behind a bearing insert result in high spots on the bearing which lead to failure.

19 Piston rings — installation

1 Before installing the new piston rings, the ring end gaps must be checked. It is assumed that the piston ring side clearance in the piston has been checked and verified correct (Section 16).

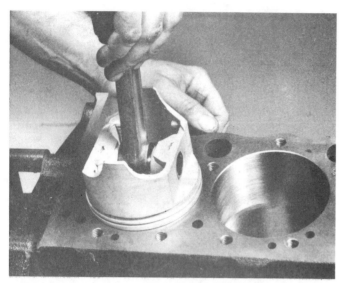

19.3a Before checking piston ring end gap the ring must be square in the cylinder bore. This is done by pushing the ring down into the cylinder with the top of a piston

19.3b With the ring square in the cylinder, measure the end gap with a feeler gauge

2   Lay out the piston/connecting rod assemblies and the new ring sets so the ring sets will be matched with the same piston and cylinder during the end gap measurement and engine assembly.

3   Insert the top (number one) ring into the first cylinder and square it up with the cylinder walls by pushing it in with the top of the piston (photo). The ring should be near the bottom of the cylinder at the lower limit of ring travel. To measure the end gap, slip a feeler gauge between the ends of the ring (photo). Compare the measurement to the Specifications.

4   If the gap is larger or smaller than specified, double-check to make sure that you have the correct rings before proceeding.

5   If the gap is too small, it must be enlarged or the ring ends may come in contact with each other during engine operation, which can cause serious damage to the engine. The end gap can be increased by filing the ring ends very carefully with a fine file. Mount the file in a vise equipped with soft jaws, slip the ring over the file with the ends contacting the file face and slowly move the ring to remove material from the ends (photo). When performing this operation, file only from the outside in.

6   Excess end gap is not critical unless it is greater than 0.040-inch (1 mm). Again, double-check to make sure you have the correct rings for your engine.

7   Repeat the procedure for each ring that will be installed in the first cylinder and for each ring in the remaining cylinders. Remember to keep rings, pistons and cylinders matched up.

8   Once the ring end gaps have been checked/corrected, the rings can be installed on the pistons.

9   The oil control ring (lowest one on the piston) is installed first. It is composed of three separate components. Slip the spacer/expander into the groove (photo), then install the lower side rail. Do not use a piston ring installation tool on the oil ring side rails, as they may be damaged. Instead, place one end of the side rail into the groove between the spacer/expander and the ring land, hold it firmly in place and slide a finger around the piston while pushing the rail into the groove (photo). Next, install the upper side rail in the same manner.

10 After the three oil ring components have been installed, check to make sure that both the upper and lower side rails can be turned smoothly in the ring groove. Refer to the accompanying illustration for proper positioning of the oil ring gaps.

11 The number two (middle) ring is installed next. It is stamped with an R mark which should face toward the top of the piston. **Note:** *Always follow the instructions printed on the ring package or box — different manufacturers may require different approaches. Do not mix up the top and middle rings, as they have different cross sections.*

12 Use a piston ring installation tool and make sure that the identification mark is facing the top of the piston, then slip the ring into the middle groove on the piston (photo). Do not expand the ring any more than

19.5 To increase ring end gap, mount a file in a vise and file the ring, from the outside in only, until the proper gap is obtained

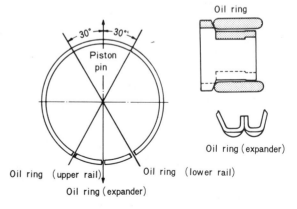

Fig. 2B.16 Oil ring installation and gap positioning
(Secs 19 and 21)

19.9a Install the oil control ring expander in the lower piston groove, making sure the ends interlock properly

19.9b Roll the oil control ring side rails into place above and below the oil control ring expander. Do not use a ring expander tool to install oil ring side rails

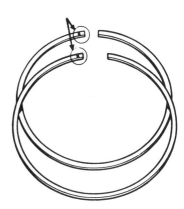

Fig. 2B.17 The piston ring markings must face up
(Sec 19)

19.12 Use a ring expander to install the compression rings. Be sure the marks are facing up, and that the number one and two rings aren't mixed up

is necessary to slide it over the piston. Feeler blades can be used instead of a ring installation tool — see Section 16.
13 Install the number one (top) ring in the same manner. Make sure the identifying mark is facing up. Be careful not to confuse the number one and number two rings. Refer to the appropriate illustration for ring gap positioning.

20 Crankshaft — installation and main bearing oil clearance check

1 Crankshaft installation is the first step in engine reassembly. It is assumed at this point that the engine block and crankshaft have been cleaned, inspected and repaired or reconditioned.
2 Position the engine with the bottom facing up.
3 Remove the main bearing cap bolts and lift out the caps. Lay them out in the proper order to ensure that they are installed correctly.
4 If they are still in place, remove the old bearing inserts from the block and the main bearing caps. Wipe the main bearing surfaces of the block and caps with a clean, lint free cloth. They must be kept spotlessly clean.
5 Clean the back sides of the new main bearing inserts and lay one bearing half in each main bearing saddle in the block. Lay the other bearing half from each bearing set in the corresponding main bearing cap. Make sure the tab on the bearing insert fits into the recess in the

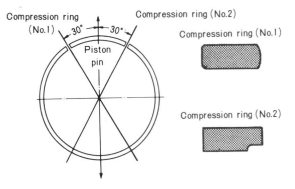

Fig. 2B.18 Compression piston ring installation and gap positioning (Secs 19 and 21)

block or cap. Also, the oil holes in the block must line up with the oil holes in the bearing insert. Do not hammer the bearing into place and do not nick or gouge the bearing faces. No lubrication should be used at this time.

6   The flanged thrust bearing must be installed in the number three (3) saddle.

7   Clean the faces of the bearings in the block and the crankshaft main bearing journals with a clean, lint free cloth. Check or clean the oil holes in the crankshaft, as any dirt here can go only one way — straight through the new bearings.

8   Once you are certain that the crankshaft is clean, carefully lay it in position (an assistant would be very helpful here) in the main bearings.

9   Before the crankshaft can be permanently installed, the main bearing oil clearance must be checked.

10   Trim several pieces of the appropriate size of Plastigage, so they are slightly shorter than the width of the main bearings, and place one piece on each crankshaft main bearing journal, parallel with the journal axis.

11   Clean the faces of the bearings in the caps and install the caps in their respective positions (do not mix them up) with the arrows pointing toward the front of the engine. Do not disturb the Plastigage.

12   Starting with the center main and working out toward the ends, tighten the main bearing cap bolts, in three steps, to the specified torque. Do not rotate the crankshaft at any time during this operation.

13   Remove the bolts and carefully lift off the main bearing caps. Keep them in order. Do not disturb the Plastigage or rotate the crankshaft. If any of the main bearing caps are difficult to remove, tap them gently from side-to-side with a soft-face hammer to loosen them.

14   Compare the width of the crushed Plastigage on each journal to the scale printed on the Plastigage container to obtain the main bearing oil clearance. Check the Specifications to make sure it is correct.

15   If the clearance is not correct, double-check to make sure you have the right size bearing inserts. Also, make sure that no dirt or oil was between the bearing inserts and the main bearing caps or the block when the clearance was measured.

16   Carefully scrape all traces of the Plastigage material off the main bearing journals and/or the bearing faces. Do not nick or scratch the bearing faces.

17   Carefully lift the crankshaft out of the engine. Clean the bearing faces in the block, then apply a thin, uniform layer of clean, high quality moly-base grease or engine assembly lube to each of the bearing surfaces. Be sure to coat the thrust flange faces as well as the journal face of the thrust bearing.

18   Make sure the crankshaft journals are clean, then lay the crankshaft back in place in the block. Clean the faces of the bearings in the caps, then apply a thin, uniform layer of clean, moly-base grease to each of the bearing faces. Install the caps in their respective positions with the arrows pointing toward the front of the engine. Install the bolts and tighten them to the specified torque, starting with the center main and working out toward the ends. Work up to the final torque in three steps.

19   On manual transaxle models, install a new pilot bearing in the end

of the crankshaft. Lubricate the crankshaft cavity and the outer circumference of the bearing with clean engine oil and place the bearing in position. Tap it evenly into the cavity using a suitable size piece of pipe and a hammer. Lubricate the inside of the bearing with grease. (See also Chapter 8, Fig. 8.11.)

20   Rotate the crankshaft a number of times by hand to check for any obvious binding.

21   The final step is to check the crankshaft end play with a dial indicator as described in Section 12.

21   Piston/connecting rod assembly — installation and bearing oil clearance check

1   Before installing the piston/connecting rod assemblies the cylinder walls must be perfectly clean, the top edge of each cylinder must be chamfered, and the crankshaft must be in place.

2   Remove the connecting rod cap from the end of the number one connecting rod. Remove the old bearing inserts and wipe the bearing surfaces of the connecting rod and cap with a clean, lint free cloth. They must be kept spotlessly clean.

3   Clean the back side of the new upper bearing half, then lay it in place in the connecting rod. Make sure that the tab on the bearing fits into the recess in the rod. Do not hammer the bearing insert into place and be very careful not to nick or gouge the bearing face. Do not lubricate the bearing at this time.

4   Clean the back side of the other bearing insert and install it in the rod cap. Again, make sure the tab on the bearing fits into the recess in the cap, and do not apply any lubricant. It is critically important that the mating surfaces of the bearing and connecting rod are perfectly clean and oil free when they are assembled.

5   Position the piston ring gaps as shown in the accompanying illustrations, then slip a section of plastic or rubber hose over the connecting rod cap bolts.

6   Lubricate the piston and rings with clean engine oil and attach a piston ring compressor to the piston. Leave the skirt protruding about 1/4-inch to guide the piston into the cylinder (photo). The rings must be compressed as far as possible.

7   Rotate the crankshaft until the number one connecting rod journal is as far from the number one cylinder as possible (bottom dead center), and apply a coat of engine oil to the cylinder walls.

8   With the notch or arrow on top of the piston facing to the front of the engine, gently place the piston/connecting rod assembly into the number one cylinder bore and rest the bottom edge of the ring compressor on the engine block. Tap the top edge of the ring compressor to make sure it is contacting the block around its entire circumference. (If there are no notches or arrows on the piston crown, check before

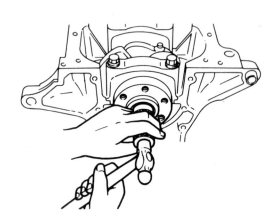

Fig. 2B.19 Installing the pilot bearing into the crankshaft (manual transaxle models) (Sec 20)

21.6 When installing the pistons and rings, leave a portion of the piston skirt extended below the ring compressor to center the piston in the cylinder

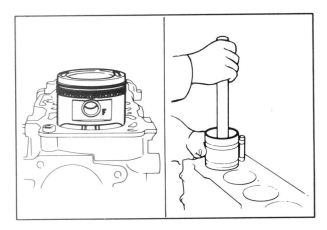

Fig. 2B.20 Installing pistons — 'F' mark must face the
front (pulley end) of the engine (Sec 21)

fitting the ring compressor that the 'F' mark next to the piston pin boss
is facing the front (pulley end) of the engine.)

9   Carefully tap on the top of the piston with the end of a wooden
hammer handle (photo) while guiding the end of the connecting rod
into place on the crankshaft journal. The piston rings may try to pop
out of the ring compressor just before entering the cylinder bore, so
keep some downward pressure on the ring compressor. Work slowly,
and if any resistance is felt as the piston enters the cylinder, stop
immediately. Find out what is hanging up and fix it before proceeding.
Do not, for any reason, force the piston into the cylinder, as you will
break a ring and/or the piston.

10 Once the piston/connecting rod assembly is installed, the connecting rod bearing oil clearance must be checked before the rod cap is
permanently bolted in place.

11 Cut a piece of the appropriate size Plastigage slightly shorter than
the width of the connecting rod bearing and lay it in place on the number
one connecting rod journal, parallel with the journal axis (photo). It must
not cross the oil hole in the journal.

12 Clean the connecting rod cap bearing face, remove the protective
hoses from the connecting rod bolts and install the rod cap. Make sure
the mating mark on the cap is on the same side as the mark on the
connecting rod. Install the nuts and tighten them to the specified
torque, working up to it in three steps. Do not rotate the crankshaft
at any time during this operation.

13 Remove the rod cap, being very careful not to disturb the
Plastigage. Compare the width of the crushed Plastigage to the scale
printed on the Plastigage container to obtain the oil clearance (photo).
Compare it to the Specifications to make sure the clearance is correct.
If the clearance is not correct, double-check to make sure that you have
the correct size bearing inserts. Also, recheck the crankshaft connecting
rod journal diameter and make sure that no dirt or oil was between
the bearing inserts and the connecting rod or cap when the clearance
was measured.

14 Carefully scrape all traces of the Plastigage material off the rod
journal and/or bearing face. Be very careful not to scratch the bearing
— use your fingernail or a piece of hardwood. Make sure the bearing
faces are perfectly clean, then apply a uniform layer of clean, high
quality moly-base grease or engine assembly lube to both of them. You
will have to push the piston into the cylinder to expose the face of
the bearing insert in the connecting rod. Be sure to slip the protective
hoses over the rod bolts first (photo).

15 Slide the connecting rod back into place on the journal, remove
the protective hoses from the rod cap bolts, install the rod cap and
tighten the nuts to the specified torque. Again, work up to the torque
in three steps.

16 Repeat the entire procedure for the remaining piston/connecting
rod assemblies. Keep the back sides of the bearing inserts and the inside
of the connecting rod and cap perfectly clean when assembling them.

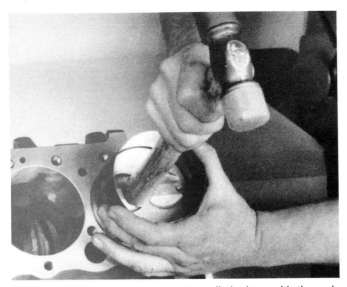

21.9   Gently drive the piston into the cylinder bore with the end
of a wooden hammer handle

21.11   Lay a piece of the proper size Plastigage across the rod
journal before installing the rod cap

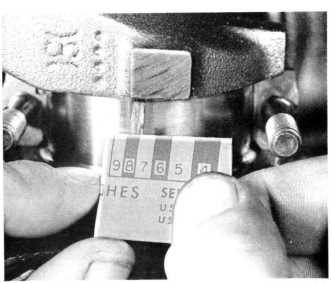

21.13   After removing the rod cap, compare the width of the
crushed Plastigage to the scale on the package to determine the
oil clearance

21.14 Use rubber boots to protect the cylinder walls and crankshaft journal from the rod bolts, and pull the rod up snugly against the rod journal

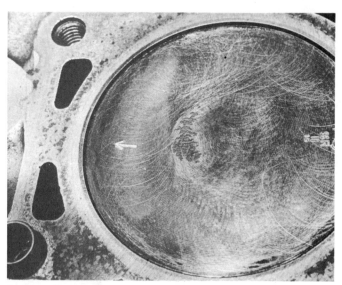

21.16a An arrow at one edge of the piston should point to the front of the engine after installation

21.16b Some pistons use a notch to indicate which side of the piston should face the front of the engine

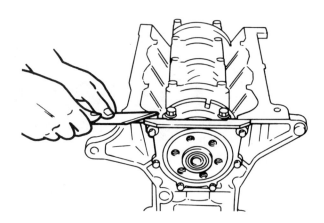

Fig. 2B.21 Cutting off the excess rear cover gasket (Sec 22)

Make sure you have the correct piston for the cylinder and that the notch, arrow or 'F' mark on the piston faces to the front of the engine when the piston is installed (photos). Remember, use plenty of oil to lubricate the piston before installing the ring compressor. Also, when installing the rod caps for the final time, be sure to lubricate the bearing faces adequately.

17 After all the piston/connecting rod assemblies have been properly installed, rotate the crankshaft a number of times by hand to check for any obvious binding.

18 As a final step, the connecting rod end play must be checked. Refer to Section 11 for this procedure. Compare the measured end play to the Specifications to make sure it is correct.

22 Rear oil seal and cover — installation

1 Lubricate the outer circumference of the oil seal lightly with assembly lube or clean engine oil and place the seal in position in the rear cover bore. Press the seal fully and evenly into the bore using a suitable size socket. The lips of the seal must face inwards when it is installed.

2 Apply gasket sealant to the gasket and rear cover contact surfaces.

3 Apply a light coat of clean engine oil to the seal lip, place the rear cover and gasket in position and install the retaining bolts. Tighten the bolts to the specified torque.

4 Carefully cut away the portion of the gasket which extends from the rear cover into the oil pan contact area as shown in the accompanying illustration.

23 Engine overhaul — reassembly sequence

1 Before beginning engine reassembly, make sure you have all the necessary new parts, gaskets and seals as well as the following items on hand:

Common hand tools
A 1/2-inch drive torque wrench
Piston ring installation tool
Piston ring compressor
Short lengths of rubber or plastic hose to fit over connecting rod bolts
Plastigage

Feeler gauges
A fine-tooth file
New engine oil
Engine assembly lube or moly-base grease
RTV-type gasket sealant
Anaerobic-type gasket sealant
Thread locking compound
2   In order to save time and avoid problems, engine reassembly must be done in the following order.
Crankshaft and main bearings
Crankshaft pilot bearing (manual transaxle models)
Piston rings
Piston/connecting rod assemblies
Rear oil seal and cover
Oil pump and oil strainer
Oil pan
Flywheel/driveplate
Front engine mount bracket
Water pump
Cylinder head, camshaft and rocker arm assembly
Front housing and oil seal
Timing belt sprockets and tensioner
Timing belt and cover
Fuel pump
Rear housing
Camshaft cover
Oil pressure switch
Oil filter
Thermostat and housing cover
Distributor, spark plug wires and spark plugs
Water hose and pipe assemblies
Intake and exhaust manifolds
Alternator and brackets
Emissions control components

24   Initial start-up and break-in after overhaul

1   Once the engine has been properly installed in the vehicle, double check the engine oil and coolant levels.
2   With the spark plugs out of the engine and the coil high tension lead grounded to the engine block, crank the engine until oil pressure registers on the gauge (if so equipped) or until the oil light goes off.
3   Install the spark plugs, hook up the plug wires and the coil high tension lead.
4   Make sure the carburetor choke plate is closed, then start the engine. It may take a few moments for the gasoline to reach the carburetor, but the engine should start without a great deal of effort.
5   As soon as the engine starts it should be set at a fast idle to ensure proper oil circulation and allowed to warm up to normal operating temperature. While the engine is warming up, make a thorough check for oil and coolant leaks.
6   Shut the engine off and recheck the engine oil and coolant levels. Restart the engine and check the ignition timing and the engine idle speed (refer to Chapter 1). Make any necessary adjustments.
7   Drive the vehicle to an area with minimum traffic, accelerate at full throttle from 30 to 50 mph, then allow the vehicle to slow to 30 mph with the throttle closed. Repeat the procedure 10 or 12 times. This will load the piston rings and cause them to seat properly against the cylinder walls. Check again for oil and coolant leaks.
8   Drive the vehicle gently for the first 500 miles (no sustained high speeds) and keep a constant check on the oil level. It is not unusual for an engine to use oil during the break-in period.
9   At approximately 500 to 600 miles, change the oil and filter, re-torque the cylinder head bolts and recheck the valve clearances.
10 For the next few hundred miles, drive the vehicle normally. Do not either pamper it or abuse it.
11 After 2000 miles, change the oil and filter again and consider the engine fully broken in.

Chapter 3
Cooling, heating and air conditioning systems

Contents

Specifications

Radiator cap pressure rating	13 ± 2 psi
Coolant capacity	
1.6 litre	12.1 Imp pints (7.3 US quarts, 6.9 litres)
2.0 litre	12.7 Imp pints (7.7 US quarts, 7.2 litres)
Thermostat rating...................................	190 °F (88 °C)
Water temperature switch	
On at	194 °F (90 °C)
Off at	206 °F (97 °C)
Cooling fan motor current.............................	8 to 11 amperes

Torque specifications

	Ft-lbs	M-kg
Fan thermo switch	22 to 29	3.0 to 4.0
Temperature gauge unit	5 to 7	0.5 to 1.0
Thermostat housing (water outlet) bolts/nuts............	14 to 22	1.9 to 3.1
Water pump-to-block bolt	14 to 19	1.9 to 2.6

1 General information

The cooling system consists of a radiator, an engine driven water pump and thermostat controlled coolant flow.

The fan is driven by an electric motor which is mounted in the radiator shroud and is activated by a temperature switch. **Warning:** *The fan can start even when the engine is Off as long as the ignition switch is On. The battery negative cable should be disconnected whenever you are working in the vicinity of the fan.*

The water pump is mounted on the front of the engine and is driven by the timing belt.

The heater utilizes the heat produced by the engine, which is absorbed by the coolant to warm the vehicle interior. The coolant passes through a heater core similar to a small radiator in the passenger compartment. The coolant flow through the core and air which is directed through the heater core and duct system to heat the vehicle interior are controlled by the driver or passenger.

Air conditioning is available as an option on these vehicles. The air conditioning system is located in the engine compartment and the compressor is driven by the crankshaft pulley by way of a drivebelt.

2 Antifreeze — general information

Warning: *Do not allow antifreeze to come in contact with your skin or painted surfaces of the vehicle. Flush contacted areas immediately with plenty of water. Antifreeze can be fatal to children and pets. They like it because it is sweet. Just a few licks can cause death. Wipe up garage floor and drip pan coolant spills immediately. Keep antifreeze containers covered and repair leaks in your cooling system immediately.*

The cooling system should be filled with a water/ethylene glycol based antifreeze solution, which will prevent freezing down to at least −20 °F (−29 °C) at all times. It also provides protection against corrosion and increases the coolant boiling point.

The cooling system should be drained, flushed and refilled at least every other year (see Chapter 1). The use of antifreeze solutions for periods of longer than two years is likely to cause damage and encourage the formation of rust and scale in the system.

Before adding antifreeze to the system, check all hose connections and retorque the cylinder head bolts. Antifreeze tends to search out and leak through very minute openings.

The exact mixture of antifreeze-to-water which you should use depends on the relative weather conditions. The mixture should contain at least 50 percent antifreeze, but should never contain more than 70 percent antifreeze.

3   Thermostat — replacement

Warning: *The engine must be completely cool before beginning this procedure. Also, when working in the vicinity of the electric fan, disconnect the negative battery cable from the battery to prevent the fan from coming on accidentally.*

1   Refer to the Warning in Section 2.
2   Disconnect the cable from the negative battery terminal (if not done previously).
3   Remove the distributor (Chapter 5) to provide access to the thermostat housing.
4   Drain the cooling system until the level is below the thermostat by loosening the radiator cap and opening the petcock at the bottom of the radiator. Close the petcock when enough coolant has drained.
5   Remove the upper radiator hose from the water outlet housing.
6   Unplug the fan thermo switch connector.

7   Remove the two housing nuts and separate the housing from the engine. It may be necessary to use a rubber mallet to break the housing gasket seal (photo).
8   Remove the thermostat from the thermostat housing (photo).
9   Before installing the thermostat, clean the gasket sealing surfaces on the water outlet and thermostat housing.
10   Apply a thin coat of sealant to both sides of the new gasket.
11   Place the thermostat in the housing, install the gasket with the printed side facing the thermostat and install the water outlet. Tighten the water outlet bolts to the specified torque.
12   Connect the upper radiator hose and tighten the hose clamp securely. Make sure the arrow on the hose aligns with the tab on the housing (photo).
13   Plug in the thermo switch connector.
14   Install the distributor.
15   Fill the cooling system with the proper antifreeze/water mixture (refer to Chapter 1).
16   Reconnect the battery cable and start the engine.
17   Run the engine with the radiator cap removed until the upper radiator hose is hot (thermostat open).
18   With the engine idling, add coolant to the radiator until the level reaches the bottom of the filler neck.
19   Install the radiator cap.

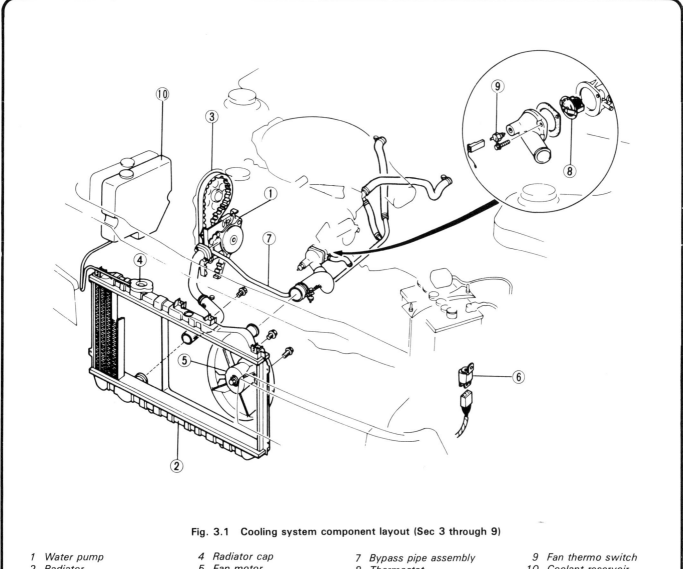

Fig. 3.1   Cooling system component layout (Sec 3 through 9)

1 Water pump	4 Radiator cap	7 Bypass pipe assembly	9 Fan thermo switch
2 Radiator	5 Fan motor	8 Thermostat	10 Coolant reservoir
3 Timing belt	6 Fan relay		

The jiggle pin should be on the upper side.

④ ③ ② ①

Fig. 3.2 Thermostat installation details (Sec 3)

1 Upper radiator hose
2 Thermostat housing
3 Gasket
4 Thermostat

3.7 Break free the thermostat housing gasket with a rubber mallet

3.8 Note the direction of installation when removing the thermostat

3.12 Make sure the arrow on the radiator hose aligns with the tab on the housing

4 Thermostat — check

1 The best way to check the operation of the thermostat is with it removed from the engine. In most cases, if the thermostat is suspect, it is more economical to simply buy and install a replacement thermostat, as they are not very costly.
2 To check, first remove the thermostat as described in Section 3.
3 Inspect the thermostat for excessive corrosion and damage. Replace it with a new one if either of these conditions is noted.
4 To check the thermostat, suspend it in a pan of water and heat the water. The thermostat must be open by the time the water boils, and must close again as the water cools. Replace the thermostat if it fails this test.

5 Radiator — removal, servicing and installation

Warning: *The engine must be completely cool before beginning this procedure. Also, when working in the vicinity of the electric fan, disconnect the negative battery cable from the battery to prevent the fan from coming on accidentally.*

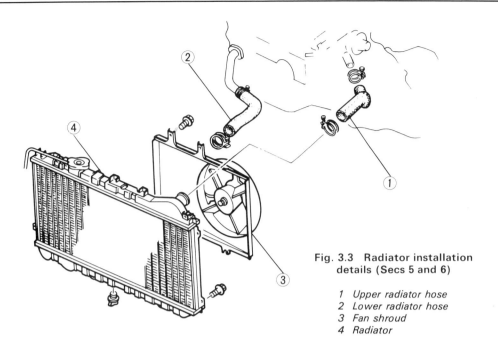

Fig. 3.3 Radiator installation details (Secs 5 and 6)

1 Upper radiator hose
2 Lower radiator hose
3 Fan shroud
4 Radiator

1 Refer to the Warning in Section 2.
2 Drain the radiator (refer to Chapter 1, if necessary).
3 For access, remove the air cleaner intake and disconnect the ignition coil wire and move it out of the way.
4 Unplug the fan motor and radiator thermo switch connectors.
5 Remove the radiator hoses from the radiator and disconnect the coolant recovery hose.
6 Remove the radiator attaching bolts and clamps and lift out the radiator. On automatic transaxle models, raise the radiator sufficiently for access to the cooler lines and disconnect and plug them. Remove the radiator from the engine compartment (photos).
7 Carefully examine the radiator for evidence of leaks and damage. It is recommended that any necessary repairs be performed by a radiator repair shop.
8 With the radiator removed, brush accumulations of insects and leaves from the fins and examine and replace, if necessary, any hoses or clamps which have deteriorated.
9 The radiator can be flushed as described in Chapter 1.
10 Replace the radiator cap with a new one of the same rating, or if the cap is comparatively new, have it tested by a service station.
11 If you are installing a new radiator, transfer the fittings from the old unit.
12 Installation is the reverse of removal, making sure the radiator seats securely in the mounts (photo).

13 After installing the radiator, refill it with the proper coolant mixture (refer to Chapter 1), then start the engine and check for leaks.
14 On automatic transaxle models, check the transmission fluid level and top up if necessary (Chapter 1).

6 Fan — removal and installation

Warning: *The engine must be completely cool before beginning this procedure. Also, when working in the vicinity of the electric fan, disconnect the negative battery cable from the battery to prevent the fan from coming on accidentally.*

1 To provide access, remove the distributor (Chapter 5) and the air cleaner assembly intake tube.
2 Unplug the fan connector.
3 Drain the coolant until the level is below the upper radiator hose by removing the drain plug at the bottom of the radiator.
4 Remove the upper radiator hose.
5 Remove the retaining bolts and lift the fan motor and cowling assembly from the radiator.
6 Installation is the reverse of removal.
7 Fill the radiator to the proper level, connect the negative battery cable and check for proper operation as the engine warms to operating temperature.

5.6a Lift the radiator for access to the automatic transaxle hose connections (arrows)

5.6b Hold the hoses out of the way and lift the radiator straight up to avoid damage to the fins

5.12 Check the radiator frame mount contact areas (arrows) for rust and damage

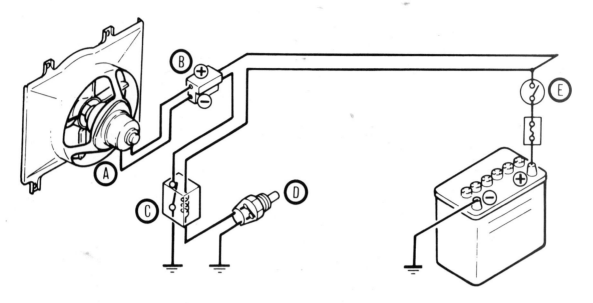

Fig. 3.4 Cooling fan electrical circuit (Sec 7)

A Fan motor
B Fan connector
C Relay

D Thermo switch
E Ignition switch

---

7 Electric cooling fan system — description, testing and component replacement

Description

1   The electric cooling fan system consists of a fan motor and blade assembly mounted in a cowling which bolts to the radiator, a fan relay located on the left inner fender panel and a thermo switch threaded into the thermostat housing.

2   When the coolant in the thermostat housing reaches operating temperature for the fan (206.6 °F/97 °C) the thermo switch opens, interrupting electrical current through the relay and turning the fan motor on. When the temperature is below 194 °F/90 °C the switch is closed and the fan motor is off. The relay contacts are normally closed, ie the relay coil must be energized to turn the motor off.

Testing and replacement

Fan motor

3   Trace the wire from the motor to the connector and separate the connector using a screwdriver.

4   Test the motor using an ammeter and battery, as shown in the accompanying illustration, to make sure the fan motor operates at the specified current.

5   If the fan motor does not operate at the specified current, replace it with a new one (Section 6).

Fan relay

6   Unplug the water thermo switch connector and check to see if the fan turns when the ignition switch is turned On, indicating that the relay is operating properly.

7   If the fan does not turn, check for a loose connection or faulty fuse. If the fuse and connections are good, replace the relay with a new one. The relay is replaced by unplugging the connector and removing the retaining screws.

Thermo switch

Note: *Do not disconnect the thermo switch with the ignition switch On or the fan will go on automatically.*

8   Drain the cooling system to below the level of the thermostat housing.

9   Disconnect the connector and remove the thermo switch.

10   Place the thermo switch in a container of hot water and check that there is continuity below 104 °F (90 °C). Heat the water and check

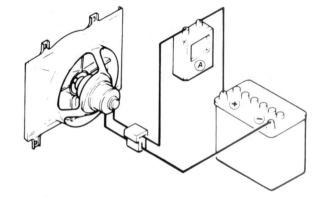

Fig. 3.5 Cooling fan motor test (Sec 7)

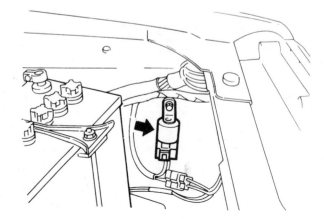

Fig. 3.6 Cooling fan relay location (arrow) (Sec 7)

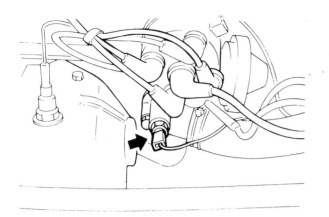

Fig. 3.7   Cooling fan thermo switch location (arrow) (Sec 7)

that the switch opens before the water boils. Replace the switch if it fails these tests.
11   When reinstalling the switch, make sure that the O-ring is installed or leaks will result.
12   Refill the cooling system on completion.

8   Water pump — check

1   A failure of the water pump can cause overheating and serious engine damage (the pump will not circulate coolant through the engine).
2   There are three ways to check the operation of the water pump

while it is still installed on the engine. If the pump is defective, it should be replaced with a new or rebuilt unit.
3   With the engine running at normal operating temperature, squeeze the upper radiator hose. If the water pump is working properly, a pressure surge will be felt as the hose is released.
4   Water pumps are equipped with *weep* or vent holes. If a pump seal failure occurs, small amounts of coolant will leak from the weep holes. It will be necessary to remove the timing belt lower cover and use a flashlight from under the vehicle to see evidence of leakage from this point on the pump body.
5   If the water pump shaft bearings fail, there may be a squealing sound emitted from the front of the engine while it is running. Shaft wear can be felt if the water pump pulley is forced up and down.
6   All the pump components are replaceable, but because press tools are required, the work should be left to a Mazda dealer or other specialist.

9   Water pump — removal and installation

Warning: *The engine must be completely cool before beginning this procedure. Also, when working in the vicinity of the electric fan, disconnect the negative battery cable from the battery to prevent the fan from coming on accidentally.*

1   Refer to the Warning in Section 2.
2   Drain the cooling system (refer to Chapter 1, if necessary).
3   Remove the timing belt covers and the belt (Chapter 2). Also remove the timing belt tensioner (idler).
4   Disconnect the water pump inlet pipe hose.
5   Remove the water pump bolts.
6   Use a large screwdriver or a suitable pry bar to pry on the water pump while using a rocking motion to disengage the pump O-ring (photo).

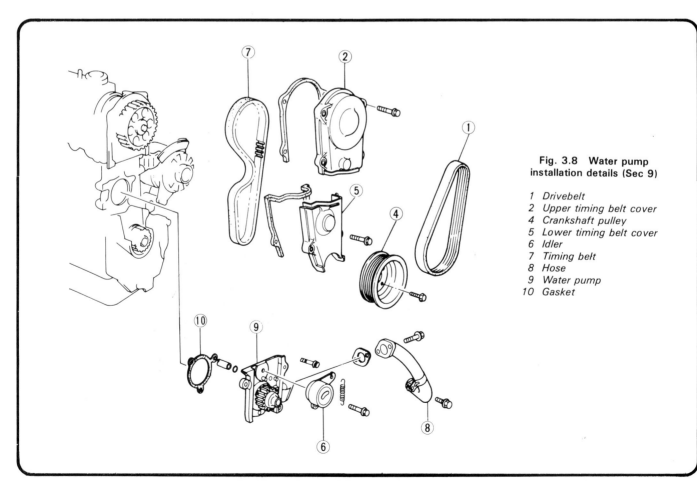

Fig. 3.8   Water pump installation details (Sec 9)

1   Drivebelt
2   Upper timing belt cover
4   Crankshaft pulley
5   Lower timing belt cover
6   Idler
7   Timing belt
8   Hose
9   Water pump
10   Gasket

9.6 Pry the water pump out from the engine with a large screwdriver

7   With the water pump leaning forward, remove the bolts and disconnect the water inlet pipe.
8   Lift the pump from the engine compartment.
9   Carefully clean all gasket material from all mounting surfaces. Clean and inspect the O-ring gasket groove.
10 Lubricate the O-ring with petroleum jelly and insert it into the groove. Coat both sides the gaskets with sealant prior to installation.
11 Place the water pump in position and bolt on the water inlet pipe. Install two of the pump retaining bolts finger tight.
12 Install the remaining bolts and then tighten all of the bolts evenly in a criss-cross pattern to the specified torque.
13 Connect the inlet pipe hose.

14 Install the timing belt tensioner, timing belt and covers.
15 Refill the cooling system with a 50/50 solution of water and the specified coolant (Chapter 1).

10 Heater fan motor — removal and installation

1   Disconnect the battery negative cable. Remove the trim from below the instrument panel on the passenger side for access to the fan motor.
2   Unplug the electrical connectors, remove the retaining screws and lift the motor from the housing (photo).
3   Installation is the reverse of removal.

11 Air conditioning system — servicing

Warning: *The air conditioning system is under high pressure. Do not disassemble any portion of the system (hoses, compressor, line fittings, etc.) without having the system depressurized by a dealer or competent repair facility. Refrigerant can cause skin or eye injury on contact, and forms a toxic gas in the presence of a naked flame or lighted cigarette.*

1   Remove the front grille cover (Chapter 11).
2   Inspect the condenser fins and brush away leaves and bugs and check the evaporator and electric fan wiring connectors (photo).
3   Check the condition of the system hoses. If there is any sign of deterioration or hardening, have them replaced by a dealer or air conditioning repair facility.
4   At the recommended intervals, check and adjust the compressor drivebelt as described in Chapter 1.
5   Because of the special tools, equipment and skills required to service air conditioning systems, and the differences between the various systems that may be installed on vehicles, major air conditioning servicing procedures cannot be covered in this manual.
6   Operate the air conditioning system for a few minutes every month, even if it is not required. This will help keep the system in good order.
7   Have the refrigerant charge checked annually by a Mazda dealer or air conditioning specialist. Operating the air conditioning with too little refrigerant can cause damage.

10.2 Removing the heater fan motor

11.2 The air conditioner fan (A), condenser (B) and evaporator (C)

Chapter 4 Fuel and exhaust systems

Contents

Specifications

Carburetor specifications

Type . . . . Downdraft, two barrel
Barrel diameters
    Primary . . . . 1.18 in (30 mm)
    Secondary . . . . 1.34 in (34 mm)
Venturi diameters
    Primary . . . . 0.925 x 0.590 x 0.315 in (23.5 x 15 x 8 mm)
    Secondary . . . . 1.142 x 0.551 x 0.276 in (29 x 14 x 7 mm)
Main nozzle
    Primary . . . . 0.083 in (2.1 mm)
    Secondary . . . . 0.110 in (2.8 mm)
Main jet
    Primary, manual transaxle . . . . 0.0429 in (1.09 mm)
    Primary, automatic transaxle . . . . 0.0425 in (1.08 mm)
    Secondary . . . . 0.0590 in (1.50 mm)
Main air bleed
    Primary, manual transaxle . . . . 0.0236 in (0.60 mm)
    Primary, automatic transaxle . . . . 0.315 in (0.80 mm)
    Secondary . . . . 0.0197 in (0.50 mm)
Slow running jet
    Primary . . . . 0.0181 in (0.46 mm)
    Secondary . . . . 0.0394 in (1.00 mm)
Slow air bleed
    Primary, No. 1 . . . . 0.0315 in (0.80 mm)
    Primary, No. 2 . . . . 0.0748 in (1.90 mm)
    Secondary, No. 1 . . . . 0.0394 in (1.00 mm)
    Secondary, No. 2 . . . . 0.0197 in (0.50 mm)
Fast idle adjustment (see text) . . . . 0.059 in (1.49 mm)
Float height adjustment (see text)
    Maximum flow position (L) . . . . 1.929 in (49 mm)
    No flow position (H) . . . . 0.394 in (10 mm)

1   General information

The fuel system consists of a rear mounted fuel tank, a mechanically operated fuel pump, a carburetor and an air cleaner assembly.

The exhaust system includes a muffler, catalytic converter, (US models) related emissions equipment and associated pipes and hardware.

2   Fuel pump — check

Warning: *Gasoline is extremely flammable, so extra precautions must be taken when working on any part of the fuel system. Do not smoke or allow open flames or bare light bulbs near the work area. Also, do not work in a garage if a natural gas-type appliance with a pilot light is present.*

1   The fuel pump bolts to the cylinder head on the back (firewall side) of the engine.
2   The fuel pump is sealed and no repairs are possible. However, it can be inspected and tested on the vehicle as follows.
3   Make sure that there is fuel in the fuel tank.
4   With the engine running, check for leaks at all gasoline line connections between the fuel tank and the carburetor. Tighten any loose connections.
5   Inspect all hoses for flat spots and kinks which would restrict the fuel flow. Air leaks or restrictions on the suction side of the fuel pump will greatly affect pump output.
6   Check for leaks at the fuel pump diaphragm flange.
7   Disconnect the ignition coil wire at the distributor, carefully ground the wire to the engine to prevent sparks, then disconnect the fuel inlet line from the carburetor and place it in a container.
8   Crank the engine a few revolutions and make sure that well defined spurts of fuel are ejected from the open end of the line. If not, the fuel line or filter is clogged or the fuel pump is defective.
9   Disconnect the fuel line at both ends and blow through it with compressed air. If the fuel line is not clogged, replace the fuel pump with a new one.

3   Fuel pump — removal and installation

Warning: *Gasoline is extremely flammable, so extra precautions must be taken when working on any part of the fuel system. Do not smoke or allow open flames or bare light bulbs near the work area. Also, do not work in a garage if a natural gas-type appliance with a pilot light is present.*

1   Disconnect the cable from the negative battery terminal.
2   Use pliers to release the clips and then remove and plug the fuel inlet and outlet hoses (photo). Also remove and plug the fuel return hose.
3   Remove the fuel pump mounting bolts, the pump, spacer and gaskets.
4   Install the pump using a new gasket on each side of the spacer.
5   Connect the fuel lines, start the engine and check for leaks.

4   Fuel line — repair and replacement

Warning: *Gasoline is extremely flammable, so extra precautions must be taken when working on any part of the fuel system. Do not smoke or allow open flames or bare light bulbs near the work area. Also, do not work in a garage if a natural gas-type appliance with a pilot light is present.*

1   If a section of metal fuel line must be replaced, only seamless steel tubing should be used, since copper or aluminum does not have enough durability to withstand normal operating vibrations.
2   If only one section of a metal fuel line is damaged, it can be cut out and replaced with a piece of rubber hose. Be sure to use only reinforced fuel resistant hose, identified by the word ''Fluroelastomer'' on the hose. The inside diameter of the hose should match the outside diameter of the metal line. The rubber hose should be cut four inches longer than the section it's replacing, so there are two inches

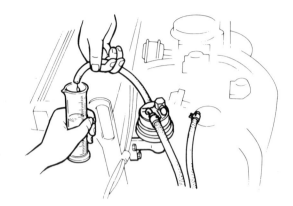

Fig. 4.1   Testing the fuel pump (Sec 2)

3.2   A bolt can be used to plug the fuel hose

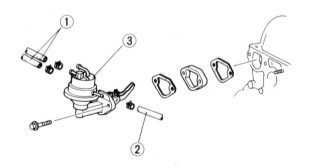

Fig. 4.2   Fuel pump installation details (Sec 3)

1   Fuel inlet and return hoses
2   Fuel outlet hose
3   Fuel pump

of overlap between the rubber and metal line at either end of the section. Hose clamps should be used to secure both ends of the repaired section.

3   If a section of metal line longer than six inches is being removed, use a combination of metal tubing and rubber hose so the hose lengths will be no longer than 10 inches.

4   Never use rubber hose within four inches of any part of the exhaust system or within 10 inches of the catalytic converter.

5   Fuel tank — removal and installation

Warning: *Gasoline is extremely flammable, so extra precautions must be taken when working on any part of the fuel system. Do not smoke or allow open flames or bare light bulbs near the work area. Also, do not work in a garage if a natural gas-type appliance with a pilot light is present. While performing any work on the fuel tank it is advisable to have a CO_2 fire extinguisher on hand and to wear safety glasses.*

1   Raise the rear of the vehicle and support it on jackstands.
2   Remove the cable from the negative battery terminal.
3   Drain all fuel from the tank into a clean container.
4   Remove the rear seat and the access panel and disconnect the fuel gauge unit wire.
5   Mark and disconnect the fuel lines and the filler pipe at the fuel tank.
6   While the tank is supported by an assistant or a floor jack, remove the five retaining bolts.
7   Carefully lower the tank and remove it from the vehicle.
8   **Warning:** *Never perform any repair work involving heat or flame on the tank until it has been purged of gas and vapors. All repair work should be performed by a professional (see the following Section).*
9   Before reinstalling the tank make sure that all traces of dirt and corrosion are cleaned from it. A coat of rust preventative paint is recommended. If the tank is rusted internally, however, it should be replaced with a new one.
10 Installation is the reverse of the removal procedure.

6   Fuel tank — repair

1   Any repairs to the fuel tank or filler neck should be carried out by a professional who has experience in this critical and potentially dangerous work. Even after cleaning and flushing of the fuel system, explosive fumes can remain and ignite during repair of the tank.
2   If the fuel tank is removed from the vehicle, it should not be placed in an area where sparks or open flames could ignite the fumes coming

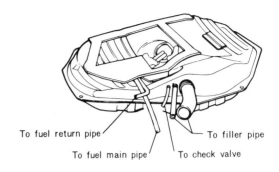

To fuel return pipe — To filler pipe
To fuel main pipe — To check valve

Fig. 4.3   Fuel tank connections (Sec 5)

from the tank. Be especially careful inside garages where a natural gas-type appliance is located, because the pilot light could cause an explosion.

7   Carburetor — removal and installation

Warning: *Gasoline is extremely flammable, so extra precautions must be taken when working on any part of the fuel system. Do not smoke or allow open flames or bare light bulbs near the work area. Also, do not work in a garage if a natural gas type appliance with a pilot light is present.*

1   Remove the cable from the negative battery terminal.
2   Remove the air cleaner assembly. (The procedure is shown in Chapter 2, Part A, Section 23.)
3   Disconnect the throttle linkage and (if equipped) cruise control cables (photos).
4   Disconnect the fuel lines.
5   Unplug the electrical harness.
6   Disconnect the choke cable (manual choke models) — see Section 11.
7   Disconnect the vacuum lines from the carburetor, noting their locations.
8   Remove the mounting nuts, lift the carburetor sufficiently to allow disconnection of the choke heater wire (automatic choke only) and remove the carburetor from the manifold.

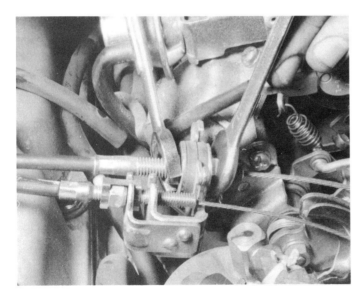

7.3a   Using two wrenches to loosen the throttle cable retaining nuts

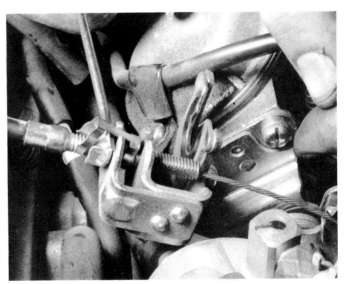

7.3b   Removing the cruise control cable spring clip

7.9   Insert a screwdriver blade under the carburetor spacer to break the gasket seal

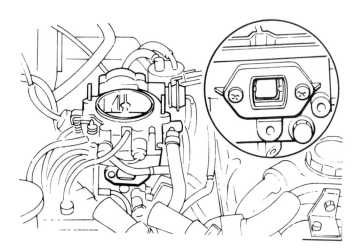

Fig. 4.4   The carburetor fuel level can be checked at the sight glass (Sec 7)

9   Remove the spacer or gasket from the manifold, using a screwdriver to break the seal (photo).
10 Installation is the reverse of the removal procedure, but the following points should be noted:
    a) By filling the carburetor bowl with fuel, the initial start-up will be easier and less drain on the battery.
    b) New gaskets should be used on both sides of the spacer.
    c) After installation, start the engine, check for leaks and make sure fuel level is even with the mark on the carburetor sight glass. If it is not, adjust the float level as described in Section 8.
    d) Idle speed and mixture settings should be checked and, if necessary, adjusted.

8   Carburetor — overhaul and adjustment

Note: *Carburetor overhaul is an involved procedure that requires some experience. The home mechanic without much experience should have the overhaul done by a dealer service department or repair shop. Because of running production changes, some details of the unit overhauled here may not exactly match those of your carburetor, although the home mechanic with previous experience should be able to detect the differences and modify the procedure.*

Check the price and availability of spare parts before starting work. A replacement carburetor may prove more satisfactory than attempting to overhaul a well worn unit.

Disassembly
1   Clean the exterior of the carburetor with solvent and dry it. Place the carburetor on a clean, well-lit workbench. Have plenty of small containers and labelling equipment handy.
2   Study the throttle, choke and accelerator pump linkages carefully. Make sketches or notes if they differ from those shown (photos).
3   Disconnect the accelerator pump lever from the throttle linkage. Unhook the lever spring.
4   Disconnect the vacuum break hose from the stub on the throttle body (photo).
5   Unhook the fast idle connecting rod from the choke shaft lever.

8.2a   View of carburetor from throttle linkage side

8.2b   View of carburetor from dashpot side. Accelerator pump lever is arrowed

8.2c View of carburetor from fuel inlet side

8.4 Disconnect the vacuum break hose (arrowed)

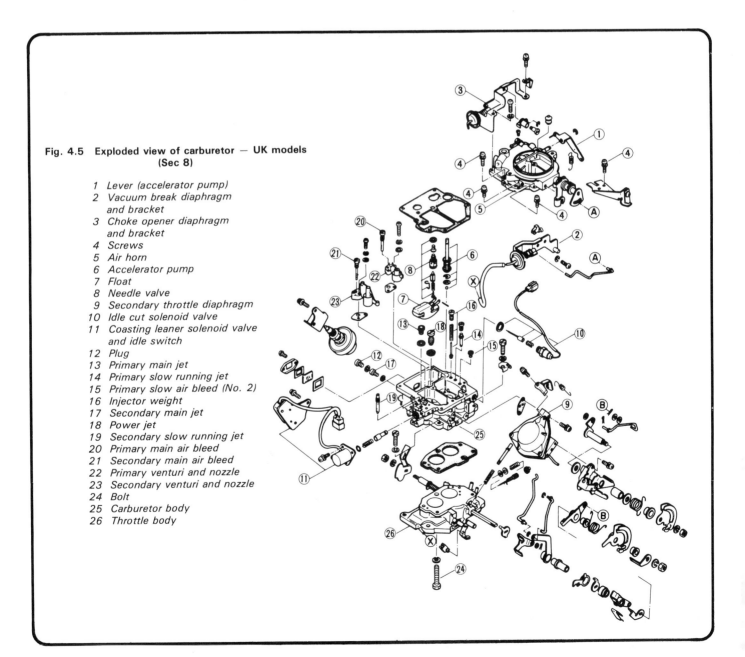

Fig. 4.5 Exploded view of carburetor — UK models
(Sec 8)

1 Lever (accelerator pump)
2 Vacuum break diaphragm
and bracket
3 Choke opener diaphragm
and bracket
4 Screws
5 Air horn
6 Accelerator pump
7 Float
8 Needle valve
9 Secondary throttle diaphragm
10 Idle cut solenoid valve
11 Coasting leaner solenoid valve
and idle switch
12 Plug
13 Primary main jet
14 Primary slow running jet
15 Primary slow air bleed (No. 2)
16 Injector weight
17 Secondary main jet
18 Power jet
19 Secondary slow running jet
20 Primary main air bleed
21 Primary main air bleed
22 Primary venturi and nozzle
23 Secondary venturi and nozzle
24 Bolt
25 Carburetor body
26 Throttle body

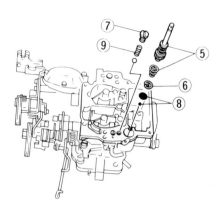

Fig. 4.6 Carburetor main body accelerating pump components (Sec 8)

5 Accelerating pump plunger assembly
6 Retaining clip
7 Check valve plug
8 Strainer and accelerating pump inlet check ball
9 Accelerating pump outlet ball and spring

8.6 Eight screws (arrowed) securing the air horn to the carburetor body

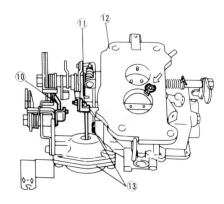

Fig. 4.7 Carburetor main body throttle link (10), vacuum diaphragm connecting rod (11), throttle body (12) and diaphragm assembly (13) (Sec 8)
Arrow shows throttle body retaining screw

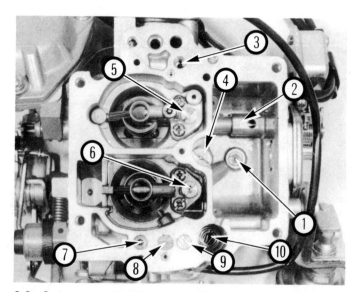

8.8 Carburetor body with air horn removed

1 Primary main jet
2 Secondary main jet (in tube)
3 Secondary slow running jet
4 Power jet
5 Secondary main air bleed
6 Primary main air bleed
7 Primary slow air bleed (No. 2)
8 Primary slow running jet
9 Injector weight
10 Accelerator pump spring

6   Remove the eight screws which secure the air horn to the carburetor body (photo). The screws are not all the same length: note their locations.
7   Lift off the air horn, freeing the wiring harness and any other obstacles. Recover the gasket. The accelerator pump piston may come out with the air horn.
8   The float bowl can now be cleaned out, and the various jets and bleeds removed for cleaning (photo).
9   The float and needle valve can be removed from the air horn by extracting the float pivot pin (photo). The needle valve seat can then be unscrewed.

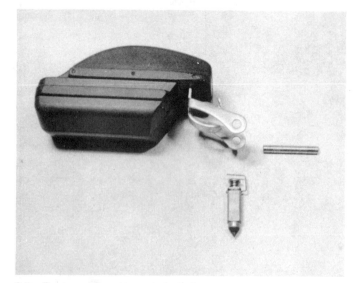

8.9 Float, needle valve and pivot pin

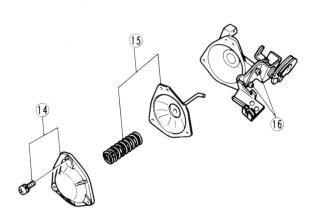

Fig. 4.8   Vacuum diaphragm components (Sec 8)

14   Cover and screws   *16   Throttle lever*
15   Spring and diaphragm

8..10   Removing the idle cut solenoid valve. Spring and plunger (arrowed) have stayed in body

10 To remove the idle cut solenoid valve, unscrew it from the car-buretor body. Recover the spring and plunger (photo.)
11 Remove the dashpot, the coasting leaner valve and the idle switch (when so equipped). Refer to Chapter 6 if necessary.
12 The secondary throttle diaphragm and choke vacuum units may be removed with their brackets if necessary. The throttle diaphragm unit may be dismantled for inspection, but individual spares are unlikely to be available.
13 If it is wished to separate the throttle body form the carburetor body, note that one of the securing screws is accessed from below, next to the secondary throttle plate.
14 Remove the idle mixture adjustment screw, counting the number of turns to give a rough setting when installing.

Cleaning and inspection

15 Wash all components in clean solvent and blow them dry with com-pressed air. A can of compressed air can be used if an air compressor is not available. Do not use a piece of wire for cleaning the jets and passages.
16 The idle cut solenoid, diaphragms and other electrical, rubber and plastic parts should not be immersed in carburetor cleaner because they will harden, swell or distort.
17 Make sure all fuel passages, jets and other metering components are free of burrs and dirt.
18 Inspect the upper and lower surfaces of the air horn, main body and throttle body for damage. Be sure all material has been removed.
19 Inspect all lever holes and plastic bushings for excessive wear and an out of round condition and replace them if necessary.
20 Inspect the float needle and seat for dirt, deep wear grooves and scoring and replace it if necessary.
21 Inspect the float, float arms and hinge pin for distortion and binding and correct or replace as necessary.
22 Inspect the rubber cup on the accelerating pump plunger for exces-sive wear and cracks.
23 Inspect the mixture adjustment screw for burrs or ridges.
24 Check the choke valve and linkage for excessive wear, binding and distortion and correct or replace as necessary.
25 Inspect the choke vacuum diaphragm for leaks and replace if necessary.
26 Check the choke valve for freedom of movement.
27 Check the solenoid operation by connecting the solenoid to the positive battery terminal with the body grounded. With the battery cur-rent applied to the solenoid, the valve stem should withdraw into the valve body. If it does not, replace the solenoid with a new one.
28 The choke opener diaphragm vacuum feed is controlled by a thermo-valve which is screwed into the intake manifold (photo). The valve should not pass air below 65 °F (19 °C), but should pass it freely above this temperature. (The tolerance for the operating temperature is ± 9 °F/3 °C.) Remove the valve for testing if wished as shown in Fig. 4.10.

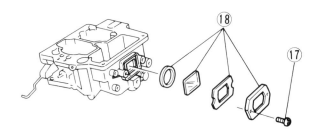

Fig. 4.9   Carburetor main body fuel bowl sight glass assembly (Sec 8)

17   Screws   *18   Cover, gasket, glass and rubber gasket*

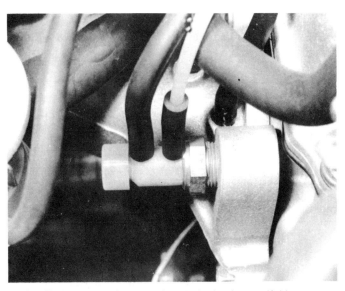

8.28   Choke opener thermo-valve on the intake manifold

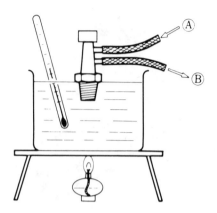

Fig. 4.10   Testing the choke opener thermo-valve (Sec 8)

A   Air in   B   Air out

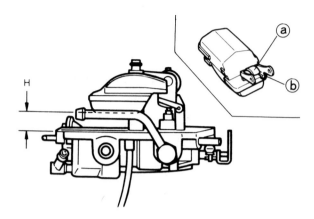

Fig. 4.11   Carburetor dry float measurement and
adjustment procedure (with body inverted) (Sec 8)

H   Clearance   a   Float tip seal
                              b   Float stopper

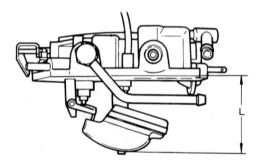

Fig. 4.12   Carburetor dry float measurement and
adjustment procedure (with air horn upright) (Sec 8)

8.30   Using a drill shank to measure float height

Assembly

29   Carburetor reassembly is basically a reversal of disassembly with
attention paid to the following points:

    a)   Use all new gaskets.

    b)   Install the mixture adjustment screw the same number of turns
        recorded during removal.

    c)   As reassembly proceeds, carry out the adjustments detailed
        in the following paragraphs.

Adjustment

Air horn dry float height

30   Prior to installation of the air horn, the float level must be measured
(without the gasket) and adjusted as follows.

    a)   With the air horn inverted, allow the float to lower by its own
        weight and measure the clearance between the float and air
        horn (photo). Compare the measurement (H in the accompany-
        ing illustration) to Specifications and bend the float tip seal
        as necessary.

    b)   Turn the air horn upright, allow the float to lower and measure
        the distance between the bottom of the float and the air horn.
        If the clearance (L in the accompanying illustration) is not as
        specified, bend the float stopper to adjust.

Choke opener diaphragm

31   Apply a vacuum of approximately 15.7 in-Hg to the choke opener
diaphragm vacuum tube. Push the choke valve lightly to close it and
measure the clearance.

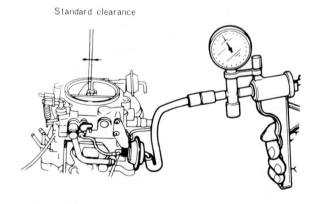

Fig. 4.13   Checking the choke opener diaphragm clearance
(Sec 8)

Standard clearance = 0.155 ± 0.006 in (3.94 ± 0.16 mm)

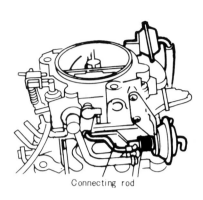

Fig. 4.14   Adjust the choke opener diaphragm clearance by bending the connecting rod (Sec 8)

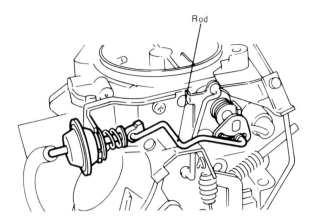

Fig 4.15   Vacuum break diaphragm connecting rod (Sec 8)

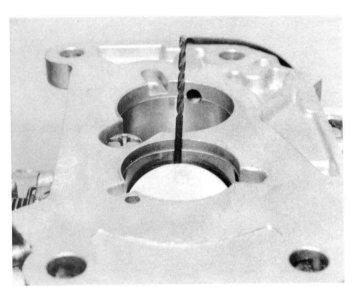

8.33   Fast idle adjustment — measuring the primary throttle valve clearance

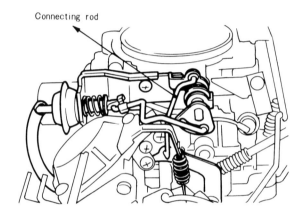

Fig. 4.16   Fast idle connecting rod (Sec 8)

Vacuum break diaphragm

32   Test as described for the choke opener diaphragm, but this time the desired choke valve clearance is 0.076 ± 0.01 in (1.94 ± 0.25 mm). Bend the connecting rod (Fig. 4.15) if necessary to adjust.

Fast idle adjustment

33   Close the choke valve fully and measure the clearance between the primary throttle valve and the barrel, using a drill shank or gauge rod (photo). The desired clearance is given in the Specifications. Adjust if necessary by bending the fast idle connecting rod.

Throttle interlock

34   Check that the secondary throttle valve is not free to open until the primary throttle valve has opened 45°. (At this angle, the clearance between the primary throttle valve and the barrel is 0.264 ± 0.020 in [6.7 ± 0.5 mm].) Also check that the secondary throttle valve is free to open fully when the primary throttle valve is fully open. Adjust if necessary by bending the interlock arm (Fig. 4.17). **Note:** *The secondary throttle plate will have to be opened manually, since it is normally opened by vacuum and not mechanically.*

Idle speed and mixture

35   Install the carburetor (Section 7), warm up the engine and adjust the idle speed and mixture (Chapter 1). Install new tamperproof caps where required on completion.

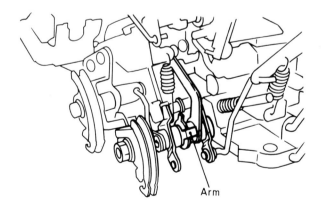

Fig 4.17   Throttle interlock arm (Sec 8)

9   Exhaust system components — removal and installation

Warning: *The vehicle's exhaust system generates very high temperatures and should be allowed to cool completely before any of*

the components are touched. Be especially careful around the catalytic converter, where the highest temperatures are generated.

1   Raise the vehicle and support it securely on jackstands.
2   Replacement of exhaust system components is basically a matter of removing the heat shields (when equipped), disconnecting the component and installing a new one.
3   The heat shields and exhaust system hangers must be reinstalled in the original locations or damage could result. Due to the high temperatures and exposed locations of the exhaust system components, rust and corrosion can ''freeze'' parts together. Penetrating oils are available to help loosen frozen fasteners. However, in some cases it may be necessary to cut the pieces apart with a hacksaw or cutting torch. The latter method should be employed only by persons experienced in this work.

10   Idle up system — checking and adjustment

1   The idle up system used on some models increases engine speed to compensate for the load placed on the engine by the air conditioner and/or power steering. The system consists of servo diaphragms (which differ according to whether the vehicle has air conditioning and power steering or just air conditioning) and a three way solenoid valve. A symptom of a fault in the idle up system is stalling of the engine at low speeds when the air conditioner and/or power steering are actuated.

Servo diaphragm

2   Remove the air cleaner assembly.
3   Turn off all accessories and disconnect the electric cooling fan.
4   Disconnect and plug the hoses of the idle compensator, reed valves and thermo sensor.
5   Warm the engine to normal operating temperature and connect a tachometer.

Models equipped with air conditioning
6   Disconnect the vacuum sensing tube (B in the accompanying illustration).
7   Apply manifold vacuum to the servo diaphragm and check that the engine idle increases to between 1200 and 1400 rpm. If the increase is not as specified, turn the adjustment screw to adjust.

Models equipped with power steering
8   Perform Steps 2 through 4. On models also equipped with air conditioning, check and adjust the servo diaphragm.
9   Disconnect the vacuum sensing tube (A in the accompanying diagram) and apply manifold vacuum to the servo diaphragm.
10   The engine speed should increase to between 800 and 1000 rpm on manual transaxle models and 1050 to 1250 rpm on automatic transaxle models. If the rpm increase is not within specification, disconnect

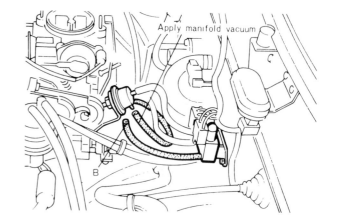

Fig. 4.18   Idle up system checking (models with air conditioning) (Sec 10)

B   Vacuum sensing tube

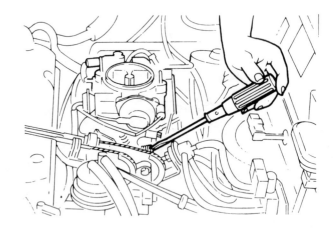

Fig. 4.19   Idle up servo adjustment (air conditioned models) (Sec 10)

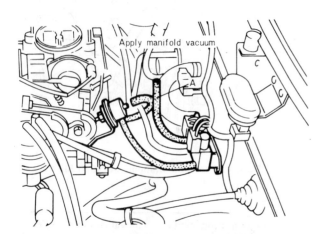

Fig. 4.20   Power steering equipped model idle up system servo diaphragm check (Sec 10)

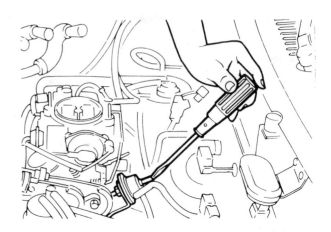

Fig. 4.21   Idle up system servo diaphragm adjustment (power steering equipped models) (Sec 10)

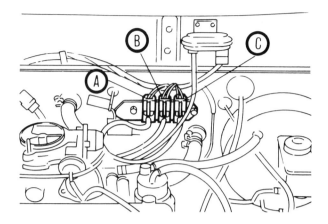

Fig. 4.22 Three-way solenoid valve locations (Sec 10)

   A Power steering   C Air conditioner
   B No. 2 ACV

Fig. 4.23 The servo diaphragm stem (arrow) should move
if the 3-way solenoid valve is operating properly (Sec 10)

the vacuum tube and rotate the adjusting screw on the diaphragm to
adjust.
11 Reconnect the vacuum tube and recheck the engine speed.

Three way solenoid valve

12 The three way solenoid valve is connected between intake manifold
and servo diaphragm. On air conditioned models the three way solenoid
valve restricts the vacuum flow in accordance with the signal sent
through the control unit from the air conditioning switch. The three
way solenoid valve on power steering equipped models restricts the
vacuum flow according to the signal from the power steering switch.
13 With the engine idling, turn on the air conditioning and check that
the servo diaphragm raises, indicating the three way solenoid is operating properly.
14 Turn the air conditioning off and turn the steering wheel full lock
to the right or left and check that the servo diaphragm raises, indicating
that the three way solenoid and power steering switch are operating
properly.

Power steering switch

15 Unplug the power steering switch connector and check for continuity as shown in the accompanying illustration. With the engine idling
turn the steering wheel full lock to the right or left to make sure there
is continuity.

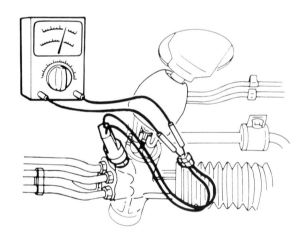

Fig. 4.24 Power steering switch continuity check (Sec 10)

---

11 Choke cable — removal, installation and adjustment

1   Disconnect the battery negative lead.
2   Remove the air cleaner assembly.
3   Disconnect the choke cable from the carburetor by slackening the
clamp screw, withdrawing the outer cable from the clamp and unhooking the inner cable (photo).
4   Working inside the vehicle, undo the ring nut which secures the
choke control to the instrument panel (photo). Turn the control knob
through 180° and remove the grub screw which secures the knob.
5   Extract the control from the instrument panel. Remove the screw
which secures the warning light switch and separate the switch from
the control (photo).
6   Free the cable from the firewall grommet and draw it into the
vehicle.
7   Installation is a reversal of removal. Adjust the position of the outer
cable in its clamp so that with the control knob pushed home, there
is a small amount of slack in the inner cable.
8   Have an assistant operate the control through its full range and
check that the choke valve plate opens and closes fully.
9   Install the air cleaner and reconnect the battery. Check the choke
warning light for correct operation.

11.3   Choke cable clamp screw (A) and inner cable nipple (B)

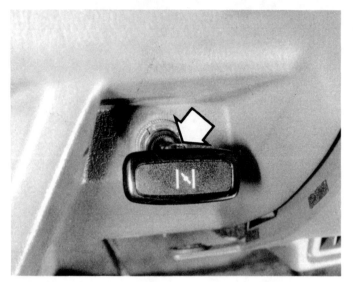

11.4 Choke control, showing ring nut and (arrowed) knob grub screw

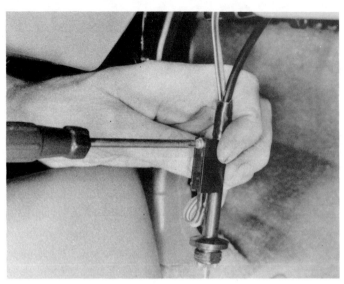

11.5 Removing the choke warning light switch

Chapter 5   Engine electrical systems

Contents

Specifications

Alternator

Rated output	12 V, 65 A
Regulated voltage	14.7 ±0.3
Brush length	
New	0.71 in (18 mm)
Wear limit	0.32 in (8 mm)
Rated resistance	3 to 4 ohms

Starter motor

Brush length wear limit	0.45 in (11.5 mm)
Pinion gap	0.02 to 0.08 in (0.5 to 2.0 mm)

Ignition coil

Primary coil resistance	1.15 ±0.12 ohms
Secondary coil resistance	10 to 30 k-ohms
Primary terminal-to-case resistance	Over 10 M-ohms

Torque specifications

	Ft-lbs	M-Kg
Alternator through-bolt	27 to 46	3.8 to 6.4
Starter motor bolt	27 to 46	3.8 to 6.4

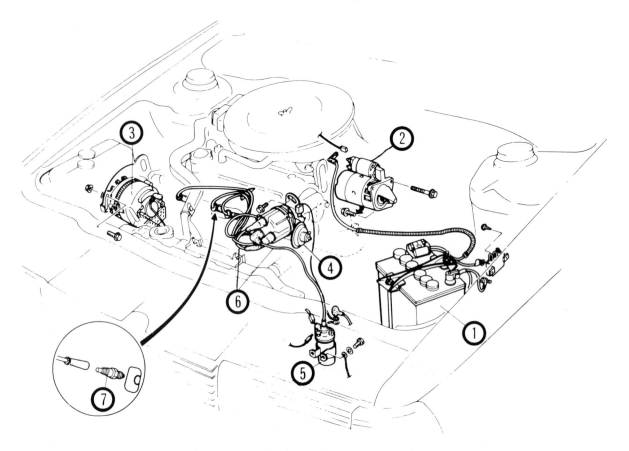

Fig. 5.1   Engine electrical system components (Sec 1)

1 Battery
2 Starter motor
3 Alternator

4 Distributor
5 Ignition coil

6 Spark plug wires
7 Spark plug

1 Ignition system — general information and precautions

The ignition system is composed of the battery, distributor, coil, ignition switch, spark plugs and the primary (low tension) and secondary (high tension) wiring circuits.

This system uses a magnetic pick up assembly located inside the distributor, which contains a rotor, a pick up coil, centrifugal advance mechanism, vacuum control unit and breaker assembly. The breaker assembly is an electronic unit; there are no contact breaker points to wear or replace.

Warning: *Because of the very high voltage generated by this system, extreme care should be taken whenever an operation involving ignition components is performed. This not only includes the distributor, coil and spark plug wires, but related items that are connected to the systems as well, such as the plug connections, tachometer, and testing equipment. Consequently, before any work is performed, the ignition should be turned off and the negative battery cable disconnected.*

2 Battery — removal and installation

1   The battery is located at the front of the engine compartment. It is held in place by a hold-down brace across the top of the case.
2   Hydrogen gas is produced by the battery, so keep open flames and lighted cigarettes away from it at all times.
3   Always keep the battery in an upright position. Spilled electrolyte should be rinsed off immediately with large quantities of water. Always wear eye protection when working around the battery.
4   Always disconnect the negative (–) battery cable first, followed by the positive (+) cable (photo).

5   After the cables are disconnected from the battery, remove the nuts and the hold-down brace.
6   Carefully lift the battery out of the engine compartment.
7   Installation is the reverse of removal. The cable and brace nuts

2.4   Hold the negative cable steady when loosening the nut as the battery post can be easily damaged

should be tight, but do not overtighten them as damage to the battery case can occur. The battery posts and cable ends should be cleaned prior to connection (Chapter 1).

3 Battery — emergency jump starting

Refer to the booster battery (jump) starting procedure at the front of this manual.

4 Battery cables — check and replacement

1   Periodically inspect the entire length of each battery cable for damage, cracked or burned insulation and corrosion. Poor battery cable connections can cause starting problems and decreased engine performance.
2   Check the cable-to-terminal connections at the ends of the cables for cracks, loose wire strands and corrosion. The presence of white, fluffy deposits under the insulation at the cable terminal connection is a sign the cable is corroded and should be replaced. Check the terminals for distortion, missing mounting bolts or nuts and corrosion.
3   If only the positive cable is to be replaced, be sure to disconnect the negative cable from the battery first.
4   Disconnect and remove the cable from the vehicle. Make sure the replacement cable is the same length and diameter.
5   Clean the threads of the starter or ground connection with a wire brush to remove rust and corrosion. Apply a light coat of petroleum jelly to the threads to ease installation and prevent future corrosion. Inspect the connections frequently to make sure they are clean and tight.
6   Attach the cable to the starter or ground connection and tighten the mounting nut securely.
7   Before connecting the new cables to the battery, make sure they reach the terminals without having to be stretched.
8   Connect the positive cable first, followed by the negative cable. Tighten the nuts and apply a thin coat of petroleum jelly to the terminal and cable connection.

5 Ignition system — check

Warning: *Because of the very high voltage generated by the ignition system, extreme care should be taken whenever an operation is performed involving ignition components. This not only includes the distributor, coil and spark plug wires, but related items that are con-*

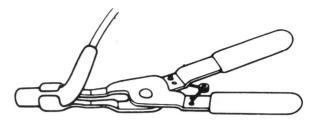

Fig. 5.2 Use an insulated tool to hold the spark plug or coil wire while testing (Sec 5)

nected to the system as well, such as the plug connections, tachometer and any test equipment. Consequently, before any work is performed, the ignition should be turned off or the battery ground cable disconnected.

1   If the engine turns over but will not start, remove the spark plug wire from a spark plug and, using an insulated tool, hold the wire about 1/4-inch from a good ground and have an assistant crank the engine.
2   If there is no spark, check another wire in the same manner. A few sparks, then no spark, should be considered as no spark.
3   If there is good spark, check the spark plugs (refer to Chapter 1) and/or the fuel system (refer to Troubleshooting).
4   If there is a weak spark or no spark, unplug the coil lead from the distributor, hold it about 1/4-inch from a good ground and check for spark as described above.
5   If there is no spark, check the coil (Section 9).
6   If there is a spark, check the distributor cap and/or rotor (refer to Chapter 1).
7   Further checks of the ignition system must be done by a dealer or repair shop.

6 Distributor — removal and installation

Removal
1   Disconnect the battery negative cable.
2   Disconnect the coil positive terminal wire.
3   Remove the two retaining screws and lift off the distributor cap.
4   Use a wrench on the crankshaft pulley bolt to rotate the engine until No. 1 piston is at TDC on the compression stroke (photos). Full details are given in Chapter 1, Section 37.

6.4a Crankshaft pulley notch in TDC position . . .

6.4b . . . and distributor rotor in No. 1 firing position

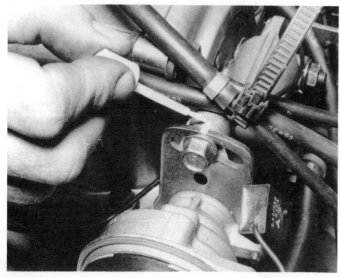

6.5   Marking the distributor-to-engine housing relationship

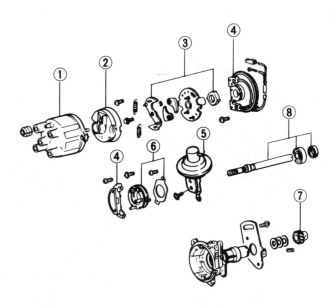

Fig. 5.3   Distributor component layout (Sec 6 through 8)

1 Cap	5 Vacuum control unit
2 Rotor	6 Breaker assembly
3 Advance mechanism	7 Driven gear
4 Pickup coil	8 Shaft

5   Mark the distributor flange to engine rear housing relationship for reference (photo).
6   Disconnect the vacuum advance hoses, remove retaining bolt and lift the distributor from the engine.

Installation if the crankshaft was not turned after distributor removal

7   Lubricate the O-ring with clean engine oil.
8   Insert the distributor into the engine rear housing with the rotor in the No. 1 firing position, align the marks made during removal and install the retaining bolt.
9   Connect the vacuum hoses and the coil wire.
10   Install the distributor cap and reconnect the battery cable.
11   Check the ignition timing (Chapter 1, Section 34).

Installation if the crankshaft was turned after distributor removal

12   Remove the number one spark plug and place your finger over the spark plug hole while turning the crankshaft with a wrench on the pulley bolt at the front of the engine. When you feel compression, continue turning the crankshaft slowly until the timing mark on the crankshaft pulley is aligned with the T on the engine timing indicator.
13   Complete the installation by referring to Steps 7 through 11.

---

7   Distributor rotor — replacement

1   Disconnect the negative battery cable.
2   Remove the distributor cap.
3   Remove the retaining screws and lift off the distributor rotor.
4   Installation is the reverse of removal.

---

8   Distributor — dismantling and reassembly

Disassembly

1   Remove the distributor (Section 6).
2   Remove the mounting tab plate from the distributor housing.
3   Mount the distributor in a vise, using a cloth to protect the surface.
4   Remove the two screws and lift off the rotor.
5   Noting their positions for ease of reassembly, remove the two advance springs (photo).
6   Remove the retaining bolt and lift the advance mechanism from the shaft (photo).
7   Remove the two screws and lift the pick up coil.

8   Use a small screwdriver to disengage the module from the pick up coil (photos)
9   Remove the two screws and extract the vacuum diaphragm assembly from the housing.
10   Remove the securing screws and lift out the breaker assembly.
11   The driven gear may be removed after driving out the roll pin. Remove the washers.
12   The distributor shaft, bearing and oil seal may now be withdrawn from the body.

Reassembly

13   Lubricate the distributor shaft with lithium grease.
14   Install the shaft, bearing and oil seal.
15   Install the washers and the driven gear. Use enough washers so that the gear has as little play as possible, without being tight. Secure the gear with a new roll pin.
16   Install the breaker assembly and secure it with the screws.
17   Insert the arm of the vacuum control unit into the distributor housing and latch it onto the mechanism in the housing base, turning the mechanism to lock the assembly in place (photos).
18   Install the pickup coil and module, making sure it locks onto the mounting tabs before tightening the screws.
19   Install the advance mechanism and reconnect the springs.
20   Install the rotor and distributor cap.

---

9   Ignition coil — testing

1   Remove the boot and disconnect the coil wires.
2   Connect an ohmmeter as shown in the accompanying illustration to check the primary circuit.
3   If the coil primary circuit is operating properly there will be continuity.
4   Measure the resistance of the coil secondary resistance with an ohmmeter as shown in the accompanying illustration and compare the reading to Specifications.
5   Measure the insulation resistance between the primary terminal and the case with a multimeter as shown in the accompanying illustration.
6   Replace the ignition coil with a new one if it fails any of the tests.

8.5   Disconnect the advance mechanism springs (arrow)

8.6   Removing the distributor advance mechanism

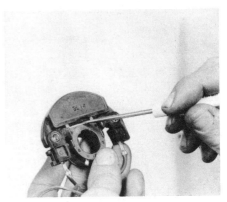

8.8a   Pry the module carefully away from the pickup coil with a small screwdriver

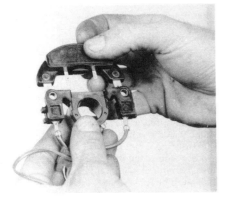

8.8b   Lift the module away from the pickup coil

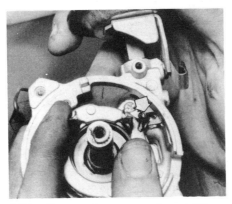

8.17a   Connect the vacuum advance arm

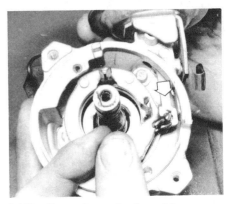

8.17b   Rotate the mechanism while engaging the arm (arrow)

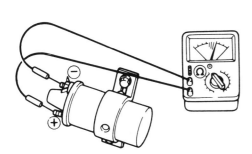

Fig. 5.4   Testing the ignition coil primary circuit (Sec 9)

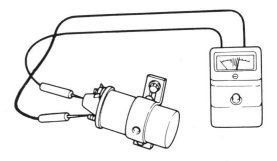

Fig. 5.5   Testing the secondary coil resistance (Sec 9)

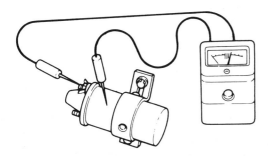

Fig. 5.6   Testing the ignition coil insulation resistance (Sec 9)

10   Ignition coil — removal and installation

Removal

1   Disconnect the battery negative cable.
2   Pull the rubber boot off and noting their positions, disconnect coil wires (photo).
3   Remove the retaining bolts and bracket and lift the coil from the radiator brace.

Installation

4   Place the coil in position, install the bracket and bolts. Tighten the bolts securely.
5   Connect the coil wires and install the boot securely on the top of the coil.

10.2   Ignition coil wire connections (arrows)

11   Charging system — general information and precautions

The charging system is made up of the alternator, voltage regulator and battery. These components work together to supply electrical power for the engine ignition, lights, radio, etc.

The alternator is turned by a drivebelt at the front of the engine. When the engine is operating, voltage is generated by the internal components of the alternator to be sent to the battery for storage.

The purpose of the voltage regulator is to limit the alternator voltage to a preset value. This prevents power surges, circuit overloads, etc., during peak voltage output. On all models with which this manual is concerned, the voltage regulator is contained within the alternator housing.

The charging system requires little periodic maintenance. The battery, drivebelts, electrical wiring and connections should, however, be inspected at the intervals suggested in Chapter 1.

Take extreme care when making circuit connections to a vehicle equipped with an alternator and note the following. When making connections to the alternator from a battery, always match correct polarity. Before using arc welding equipment to repair any part of the vehicle, disconnect the wires from the alternator and the battery terminal. Never start the engine with a battery charger connected. Always disconnect both battery leads before using a battery charger. Do not run the engine with the alternator disconnected, nor disconnect battery leads while the engine is running.

12   Charging system — check

1   If a malfunction occurs in the charging circuit, do not immediately assume that the alternator is causing the problem. First check the following items:
a)   The battery cables where they connect to the battery (make sure the connections are clean and tight).

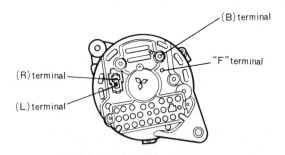

Fig. 5.8   Alternator terminal locations (Sec 12)

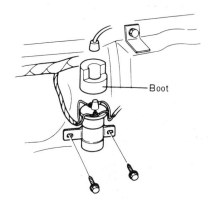

Fig. 5.7   Ignition coil installation details (Sec 10)

b)   The battery electrolyte specific gravity (if it is low, charge the battery).
c)   Check the external alternator wiring and connections (they must be in good condition).
d)   Check the drivebelt condition and tension (see Chapter 1).
e)   Check the alternator mount bolts for tightness.
f)   Run the engine and check the alternator for abnormal noise.

2   Using a voltmeter, check the battery voltage with the engine off at the B terminal. It should be approximately 12 volts. **Caution:** *When checking the alternator, do not ground the L terminal while the engine is running or start the engine with the L and R terminals disconnected.*

3   To check the charging system, make the connections shown in Fig. 5.9. With the ignition off, check the voltage between the alternator L terminal and ground. If the reading is not 0 volts, the alternator is faulty. Turn the ignition On and check the voltage. If the reading is 0 volts, there is a fault in the alternator or wiring. If the voltage is close to battery voltage (12 volts), short circuit between the F terminal and alternator rear bracket and check the voltage. There is a fault in the IC regulator if the voltage drops.

4   To check the no-load adjustment voltage, make sure the battery is fully charged and connect an ammeter and voltmeter as shown in Fig. 5.9. The voltmeter reading should be 0 volts (ignition off).

5   Turn the ignition On and make sure the reading is between 1 and 3 volts lower than the battery voltage. A fault in the alternator is indicated if the voltage reading is the same as battery voltage. Short circuit the

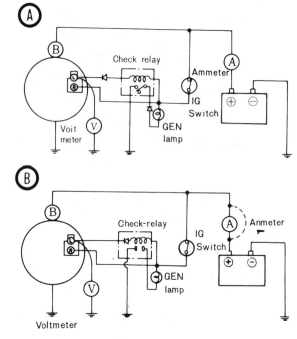

Fig. 5.9   Alternator check connections (Sec 12)

A   System check   B   No load adjustment check

terminals of the ammeter, start the engine and discontinue short circuiting. **Caution:** *When starting the engine, make sure that the starter motor current doesn't flow to the ammeter.*

6   Increase the engine speed to approximately 2500 rpm and check the ammeter and voltmeter readings. The ammeter should read 5A or less and the voltmeter should read 14.7 ± 0.3 V (at 68°F/20°C).

7   To check the alternator output, disconnect the negative battery cable and connect an ammeter and voltmeter as shown in Fig. 5.10.

8   Connect the negative battery cable, start the engine and apply a load by turning on the headlights. Increase the engine speed gradually and check the current output. The system is operating properly if the voltage is higher than battery voltage and there is output current.

13   Alternator — removal and installation

Removal

1   Disconnect the battery negative cable.
2   Remove the adjustment bolt.
3   Unplug the terminal plugs and disconnect the wire harness from the clip.
4   Remove the drivebelt.

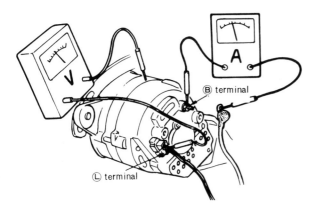

Fig. 5.10   Alternator output check (Sec 12)

5   Remove the through bolt and nut and lift the alternator from the engine.

Installation

6   Place the alternator in position and install the through bolt and nut. Install the adjusting bolt.
7   Install the drivebelt and adjust the tension (Chapter 1).
8   Plug in the alternator connectors.
9   Connect the battery negative cable.

14   Alternator — brush replacement

Note: *A soldering iron, and some skill in its use, will be required for this procedure.*

1   Remove the alternator as described in Section 13.
2   Remove the three screws which hold the two end casings together.

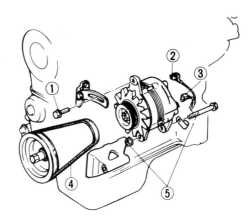

Fig. 5.11   Alternator installation details (Sec 13)

1 Adjustment bolt   4 Drivebelt
2 B terminal connection   5 Through bolt and nut
3 L and R terminal connections

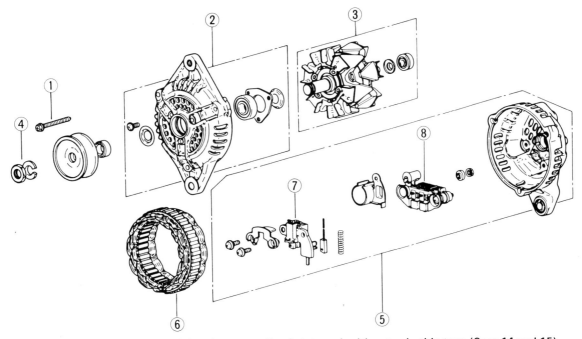

Fig. 5.12   Exploded view of the alternator. Fan is integral with rotor in this type (Secs 14 and 15)

1 Housing screw
2 Drive end housing, bearing and retainer
3 Rotor and slip ring end bearing
4 Pulley nut and washer
5 Slip ring end housing and associated components
6 Stator
7 Voltage regulator/brush carrier
8 Rectifier

3   Apply heat to the slip ring end bearing housing, using a 200 W soldering iron for 3 or 4 minutes, or a hot air blower for a longer period. The aim is to heat the bearing housing to 122° to 144°F (50° to 60°C) without overheating other components.

4   While the bearing housing is still hot, remove the drive end housing and rotor by prying between the drive end housing and the stator laminations. Be careful not to damage the stator windings. Make sure that the slip ring and bearing retainer is not lost. Clean the slip rings with some solvent and a soft rag.

5   Remove the voltage regulator/brush carrier screw (photo). Also remove the ''B'' terminal nut and washer.

6   Unsolder the connecting links from the rectifier to free the voltage regulator/brush carrier (photo). Carry out the unsoldering quickly, so as not to damage the rectifier with excess heat.

7   Remove the voltage regulator/brush carrier unit. Unsolder the old brushes and solder in the new ones (photos). When the new brushes are correctly installed, the wear limit line should project from the brush holder by 0.08 to 0.12 in (2 to 3 mm).

8   Install the voltage regulator/brush carrier and solder in the connecting links. Install the 'B' terminal nut and washer and the securing screw.

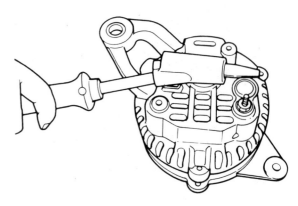

Fig. 5.13   Heating up the slip ring end bearing housing
(Secs 14 and 15)

14.5   Removing the voltage regulator/brush carrier screw

14.6   Unsolder the connecting links (arrowed)

14.7a   Soldering in a new brush

14.7b   Brushes correctly installed

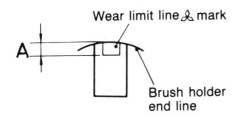

Fig. 5.14 Alternator brush installation dimension (Sec 14)
A = 0.08 to 0.12 in (2 to 3 mm)

9   Carefully raise the brushes, and keep them raised by inserting a thin rod or twist drill through the hole in the slip ring end casing (photo). New brushes have holes in them, through which this rod will pass.
10   Make sure that the slip ring end bearing retainer is still in place in the bearing groove. Heat the bearing housing as was done for removal, and install the rotor and drive end housing.
11   Install the three screws which hold the two end casings together and tighten them.
12   Extract the rod which was used to hold up the brushes (photo).
13   Install the alternator (Section 13).

15 Alternator — overhaul

Note: *If the alternator has seen much service, installation of a replacement unit may be more satisfactory than attempting to overhaul the old unit. Check the availability and cost of spares before proceeding. A soldering iron, and skill in its use, will also be required.*

1   Remove the alternator as described in Section 13.
2   Remove the pulley nut and washer (photo). Clamp an old drivebelt around the pulley to restrain it while the nut is undone.
3   Remove the pulley, fan (if externally mounted), spacer and dished washer (photos). Note the orientation of the dished washer.
4   Remove the three casing securing screws (photo). Heat the slip ring and bearing housing and pull off the drive end housing and rotor, as described in the previous Section.
5   Tap the rotor out of the drive end bearing.
6   Remove the 'B' terminal nut and washer. From inside the slip ring end casing, remove the three screws which secure the rectifier and

14.9   Twist drill (arrowed) used to keep brushes raised

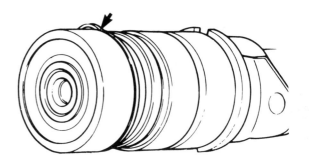

Fig. 5.15 Make sure that the slip ring end bearing retainer (arrowed) is in place (Secs 14 and 15)

14.12   Extract the drill to release the brushes

15.2   Removing the pulley nut and washer

15.3a   Remove the pulley . . .

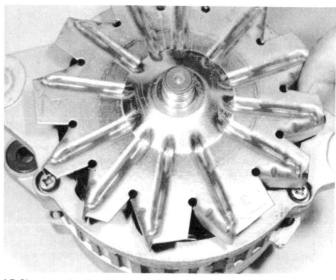

15.3b   . . . the fan (if mounted externally) . . .

15.3c   . . . the spacer . . .

15.3d   . . . and the outer dished washer

15.4   Removing a casing securing screw — the other two screws are arrowed

voltage regulator/brush carrier. Withdraw the stator, rectifier, etc. from the slip ring end casing.

7   If electrical tests are to be made on the stator or rectifier, separate them by unsoldering their leads. Note the arrangement of the leads for installation. Be quick with the soldering iron, so as not to damage the rectifier with excess heat.

8   For brush replacement see Section 14.

9   Use a multi-meter or self-powered 12 volt test lamp to check for continuity between the stator leads. There should be continuity between any pair of leads. Also check for continuity between the stator laminations and each stator lead: there should be no continuity. Replace the stator if it fails these tests, or if it is obviously damaged or burnt.

10   Inspect the rotor for visible damage, paying particular attention to the slip rings (photo). Slight burning may be polished out with fine abrasive paper, followed by solvent and a soft rag. If there is serious damage, the rotor must be replaced.

11   Use the multi-meter or test lamp to check for continuity between the slip rings. If a meter of sufficient accuracy is available, compare the rotor winding resistance with that given in the Specifications. Also check for continuity between each slip ring and the rotor laminations: there should be none. Replace the rotor if it fails these tests.

12   Check the rotor bearings for roughness and shake. Replace them if their condition is doubtful. Make sure that the slip ring end bearing is installed the right way around (with the retainer groove nearest the slip rings).

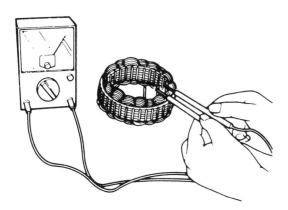

Fig. 5.16   Checking the stator windings for continuity
(Sec 15)

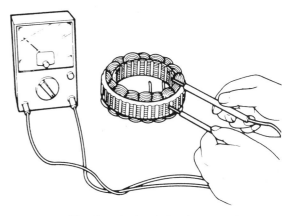

Fig. 5.17   Checking the insulation between the stator
windings and the laminations (Sec 15)

15.10   Check the slip rings (arrowed) for damage

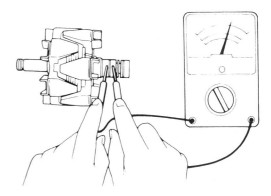

Fig. 5.18   Measuring the rotor winding resistance (Sec 15)

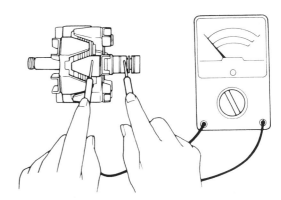

Fig. 5.19   Checking the insulation between the rotor
windings and the laminations (Sec 15)

13   Use the multi-meter or test lamp to check the rectifier for continuity. Each pair of terminals should show continuity when the test probes are applied one way around, and no continuity when the probes are reversed. If any pair shows continuity or discontinuity in both directions, replace the rectifier complete.

14   Commence reassembly by soldering the voltage regulator/brush carrier, stator and rectifier together. Install the assembly to the slip ring end casing and secure it with the screws and the 'B' terminal nut and washer.

15   Raise and retain the brushes as described in the previous Section. Make sure that the slip ring end bearing retainer is in place in the bearing groove, then heat the slip ring end bearing housing and install the rotor (photo).

15.15   Installing the rotor

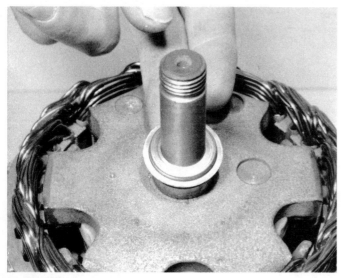

15.16   Correct installation of the inner dished washer

16   Place a dished washer on the rotor shaft, making sure it is the right way around (photo). Place the drive end casing over the rotor and tap it home. Install and tighten the three casing screws.
17   Install the other dished washer, the spacer, fan and pulley. Clamp the pulley and install the washer and nut.
18   Release the brushes, then install the alternator (Section 13).

16   Starting system — general information

The function of the starting system is to crank the engine. This system is composed of a starting motor, solenoid and battery. The battery supplies the electrical energy to the solenoid, which then completes the circuit to the starting motor, which does the actual work of cranking the engine.
The solenoid and starting motor are mounted together on the lower rear (firewall) side of the engine. No periodic lubrication or maintenance is required.
The electrical circuitry of the vehicle is arranged so that the starter motor can only be operated when the transmission selector lever is in Park or Neutral (automatic transaxle).
Never operate the starter motor for more than 30 seconds at a time without pausing to allow it to cool for at least two minutes. Excessive cranking can cause overheating, which can seriously damage the starter.

17   Starter motor — testing in vehicle

1   If the starter motor does not turn at all when the switch is operated, make sure that the shift lever is in Neutral or Park (automatic transaxle).
2   Make sure that the battery is charged and that all cables, both at the battery and starter solenoid terminals, are secure.
3   If, when the switch is actuated, the starter motor does not operate at all but the solenoid clicks, and the battery is fully charged, then the problem is in the main solenoid contacts or the starter motor itself.
4   If the solenoid plunger cannot be heard when the switch is actuated, the solenoid itself is defective or the solenoid circuit is open.
5   To check the motor, connect a jumper lead between the battery (B) and the M terminal on the solenoid (Fig.5.20). If the starter motor now operates, the motor is OK and the problem is in the solenoid, ignition switch, neutral start switch or in the wiring. (Note that the motor will spin without cranking the engine during this check, since the solenoid — which moves the starter pinion into mesh with the ring gear — is being bypassed by the jumper lead.)
6   If the starter motor still does not operate, remove the starter/solenoid assembly for disassembly, testing and repair or replacement.

18   Starter motor — removal and installation

1   Disconnect the negative battery cable.
2   Remove the air cleaner.
3   Disconnect the solenoid wires and battery cable from the starter motor.
4   Remove the retaining bolts and detach the starter motor from the engine.
5   Installation is the reverse of the removal procedure.

19   Starter solenoid — removal and installation

Removal
1   After removing the starter motor (Section 18), disconnect the motor strap.
2   Remove the two or three screws which secure the solenoid housing to the starter end frame.
3   Twist the solenoid to disengage it and remove it from the starter body, taking care not to lose any of the shims.

Installation
4   Place the solenoid with shims in place and rotate it into position in the starter end frame.
5   Install the two solenoid screws and connect the motor strap.
6   If new components have been installed, the starter motor will have to be removed to check the pinion gap. Refer to Sections 18 and 21.

20   Starter motor — brush replacement

Note: *A soldering iron will be required for this operation.*
1   Remove the starter motor as described in Section 18 and clean it externally.
2   Remove the two through-bolts and the two short screws from the armature cover. Carefully pull off the cover (photos). Recover the shim washer(s) from the armature.
3   The brushes may now be extracted from their holders one by one, by lifting up the brush springs and pulling out the brush (photos). Only remove one brush at a time so as not to leave the brush plate unsecured. Measure the brushes and compare their length with that given in the Specifications.
4   Brushes are replaced by cutting the old brush leads and soldering the new leads onto the old ones. Make sure that the field brushes are still insulated on completion. Do not allow a lot of solder to run up the leads, as this will impair their flexibility.
5   Clean the commutator with solvent and a soft rag.
6   Assemble the motor in the reverse order to dismantling.

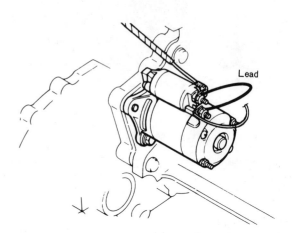

Fig. 5.20   Starter motor check (Sec 17)

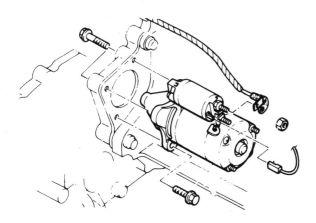

Fig. 5.21 Starter motor installation details (Sec 18)

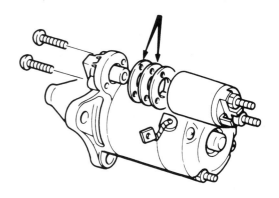

Fig. 5.22 Starter solenoid and shims (arrows) installation
details (Sec 19)

20.2a Remove the starter motor
through-bolts . . .

20.2b . . . and the armature cover screws

20.2c Removing the armature cover

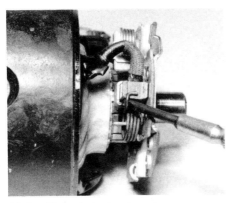

20.3a. Unhook the brush spring . . .

20.3b . . . and lift out the brush

21 Starter motor — overhaul and bench testing

Note: *If the starter motor has seen much service, installation of a replacement unit may be more satisfactory than attempting to overhaul the old one. Check the availability and cost of spare parts before proceeding.*

Dismantling

1   With the motor removed from the vehicle (Section 18), clean it externally.

2   Remove the nut which secures the motor strap to the solenoid. Free the strap.
3   Remove the two or three screws which secure the solenoid to the drive end housing. Withdraw the solenoid yoke and recover the shims, noting their number and location. Recover the spring.
4   Unhook the solenoid plunger from the operating lever.
5   Remove all three brushes as described in the previous Section. Lift off the brush carrier plate.
6   Carefully draw the yoke off the armature. Support the armature, and be prepared for the release of the operating lever springs and washers.

7   Unhook the operating lever from the pinion clutch.
8   Remove the armature, clutch and pinions from the drive end housing.
9   To remove the pinion/clutch assembly from the armature, secure the armature in a vise with padded jaws. Use a hammer and a piece of tube to drive the spring ring collar towards the pinion until the spring ring is exposed. Remove the spring ring, collar and pinion/clutch.

Inspection

10   Use a multi-meter to check the insulation resistance of the armature. Resistance between any commutator segment and the armature laminations should be infinite (open-circuit).
11   Inspect the commutator for burning or other damage. Machining down to good metal is sometimes possible, but this is specialist work.

Scrape carbon and other debris from between the commutator segments with a ground-down hacksaw blade or similar tool. Undercutting of the segments should be to the depth shown in Fig. 5.26.
12   Check the insulation resistance between the field coil connector and the yoke. It should be infinite (make sure the field brushes are not touching the yoke). Check the resistance between the field brush wires — it should be negligible. Replace the yoke if it fails these tests, or if there is burning or other obvious damage to the field coils. The coils are not available separately.
13   Check the resistance between the brush carrier plate and each field (positive) brush holder — it should be infinite. Replace the brush carrier plate if not.
14   Examine the brushes and replace them if necessary as described in the previous Section.

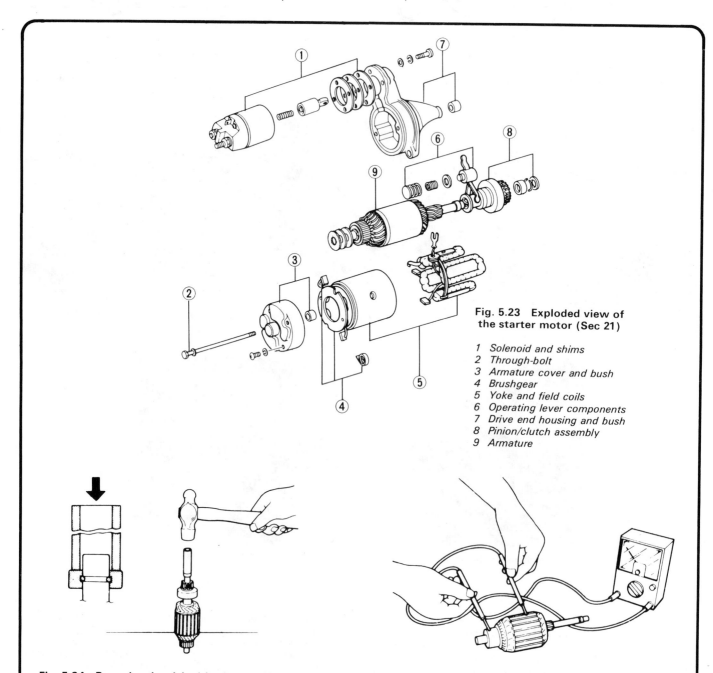

Fig. 5.23   Exploded view of the starter motor (Sec 21)

1   Solenoid and shims
2   Through-bolt
3   Armature cover and bush
4   Brushgear
5   Yoke and field coils
6   Operating lever components
7   Drive end housing and bush
8   Pinion/clutch assembly
9   Armature

Fig. 5.24   Removing the pinion/clutch assembly (Sec 21)

Fig. 5.25   Checking the armature insulation resistance (Sec 21)

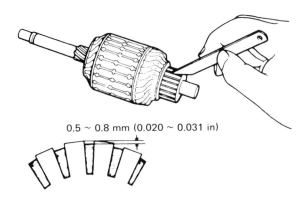

0.5 ~ 0.8 mm (0.020 ~ 0.031 in)

Fig. 5.26 Undercutting the commutator (Sec 21)

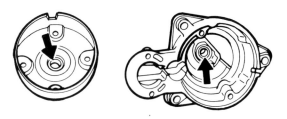

Fig. 5.27 Armature and bushes (arrowed) (Sec 21)

15 The armature end brushes can be removed from their respective housings and new ones installed if necessary. Some such brushes need to be soaked in engine oil for a period before installation — seek advice when buying them.
16 Inspect the solenoid components for visible damage and clean any corrosion from the plunger. Functional testing will be described later.

Reassembly

17 Commence reassembly by securing the pinion/clutch to the armature shaft. Place the pinion/clutch on the shaft, followed by the spring ring collar. Install a new spring ring into the shaft groove and secure it by levering the collar up over the ring, using a couple of open-ended spanners.
18 Install the armature into the drive end housing. Engage the operating lever with the pinion clutch. Install the washer and springs to the operating lever pivot and carefully slide the yoke into position.
19 Install the brushgear, shims, commutator end cover and through-bolts, as described in the previous Section.
20 Hook the solenoid plunger onto the operating lever. Install the spring, yoke and shims, using the same number of shims as noted when dismantling. Install and tighten the solenoid securing screws, but do not connect the motor strap yet.

Bench testing

21 With a 12 volt battery and some test leads, check the solenoid functions and the pinion gap as follows.
22 Check the pull-in function by connecting the battery negative terminal to the solenoid yoke and to the 'M' (large lower) terminal. Connect the battery positive terminal to the 'S' (spade) terminal: the solenoid should operate and the pinion be moved outwards. Do not apply battery voltage for more than ten seconds.
23 Check the hold-in function of the solenoid by repeating the above test, but disconnect the 'M' terminal wire whilst leaving the yoke and 'S' terminal connected. The pinion must stay in its outward position.
24 Check the return function by connecting the battery positive terminal to the 'M' terminal, leaving the negative terminal connected to the yoke. Pull the pinion outwards by hand and release it: it must return immediately.
25 Replace the solenoid if it fails any of the above tests. When it is functioning correctly, check the pinion gap as follows:
26 Connect the negative terminal to the solenoid yoke and the battery positive terminal to the solenoid 'S' terminal.
27 The pinion gap is altered by adding or removing shims between the solenoid yoke and the drive end housing. Adding shims decreases the gap, and vice versa.
28 With the solenoid function and the pinion gap both correct, reconnect the motor strap to the solenoid 'M' terminal and secure it with the nut.
29 If suitable test instruments are available, measure the light running current of the starter motor. Make the connections as shown in Fig. 5.32 and secure the starter motor in a vise. At 11.5 volts, current should not exceed 60 amps and the motor speed should be in excess of 6500 rpm. Do not run the motor for long periods at this speed.

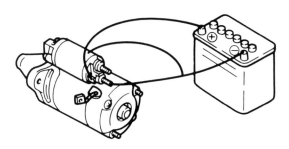

Fig. 5.28 Checking the solenoid pull-in function (Sec 21)

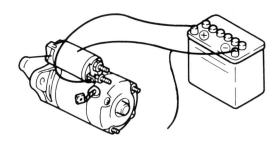

Fig. 5.29 Checking the solenoid hold-in function (Sec 21)

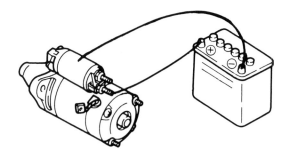

Fig. 5.30 Checking the solenoid return function (Sec 21)

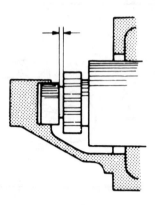

Fig. 5.31 Pinion gap is measured between arrows
(Sec 21)

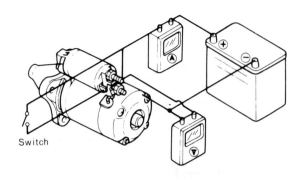

Switch

Fig. 5.32 Wiring connections for measuring starter motor
light running current (Sec 21)

Chapter 6 Emissions control systems

Contents

1 General information

To prevent pollution of the atmosphere from burned and evaporating gases, a number of emissions control systems are incorporated on the vehicles covered by this manual. The combination of systems used depends on the year in which the vehicle was manufactured, the locality to which it was originally delivered and the transaxle type. By reading the descriptions and looking at the illustrations it will become obvious which systems are incorporated on your vehicle. The major systems incorporated on the vehicles with which this manual is concerned include the:

Electronic ignition system
Air injection system
Coasting leaner system
Deceleration control system
Air inlet temperature control system
Positive Crankcase Ventilation (PCV)

The economy drive indicator system, though not strictly speaking related to emissions, shares a control unit with the coasting leaner system and so it is included in this Chapter.

The Sections in this Chapter include general descriptions, checking procedures (where possible) and component replacement procedures (where applicable) for each of the systems listed above.

Before assuming that an emissions control system is malfunctioning, check the fuel and ignition systems carefully. In some cases special tools and equipment, as well as specialized training, are required to accurately diagnose the causes of a rough running or difficult to start engine. If checking and servicing become too difficult, or if a procedure is beyond the scope of the home mechanic, consult your dealer service department. This does not necessarily mean, however, that the emissions control systems are particularly difficult to maintain and repair. You can quickly and easily perform many checks and do most (if not all) of the regular maintenance at home with common tune-up and hand tools. **Note:** *The most frequent cause of emissions system problems is simply a loose or broken vacuum hose or wiring connection. Therefore, always check the hose and wiring connections first.*

Pay close attention to any special precautions outlined in this Chapter. It should be noted that the illustrations of the various systems may not exactly match the system installed on your particular vehicle due to changes made by the manufacturer during production or from year to year.

2 Electronic ignition system

1 The electronic ignition system used on all engines with which this manual is concerned controls the spark for optimum operation of the engine for proper driveability and emissions. The distributor contains both vacuum and centrifugal advance mechanisms to control advance.
2 For further information and checking and component replacement procedures regarding the distributor, refer to Chapter 5.

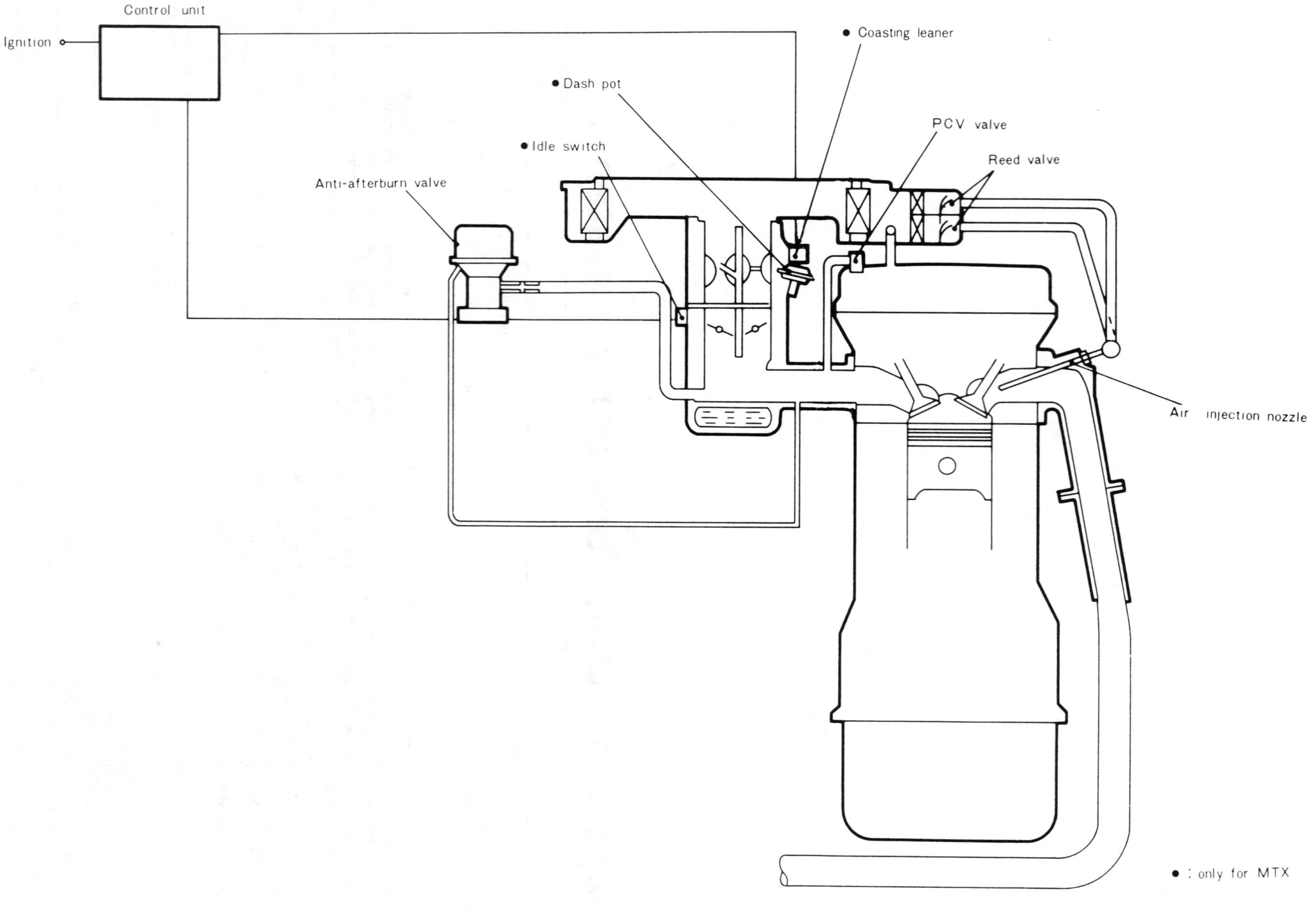

Fig. 6.1 Emissions control systems components (Sec 1)

Air injection nozzle

Reed valve

PCV valve

Coasting leaner

Dash pot

Idle switch

Anti-afterburn valve

Control unit

Ignition

● : only for MTX

3 Air injection system

General description

1   The air injection system helps reduce hydrocarbons and carbon monoxide levels in the exhaust by injecting air into the exhaust ports of each cylinder.
2   The air injection system uses exhaust pressure pulses to draw air into the exhaust system and utilizes fresh air that is filtered by the air cleaner.
3   Components utilized in the system include the reed valves located in the air cleaner assembly and external tubes and hoses.

Checking

4   Exhaust gas blowing back through the air cleaner assembly is a symptom of a fault in the air injection system. Begin any inspection by carefully checking all hoses. Be sure they are in good condition and that all connections are tight and clean.

5   A simple, functional test of this system can be performed with the engine running.
6   Remove the top of the air cleaner assembly and the filter element.
7   With the engine idling at normal operating temperature, place a piece of paper over the reed valve inlet port. With the engine idling there should be a steady stream of air being sucked into the valve. Have an assistant apply throttle, and as the engine gains speed, see if the suction increases.
8   If this does not occur, the hoses are leaking or restricted or the reed valves are faulty.
9   Increase the engine speed to approximately 1500 rpm and check for exhaust gas leakage at the air inlet fitting.
10   Replace the reed valve with a new one if it fails either test.

Component replacement

11   Remove the air cleaner — see Chapter 2, Part A, Section 23.
12   Remove the reed valve housing cover retaining screws and lift the valves and filters from the housing (photos).
13   Installation is the reverse of removal.

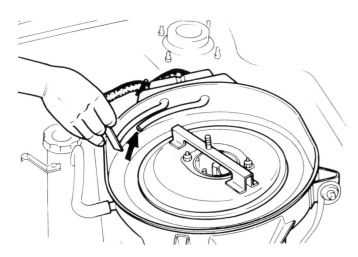

Fig. 6.2   Checking the air injection system reed valve operation with a piece of paper (Sec 3)

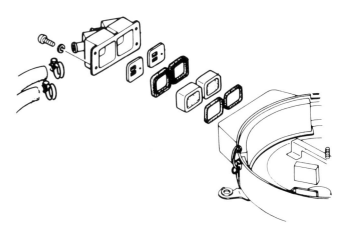

Fig. 6.3   Reed valve components (Sec 3)

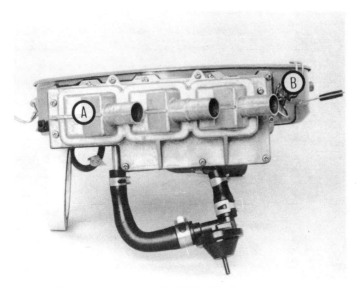

3.12a   The reed valve assembly (A) is attached to the air cleaner housing (B) by screws

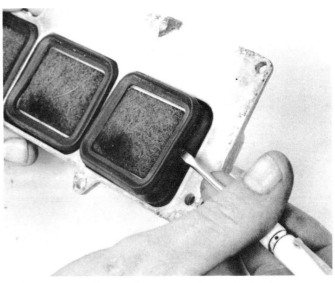

3.12b   Use a small screwdriver to pry the reed valve loose

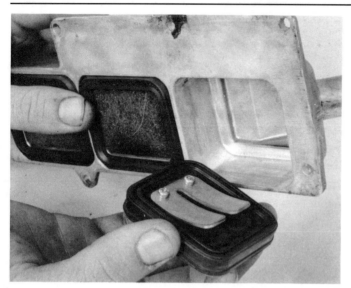

3.12c Removing the reed valve from the housing

4 Coasting leaner system

General description

1   The coasting leaner valve is fitted to UK vehicles with a manual transaxle. Its function is to supply additional air to the intake manifold during deceleration, so reducing HC and CO emissions.
2   Malfunction of the coasting leaner system can cause rough idling, excessive idle speed and running-on.

Checking

3   Checking of the coasting leaner system is described in Chapter 1, Section 39.

Component replacement

Coasting leaner valve
4   Remove the air cleaner and disconnect the battery negative lead.
5   Remove the screws which secure the coasting leaner valve to the carburetor. Disconnect the wiring from the valve and withdraw it (photo). Recover the O-ring.
6   Install the new valve in the reverse order to removal.

Idle switch
7   Remove the air cleaner and disconnect the battery negative lead.
8   Remove the screws which secure the idle switch to the carburetor. Disconnect the wiring from the switch and withdraw it.
9   Install the new switch in the reverse order to removal. Before installing the air cleaner, check the adjustment of the switch as described in Chapter 1, Section 39.

Control unit
10   Refer to Section 8.

5 Positive Crankcase Ventilation (PCV) system

General description

1   The positive crankcase ventilation system reduces hydrocarbon emissions by circulating fresh air through the crankcase to pick up blow by gases, which are then rerouted through the intake manifold to be burned in the engine.
2   The main components of this system are vacuum hoses and a PCV valve, which regulates the flow of gases according to engine speed and manifold vacuum.

Checking

3   The PCV system can be checked quickly and easily for proper operation. This system should be checked regularly, as carbon and gunk deposited by the blow by gases will eventually clog the PCV valve and/or system hoses. When the flow of the PCV system is reduced or stopped, common symptoms are rough idling or reduced engine speed at idle.
4   To check for proper vacuum in the system, remove the top plate of the air cleaner and locate the small PCV filter on the inside of the air cleaner housing.
5   Disconnect the hose leading to this filter.
6   With the engine idling, place your thumb over the end of the hose. You should feel a slight vacuum. The suction may be heard as your thumb is released. This will indicate that air is being drawn all the way through the system. If a vacuum is felt, the system is functioning properly. Check that the filter inside the air cleaner housing is not clogged or dirty. If in doubt, replace the filter with a new one, an inexpensive safeguard (refer to Chapter 1).
7   If there is very little vacuum or none at all at the end of the hose, the system is clogged and must be inspected further.
8   Shut off the engine and locate the PCV valve. Carefully pull it from its rubber grommet. Shake it and listen for a clicking sound. That is the rattle of the check ball. If the valve does not click freely, replace it with a new one.
9   Start the engine and run it at idle speed with the PCV valve removed. Place your thumb over the end of the valve and feel for suction. This should be a relatively strong vacuum which will be felt immediately. See also Chapter 1, Section 31.
10   If little or no vacuum is felt at the PCV valve, turn off the engine and disconnect the vacuum hose from the other end of the valve. Run the engine at idle speed and check for vacuum at the end of the hose just disconnected. No vacuum at this point indicates that the vacuum hose or inlet fitting at the engine is plugged. If it is the hose which is blocked, replace it with a new one or remove it from the engine and blow it out sufficiently with compressed air. A clogged passage at the carburetor or manifold requires that the component be removed and thoroughly cleaned to remove carbon build up. A strong vacuum felt going into the PCV valve, but little or no vacuum coming out of the valve, indicates a failure of the PCV valve requiring replacement with a new one.
11   When purchasing a new PCV valve, make sure it is the correct one for your engine. An incorrect PCV valve may pull too little or too much vacuum, possibly leading to engine damage.

Component replacement

12   The replacement procedures for both the PCV valve and filter are covered in Chapter 1.

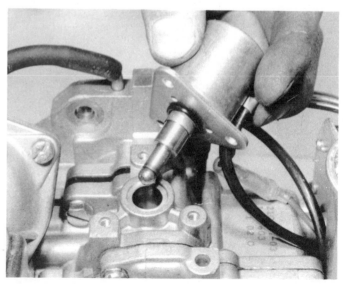

4.5 Removing the coasting leaner valve (carburetor removed)

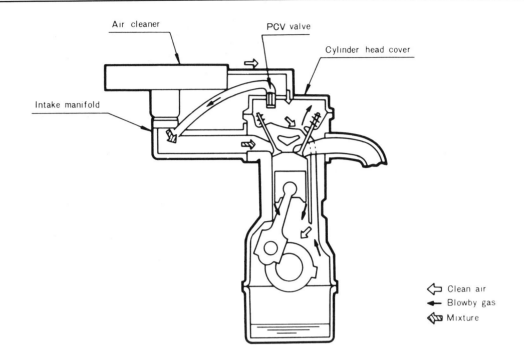

Fig. 6.4 PCV system diagram (Sec 5)

6 Air inlet temperature control system

General description

1   The air inlet temperature control system is provided to improve engine efficiency and reduce hydrocarbon emissions during the initial warm-up period by maintaining a controlled air temperature at the carburetor. This temperature control of the incoming air allows leaner carburetor and choke calibrations.

2   The system uses a damper assembly, located in the snorkel of the air cleaner housing, to control the ratio of cold and warm air directed into the carburetor. This damper is controlled by a vacuum diaphragm which is, in turn, modulated by a thermo sensor in the air cleaner.

3   It is during the first few miles of driving (depending on outside temperature) that this system has its greatest effect on engine performance and emissions output. When the engine is cold, the damper flap blocks off the air cleaner inlet snorkel, allowing only warm air from around the exhaust manifold to enter the carburetor. Gradually, as the engine warms up, the flap opens the snorkel passage, increasing the amount of cold air allowed in. Once the engine reaches normal operating temperature, the flap opens completely, allowing only cold, fresh air to enter.

4   Because of this cold-engine-only function, it is important to periodically check this system to prevent poor engine performance when cold or overheating of the fuel mixture once the engine has reached operating temperatures. If the air cleaner valve sticks in the *no heat* position, the engine will run poorly, stall and waste gas until it has warmed up on its own. A valve sticking in the *heat* position causes the engine to run as if it is out of tune due to the constant flow of hot air to the carburetor.

Checking

5   Refer to Chapter 1 for maintenance and checking procedures for this system. If problems were encountered in the system's performance while performing the routine maintenance checks, refer to the procedures which follow.

6   If the damper door did not close off snorkel air when the cold engine was first started, disconnect the vacuum hose at the snorkel vacuum diaphragm and place your thumb over the hose end, checking for vacuum. If there is vacuum going to the diaphragm, check that the damper door and link are not frozen or binding within the air cleaner

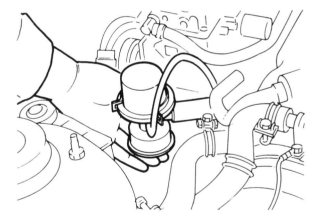

Fig. 6.5 Checking the anti-afterburn valve (Sec 7)

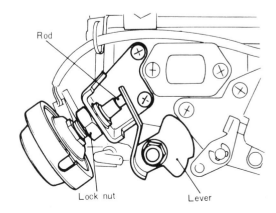

Fig. 6.6 Dashpot and associated components (Sec 7)

snorkel. If a vacuum pump is available, disconnect the vacuum hose and apply vacuum to the motor to make sure the damper door actuates. Replace the vacuum diaphragm if the application of vacuum does not open the door and the hose routing is correct but the damper door moves freely.

7   If there was no vacuum going to the diaphragm in the above test, check the hoses for cracks, crimps and proper connection. If the hoses are clear and in good condition, replace the thermo sensor inside the air cleaner housing.

Component replacement

Air cleaner vacuum diaphragm
8   Disconnect the vacuum hose from the diaphragm.
9   Remove the retaining screw, unhook the linkage and rotate the diaphragm up and out of the air cleaner housing.
10   To install, insert the diaphragm in the housing, rotate it into position, connect the linkage and install the retaining screw.
11   Connect the vacuum hose.

Air cleaner thermo sensor
12   Remove the air cleaner for access to the underside.
13   Mark their locations and disconnect the vacuum hoses at the sensor.
14   Carefully note the position of the sensor as it must be installed in exactly the same position. Lift the sensor from the air cleaner (photo).
15   Install the new sensor in the same position as the old one and connect the vacuum hoses.
16   Install the air filter element and the air cleaner top plate.

6.14   The air inlet thermo sensor can be lifted straight up (arrow) after disconnecting the vacuum hoses under the air cleaner assembly

7   Deceleration control system

General description

1   The deceleration control system gradually closes the throttle during sudden deceleration so that excessive unburned fuel is not dumped into the exhaust, causing increased emissions.
2   The components of this system are an anti-afterburn valve and (on manual transaxle models) a dashpot on the carburetor which operates the throttle.
3   A symptom of a fault in the dashpot is immediate closing of the throttle on deceleration. Malfunction of the anti-afterburn valve can cause backfiring and running-on.

Component checking

Anti-afterburn valve
4   Run the engine and place a hand under the anti-afterburn valve.
5   Increase the engine speed to approximately 3000 rpm and then release the throttle suddenly. If air is felt coming from the valve it is functioning correctly.
6   Allow the engine to idle. Disconnect the air hose from the valve and plug the open end of the hose. If the idle speed differs greatly from that obtained before disconnecting the hose, the valve is leaking and must be replaced.

Dashpot
7   Pull the throttle lever sharply away from the dashpot and check that the dashpot rod immediately extends fully. Release the throttle lever and make sure that it slowly returns to the idle position after contacting the dashpot rod.
8   To adjust the dashpot, run the engine at idle at normal operating temperature and connect a tachometer. Slowly increase the engine speed and check that the dashpot rod separates from the lever at approximately 2200 rpm. Loosen the locknut and turn the dashpot to adjust.
9   If adjustment does not bring the dashpot into specification, replace it with a new one.

Component replacement

Anti-afterburn valve
10   Remove the air hose and unsnap the valve from the bracket.
11   Install the new valve in the bracket and reconnect the air hose.

Dashpot
12   Loosen the locknut and unscrew the dashpot from the bracket.
13   Install the new dashpot and adjust it as just described.

8   Economy drive indicator system

General description

1   Some manual transaxle models are equipped with the economy drive indicator system. Two lights on the instrument cluster advise the driver to shift to a higher gear and/or to ease up on the throttle. Enhanced fuel economy will result from obeying the lights.
2   The lights do not operate in 5th (high) gear, nor when decelerating. (On 1984 and later models, the excessive throttle indicator light operates in all forward gears.)
3   Besides the lights themselves, the main components of the system are a control unit, located under the instrument panel or behind the instrument cluster; a vacuum switch, connected to the intake manifold via a delay valve; a 5th gear switch on the transaxle and an idle switch on the carburetor.
4   The control unit and the idle switch are shared with the coasting leaner system (Section 4).
5   The control unit receives inputs from the switches already mentioned, plus a power input and an input from the ignition coil. The coil input allows the unit to monitor engine speed.

Checking

Shift-up indicator
6   Start the engine and allow it to idle.
7   Increase the engine speed gradually and check that the shift-up indicator lights up at approximately 2800 rpm, and stays lit at higher engine speeds.
8   Disconnect the 5th gear switch connector (near the battery) and repeat the check. The indicator should not light up at any time. Reconnect the 5th gear switch connector.

Excessive throttle indicator
9   A vacuum pump and gauge will be needed for this check.
10   Disconnect the vacuum hose from the switch and connect the vacuum pump and gauge instead. Switch on the ignition. Have an assistant watch the indicator whilst vacuum is applied to the switch. The indicator should light up when vacuum is in the range 0 to 4.7 in (0 to 120 mm) Hg, and go out at higher values.
11   On pre-1984 models, disconnect the 5th gear switch connector and repeat the check. The indicator should not light up at any time. Reconnect the 5th gear switch connector, and reconnect the vacuum hose to the switch.

Component replacement

Indicator lights
12   Proceed as described in Chapter 12, Section 10, for instrument cluster bulb replacement.

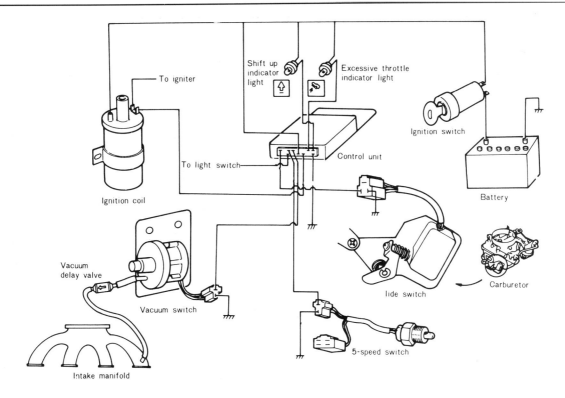

Fig. 6.7   Components of the economy drive indicator system (Sec 8)

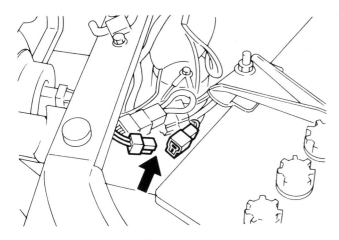

Fig. 6.8   Economy drive 5th gear switch connector (arrowed) (Sec 8)

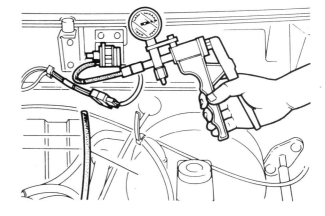

Fig. 6.9   Checking the economy drive vacuum switch (Sec 8)

Vacuum switch
13   Disconnect the vacuum hose and the wiring connector from the switch. Release the switch from its bulkhead mounting.
14   Install the new switch and connect the hose and wiring.

Idle switch
15   Idle switch replacement is described in Section 4.

5th gear switch
16   Separate the 5th gear switch connector and follow the wiring back to the transaxle.
17   Unscrew the switch from the transaxle. Be prepared for oil spillage.
18   Install and connect the new switch, then check the transaxle oil level (Chapter 1, Section 4).

Control unit
19   No specific information on the location of the control unit was available at the time of writing. Access is by removing the instrument panel lower trim, the instrument panel or the instrument cluster.

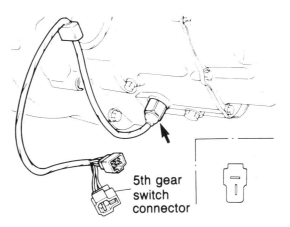

Fig. 6.10   5th gear switch (arrowed) and wiring (Sec 8)

Chapter 7 Part A   Manual transaxle

Contents

Specifications

Reverse lever-to-idler clearance	0.004 to 0.013 in (0.1 to 0.32 mm)
Service limit	0.020 in (0.5 mm)
Shift fork-to-clutch sleeve clearance	0.008 to 0.018 in (0.2 to 0.46 mm)
Service limit	0.020 in (0.5 mm)
Gear synchronizer ring-to-gear clearance	0.059 in (1.5 mm)
Service limit	0.031 in (0.80 mm)
Thrust clearances	
First gear	0.002 to 0.021 in (0.05 to 0.53 mm)
Service limit	0.024 in (0.6 mm)
Second gear	0.02 to 0.039 in (0.5 to 1.0 mm)
Service limit	0.039 in (1.0 mm)
Third gear	0.002 to 0.017 in (0.05 to 0.43 mm)
Service limit	0.020 in (0.5 mm)
Fourth gear	0.01 to 0.014 in (0.25 to 0.355 mm)
Service limit	0.020 in (0.5 mm)
Primary shaft gear bearing preload	0.4 to 1.7 in-lb (0.5 to 2.0 cm-kg)
Differential side bearing preload	0.69 to 1.56 in-lb (0.8 to 1.8 cm-kg)
Side gear and pinion gear backlash	0.004 in (0.1 mm)

Torque specifications

	Ft-lbs	M-kg
Rear crossmember		
Front nuts and bolts	32 to 40	4.4 to 5.5
Rear bolt	69 to 85	9.5 to 11.8
Lower balljoint bolt	32 to 40	4.4 to 5.5
Transaxle		
Case bolts	27 to 39	3.7 to 5.5
Gate lock bolt	8.7 to 11.6	1.2 to 1.6
Gear shaft locknut	94 to 152	13 to 21
Guide bolt	6 to 10	0.9 to 1.4
Rear cover bolt	6 to 8	0.9 to 1.1
Reverse idle shaft lock bolt	15 to 22	2.1 to 3.1
Transaxle-to-engine bolts	65 to 87	9.1 to 11.9
Transaxle mount-to-engine bolts	40	5.5
Transaxle mount-to-transaxle bolts and nuts	27 to 38	3.8 to 5.4
Transaxle mount-to-body nuts	32 to 40	4.4 to 5.5

1 General information

All manual transmission models are equipped with either a 4-speed or 5-speed transaxle which incorporates the transmission and differential into one unit. Power from the engine passes through the transaxle gears and then to the differential gears, which drive the axleshafts.

All forward gears are synchromesh and the floor mounted gear shift lever operates the transaxle internal shift mechanism by way of a shift control rod.

The transaxle shown in the photographs in this Chapter was installed on a US specification vehicle. The transaxle installed on UK vehicles may differ slightly.

Dismantling and reassembly procedures are based on the assumption that bearings are not to be renewed, and that press-fitted components are reinstalled to the same positions. Installation of new bearings or shafts means that preload shim thicknesses will have to be determined, using special tools and techniques not available to the home mechanic.

In view of the above points, if the transaxle develops a fault or is generally worn, installation of a new or reconditioned unit may be the best course.

2 Transaxle mounts — check and replacement

Checking

1 Watch the mount as an assistant pulls up and pushes down on the transaxle. If the rubber separates from the plate or the case moves up but not down, indicating the mount is bottomed out, replace the mount with a new one.

Replacement

2 Disconnect the battery negative cable.
3 Support the transaxle with a jack.
4 Remove the transaxle mount-to-engine or mount-to-transaxle bolts.
5 Remove the mount-to-body nuts and remove the mount.
6 Place the new mount in position and install the mount-to-transaxle or mount-to-engine bolts. Tighten the bolts to the specified torque.
7 Install the mount-to-body nuts and tighten them to the specified torque.
8 Remove the jack and connect the battery negative cable.

3 Transaxle shift lever assembly — removal and installation

1 Inside the vehicle passenger compartment, remove the shift lever knob, shift boot and the front and rear consoles (Chapter 11).
2 Raise the front of the vehicle and support it securely on jackstands.
3 Remove the retaining nuts and bolts and lower the change rod from the vehicle.
4 Remove the shift lever spring clip with a screwdriver as shown in the accompanying illustration and lift the lever assembly from the vehicle.
5 Remove the extension bar retaining nuts and bolts and remove the bar, bracket and gasket assembly.
6 Installation is the reverse of removal. Apply lithium-based grease to the moving and rubbing parts of the assembly.

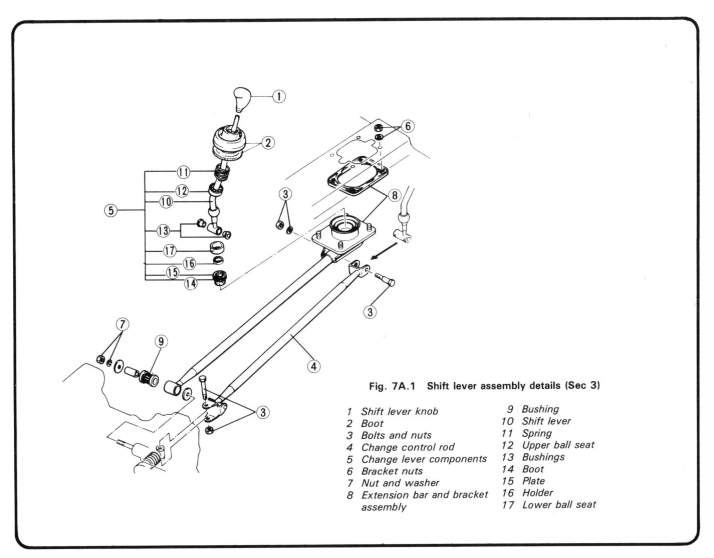

Fig. 7A.1 Shift lever assembly details (Sec 3)

1 Shift lever knob	9 Bushing
2 Boot	10 Shift lever
3 Bolts and nuts	11 Spring
4 Change control rod	12 Upper ball seat
5 Change lever components	13 Bushings
6 Bracket nuts	14 Boot
7 Nut and washer	15 Plate
8 Extension bar and bracket	16 Holder
assembly	17 Lower ball seat

12 Remove the joint shaft (Chapter 8). Insert a wooden dowel or similar item to retain the differential side gear.
13 Separate the change control rod from the change rod and remove the extension bar from the transaxle.
14 Remove the transaxle under cover.
15 Unbolt and remove the crossmember and lower left-hand suspension arm assembly.
16 Support the transaxle with a jack and fasten the transaxle to the jack.
17 Remove the two remaining bolts, separate the transaxle from the engine and lower the transaxle from the vehicle. Do not allow the weight of the transaxle to hang on the primary shaft as the transaxle is withdrawn from the engine. Steady the transaxle as it is lowered in case it falls off the jack.

Installation

18 Apply a thin coat of moly grease to the transaxle input shaft splines.
19 Raise the transaxle into position and install the bolts. Tighten the bolts to the proper torque.
20 Install the extension bar onto the transaxle and the change rod to the change control rod.
21 Install the crossmember and lower arm assembly.
22 Install the transaxle under cover.
23 Install the joint shaft (Chapter 8).
24 Install the left driveaxle (Chapter 8).
25 Connect the lower balljoints to the knuckles and install the nuts and bolts, tightening them to the specified torque.
26 Connect the stabilizer bar links.
27 Install the splash shields and the front wheels. Install the oil pan protector plate, when applicable.
28 Install the starter motor.
29 Remove the jack from the transaxle and lower the vehicle.
30 Install the four transaxle-to-engine retaining bolts. Tighten the bolts to the specified torque.
31 Install the wiring harness clips and the ground cable bolt and connect the clutch cable.
32 Fill the transaxle with the specified oil (Chapter 1).

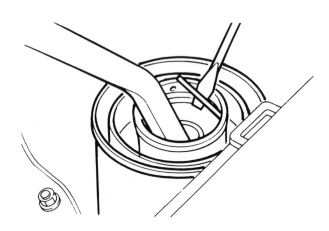

Fig. 7A.2   Release the shift lever spring clip with a screwdriver (Sec 3)

4   Transaxle — removal and installation

Removal

1   Disconnect the battery negative cable.
2   Disconnect the speedometer cable, the backup light switch and (when equipped) the 5th gear switch.
3   Remove the mounting bolts from the clutch cable bracket and disconnect the clutch cable from the release lever.
4   Remove the ground cable retaining bolt and the wire harness clip.
5   Remove the starter motor (Chapter 5).
6   There are two principal ways of supporting the weight of the engine during the removal of the crossmember and transaxle. A special support fixture can be obtained which rests on the suspension strut towers, or an engine hoist can be used. If the engine support fixture is being used, install it at this time. If the engine hoist is being used to support the engine, the hood must be removed to gain sufficient clearance (Chapter 11).
7   Remove the four top transaxle-to-engine mounting bolts.
8   Raise the front of the vehicle, support it securely on jackstands and drain the transaxle oil (Chapter 1).
9   Remove the front wheels and splash panels and disconnect the stabilizer bar control links. Remove the oil pan protector plate, when applicable.
10 Remove the lower balljoint and steering knuckle coupling bolts and separate the lower suspension arms from the knuckles (Chapter 10).
11 Remove the left driveaxle from the transaxle (Chapter 8).

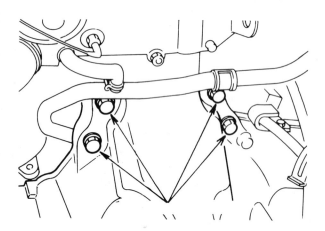

Fig. 7A.3   Upper transaxle bolt locations (arrows) (Sec 4)

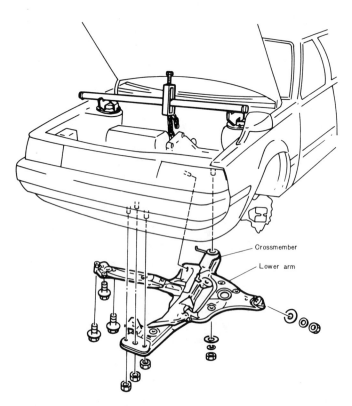

Crossmember

Lower arm

Fig. 7A.4   Crossmember and lower suspension arm assembly installation details (Sec 4)

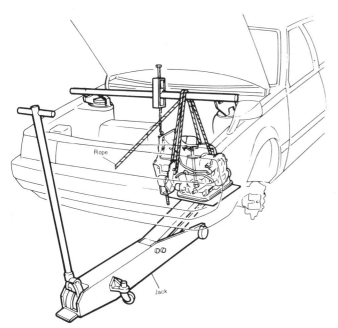

Fig. 7A.5 Removing the transaxle using the factory engine support, and a jack and rope to steady the transaxle as it is lowered (Sec 4)

33 Connect the speedometer cable, the backup light switch and (when equipped) the 5th gear switch.
34 Connect the battery negative cable.

5 Transaxle — disassembly

1 Unbolt and remove the rear cover (5-speed).
2 Use a punch to drive the locknut collar back from the groove on each of the locknuts (5-speed).
3 Carefully lock the gear teeth with a screwdriver or similar tool and remove the locknuts (photos).
4 Remove the 5th gear shift fork retaining pin and the shift fork (photo).
5 Remove the 5th gear stop plate, clutch hub, synchro ring, gear sleeve and gear.
6 Remove the lock bolt from the transaxle case (photo).

5.4 Drive out the shift fork retaining pin with a hammer and punch

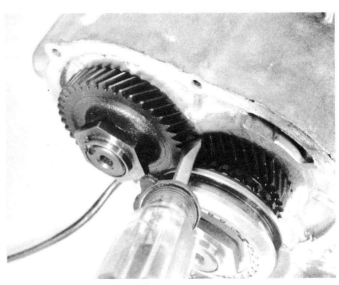

5.3a Insert a screwdriver into the gear teeth to lock the shaft

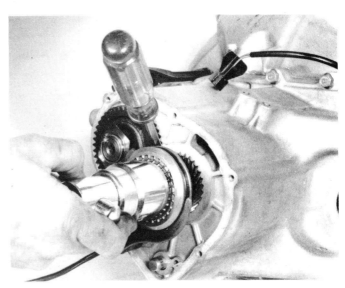

5.3b Make sure the screwdriver doesn't slip while removing the locknuts

5.6 Remove the lock bolt

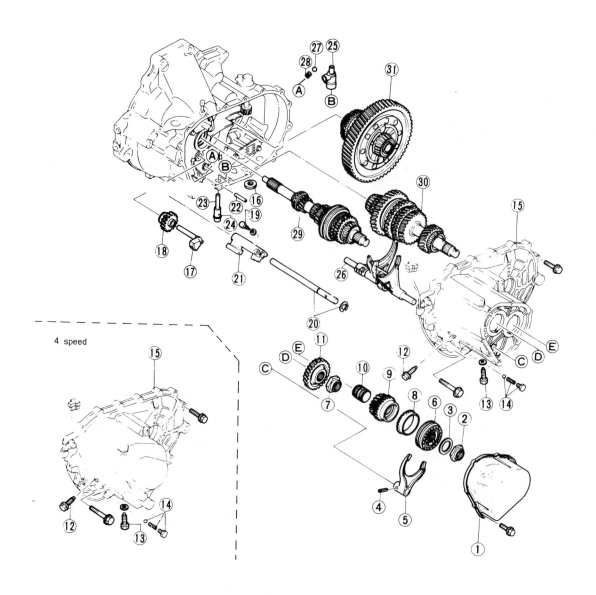

Fig. 7A.6 Transaxle component layout (Sec 5)

1 Rear cover (5-speed)
2 Locknut (5-speed)
3 Stop plate (5-speed)
4 Springpin (5-speed)
5 Shift fork (5-speed)
6 Clutch hub assembly
   (5-speed)
7 Locknut (5-speed)
8 Synchronizer ring (5-speed)
9 5th gear (5-speed)
10 Gear sleeve (5-speed)
11 Primary gear (5-speed)

12 Lock bolt
13 Guide bolt
14 Lock bolt and ball and spring
15 Transaxle case assembly
16 Magnet
17 Reverse idle shaft
18 Reverse idle gear
19 Lock bolt
20 Shift rod (5th and reverse)
   and clip
21 Gate
22 Springpin

23 Crank lever shaft
24 O-ring
25 Crank lever assembly
26 Shift fork and shift
   rod assembly
27 Steel ball
28 Spring
29 Primary shaft gear assembly
30 Secondary shaft gear
   assembly
31 Ring gear and differential
   assembly

4 speed

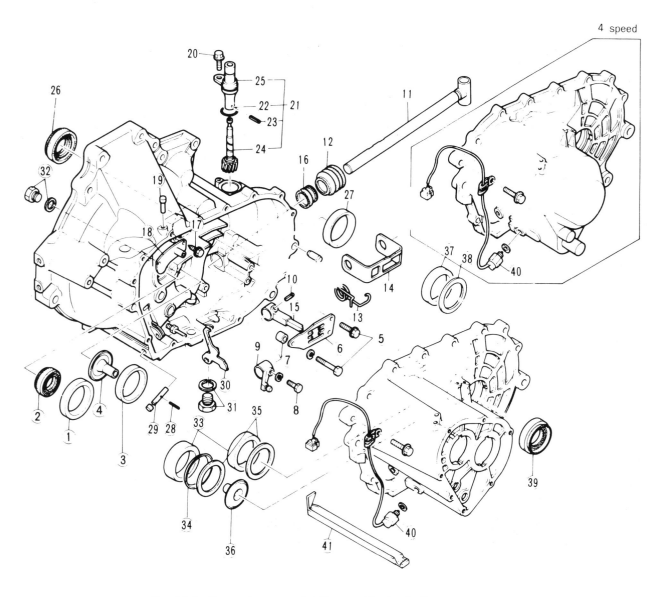

Fig. 7A.7 Transaxle case and shift assembly details (Sec 5 through 9)

1 Bearing outer race	12 Boot	22 O-ring	32 Bolt and washer
2 Oil seal	13 Spring (5-speed)	23 Springpin	33 Bearing outer race
3 Bearing outer race	14 Reverse gate (5-speed)	24 Driven gear	34 Diaphragm spring
4 Funnel	15 Selector	25 Gear case	35 Adjusting shim
5 Bolts	16 Oil seal	26 Driveaxle oil seal	36 Funnel
6 Guide plate	17 Bolts	27 Bearing outer race	37 Bearing outer race
7 Pipe	18 Breather cover	28 Springpin	38 Adjusting shim
8 Bolt	19 Breather	29 Reverse lever shaft	39 Oil seal
9 Change arm	20 Bolts	30 Reverse lever	40 Backup light switch
10 Springpin	21 Speedometer driven gear	31 Drain bolt and washer	41 Oil passage
11 Change rod	assembly		

7   Remove the guide bolt from the the case (photo). Remove the lock bolt, ball and spring.

8   Unscrew the backup light connector from the case.

9   Mark the location of the wiring clamp for ease of reassembly and remove the transaxle bolts.

10 Carefully separate the halves of the case (photos).

11 Remove the 5th gear oil passage (photo).

12 Remove the magnet from the case.

13 Remove the idler shaft and gear (photo).

14 Remove the lock bolt from the 5th gear and the reverse lock plate (photo).

15 On 4-speed models, remove the shift gate and reverse lever as as a unit, with the shifter in Neutral.

16 Remove the 5th gear and reverse rod (photo).

17 Remove the 5th and reverse gear shift gate (photo).

18 Drive out the crank lever retaining pin and remove the pin (5-speed) (photos).

19 Remove the crank lever assembly while moving the shift rod to assist in its release (5-speed) (photo).

20 Making sure the interlock sleeve end surface is flush with the control lever end surface, turn the change rod counterclockwise as far as it will go (photo).

5.7 Remove the guide bolt from the case

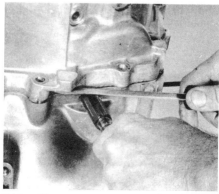

5.10a Use two screwdrivers to carefully separate the transaxle case halves

5.10b Carefully lift the case half off the shafts

5.11 Use a scraper to remove the 5th gear oil passage which is held in place with gasket sealant

5.13 Lift out the reverse idle shaft and remove the gear

5.14 Remove the 5th gear and reverse lock plate bolt

5.16 Use a screwdriver to lift out the 5th gear and reverse rod

5.17 Remove the 5th gear and reverse shift gate

5.18a Use a punch to drive out the crank lever retaining pin

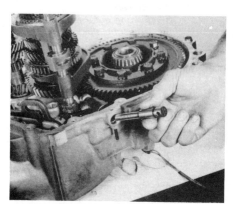

5.18b Remove the crank lever pin

5.19 Lift out the crank lever while moving the shifter

5.20 Rotate the control rod counterclockwise

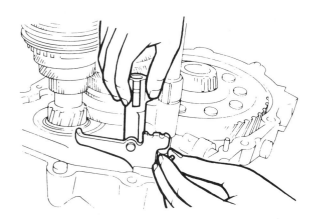

Fig. 7A.8 The 4-speed gearshift and lever are removed as a unit (Sec 5)

21 Pull up on the change rod. It may be necessary to pry upward on the interlock ball.
22 Drive out the retaining pin from the change rod (photo).
23 Place the transaxle in 4th gear by pulling upward on the upper shift fork (photo).
24 Pull the shift rod carefully out of the housing. When the rod is clear of the housing, the steel ball will fall from the reverse lever shaft.
25 Lift the secondary gear shaft and shift fork assembly from the transaxle case (photo).
26 Remove the primary gear assembly.
27 Remove the differential assembly (photo).
28 Remove the Neutral switch or 5th gear switch.
29 Remove the input shaft oil seals and bearing races.
30 Remove the funnel from the transaxle case.
31 Unbolt and remove the shifter guide plate and arm.
32 Drive out the shift arm retaining pin, making sure the selector lever is centered.
33 Remove the change shaft boot from the transaxle housing and withdraw the shaft (photo).
34 Remove the reverse gate spring bushing and selector.
35 Carefully drive out the bearing races (photo).
36 Remove the change rod seal from the case.
37 Remove the driveaxle seals from the case by tapping them out with a hammer and punch, working around the circumference.
38 Remove the differential bearing race.
39 Remove the breather baffle.
40 Remove the control lever spring.

5.22 Use a punch to drive the retaining pin from the control end of the rod

5.23 Shift into 4th gear by pulling the shift fork upward

5.25 Remove the secondary gearshaft assembly by lifting it carefully upward

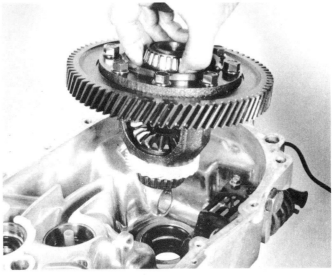

5.27 Lift the differential assembly from the transaxle case

5.33 Withdraw the boot and change shaft

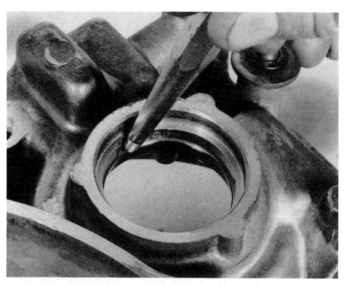

5.35 Drive the bearing race out by tapping evenly around the circumference with a punch and hammer

6 Secondary gear shaft assembly — inspection and overhaul

1   Remove the secondary gear shaft from the transaxle (Section 5).
2   Place the shaft in a vise, using two blocks of wood to protect it from damage. Check the gear thrust clearances with a feeler gauge and check them against Specifications (photo).
3   Use a puller to remove the roller bearing from the end of the shaft and lift off 4th gear.
4   Remove the synchronizer ring.
5   Remove the 3rd and 4th gear clutch hub assembly retaining rings.
6   Carefully pry the 3rd and 4th gear clutch hub assembly off the shaft.
7   Remove the 3rd gear synchronizer ring.
8   Remove the 3rd gear assembly.
9   Remove the thrust washer retaining ring, followed by the thrust washers.
10 Remove 2nd gear.
11 Remove the synchronizer ring.
12 Remove the 1st gear retaining ring.
13 Special tools are required to press off the 1st gear and the 1st and 2nd gear synchronizer assembly. This operation will have to be performed by your dealer or a properly equipped shop.
14 Remove the bearing with a puller.

15 Inspect the gears for worn or damaged synchro cones, hub sleeve wear, worn or damaged teeth or worn surfaces.
16 Check the secondary shaft for worn or damaged sliding and contact surfaces, splines or teeth as well as for clogged oil passages.
17 Check the synchro rings by pressing them into position and then rotating them to make sure they slide smoothly. Measure the clearance with a feeler gauge and compare them to Specifications (photo).
18 Inspect the clutch hub assembly and shifter for grooves, galling and wear.
19 Disassemble the synchronizer hub and inspect the splines and surfaces for wear and the springs to make sure they are not bent or weak.
20 Reassemble the hub with the raised portion of the key facing the outer edge of the hub. When installing the spring, make sure it is in the center indentation of the keys.
21 Check the clutch hub-to-shifter clearance with a feeler gauge (photo).
22 Replace any worn or damaged components with new ones.
23 Install the bearing on the gear end of the shaft.
24 Invert the shaft and install 1st and 2nd gear clutch hubs assembly with the shift fork groove downward.
25 Install the 1st and 2nd gear assembly snap rings.
26 Install the synchro ring into the hub, aligning the groove with the keys in the hub.
27 Install 2nd gear.

6.2 Check gear thrust clearances with a feeler gauge

6.17 Check the synchro ring for free movement

6.21 Check the clutch hub and shifter clearance

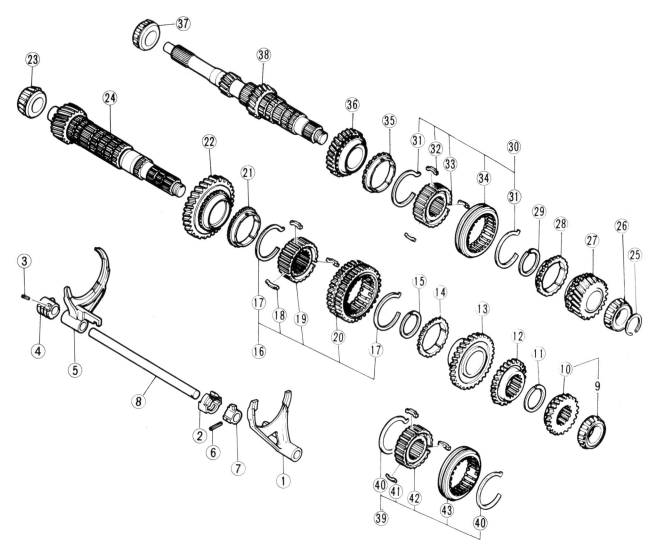

Fig. 7A.9 Primary and secondary gearshaft component layout (Sec 6)

1 Shift fork (3rd and 4th gears)
2 Interlock sleeve
3 Springpin
4 Control end
5 Shift fork (1st and 2nd gears)
6 Springpin
7 Control lever
8 Control rod
9 Bearing outer race
10 4th gear
11 Retaining ring
12 3rd gear

23 Bearing inner race
24 Secondary shaft
25 Snap ring (4-speed)
26 Bearing inner race
27 4th gear
28 Synchronizer ring
29 Retaining ring
30 3rd and 4th gear clutch
      hub assembly
31 Synchronizer spring
32 Synchronizer key

13 2nd gear
14 Synchronizer ring
15 Retaining ring
16 Clutch hub assembly
17 Synchronizer spring
18 Synchronizer key
19 Clutch hub
20 Reverse gear clutch
      hub sleeve
21 Synchronizer ring
22 1st gear

33 Clutch hub
34 Clutch hub sleeve
35 Synchronizer ring
36 3rd gear
37 Bearing inner race
38 Primary shaft
39 Clutch hub assembly
40 Synchronizer spring
41 Synchronizer key
42 Clutch hub
43 Clutch hub sleeve

28 Install the synchro ring into the hub, aligning the groove with the keys in the hub.
29 Install the thrust washer retaining rings.
30 Install 3rd gear and the 3rd gear synchro ring.
31 Install the 3rd/4th gear synchro with the grooved surfaces downward and the keys aligned. Installation may require the use of a press.
32 Install the 3rd/4th gear retaining ring.
33 Install the 4th gear synchro ring, followed by 4th gear.
34 Take the shaft to a dealer or properly equipped shop to have the bearing pressed onto the shaft.

7 Primary gear shaft assembly — inspection and overhaul

1 Remove the assembly and place it securely in a vise using wood blocks to protect the shaft surface.
2 Use a puller to remove the bearings from both ends of the shaft (photo).
3 Inspect the shaft and gears for worn or damaged splines, sliding surfaces or damaged teeth.
4 Inspect the bearings for wear, looseness, galling or pitting of the bearing rollers.

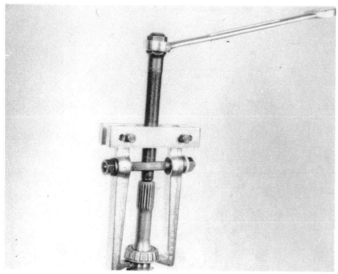

7.2   Remove the primary shaft bearing with a puller tool

5   Replace any worn components with new ones.
6   Press the bearings onto the shaft and reinstall the assembly.

---

8   Differential — inspection and overhaul

1   Remove the differential from the transaxle (Section 5) and place it securely in a vise, using wood blocks to protect the surface.
2   Remove the bolts and lift the ring gear from the gear case. (The ring gear may be secured to the case by rivets, in which case it cannot be removed.)
3   Remove the pinion shaft spring pin by driving it out from the opposite side of the gear case.
4   Remove the pinion shaft, gears and thrust washers.
5   Remove the gear case bearing inner race using a press and bearing removal tool.
6   Remove the remaining bearing with a puller.
7   Remove the speedometer drive gear.
8   Inspect the gears and sliding and contact surfaces for wear, cracks and galling.
9   Check the side and pinion gear assembly. This is done with the driveaxles inserted in the differential assembly. With the axles supported on B-blocks, measure the backlash of both pinion gears by manually moving them the full distance of free travel. If the backlash exceeds specification, obtain a thrust washer of the proper thickness from your dealer and install it between the differential case and side gears. The thrust washers should be of similar thickness.
10   Prior to reassembly, wash each part thoroughly in solvent.
11   During reassembly, apply clean transmission oil to all sliding surfaces and replace with new ones any spring pins which were removed.
12   Install the speedometer drive gear.
13   Install the side bearings, using the approved special tool and hydraulic press or take the assembly to your dealer or a suitably equipped shop to have this operation performed.
14   Install the pinion and side gears, using the appropriate thrust washers.
15   Install the pinion shaft, making sure the spring pin hole is aligned with the hole in the gear case.
16   Install the spring pin by tapping it in place with a hammer and drift, working from the speedometer gear side.
17   Install the ring gear and tighten the bolts (if applicable).
18   Install the differential assembly in the transaxle.

---

9   Transaxle — reassembly

1   Install the drain plug in the case.
2   Install the secondary shaft outer bearing race by placing it in posi-

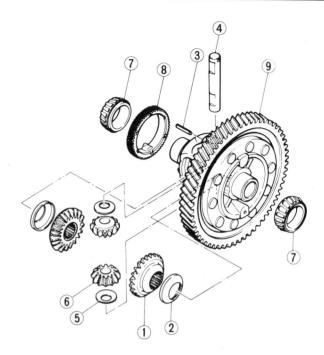

Fig. 7A.10   Differential assembly component layout (Sec 8)

1 Side gears	6 Pinion gears
2 Thrust washer	7 Side bearing inner races
3 Springpin	8 Speedometer drive gear
4 Pinion shaft	9 Ring gear and gear case
5 Thrust washer	assembly

tion with its shim. Tap lightly around the circumference with a drift punch and a hammer until the race is seated.
3   Install the differential bearing race and shims, matching the numbers on the shims with those on the removed items.
4   Install the primary shaft shim spring (raised portion up), followed by the spring.
5   Install the reverse lever shaft and spring.
6   Install the oil deflector.
7   Install the shift rod oil seal.
8   Insert the shift rod and install the shifter, making sure the spring pin is in the proper position.
9   Place the selector rod tip through the right hole of the reverse gate and lower the assembly into position so that the shift rod can be inserted.
10   Place the reverse gate spring in position and insert the reverse shift rod through the spring on the end of the gate.
11   Position the shift arm onto the end of the shift rod.
12   Secure the selector to the shift rod with the spring pin.
13   Secure the selector guide plate with the three bolts. The bolts are dissimilar and the one without a washer is installed at the upper right corner. The reverse gate spring must be installed around the rear bolt spacer.
14   Install the lock bolt and washer onto the shift arm.
15   Install the gear lube funnel, followed by the secondary shaft bearing race.
16   Install the primary shaft seal with the open end upward.
17   Install the primary shaft bearing into the case and tap it into place.
18   Place the magnet in the slot in the transaxle case.
19   Install the differential in the case.
20   Lubricate the inner lip of the differential seal with clean transaxle oil and install it in the case.
21   Install the spring in the reverse lever shaft.
22   Position the shift fork assembly on the secondary shaft gear assembly. Use care when installing and make sure the gears are properly meshed with the differential and primary shaft. The shift fork

assembly must be inserted into the proper boss in the transaxle case.

23 Carefully pull the shift fork assembly slightly upward and outward of its boss by tilting the secondary gear shaft assembly. Slide the control up as far as it will go and rotate it 90° from the Neutral position. Place the ball in the end of the reverse lever shaft and rotate the rod into the Neutral position. Carefully reinsert the rod into its transaxle case boss.

24 Install the spring pin into the shift fork assembly rod control end and tap it into place.

25 Install the crank lever assembly which connects the shift arm to the shift fork assembly rod control end.

26 Install a new O-ring on the crank lever shaft. Lubricate the crank lever with clean transaxle oil and install it. Secure the lever with the spring retaining pin.

27 Place the reverse gate in place and slide the 5th gear and reverse rod into position with the dimple on the rod facing out. The hole in the shift rod must be aligned with the reverse gate.

28 Install the reverse idler gear and shaft. Place the gear in position, insert the shaft with the shaft hole lined up with the rib in the transaxle case.

29 On 5-speed models, use RTV-type sealant to install the oil passage on the transaxle case.

30 Install the transaxle case onto the differential case, carefully placing it so the primary and secondary gear shafts seat in their bosses. It may be necessary to align the magnet with the slot in the upper case half.

31 Install the transaxle case retaining bolts and tighten them to the specified torque in a criss-cross pattern.

32 Install the primary shift rod lock bolt and seal washer. It may be necessary to lift up on the secondary shift shaft to properly align the lock bolt. Tighten the bolt securely (5-speed).

33 Install the reverse idler shaft lock bolt (5-speed).

34 Install the primary gear and locknut, with the nut finger tight (5-speed).

35 Lubricate the primary shaft gear sleeve with clean transaxle fluid and slide it into place (5-speed).

36 Lubricate and install the 5th gear.

37 Install the 5th speed synchronizer ring.

38 Install the clutch hub assembly and shift fork, aligning the keys with the slots in the synchronizer ring securing the fork with the roll pin (5-speed).

39 Install the synchronizer stopper plate (5-speed).

40 Install the secondary shaft lock nut finger tight (5-speed).

41 Tighten both locknuts and use a punch and hammer to peen the nut collars into the shaft grooves to keep them from turning (5-speed).

42 Apply sealant to the transaxle 5th speed cover and install the cover and bolts, tightening to the specified torque.

43 Install the axleshaft seals.

44 Install the backup light switch in the case.

45 Lightly lubricate the O-ring with clean transaxle oil, install it on the speedometer gear assembly. Install the speedometer gear assembly.

46 Install the transaxle (Section 4).

10 Transaxle seals — replacement

1   The primary shaft oil seal can only be replaced after removing the transaxle. The driveaxle oil seals can be replaced with the transmission installed. Proceed as follows.

2   Remove the driveaxle or joint shaft from the transaxle as described in Chapter 8.

3   Carefully pry out the old oil seal, using a blunt screwdriver or similar tool.

4   Coat the new seal with transaxle oil. Install the seal, open lip facing into the transaxle, and use a piece of pipe or a large socket to seat it.

5   Install the driveaxle or joint shaft as described in Chapter 8.

Chapter 7 Part B Automatic transaxle

Contents

Specifications

Torque specifications

	Ft-lbs	M-kg
Crossmember		
All 10 mm bolts	32 to 40	4.4 to 5.5
12 mm bolt	69 to 85	9.5 to 11.8
Inhibitor switch	14 to 19	1.9 to 2.6
Oil pan bolts	4 to 6	0.5 to 0.8
Torque converter bolts	25 to 36	3.5 to 5.0
Transaxle-to-engine bolts	66 to 86	9.1 to 11.9

---

1 General information

Due to the complexity of the clutches and the hydraulic control system, and because of the special tools and expertise required to perform an automatic transaxle overhaul, this should not be undertaken by the home mechanic. Therefore, the procedures in this Chapter are limited to general diagnosis, routine maintenance and adjustment, transaxle removal and installation and replacement of the input and output shaft seals.

If the transaxle requires major repair work, it should be left to a dealer service department or a transmission repair shop. You can, however, remove and install the transaxle yourself and save the expense, even if the repair work is done by a transmission specialist.

Adjustments that the home mechanic can perform include those involving the kickdown switch and solenoid, the inhibitor (neutral start) switch, vacuum diaphragm and the shift linkage. **Caution:** *Never tow a disabled vehicle at speeds greater than 30 mph or distances over*

50 miles unless the front wheels are off the ground. Failure to observe this precaution may result in severe transmission damage caused by lack of lubrication.

---

2 Diagnosis — general

Automatic transmission malfunctions may be caused by four general conditions: poor engine performance, improper adjustments, hydraulic malfunctions and mechanical malfunctions. Diagnosis of these problems should always begin with a check of the easily repaired items: fluid level and condition, shift linkage adjustment and throttle linkage adjustment. Next, perform a road test to determine if the problem has been corrected or if more diagnosis is necessary. If the problem persists after the preliminary tests and corrections are completed, additional diagnosis should be done by a dealer service department or a transmission repair shop.

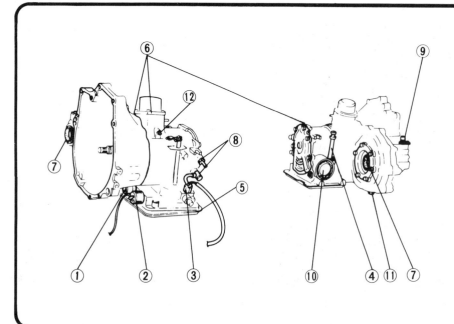

Fig. 7B.1 Automatic transaxle details (Sec 2)

1 Vacuum diaphragm
2 Kickdown solenoid
3 Inhibitor switch
4 Oil level tube
5 Oil pan
6 Case
7 Oil seal
8 Oil pipe
9 Speedometer gear
10 Servo retainer
11 Drain plug
12 Fluid pressure detection plug

3 Vacuum diaphragm — testing and replacement

1 Symptoms of a fault in the vacuum diaphragm include vibration during shifts and incomplete shifts.
2 Drain approximately one quart of fluid from the transaxle so the level will be below the vacuum diaphragm (Chapter 1).
3 Disconnect the vacuum hose and remove the vacuum diaphragm from the transaxle.
4 Connect a vacuum pump to the diaphragm and check that the rod moves when vacuum is applied. If the rod does not move or moves less than one inch, replace the diaphragm with a new one.
5 Apply sealant to the diaphragm threads 'before installation.
6 After installation, check the fluid level and add as necessary (Chapter 1).

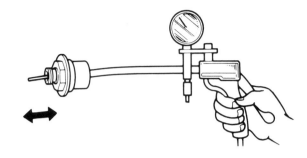

Fig. 7B.2 Checking the vacuum diaphragm (Sec 3)

4 Kickdown switch — checking and adjustment

1 If the transaxle will not shift down when the throttle pedal is fully depressed and the kickdown solenoid is operating properly (Section 5), the kickdown switch could be faulty or out of adjustment.

Checking

2 With the throttle pedal completely depressed, use an ohmmeter to make sure there is continuity between the terminals as shown in the accompanying illustration.

Adjustment

3 Loosen the locknut and turn the kickdown switch until the ohmmeter indicates continuity when the throttle pedal is depressed seven-eighths of full travel. Tighten the locknut.

5 Kickdown solenoid — checking

1 A fault in the kickdown solenoid is indicated if the transaxle will not shift down when the throttle is depressed or if the downshift is hesitant or rough.
2 Raise the front of the vehicle and support it securely on jackstands. Drain approximately one quart of fluid from the transaxle (Chapter 1).
3 Trace the wire to the connector near the battery and unplug it.
4 Unscrew the switch with a large pair of pliers (photo) and plug the opening with a rag.
5 Hold your finger on the solenoid plunger. Place the switch on the

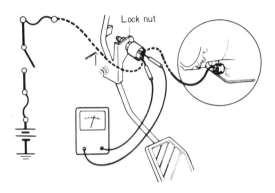

Fig. 7B.3 Checking the kickdown switch for continuity (Sec 4)

battery negative post and touch the connector to the positive post to make sure the plunger retracts (photo).
6 Replace the solenoid with a new one if there is any doubt about its condition.
7 Apply sealant to the solenoid threads before installation.
8 After installation, check the fluid level and add as necessary.

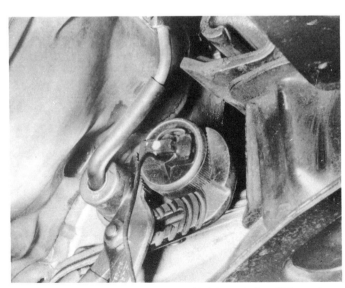

5.4 Use large pliers to unscrew the kickdown solenoid from the transaxle case

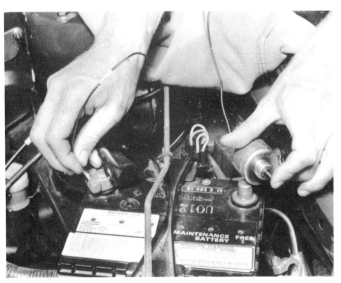

5.5 Testing the kickdown solenoid

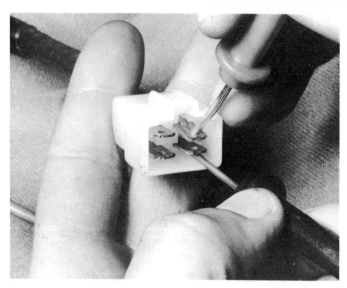

6.3   Checking the inhibitor switch

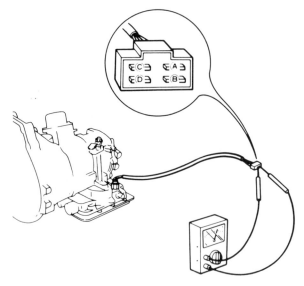

Fig. 7B.4   Inhibitor switch terminals (Sec 6)

6   Inhibitor switch — checking and replacement

Checking

1   Check the inhibitor switch for proper operation by making sure that the engine starts only with the shifter in the Park and Neutral positions.
2   Trace the wire from the switch to the connector and unplug the connector.
3   Check the switch connector terminals for continuity in Park, Reverse and Neutral with an ohmmeter (photo).
4   With the ignition on and the shifter in the noted positions, there should be continuity between:

Park position — A and B terminals
Reverse position — C and D terminals
Neutral position — A and B terminals

Replacement

5   Unplug the connector and unscrew the switch from the transaxle. Installation is the reverse of removal. Apply sealant to the switch threads before installation.

7   Transaxle — removal and installation

Removal

1   Disconnect the battery negative cable.
2   Disconnect the speedometer cable.
3   Disconnect the shift control cable from the transaxle (photo).
4   Disconnect the battery negative cable and ground wires from the transaxle.
5   Disconnect the inhibitor switch and kickdown solenoid.
6   Remove the starter motor (Chapter 5).
7   There are two principal ways of supporting the weight of the engine during the removal of the transaxle. A special support fixture can be obtained which rests on the suspension strut mount towers or an engine hoist can be used. If the engine support fixture is being used, install it at this time. If the engine hoist is being used to support the engine, the hood must be removed to gain sufficient clearance (see Chapter 11).
8   Connect the support to the engine and raise the vehicle to provide sufficient clearance for lowering the transaxle and support it securely on jackstands (photo).

7.3   Use needle nose pliers to remove the shift cable retaining clip

7.8   The engine must be supported during transaxle removal

9   Disconnect the oil cooler lines at the transaxle.
10 Disconnect and tag any remaining vacuum or electrical connectors that are attached to the transaxle or will interfere with the removal of the transaxle.
11 Remove the upper transaxle-to-engine bolts (photo).
12 Remove the front wheels and splash shields. Also remove the oil pan protector plate (when equipped).
13 Disconnect the stabilizer bar, remove the lower balljoint-to-steering knuckle bolts and nuts and separate the balljoints from the knuckles (Chapter 10).
14 Disconnect the left driveaxle from the transaxle (Chapter 8). Use a piece of wire to fasten the left driveaxle out of the way.
15 Remove the joint shaft and bracket assembly (Chapter 8). Insert a wooden dowel or similar item to retain the differential side gears.
16 Remove the torque converter access plate and separating plate (photo).
17 With an assistant rotating the engine with a wrench on the crankshaft pulley bolt to bring them into position, remove the torque converter bolts (photo).
18 Remove all but two of the crossmember assembly bolts.
19 Place a jack under the crossmember, remove the bolts and lower the crossmember assembly.
20 Support the transaxle with the jack.
21 Making sure the engine weight is supported by the lift, remove the two lower transaxle-to-engine bolts.
22 Slide the transaxle away from the engine and carefully lower the jack until until it is clear of the vehicle (photo).

Installation

23 Raise the transaxle into position while an assistant guides it, making sure the torque converter is not dislodged.
24 Install the transaxle-to-engine mounting bolts, tightening to the specified torque.
25 Install the engine crossmember.
26 The rest of the installation procedure is the reverse of the removal procedure with the following notes:
  a) Make sure all nuts and bolts are torqued to the proper value.
  b) Check the transaxle fluid level (Chapter 1).

---

8   Transaxle seals — replacement

Input shaft seal

1   Remove the transaxle (Section 7).
2   Remove the torque converter from the input shaft.
3   Pry the old seal out using a small screwdriver or punch (photo).
4   Coat the inner circumference of the seal with clean engine oil and

7.11   Transaxle bolt locations (arrows)

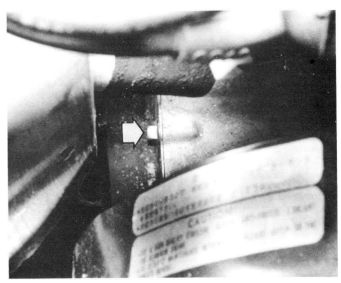

7.16   Torque converter access cover bolt location (arrow)

7.17   Lock the flywheel gear teeth with a screwdriver when removing the torque converter bolts

7.22   Lower the transaxle carefully because it can easily topple off the jack

8.3   Use a punch or similar tool to pry the input shaft seal out of its bore

8.4   The head of the punch and hammer can be used to seat the new seal fully into the bore

tap it into the bore until it is flush with the housing (photo). The open lip of the seal should face inwards.
5   Install the torque converter.
6   Install the transaxle.

Axleshaft seals

7   Disconnect the left-hand driveaxle or remove the joint shaft (Chapter 8). If both the driveaxle and the joint shaft are to be disconnected, insert a wooden dowel or similar item to retain the differential side gears. Do not introduce dirt into the transaxle.
8   Pry the old seal out with a screwdriver (photo).
9   Lubricate the inner circumference of the new seal with clean engine oil or white lithium base grease. Using a piece of pipe or a large socket of 1-3/4 inch (45 mm) diameter, tap the seal evenly into the bore (photo). The open lip of the seal must face inwards.
10   Install the driveaxle or joint shaft (Chapter 8).

8.8   Pry out the old axleshaft seal with a screwdriver

9   Shift linkage — check and adjustment

1   Move the shifter through each position, making sure the movement into each detent is positive and corresponds to the shifter plate. Slight resistance should be felt entering each detent.
2   The shifter should move between Drive and Neutral without the need to depress the button on the shifter handle. The button must be depressed when moving from Drive to Reverse.
3   If the button is loose or if the shifter can be moved from Drive to Reverse without pressing the button, adjust the shifter knob. Loosen the locknut, twist the shifter knob until proper operation of the linkage is attained and tighten the locknut.

10   Oil pan gasket — replacement

1   Drain the fluid from the transaxle (Chapter 1, Section 28). **Warning:** *The fluid may be very hot.*
2   Remove the oil pan securing bolts and the oil pan itself. Be prepared for further fluid spillage.
3   Scrape the remains of the old gasket off the oil pan and/or transaxle case. Be careful not to gouge the metal, nor to introduce dirt into the transaxle.
4   Install the new gasket on the transaxle case, using a smear of clean grease to hold it in position.
5   Install the oil pan and secure it with the bolts. Tighten the bolts progressively to the specified torque.
6   Install the drain plug, then fill the transaxle with fresh fluid (Chapter 1, Section 28).
7   Check for leaks when the vehicle is next run.

8.9   Use a socket and rubber mallet to tap the new axleshaft seal fully into the transaxle case bore

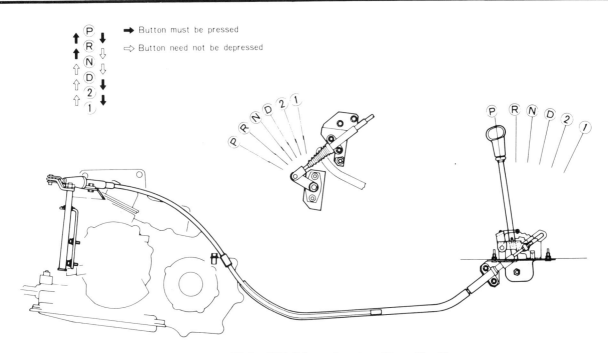

→ Button must be pressed

⇨ Button need not be depressed

Fig. 7B.5   Shift linkage detent positions (Sec 9)

**Fig. 7B.6   Automatic transaxle shifter component layout
(Sec 9)**

1 Knob
2 Knob locknut
4 Cable locknut
6 Shifter lever bracket
7 Nut and washer
8 Lever mounting bolt
9 Guide pin
10 Push rod
11 Shifter lever
12 Cable-to-transaxle pin
13 Shifter cable

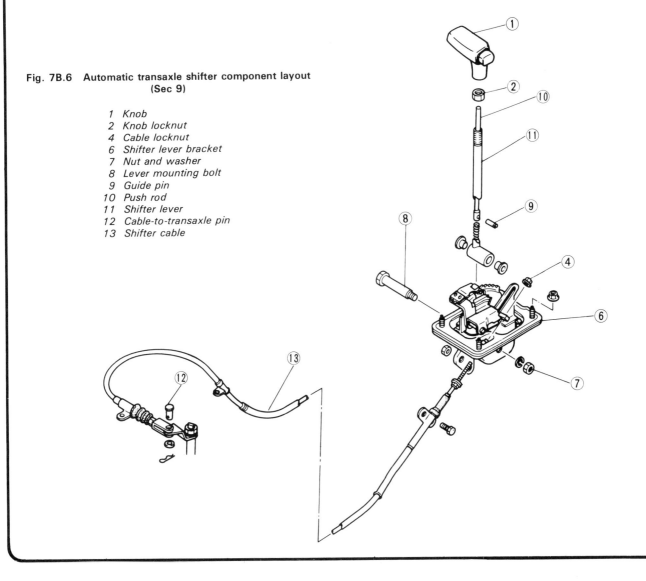

Chapter 8 Clutch and driveaxles

Contents

Specifications

Clutch pilot bearing-to-crankshaft end surface clearance
(Dimension A in Fig. 8.11) .... 0.087 to 0.110 in (2.5 to 2.8 mm)

Torque specifications

	Ft-lbs	M-kg
Clutch release lever and fork bolt	8	1.1
Clutch pressure plate-to-flywheel bolts	15 to 20	2.2 to 2.7
Driveaxle (hub) nut	116 to 174	16.0 to 24.0
Flywheel bolts	71 to 76	9.8 to 10.5
Stabilizer bar nut	9 to 13	1.2 to 1.8
Steering knuckle-to-shock absorber bolt	69 to 86	9.5 to 11.9
Steering knuckle-to-balljoint	32 to 40	4.4 to 5.5
Wheel nut	65 to 87	9.0 to 12.0

1 Clutch — general information

Manual transaxle equipped vehicles use a single dry plate, diaphragm spring-type clutch. Operation is through a foot pedal, cable, release lever and fork assembly and a release bearing.

2 Clutch operation — checking

1   Before performing any operations on the clutch, several checks can be made to determine if there is actually a fault in the clutch itself.
2   With the engine running and the brake applied, hold the clutch pedal approximately 1/2-inch from its lower limit of travel and shift back and forth several times. If the shifts are smooth, the clutch is releasing properly. If it is not the clutch is not releasing fully and the linkage should be checked.
3   Inspect the clutch pedal bushings for wear or binding.
4   Refer to Chapter 1 for further information on clutch and clutch pedal adjustment.

3 Clutch pedal — removal and installation

Removal

1   Remove the under dash air duct or other trim for access.
2   Remove the clip and disconnect the upper end of the clutch pedal rod.
3   Remove the pedal through bolt and nut, disengage the clutch cable and remove the pedal and rod assembly from the vehicle.

Installation

4   Prior to installation, lubricate the pedal bushing and cable hook liberally with lithium base grease.
5   Place the pedal in position, install the through bolt and nut and connect the clutch cable.
6   Connect the pedal rod.
7   Refer to Chapter 1 and check the clutch pedal height and free play, adjusting as necessary.
8   Adjust the length of the assist spring, by turning the nut on the rod, until the distance between the spring seat and the assist seat is 1.34 ± 0.20 inch.
9   Install the air duct or other trim.

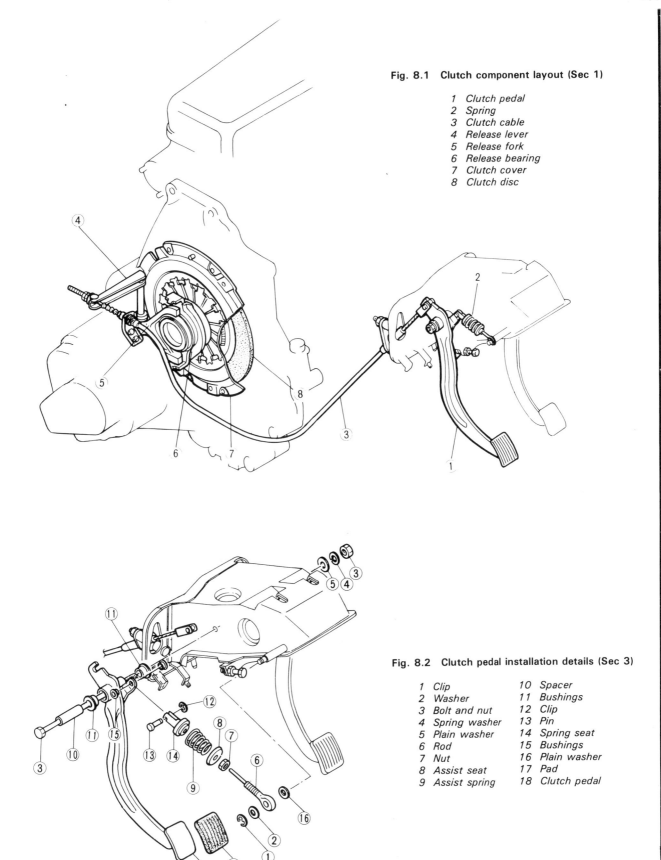

Fig. 8.1   Clutch component layout (Sec 1)

1   Clutch pedal
2   Spring
3   Clutch cable
4   Release lever
5   Release fork
6   Release bearing
7   Clutch cover
8   Clutch disc

Fig. 8.2   Clutch pedal installation details (Sec 3)

1	Clip	10	Spacer
2	Washer	11	Bushings
3	Bolt and nut	12	Clip
4	Spring washer	13	Pin
5	Plain washer	14	Spring seat
6	Rod	15	Bushings
7	Nut	16	Plain washer
8	Assist seat	17	Pad
9	Assist spring	18	Clutch pedal

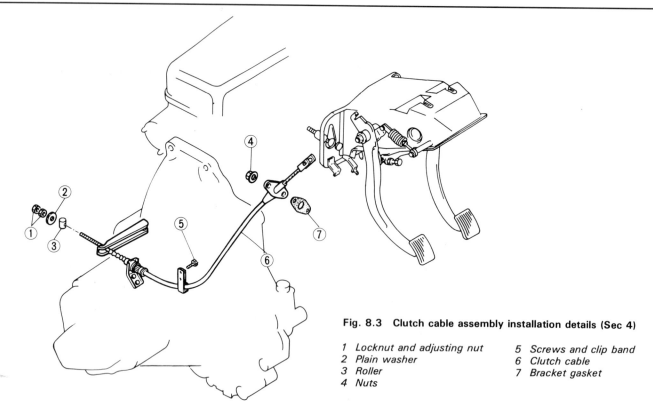

Fig. 8.3 Clutch cable assembly installation details (Sec 4)

1 *Locknut and adjusting nut*   5 *Screws and clip band*
2 *Plain washer*   6 *Clutch cable*
3 *Roller*   7 *Bracket gasket*
4 *Nuts*

4 Clutch cable — removal and installation

Removal

1   In the engine compartment, remove the locknut, adjusting nut and washer from the end of the cable and disengage it from the release lever (photo).
2   Pull the cable from the bracket on the transaxle.
3   Remove the clip band and bracket retaining the cable. Also remove the nuts which hold the cable to the firewall.
4   Inside the passenger compartment remove the under dash air duct or other trim for clearance.
5   Disengage the cable from the pedal and remove it from the vehicle.

Installation

6   Prior to installation, lubricate the contact surfaces of the roller and the release lever.
7   Insert the cable through the firewall and connect it to the clutch pedal. Install the nuts holding the cable to the firewall.
8   Insert the cable in the release arm and install the bracket and clip band.
9   Install the washer, adjusting nut and locknut.
10   Adjust the pedal free play (Chapter 1).
11   Install the air duct or other trim.

4.1   Clutch cable at transaxle end. Adjusting nut and locknut are arrowed

5 Clutch — removal, inspection and installation

Removal

1   Remove the transaxle (Chapter 7).
2   Mark the pressure plate-to-flywheel relationship so that it can be installed in the same position.
3   Use an alignment tool or screwdriver handle to hold the clutch disc during removal of the pressure plate.
4   Lock the flywheel ring gear and loosen the pressure plate retaining bolts evenly, one turn at a time, in a criss-cross pattern so as not to warp the cover.

5   Remove the pressure plate and clutch disc.
6   Handle the disc carefully, taking care not to touch the lining surface, and set it aside.
7   Disconnect the return spring from the release fork hook, twist the release lever and remove the release bearing.
8   Remove the release fork bolt and lift the fork and lever away as a unit.

Inspection

9   Clean the dust out of the clutch housing using a vacuum cleaner or clean cloth. Do not use compressed air as the dust can endanger your health if inhaled.

Fig. 8.4 Clutch component layout (Sec 5)

1 Transaxle   4 Flywheel
2 Clutch cover   5 Release bearing
3 Clutch disc

10 Inspect the pressure plate for damage and wear of the diaphragm spring, scratches, scoring or color changes (indicating overheating) of the friction surface and damage or distortion of the cover. Although minor imperfections of the friction surface can be removed with fine sandpaper, the pressure plate should be replaced with a new unit if there is any doubt as to its condition.

11 Inspect the surface of the flywheel for signs of uneven contact, indicating improper mounting or damaged clutch springs. Check the surface for burned areas, grooves, cracks or other signs of wear. It may be necessary to remove a badly grooved flywheel and have it machined to restore the surface. Light glazing of the flywheel surface can be removed with fine sandpaper.

12 Inspect the clutch lining for contamination by oil, grease or any other substance and replace the disc with a new one if any is present. Check for wear by measuring the distance from the rivet head to the material surface. Replace the disc with a new one if the linings are worn to the limit shown in Fig. 8.6.

13 Inspect the disc for distortion, wear, loose rivets, weak springs

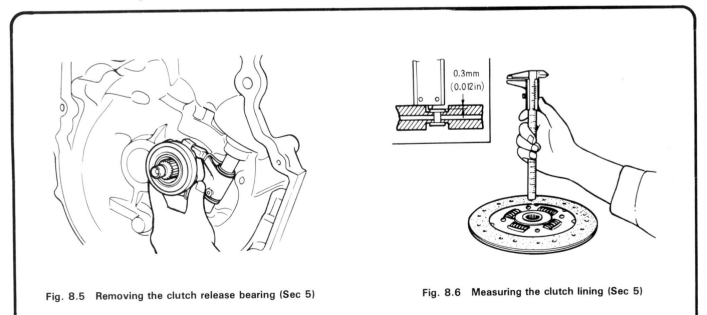

Fig. 8.5 Removing the clutch release bearing (Sec 5)

Fig. 8.6 Measuring the clutch lining (Sec 5)

0.3mm
(0.012in)

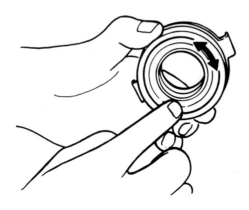

Fig. 8.7   Check the release bearing to make sure that it
rotates smoothly (Sec 5)

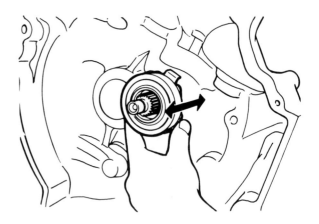

Fig. 8.8   The release bearing must slide back and forth
smoothly in the directions shown (Sec 5)

and damaged splines. Slide the disc onto the input shaft temporarily
to make sure the fit is snug and the splines are not burred or worn.
Replace the disc with a new one if there is any question as to its
condition.

14   Check the release bearing for wear and distortion and make sure
that it turns and slides easily on the input shaft. Unless the vehicle
has very low miles, it is a good idea to replace the bearing with a new
one whenever the clutch is removed.

15   Inspect the clutch housing mounting surface, release lever and
return spring for wear, cracking, distortion, damage and fatigue, replacing as necessary.

16   Check the pilot bearing in the crankshaft to make sure it turns easily
and smoothly by applying force with your finger and rotating it. Replace
the bearing if necessary by removing it with a slide hammer and tapping
a new one into the crankshaft bore using a socket or piece of pipe and
a hammer. Lubricate the new bearing before installation, and observe
the installation dimension shown in Fig. 8.11.

Installation

17   Prior to installation, lubricate the clutch release bearing, input shaft
and clutch disc splines lightly with moly-base grease. Take care to keep
grease off the friction surfaces of the clutch disc, flywheel and pressure
plate.

18   Offer the clutch disc to the flywheel, making sure that it is the
right way around (Fig. 8.12). Hold the disc in place with an alignment
tool or other round bar and install the pressure plate, aligning any marks
made during removal.

19   Install the pressure plate bolts and tighten them in a criss-cross
pattern until the pressure plate starts to grip the clutch disc. Center

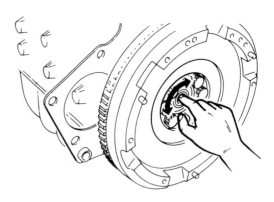

Fig. 8.9   Check the pilot bearing for smooth rotation
(Sec 5)

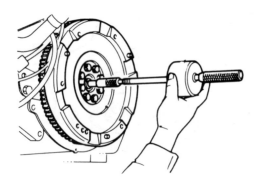

Fig. 8.10   Removing the pilot bearing with a slide hammer
(Sec 5)

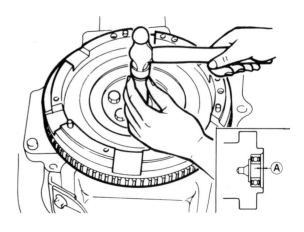

Fig. 8.11   Tap the pilot bearing assembly into place in the
crankshaft (Sec 5)
A = 0.098 ± 0.012 in

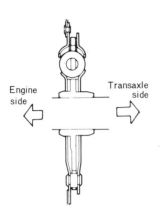

Fig. 8.12 Sectional view of clutch disc showing correct orientation (Sec 5)

5.19 A socket can be used as a clutch alignment tool

the disc relative to the pilot bearing, using a proprietary alignment tool or a round bar or similar item (photo). **Note:** *If the disc is not centered accurately, it will be impossible to install the transaxle.*

20 Tighten the pressure plate bolts, half a turn at a time and in a criss-cross pattern, to the specified torque. Keep the clutch disc centered during this tightening.

21 Install the release lever, fork, spring and bearing.

22 Remove the alignment tool and install the transaxle.

6 Driveaxle — general information

Power is transmitted from the transaxle to the front wheels by drive-axles, which consist of splined solid axles with constant velocity (CV)

joints at each end. The driveaxles are of equal length with a joint shaft located between the transaxle and the right driveaxle. The CV joints are protected by rubber boots which are retained by straps to keep the joints from being contaminated by water and dirt.

The boots should be inspected periodically (Chapter 1) for damage, leaking lubricant or cuts. Damaged CV joint boots must be replaced immediately or the joints can be damaged. Boot replacement involves removing the driveaxles (Section 7).

The most common symptom of worn or damaged CV joints besides lubricant leaks are a clicking noise in turns, a *clunk* when accelerating from a coasting condition or vibration at highway speeds.

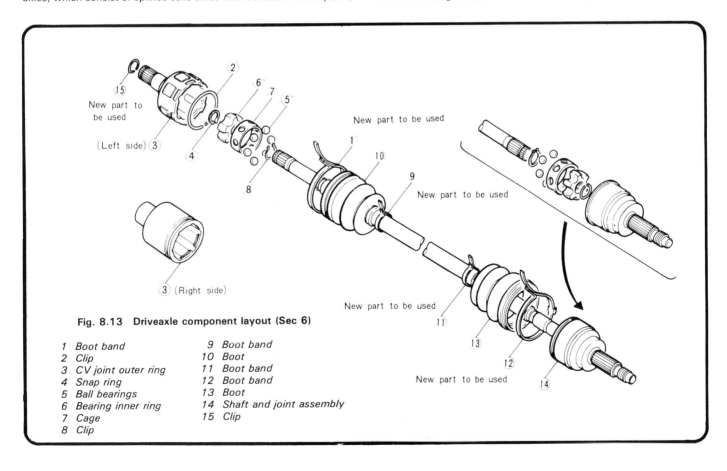

Fig. 8.13 Driveaxle component layout (Sec 6)

1 Boot band
2 Clip
3 CV joint outer ring
4 Snap ring
5 Ball bearings
6 Bearing inner ring
7 Cage
8 Clip
9 Boot band
10 Boot
11 Boot band
12 Boot band
13 Boot
14 Shaft and joint assembly
15 Clip

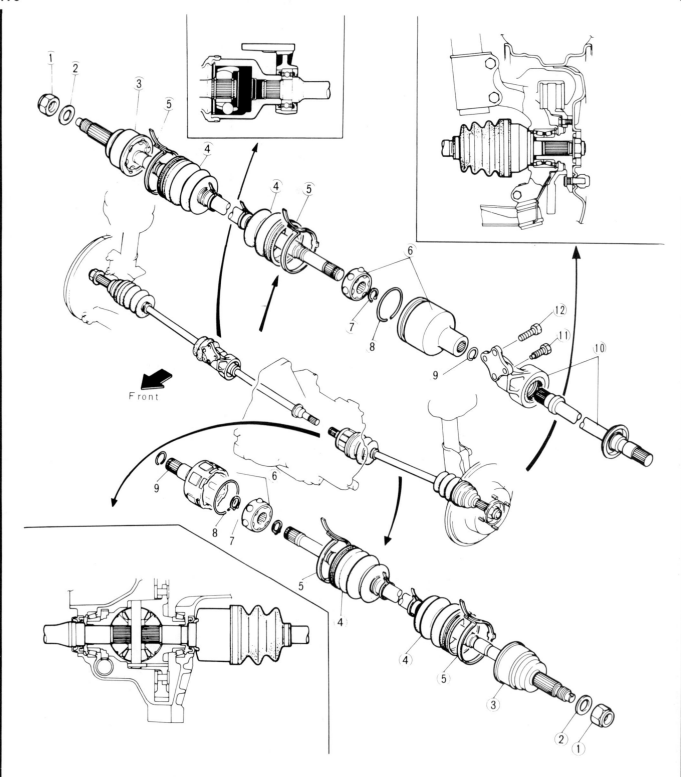

Fig. 8.14 Manual transaxle driveaxle component layout details (Sec 6)

1 Locknut
2 Washer
3 Outer joint assembly
4 Boot
5 Boot band
6 Differential side joint
   assembly
7 Snap ring
8 Clip
9 Clip
10 Joint shaft assembly
11 Reamer bolt
12 Joint shaft bracket
   mounting bolt

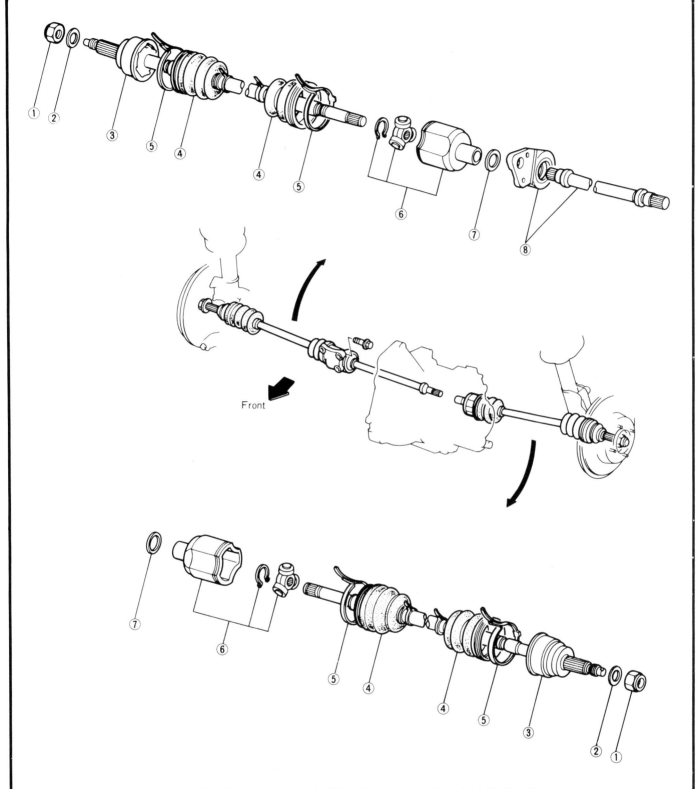

Fig. 8.15 Automatic transaxle driveaxle component layout details (Sec 6)

1 Locknut
2 Washer
3 Outer joint assembly

4 Boot
5 Boot band
6 Tripod joint assembly

7 Clip
8 Joint shaft assembly

7 Driveaxle and joint shaft — removal and installation

Removal

Driveaxle

1   Raise the front of the vehicle, support it securely on jackstands, remove the front wheels and splash shields and drain the transaxle.
2   Lock the brake disc with a screwdriver, relieve the staking and remove the hub nut (photo). This nut is very tight. A new nut will be needed for installation.
3   Disconnect the stabilizer link, remove the balljoint and steering knuckle nuts and bolts and disconnect the strut from the balljoint (Chapter 10).
4   Free the inner end of the driveaxle from the transaxle or joint shaft as shown in the illustrations. Be careful not to damage the transaxle oil seal. On automatic transaxle models it may be necessary to insert a chisel between the driveaxle and housing, tapping the end of the chisel lightly to disengage the driveaxle from the differential. Pull the hub outwards and support the inner joint to disconnect the inner end of the driveaxle.
5   Disengage the driveaxle from the hub, if necessary, using a puller (photo).
6   Support the CV joints and remove the driveaxle from the vehicle (photo).

Joint shaft

7   Disconnect the right-hand driveaxle inner joint as described in paragraphs 1, 3 and 4. Remove the retaining bolts, disengage the joint shaft from the transaxle and lower it from the vehicle. **Note:** *Plug the hole in the transaxle case whenever the driveaxle is removed. When both the driveaxle and the joint shaft are removed, take care not to move the transaxle differential side gear splines. Insert a wooden dowel or similar item to prevent displacement of the side gears.*
8   Disassembly of the joint shaft and replacement of the bearing requires press tools and should be left to a Mazda dealer or suitably equipped workshop.

Installation

Joint shaft

9   Prior to installation, install new clips (available at your dealer) in the driveaxle and joint shaft grooves and lubricate the splines with transaxle lubricant.
10 Insert the joint shaft into the transaxle, install the retaining bolts and tighten them.

Driveaxle

11 Raise the driveaxle into position while supporting the CV joints and insert the splined ends into the hub and transaxle or joint shaft.
12 Seat the driveaxle into the differential by gently tapping it with a piece of wood and a hammer (photo). Pull the hub outwards to check that the driveaxle is securely engaged in the transaxle.
13 Place the steering knuckle in position and install the bolts (Chapter 10).
14 Install the new hub nuts.

7.2   A screwdriver inserted into the rotor through the caliper will hold the hub stationary when loosening and tightening the hub locknut

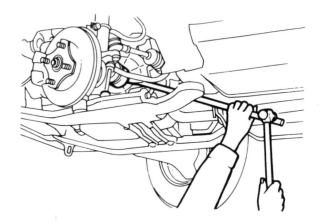

Fig. 8.16   **Disconnect the left driveaxle from the manual transaxle by tapping it out (Sec 7)**

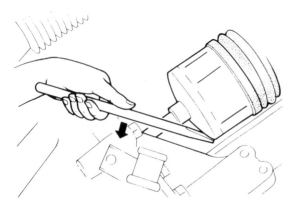

Fig. 8.17   **Disengaging the left driveaxle from the transaxle differential on automatic transaxle models (Sec 7)**

7.5   Using a puller to disengage the driveaxle from the hub

7.6 Support the CV joints and carefully withdraw the driveaxle past the hub assembly

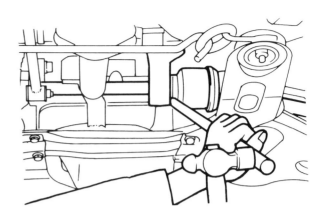

Fig. 8.18 Use a lever and hammer as shown to disengage the right driveaxle and joint shaft from the transaxle (Sec 7)

New clip

Fig. 8.19 The clip must be replaced with a new one whenever the driveaxles or joint shafts are removed (Sec 7)

7.12 Use a hammer and a piece of wood to seat the driveaxle in the transaxle

15 Lock the disc so that it cannot turn, using a screwdriver or punch inserted through the caliper into a disc cooling vane, and tighten the hub nut (Chapter 10).

16 Use a hammer and punch to peen the locknut collar into the groove in the driveaxle.

17 Connect the stabilizer bar, install the splash shields and wheels, fill the transaxle with the specified fluid (Chapter 1) and lower the vehicle.

8 Driveaxle boot — replacement

Note: *Prior to beginning work, obtain the proper boot kit from your dealer. The boot kit contains special moly-base lubricant required for use on Constant Velocity (CV) joints, and no other type should be used.*

1   Remove the driveaxle (Section 7).

2   Place the driveaxle assembly in a vise, using blocks of wood to protect the surface from damage.

3   Cut the boot retaining bands and discard the bands (photo).

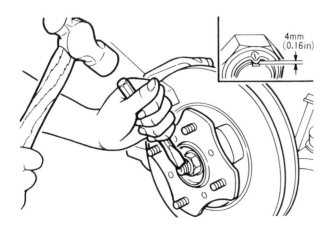

4mm (0.16in)

Fig. 8.20 Peen the locknut collar into the driveaxle groove with a hammer and punch or dull chisel (Sec 7)

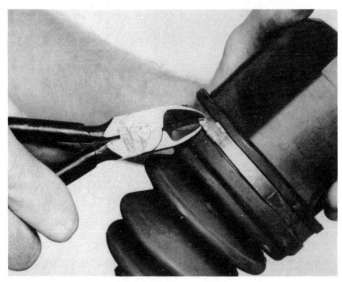

8.3   Cut the driveaxle boot retaining band with a pair of wire cutters

8.5a   Remove the CV joint outer ring retaining clip with a screwdriver

8.5b   Remove the outer ring

4   Pry back the boot and slide it down the shaft, away from the CV joint.
5   Remove the joint outer ring retaining clip (if equipped) with a screwdriver and slide the ring off (photos).
6   Remove the snap ring and slide the bearing assembly off the axleshaft splines (photo).
7   Slide the boot off the axle.
8   Due to the work involved in driveaxle removal and installation, it is a good idea to replace both boots even if only one boot is damaged, unless the vehicle has covered very few miles.
9   Clean the bearing assembly and shaft splines carefully and inspect for wear, damage, and contamination by dirt and water. Replace any damaged components with new ones.
10   Wrap tape around the shaft splines to avoid damaging the sealing surface of the new boot during installation. Lightly lubricate the inner diameter of the new boot and slide it onto the driveaxle. **Note:** *Different boots are used on the wheel and differential sides, which should not be mixed up.*
11   Remove the tape, apply a light coat of grease to the splines and install the bearing assembly and snap ring with the tapered edge facing the shaft (photo).
12   Pack the bearing cavity with the special moly base grease (photo).
13   Install the outer ring.
14   Seat the boot in the grooves.
15   Install the boot retaining bands so that the tightening tab folds in the opposite direction of driveshaft rotation when the vehicle is moving forward.
16   Pull the band tight with a pair of pliers and lock it tightly in place by bending the tabs over and securing them with a blunt tool such as a large punch (photo).
17   Install the driveaxle.

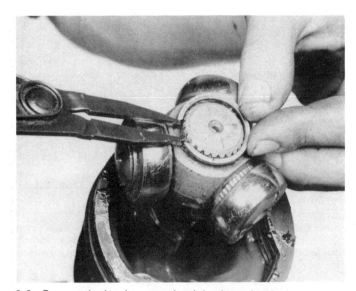

8.6   Remove the bearing snap-ring (tripod-type bearing)

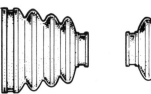 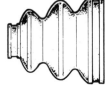

Fig. 8.21   The wheel side (left) and differential side driveaxle boots are different and should not be interchanged (Sec 8)

8.11   The chamfer (arrow) must face toward the axle

8.12a   Carefully pack grease into the cavity

8.12b   Cover the bearing cavity

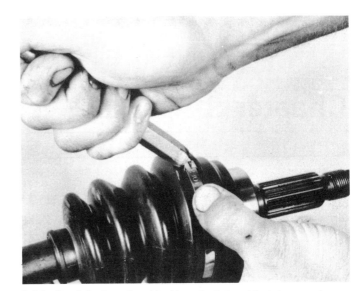

8.16   Bend the boot band locking clip flat and lock it securely with a punch

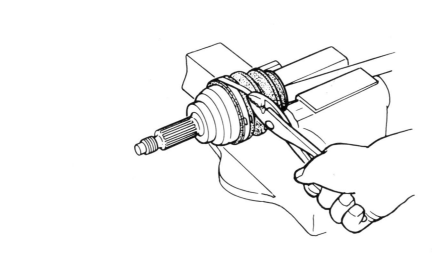

Fig. 8.22   Use pliers to pull the boot band tight (Sec 8)

Chapter 9 Brakes

Contents

Specifications

Disc brakes

Pad lining thickness	0.39 in (10 mm)
Service limit	0.04 in (1.0 mm)
Caliper bore	2.160 in (55 mm)
Rotor	
Thickness	0.55 in (14 mm)
Service limit	0.49 in (12.5 mm)
Runout (maximum)	0.0039 in (0.1 mm)

Rear drum brakes

Lining thickness	0.19 in (5.0 mm)
Service limit	0.04 in (1.0 mm)
Drum diameter	
Standard	7.87 in (200 mm)
Service limit	7.91 in (201 mm)
Wheel cylinder	
Bore	0.748 in (19 mm)
Piston-to-bore clearance	0.002 to 0.005 in (0.05 to 0.127 mm)
Service limit	0.006 in (0.15 mm)

Master cylinder

Bore diameter	0.875 in (22.22 mm)
Piston-to-bore clearance	0.002 to 0.005 in (0.05 to 0.127 mm)
Wear limit	0.006 in (0.15 mm)

Torque specifications

	Ft-lbs	M-kg
Brake pedal-to-bracket	14.5 to 25.3	2 to 3.5
Disc brake caliper mounting bolts		
Upper	12 to 18	1.6 to 2.5
Lower	14.5 to 21.7	2 to 3
Steering knuckle bolts	36 to 55	5 to 7.6
Flexible brake hose-to-caliper		
Front	16 to 19	2.2 to 2.6
Rear	17 to 25	2.3 to 3.5
Wheel cylinder retaining bolt	7 to 11	1 to 1.5
Rear spindle-to-backing plate bolts	50	6.9
Brake pipe flare nut	9.4 to 16	1.3 to 2.2
Wheel lug nuts	65 to 87	9 to 12

1 General information

All vehicles covered by this manual are equipped with hydraulically operated front and rear brake systems. All front brake systems are disc type while the rear brakes are drum type.

All brakes are self adjusting. The front disc brakes automatically compensate for pad wear while the rear drum brakes incorporate an adjustment mechanism which is activated as the brakes are applied until the thickness of the brake lining decreases to less than 0.078 in (2 mm).

The hydraulic system consists of two separate circuits. The master cylinder has separate reservoirs for the two circuits and in the event of a leak or failure in one hydraulic circuit, the other circuit will remain operative. A dual proportioning valve modulates the hydraulic pressure between the front and rear braking systems to prevent wheel lockup. A visual warning of low fluid level is given by a warning light activated by a switch in the master cylinder reservoir.

The parking brake mechanically operates the rear brakes only. It is activated by a pull handle in the center console between the front seats.

The power brake booster, located in the engine compartment on the firewall, uses engine manifold vacuum and atmospheric pressure to provide assistance to the hydraulically operated brakes.

After completing any operation involving the disassembly of any part of the brake system, always test drive the vehicle to check for proper braking performance before resuming normal driving. Test the brakes while driving on a clean, dry, flat surface. Conditions other than these can lead to inaccurate test results. Test the brakes at various speeds with both light and heavy pedal pressure. The vehicle should stop evenly without pulling to one side or the other. Avoid locking the brakes

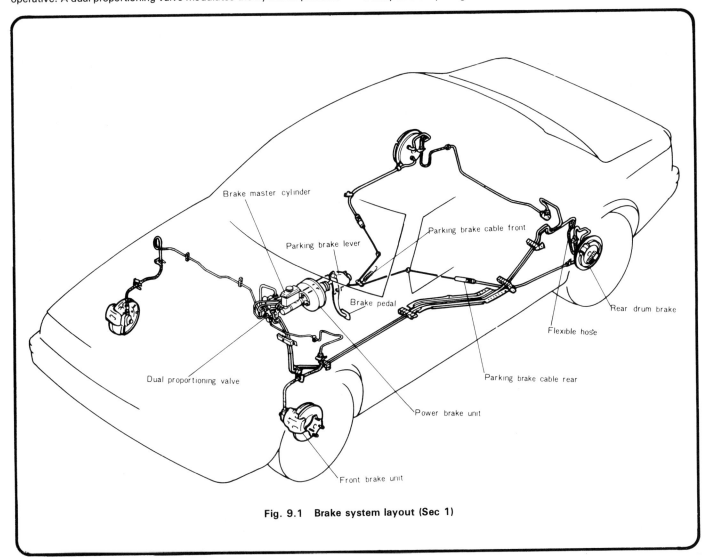

Fig. 9.1 Brake system layout (Sec 1)

because this slides the tires and diminishes braking efficiency and control.

Tires, vehicle load and front end alignment are factors which also affect braking performance.

2   Disc brake pads — replacement

Note: *Disc brake pads should be replaced on both wheels at the same time. Work on one brake at a time, using the other, assembled brake, for reference if necessary.*

1   Whenever you are working on the brake system, be aware that asbestos dust is present and be careful not to inhale any of it as this could be harmful to your health.
2   Remove the cover from the brake fluid reservoir and siphon off about two ounces of the fluid into a container and discard it.
3   Loosen the front wheel bolts, raise the front of the vehicle, support it securely on jackstands and remove the front wheels.
4   Remove the two caliper bolts (photo).
5   Rotate the caliper up, clear of the disc. Support the caliper by hand, or tie it to the suspension strut with string or wire — do not allow it to hang on its hose.
6   Release the clips with a screwdriver and remove the outer pad (photo). Recover the anti-squeal shim from the back of the pad.
7   Remove the inner pad by lifting it from the caliper. Again, recover the anti-squeal shim.
8   Inspect the caliper boot by gently peeling back the edge and checking for signs of fluid leakage (photo). If leakage is found, remove the caliper for overhaul or replacement.
9   Push the caliper back into the piston until it bottoms, using a C-clamp (photo).
10 Install the anti-squeal shims to the new pads. For more information see Fig. 9.3.
11 Place the inner pad in position and snap it into the piston (photo).
12 Slide the outer pad into place and snap it into the caliper.

2.4   The two caliper retaining bolts (arrows)

13 Rotate the caliper back into position.
14 Install the bolts and tighten them to the specified torque.
15 Pump the brake pedal several times to bring the pads up to the disc, then top up the brake fluid reservoir.
16 Install the wheels and lower the vehicle. Tighten the wheel nuts.
17 Avoid harsh braking as far as possible for the first few hundred miles until the new pads have bedded in.

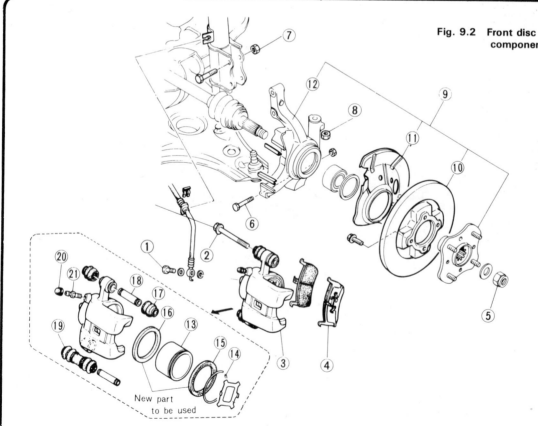

Fig. 9.2   Front disc brake and steering knuckle component layout (Sec 2)

1   Brake hose bolt
2   Caliper retaining bolts
3   Caliper housing
4   Outer brake pad
5   Hub nut
6   Bolt and nut
7   Bolts and nuts
8   Nut
9   Front hub assembly
10 Brake disc
11 Dust cover
12 Steering knuckle
13 Piston
14 Retainer
15 Dust seal
16 Piston seal
17 Dust boot
18 Pin
19 Bushing
20 Rubber cap
21 Bleeder screw

New part to be used

2.6   Remove the outboard pad by unsnapping the clips with a screwdriver

2.8   Carefully peel back the edge of the piston boot and check for corrosion and leaking fluid

2.9   Push the caliper piston back with a C-clamp

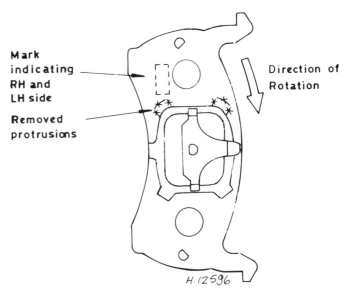

Mark indicating RH and LH side

Removed protrusions

Direction of Rotation

H.12596

Fig. 9.3   Correct installation of brake pad anti-squeal shim. Early models may not have protrusions removed (Sec 2)

2.11   Install the inner pad by snapping the clip into the piston

3   Disc brake caliper — removal and installation

Removal

1   If the caliper is to be removed from the vehicle, remove the cover from the brake fluid reservoir and siphon off two-thirds of the fluid into a container and discard it.

2   Loosen the front wheel nuts, raise the front of the vehicle, support it securely on jackstands and remove the front wheels.

3   If the caliper is to be removed from the vehicle, remove the brake line hose inlet fitting bolt and disconnect the fitting.

4   Remove the two mounting bolts and lift the caliper from the vehicle. If the caliper is not to be removed from the vehicle, hang it out of the way with a piece of wire so the brake hose will not be damaged.

Installation

5   Inspect the mounting bolts for excessive corrosion and the rubber bushings and dust boots for tears and damage, replacing with new

ones if necessary. Lubricate the contact surfaces of the bolts, bushings and dust boots with white lithium base grease prior to installation.

6   Place the caliper in position over the rotor and steering knuckle, install the bolts and tighten them to the specified torque.

7   Connect the inlet fitting (if removed) and install the retaining bolt. It will be necessary to bleed the brakes (Section 15) if the fitting was disconnected.

8   Install the wheels and lower the vehicle. Tighten the wheel nuts.

9   If the brakes did not have to be bled, pump the brake pedal a few times to bring the pads up to the disc. Check the brake fluid level and top up if necessary.

4   Disc brake caliper — overhaul

Note: *Purchase a brake caliper overhaul kit for your particular vehicle before beginning this procedure.*

1   Remove the caliper (Section 3) and brake pads (Section 2). There are two methods of removing the caliper piston. Step 4 details the procedure for removal with the caliper off the vehicle. With the brake line still connected and the pads removed, the piston can be pushed out, using hydraulic pressure. Protect the caliper with a piece of wood or

4.1   Use a block of wood to protect the caliper when using hydraulic pressure to force the piston out. Be sure to keep your fingers out of the way

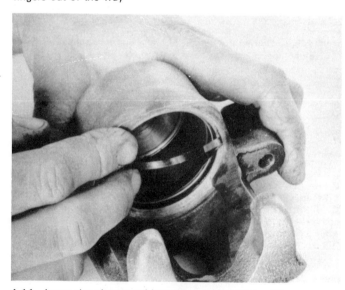

4.11   Insert the piston seal into the groove of the caliper

folded rags and take care to not place your fingers between the piston and the caliper. Have an assistant very slowly apply the brakes to push the piston out and be prepared for a rush of brake fluid as the piston is ejected (photo).

2   Clean the exterior of the brake caliper with brake fluid, denatured alcohol or brake system cleaner (never use gasoline or kerosene), then place the caliper on a clean workbench.

3   Remove the caliper bleed screw.

4   If the piston has not been removed, place a wooden block or shop rag in the caliper as a cushion, then use compressed air to remove the piston from the caliper. Use only enough air pressure to ease the piston out of the bore. If the piston is blown out, even with the cushion in place, it may be damaged. **Warning:** *Never place your fingers in front of the piston in an attempt to catch or protect it when applying compressed air. Serious injury could occur.*

5   Remove the retainer and dust seal from the piston caliper bore.

6   Using a wood or plastic tool, remove the piston seal from the groove in the caliper bore. Metal tools may cause bore damage.

7   Remove the dust boots, pins and bushings from the caliper ears.

8   Clean the remaining parts with brake fluid. Allow them to drain and then shake them vigorously to remove as much fluid as possible.

9   Carefully examine the piston and caliper bore for nicks, burrs, corrosion and loss of plating. If surface defects are present, parts must be replaced although the caliper bore can be lightly polished with crocus cloth to remove light corrosion and stains. Inspect the mounting bolts, pins and bushings for corrosion and damage, replacing with new parts as necessary.

10   When assembling, lubricate the piston bore and seal with clean brake fluid. Apply the red grease in the seal kit to the piston seal.

11   Position the seal in the caliper bore groove (photo).

12   Assemble the dust seal to the piston. Apply some of the orange grease in the seal kit to the dust seal, then install the piston and dust seal to the caliper bore. Install the dust seal retainer.

13   Install the caliper bleed screw.

14   Lubricate the dust boots, bushings and pins with the orange grease and install the caliper.

15   Lubricate the brake pad shims with a light coat of disc brake grease (to Mazda spec 8175 49 248) or proprietary anti-squeal compound. Keep the grease off the friction surfaces. Install the brake pads.

16   Install the caliper and bleed the brakes (Section 15).

5   Disc brake rotor — inspection, removal and installation

1   Raise the vehicle and place it securely on jackstands.

2   Remove the wheel and tire.

3   Remove the brake caliper assembly (refer to Section 3). **Note:** *It is not necessary to disconnect the brake hose. After removing the caliper mounting bolts, hang the caliper out of the way on a piece of wire. Never hang the caliper by the brake hose because damage to the hose will occur.*

4   Inspect the rotor surfaces. Light scoring or grooving is normal, but deep grooves or severe erosion is not. If pulsating has been noticed during application of the brakes, suspect disc runout or worn wheel bearings.

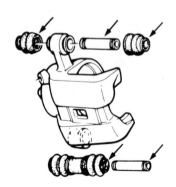

Fig. 9.4   Caliper boot, bushing and pin lubrication points (arrows) (Sec 4)

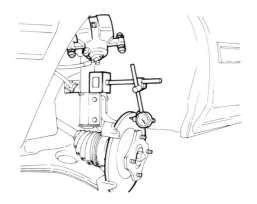

Fig. 9.5 Checking the brake disc runout (Sec 5)

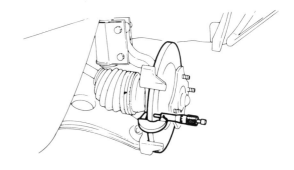

Fig. 9.6 Measuring the brake disc thickness (Sec 5)

5   Attach a dial indicator to the caliper mounting bracket, turn the rotor and note the amount of runout. Check both inboard and outboard surfaces. If the runout is more than the maximum allowable and the bearings are OK, the rotor must be removed from the vehicle and taken to an automotive machine shop for resurfacing. (Some machine shops can resurface the rotors without removing them — ask about this beforehand).

6   Using a micrometer, measure the thickness of the rotor. If it is less than the minimum specified, replace the rotor with a new one. Also measure the disc thickness at several points to determine variations in the surface. Any variation over 0.0005-inch may cause pedal pulsations during brake application. If this condition exists and the disc

thickness is not below the minimum, the rotor can be removed (if necessary) and taken to an automotive machine shop for resurfacing.

7   Special tools and techniques are required to remove the disc from the hub. Consequently, the hub should be removed (Chapter 10) and the assembly taken to your dealer or a properly equipped shop to have the disc turned or replaced.

6   Drum brake shoes — replacement

1   Whenever working on the brake system, be aware that asbestos dust is present. It has been proven to be harmful to your health, so be careful not to inhale it.

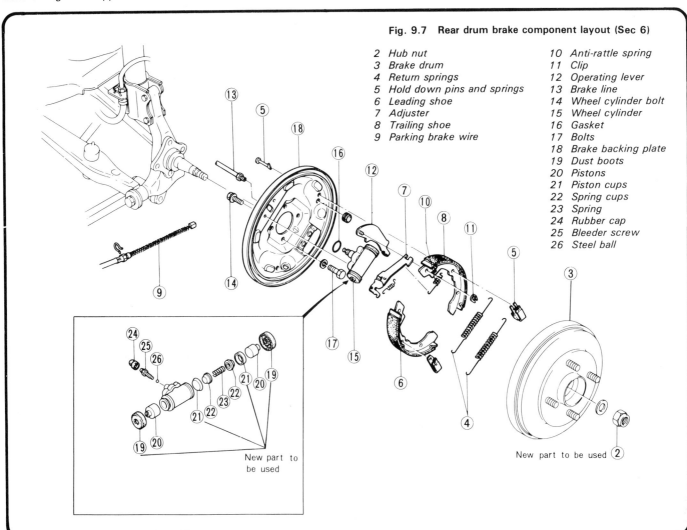

Fig. 9.7 Rear drum brake component layout (Sec 6)

2   Hub nut
3   Brake drum
4   Return springs
5   Hold down pins and springs
6   Leading shoe
7   Adjuster
8   Trailing shoe
9   Parking brake wire
10   Anti-rattle spring
11   Clip
12   Operating lever
13   Brake line
14   Wheel cylinder bolt
15   Wheel cylinder
16   Gasket
17   Bolts
18   Brake backing plate
19   Dust boots
20   Pistons
21   Piston cups
22   Spring cups
23   Spring
24   Rubber cap
25   Bleeder screw
26   Steel ball

New part to be used

New part to be used (2)

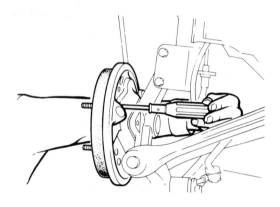

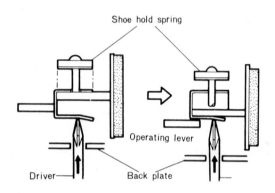

Fig. 9.8 Release the shoe hold down springs by inserting a screwdriver through the backing plate (Sec 6)

6.5   Use pliers to remove the return springs

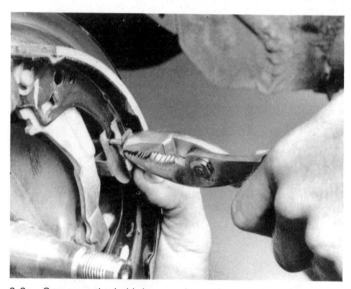

6.6a   Compress the hold down spring and rotate the pin to release it from the spring

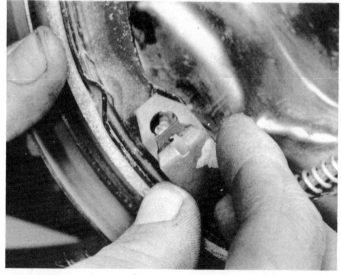

6.6b   With the tension released, the hold down spring can be lifted off

2   Raise the vehicle and support it securely on jackstands.
3   Remove the wheel. **Note:** *All four rear shoes should be replaced at the same time, but to avoid mixing up parts, work on only one brake assembly at a time.*
4   Remove the drum/hub assembly (Chapter 1). If the drum cannot be removed easily, remove the plug in the backing plate, insert a screwdriver through the hole and press on the hold spring to widen the shoe clearance as shown in the accompanying illustration. If this doesn't allow drum removal, loosen the parking brake lever adjusting nut to increase the stroke.
5   Remove the brake shoe return springs (photo).
6   Remove the hold down springs and pins (photos).
7   Remove the leading shoe and the adjuster. It may be necessary to release the adjuster using a screwdriver as shown in the accompanying illustration. This will ease the removal of the leading shoe.
8   Remove the trailing shoe and disconnect the parking brake wire.
9   Remove the clip and disconnect the operating lever from the shoe (photo).
10   Lightly lubricate the contact surfaces of the brake backing plate with white lithium base grease at the points shown in the accompanying illustration. Take care to keep grease and other contaminants off the friction surfaces.
11   Install the operating lever on the new trailing shoe.
12   Install the trailing shoe with the anti-rattle spring in place.
13   Connect the parking brake wire.
14   Assemble the leading shoe and adjuster, connect the adjuster to the anti-rattle spring and rotate the assembly into position (photo).
15   Install the hold down springs.
16   Install the return springs.
17   Center the shoe assembly (photo).
18   Inspect the brake drum for cracks, score marks, deep scratches and hard spots, which will appear as small discolored areas. If the hard spots cannot be removed with a fine emery cloth and/or if any of the

other conditions listed above exist, the drum must be taken to an automotive machine shop to have it turned. If the drum will not "clean up" before the maximum drum diameter is reached in the machining operation, the drum will have to be replaced with a new one. **Note:** *The maximum diameter is cast into each brake drum (photo).*
19 Install the brake drum/hub assembly and adjust the wheel bearings (Chapter 1).

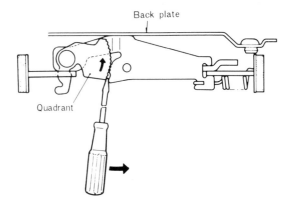

Fig. 9.9 Insert a screwdriver into the adjuster quadrant and turn in the direction shown (arrows) to release the adjuster (Sec 6)

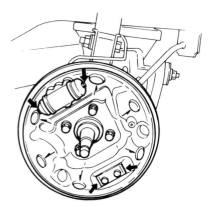

Fig. 9.10 Backing plate and wheel cylinder boot lubrication points (Sec 6)

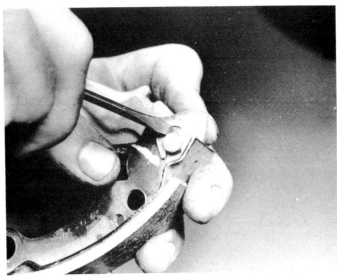

6.9 Use a small screwdriver to remove the clip retaining the operating lever to the trailing shoe

6.14 Connect the anti-rattle spring to the adjuster using pliers

6.17 With all of the components installed, center the brake assembly with clean hands

6.18 The maximum diameter allowed is marked inside the brake drum

20 Mount the wheel, install the wheel lugs and tighten to the specified torque, then lower the vehicle.
21 Pump the brake pedal to adjust the brakes until a satisfactory pedal action is obtained.
22 Check the parking brake operation and adjust if necessary.
23 If new brake shoes have been installed, avoid harsh braking as far as possible for the first few hundred miles until the linings have bedded in.

7   Drum brake wheel cylinder — removal, overhaul and installation

Removal

1   Raise the rear of the vehicle and support it securely on jackstands.
2   Remove the brake shoe assembly (Section 6).
3   Carefully clean all dirt and foreign material from around the wheel cylinder.
4   Disconnect and plug the fluid inlet tube and remove the wheel cylinder retaining bolts (photo).
5   Remove the wheel cylinder from the brake backing plate and place it on a clean workbench.

Overhaul

6   Obtain a wheel cylinder rebuild kit from your dealer or an automotive parts store.
7   Remove the bleeder screw and steel ball. It may be necessary to tap the wheel cylinder body on a block of wood to dislodge the ball.
8   Remove the dust boots and pistons from the cylinder bore and then separate the boots from the pistons.
9   Push from one end of the bore to remove the piston and spring cups and the spring from the bore.
10 Clean the wheel cylinder with brake fluid, denatured alcohol or brake system cleaner. Do not, under any circumstances, use petroleum based solvents to clean brake parts.
11 Use compressed air to remove excess fluid from the wheel cylinder and to blow out the passages.
12 Check the cylinder bore for corrosion and scoring. Crocus cloth or steel wool may be used to remove light corrosion and stains, but the cylinder must be replaced with a new one if the defects cannot be removed easily, or if the bore is scored.
13 Lubricate the new cups and the cylinder bore with clean brake fluid.
14 Install the spring, spring cups and piston cups into the cylinder bore. Make sure the cups are the right way around (open ends facing inwards).
15 Install the new boots to the pistons. Lubricate the pistons with clean brake fluid. If the rebuild kit includes a packet of brake grease, apply it to the insides of the boots (or as instructed).
16 Install the pistons and boots to the cylinder bore, making sure the boots are properly seated.
17 Install the steel ball and bleeder screw.

Installation

18 Place the wheel cylinder in position and screw the fluid inlet nut into the cylinder finger tight, making sure it is not cross threaded.
19 Install the retaining bolts and tighten them securely.
20 Tighten the inlet nut securely and install the brake shoe assembly.
21 Install the brake drum and adjust the hub bearings (Chapter 1). Mount the wheel and install the lug nuts.
22 Bleed the brakes (Section 15) and lower the vehicle.
23 Tighten the lug nuts to the specified torque.

8   Master cylinder — removal, overhaul and installation

1   A master cylinder overhaul kit should be purchased before beginning this procedure. The kit will include all the replacement parts necessary for the overhaul procedure. The rubber replacement parts, particularly the seals, are the key to fluid control within the master cylinder. As such, it's very important that they be installed securely and facing in the proper direction. Be careful during the rebuild procedure that no grease or mineral-based solvents come in contact with the rubber parts.
2   Completely cover the front fender and cowling area of the vehicle, as brake fluid can ruin painted surfaces if it is spilled.

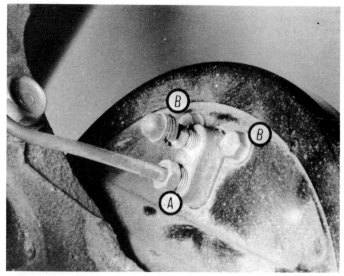

7.4   Wheel cylinder inlet tube (A) and retaining bolts (B)

3   Disconnect the brake line connections. Rags or newspapers should be placed under the master cylinder to soak up the fluid that will drain out. Unplug the fluid level sensor connector, remove the two master cylinder mounting nuts and lift the master cylinder from the vehicle (photo).
4   Drain any remaining fluid from the reservoir. Remove the reservoir by grasping the master cylinder firmly and rocking the reservoir from side to side (photo).
5   Place the master cylinder in the vertical position (with the front end down), depress the primary piston and remove the snap ring.
6   Remove the primary piston and discard it. The overhaul kit will have a replacement unit.
7   Use a wooden dowel to depress the secondary piston. Remove the O-ring and retaining screw.
8   With the master cylinder in the vertical position with the rear end downward, tap it on a block of wood to remove the secondary piston.
9   Remove the spring from the front of the secondary piston.
10 From the secondary piston, remove the rear spreader and cylinder cup seal, the valve shims and the two seals from the rear of the piston.

8.3   Master cylinder retaining nuts (A), fluid pipe connections (B) and level sensor connector (C)

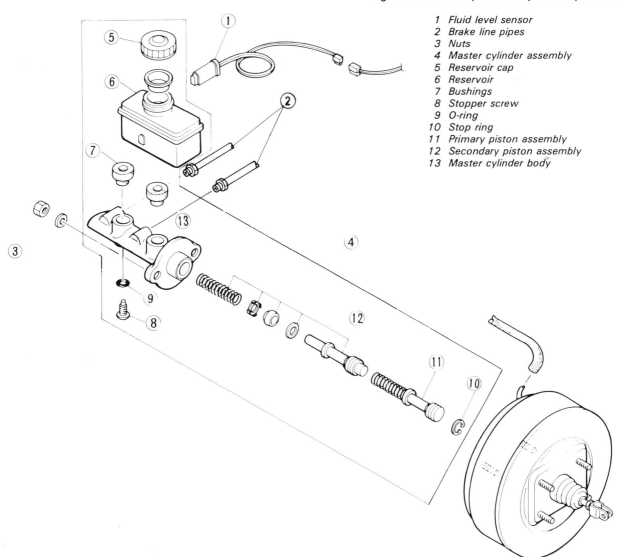

Fig. 9.11 Master cylinder component layout (Sec 8)

1 Fluid level sensor
2 Brake line pipes
3 Nuts
4 Master cylinder assembly
5 Reservoir cap
6 Reservoir
7 Bushings
8 Stopper screw
9 O-ring
10 Stop ring
11 Primary piston assembly
12 Secondary piston assembly
13 Master cylinder body

11 Remove the reservoir bushings, cap and float.
12 Clean the master cylinder and inspect the bore for corrosion and damage. If any corrosion or damage is found, replace the master cylinder body with a new one unless the imperfections are very minor.
13 Inspect the reservoir for cracks and worn bushings, replacing with new components as necessary.
14 Lubricate all components prior to assembly with clean brake fluid.
15 Install the valve shim on the front of the secondary piston. Place the seal (open end forward) on the piston.
16 Install the center seal onto the secondary piston with the open end forward.
17 Install the rear secondary piston seal with the open end toward the rear.

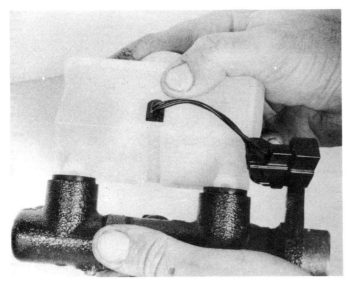

8.4 Grasp the master cylinder firmly and rock the reservoir from side to side to remove it

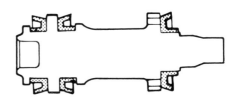

Fig. 9.12 Secondary piston seals (shaded areas) installation (Sec 8)

18 Place the O-ring on the secondary piston retaining screw.
19 Lubricate the primary and secondary pistons with clean brake fluid.
20 Push the secondary piston assembly into the bore using a wooden dowel. Depress the spring slightly and insert the set screw.
21 Insert the primary piston with the spring facing forward. Depress it slightly and then install the snap ring.
22 Lubricate the reservoir bushings, lay the reservoir on a hard surface and press the master cylinder body onto the reservoir, using a rocking motion.
23 Install the reservoir level float and baffle assembly.
24 In theory the clearance between the primary piston and the brake booster pushrod must be checked. The makers have a special tool for this purpose, No. 49 B002 765. In the absence of the special tool, use a depth gauge or similar to measure the depth of the recess in the primary piston and the protrusion of the booster pushrod. The desired clearance between the two, with no vacuum applied to the booster, is 0.016 to 0.024 inch. Adjustment is made by rotating the booster pushrod, which is secured by a locknut.
25 Whenever the master cylinder is removed, the complete hydraulic system must be bled. The time required to bleed the system can be reduced if the master cylinder is filled with fluid and primed or "bench bled" before the master cylinder is installed on the vehicle. Fill the reservoir with brake fluid and slowly push the piston all the way in using the wood dowel or a Phillips screwdriver. Before releasing the piston block the brake line ports to keep air from being drawn back into the master cylinder, then release the piston. Repeat the procedure until only brake fluid (no air) is expelled from the brake line ports. Be careful not to let the reservoir run dry during the bleeding process.
26 Place the master cylinder in position over the power brake reservoir studs and install the brake line flare nuts finger tight, making sure not to cross thread them.
27 Install the master cylinder retaining nuts, tightening them securely.
28 Tighten the brake line flare nuts securely and plug in the level sensor connector.
29 Bleed the brakes at the wheel bleed valves (refer to Section 15).

9 Hydraulic brake hoses and lines — inspection and replacement

1 About every six months, with the vehicle raised and placed securely on jackstands, the flexible hoses which connect the steel brake lines with the front and rear brake assemblies should be inspected for cracks, chafing of the outer cover, leaks, blisters and other damage. These are important and vulnerable parts of the brake system and inspection should be complete. A light and mirror will prove helpful for a thorough check. If a hose exhibits any of the above conditions, replace it as follows:

Front brake hose

2 When disconnecting a flexible hose and a brake line pipe, use a back-up wrench and loosen the flare nut, then remove the clip. When connecting, install the clip, then tighten the flare nut.
3 When installing make sure all bolt threads are clean.
4 When the brake hose installation is complete, there should be no kinks in the hose. Also, make sure the hose does not contact any part of the suspension. Check this by turning the wheels to the extreme left and right positions. If the hose makes contact, remove the hose and correct the installation as necessary.
5 Bleed the system on completion (Section 15).

Rear brake hose

6 Using a back-up wrench, disconnect the hose at both ends, being careful not to bend the bracket or steel lines.
7 Remove any clips with pliers and separate the female fittings from the brackets.
8 Unbolt the hose retaining clip and remove the hose.
9 Without twisting the hose, install the female ends of the hose in the frame brackets.
10 Install the clips retaining the female end to the bracket.
11 Using a back-up wrench, attach the steel line fittings to the female fittings. Again, be careful not to bend the bracket or steel line.
12 Check that the hose installation did not loosen the frame bracket. Retorque the bracket if necessary.
13 Fill the master cylinder reservoir and bleed the system (refer to Section 15).

Steel brake lines

14 When it becomes necessary to replace steel lines, use only double wall steel tubing or other approved material. If copper alloy pipes are used, follow the maker's instructions carefully concerning the installation of additional support clips.
15 Auto parts stores and brake supply houses carry various lengths of prefabricated brake line.
16 If prefabricated lengths are not available, obtain the recommended tubing and fittings to match the line to be replaced. Determine the correct length by measuring the old brake line, and cut the new tubing to length, leaving about 1/2-inch extra for flaring the ends.
17 Install the fittings onto the cut tubing and flare the ends using an ISO flaring tool.

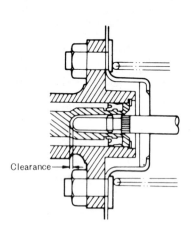

Fig. 9.13   Master cylinder-to-booster clearance (Sec 8)

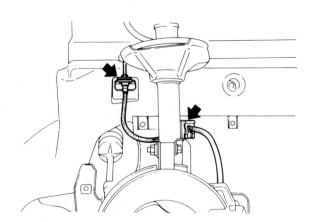

Fig. 9.14   Front disc brake hose clip locations (Sec 9)

18 Using a tubing bender, bend the tubing to match the shape of the old brake line.
19 Tube flaring and bending can usually be performed by a local auto parts store if the proper equipment is not available.
20 When installing the brake line, leave at least 3/4-inch clearance between the line and any moving parts.
21 Bleed the system on completion (Section 15).

---

10 Parking brake — checking and adjustment

Checking

1 Pull up on the parking brake handle and make sure that sure that full engagement takes place between 7 and 9 clicks.

Adjustment

2 Start the engine, pump the brake pedal two or three times and shut the engine off.
3 Remove the parking brake cover and use a screwdriver to turn the adjusting nut until the lever stroke is within specification. The parking brake warning light on the dash should illuminate after the lever is pulled one notch.
4 Release the parking brake and check that the rear brakes are not binding by pushing the vehicle back and forth, or by turning the rear wheels if they are off the ground.

---

11 Brake pedal assembly — removal and installation

1 Remove the under dash air duct or other trim for access.
2 Remove the split pin and withdraw the clevis pin.
3 Remove the through bolt, nut and washers.
4 Disconnect the return spring and lift the pedal from the vehicle.
5 Inspect the assembly for worn bushings, bent or damaged pedal, worn or deteriorated pad, bent through bolt and damaged or weak return spring.
6 Prior to installation, lubricate the contact surfaces of the through bolt, bushings and clevis pin with white lithium base grease.
7 Installation is the reverse of removal.

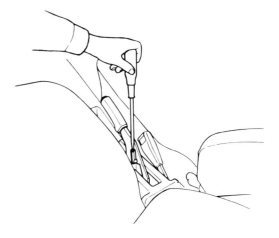

Fig. 9.15 Adjusting the parking brake stroke (Sec 10)

8 After installation, adjust the pedal height and play as follows.
9 Measure the pedal height: it should be 8.43 to 8.47 inch. If adjustment is necessary, disconnect the wiring from the brake light switch, release the switch locknut and turn the body of the switch until the correct pedal height is achieved. Tighten the locknut and reconnect the switch.
10 Depress the brake pedal a few times with the engine stopped to disperse any vacuum in the booster, then check the pedal free play: it should be 0.28 to 0.35 inch. Adjust if necessary by slackening the clevis locknut and turning the pushrod. Tighten the locknut when adjustment is correct.
11 Still with the engine stopped, depress the pedal as far as it will go and measure the pedal-to-floor clearance. Under a load of 132 lb, the clearance should be at least 4.53 inch. If it is less than this, first bleed the hydraulic system to expel any air, then check the condition of the rear brake linings and automatic adjusters. Also check that the flexible hoses are not 'ballooning' under pressure.

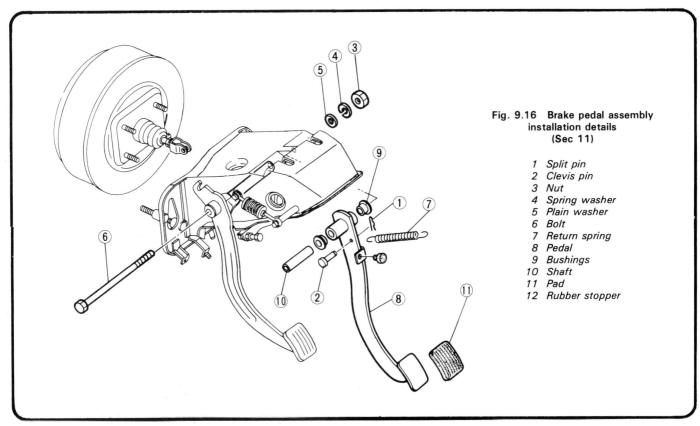

Fig. 9.16 Brake pedal assembly installation details (Sec 11)

1 Split pin
2 Clevis pin
3 Nut
4 Spring washer
5 Plain washer
6 Bolt
7 Return spring
8 Pedal
9 Bushings
10 Shaft
11 Pad
12 Rubber stopper

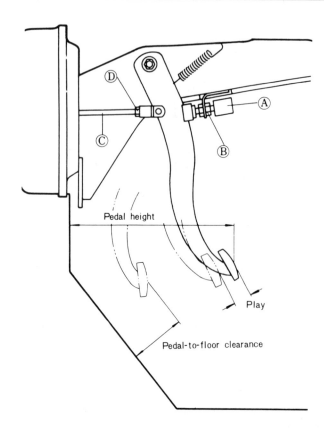

Fig. 9.17 Brake pedal height and free play adjustment (Sec 11)

A   *Brake light switch*   C   *Pushrod*
B   *Switch locknut*   D   *Clevis locknut*

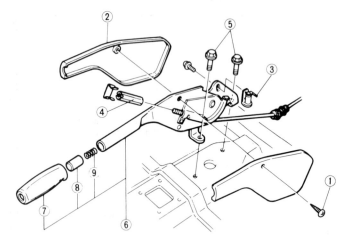

Fig. 9.18 Parking brake lever assembly details (Sec 12)

1 *Screw*	5 *Bolts*
2 *Covers*	6 *Parking brake lever assembly*
3 *Parking brake switch*	7 *Grip*
connector	8 *Push button*
4 *Adjusting nut*	9 *Return spring*

12   Parking brake assembly — removal and installation

1   Remove the parking brake cover.
2   Disconnect the switch.
3   Remove the adjustment nut.

4   Remove the retaining bolts, disconnect the parking brake cable and lift the handle assembly from the vehicle.
5   Inspect the sector and ratchet pawl for damaged teeth and check the return spring to make sure it is not weak or damaged, replacing as necessary with new components.
6   Lubricate the sector and ratchet teeth lightly with white lithium base grease prior to installation.
7   Installation is the reverse of removal. Adjust the parking brake on completion.

13   Parking brake cables — removal and installation

Rear cables

1   Raise the rear of the vehicle and support it securely on jackstands.
2   Remove the cable clip.
3   Remove the trailing brake shoe assembly (Section 6) and disconnect the cable from the shoe operating lever.
4   Remove the retaining bolts and the adjusting nut and remove the cable assembly from the vehicle.
5   Installation is the reverse of removal. Prior to installation, apply white lithium base grease to the cable grommet. After installation, turn the adjusting nut until the equalizer is at a 90° angle to the front brake cable.
6   Adjust the parking brake lever stroke if necessary.

Front cable

7   Remove the parking brake lever cover. Unscrew and remove the adjustment nut.
8   Raise the rear of the vehicle and support it securely on jackstands.
9   Withdraw the front cable from below the vehicle, unhooking the rear cables from the equalizer.
10   Installation is the reverse of removal. Adjust the parking brake lever stroke on completion.

14   Power brake booster — inspection, removal and installation

1   The power brake unit requires no special maintenance apart from periodic inspection of the hoses and inspection of the air filter beneath the boot at the pedal pushrod end.
2   Dismantling of the power brake unit requires special tools. If a problem develops, it is recommended that a new or factory exchange unit be installed rather than trying to overhaul the original booster.
3   Remove the mounting nuts which hold the master cylinder to the power brake unit. Unplug the brake fluid level sensor connector and position the master cylinder out of the way, being careful not to strain the lines leading to the master cylinder. If there is any doubt as to the flexibility of the lines, disconnect them at the cylinder and plug the ends.
4   Disconnect the vacuum hose leading to the front of the power brake booster. Cover the end of the hose.
5   Inside the vehicle, remove the under dash blower air duct or other trim for access. Remove the split pin and clevis pin and disconnect the power brake pushrod from the brake pedal. Do not force the pushrod to the side when disconnecting it.
6   Now remove the four booster mounting nuts and carefully lift the unit out of the engine compartment.
7   If a new booster unit is to be installed, check the clearance between the master cylinder primary piston and the booster pushrod — see Section 8, paragraph 24.
8   When installing, loosely install the four mounting nuts and then connect the pushrod to the brake pedal. Tighten the nuts and reconnect the vacuum hose and master cylinder. If the hydraulic brake lines were disconnected, the entire brake system should be bled to eliminate any air which has entered the system (refer to Section 15).
9   Check the brake pedal height and free play, and adjust if necessary — see Section 11, paragraph 8 onwards.

15   Hydraulic system — bleeding

1   Bleeding of the hydraulic system is necessary to remove air whenever it is introduced into the brake system.
2   It may be necessary to bleed the system at all four brakes if air

**Fig. 9.19 Parking brake rear cable
installation details (Sec 13)**

1 Clip
2 Cable connector to shoe
   operating lever
3 Bolts
4 Adjusting nut
5 Cable assembly

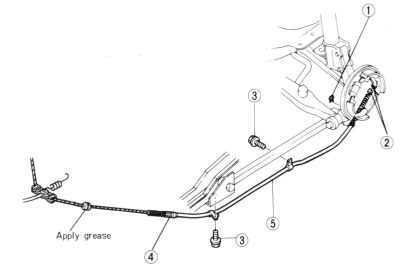

Apply grease

New part to be used

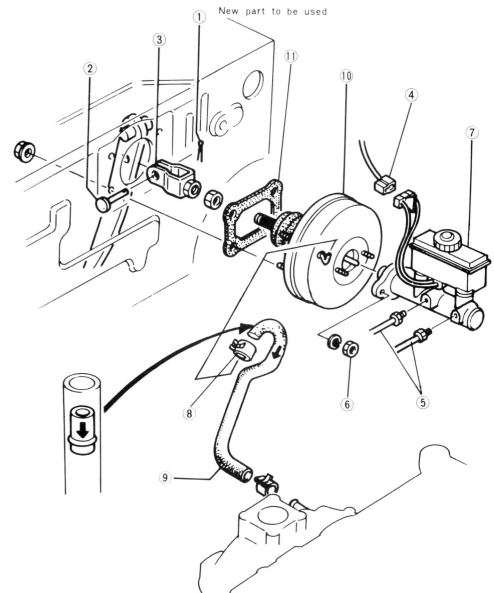

**Fig. 9.20 Power brake
booster installation details
(Sec 14)**

1 Split pin
2 Clevis pin
3 Fork and nut
4 Fluid level sensor connector
5 Brake line pipes
6 Nuts
7 Master cylinder assembly
8 Hose clamps
9 Vacuum hose
10 Booster unit
11 Gasket

has entered the system due to low fluid level, or if the brake lines have been disconnected at the master cylinder.

3   If a brake line was disconnected only at a wheel, then only that wheel cylinder (or caliper) must be bled.

4   If a brake line is disconnected at a fitting located between the master cylinder and any of the brakes, that part of the system served by the disconnected line must be bled.

5   If the master cylinder has been removed from the vehicle, refer to Section 8 for the bench bleeding procedure before proceeding with the procedure which follows.

6   If the master cylinder is installed on the vehicle but is known to have, or is suspected of having air in the bore, the master cylinder must be bled before any wheel cylinder (or caliper) is bled. Follow Steps 7 through 16 to bleed the master cylinder while it is installed on the vehicle.

7   Remove the vacuum reserve from the brake power booster by applying the brake several times with the engine off.

8   Remove the master cylinder reservoir cover and fill the reservoirs with brake fluid, then keep checking the fluid level often during the bleeding operation, adding fluid as necessary to keep the reservoirs full. Reinstall the cover.

9   Disconnect the forward brake line connection at the master cylinder.

10   Allow brake fluid to fill the master cylinder bore until it begins to flow from the forward line connector port. Have a container and shop rags handy to catch and clean up spilled fluid.

11   Reconnect the forward brake line to the master cylinder.

12   Have an assistant depress the brake pedal very slowly (one time only) and hold it down.

13   Loosen the forward brake line at the master cylinder to purge the air from the bore, retighten the connection, then have the brake pedal released slowly.

14   Wait 15 seconds (important).

15   Repeat the sequence, including the 15 second wait, until all air is removed from the bore.

16   After the forward port has been completely purged of air, bleed the rear port in the same manner.

17   To bleed the individual wheel cylinders or calipers, first refer to Steps 7 and 8.

18   Have an assistant on hand, as well as a supply of new brake fluid, an empty clear plastic container, a length of 3/16-inch plastic, rubber or vinyl tubing to fit over the bleeder valve and a wrench to open and close the bleeder valve. The vehicle may have to be raised and placed on jackstands for clearance.

19   Beginning at the right rear wheel, loosen the bleeder valve slightly, then tighten it to a point where it is snug but can still be loosened quickly and easily.

20   Place one end of the tubing over the bleeder valve and submerge the other end in brake fluid in the container.

21   Have the assistant pump the brakes a few times to get pressure in the system, then hold the pedal firmly depressed.

22   While the pedal is held depressed, open the bleeder valve just enough to allow a flow of fluid to leave the valve. Watch for air bubbles to exit the submerged end of the tube. When the fluid flow slows after a couple of seconds, close the valve again and have your assistant release the pedal.

23   Repeat Steps 21 and 22 until no more air is seen leaving the tube, then tighten the bleeder valve and proceed to the left rear wheel, the right front wheel and the left front wheel, in that order, and perform the same procedure. Be sure to check the fluid in the master cylinder reservoir frequently.

24   Never use old brake fluid because it attracts moisture which will deteriorate the brake system components.

25   Refill the master cylinder with fluid at the end of the operation.

26   If any difficulty is experienced in bleeding the hydraulic system, or if an assistant is not available, a pressure bleeding kit is a worthwhile investment. If connected in accordance with the instructions, each bleeder valve can be opened in turn to allow the fluid to be pressure ejected until it is clear of air bubbles without the need to replenish the master cylinder reservoir during the process.

16   Brake fluid level sensor — checking

1   To check the operation of the fluid level sensor, remove the master cylinder reservoir cap. Switch on the ignition. Have an assistant observe the fluid level warning light on the instrument cluster.

2   Depress the float in the master cylinder reservoir, using a clean screwdriver or similar. The warning light should be lit when the float is below the 'MIN' mark, and extinguished when the float is above it.

3   The level sensor can also be checked by connecting a continuity tester to its electrical connector. There should be continuity when the float is below the 'MIN ' mark, and no continuity when the float is above it.

4   Remake the original wiring connections and install the reservoir cap on completion.

17   Dual proportioning valve — checking, removal and installation

1   The dual proportioning valve is located on the firewall. Accurate checking requires special test equipment, but malfunction may be suspected if the rear wheels lock prematurely under heavy braking, or if the rear brakes seem not to be working at all.

2   To remove the valve, first clean it externally, then unscrew the hydraulic unions from it. Have rags ready to catch the hydraulic fluid which will be released, taking care to keep it off the paintwork.

3   Unbolt the valve from the firewall and remove it.

4   Install by reversing the removal operations. Bleed the entire hydraulic system on completion (Section 15).

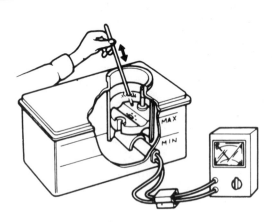

Fig 9.21   Checking the brake fluid level sensor with a continuity tester (Sec 16)

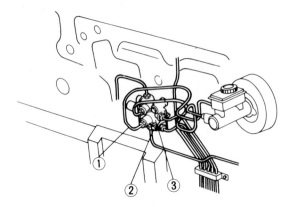

Fig. 9.22   Dual proportioning valve. LHD shown, RHD similar (Sec 17)

1 Hydraulic pipe   3 Valve
2 Bolt

Chapter 10 Suspension and steering

Contents

Specifications

Front suspension alignment

Toe . . . . 0 ± 0.12 in (0 ± 3.0 mm)
Camber . . . . +0°20′ ± 30′
Caster . . . . +1°40′ + 45′

Rear suspension alignment

Toe . . . .   0 ± 0.12 in (0 ± 3.0 mm)

Tire pressures

All models with 14-inch wheels
  Normal and heavy load
    Front . . . .   28 psi (2.0 bar)
    Rear . . . .   26 psi (2.0 bar)
All models with 13-inch wheels
  Normal load
    Front . . . .   28 psi (2.0 bar)
    Rear . . . .   26 psi (2.0 bar)
  Heavy load
    Front . . . .   30 psi (2.1 bar)
    Rear . . . .   27 psi (1.9 bar)

Torque specifications

	Ft-lbs	M-kg
Front suspension		
Driveaxle locknut	116 to 174	16 to 24
Upper strut mounting nuts	17 to 22	2.3 to 3.0
Strut piston rod nut	47 to 59	6.5 to 8.2
Lower strut damper nuts and bolts	69 to 86	9.5 to 11.9
Balljoint-to-steering knuckle bolt and nut	32 to 40	4.4 to 5.5
Lower suspension arm through-bolts and nuts	69 to 86	9.5 to 11.9
Stabilizer bar bracket bolts	32 to 40	4.4 to 5.5
Rear suspension		
Upper strut mounting nuts	16 to 20	2.2 to 2.7
Strut piston rod nut	41 to 59	5.6 to 8.2
Lower strut damper bolts and nuts	69 to 86	9.5 to 11.9
Lateral link through-bolt	46 to 55	6.1 to 7.5
Lateral link-to-crossmember	69 to 86	9.5 to 11.9
Lateral link-to-rear hub spindle	69 to 86	9.5 to 11.9
Trailing link-to-body	43 to 54	6.0 to 7.5
Trailing link-to-rear hub spindle	40 to 50	5.5 to 6.9
Trailing link-to-stabilizer bar	23 to 34	3.2 to 4.7
Steering		
Tie rod end nut	22 to 33	3.0 to 4.5
Intermediate shaft nut	13 to 20	1.8 to 2.7
Rack and pinion body-to-chassis	23 to 34	3.2 to 4.7
Steering wheel nut	29 to 36	4.0 to 5.0
Steering column bracket nuts/bolts	12 to 17	1.6 to 2.3
Wheel lug nuts	65 to 87	9.0 to 12.0

1 Wheels and tires — general information

1   These models are equipped with metric size steel belted radial tires. Do not mix different types of tires, such as radials and bias belted, on the same car, as handling may be seriously affected. In the UK it is illegal to mix tires of different construction on the same axle.

2   It is recommended that tires be replaced in pairs on the same axle, but if only one tire is being replaced, be sure it is of the same size, structure and tread design as the other.

3   Because tire pressure has a substantial effect on handling and wear, the pressure on all tires should be checked at least once a month or before any extended trips and set to the correct pressure. Tire pressure should be checked and adjusted with the tires cold.

4   If it is wished to rotate the tires to even out wear, refer to Chapter 1.

5   The tires should be replaced when the depth of the tread pattern is worn to a minimum of 1/16-in (1.5 mm). The tires incorporate wear indicators which appear as bands across the tread when the tire is worn beyond limits. Correct tire pressures and driving techniques have an important influence on tire life. Hard cornering, excessively rapid acceleration or deceleration and heavy braking increase tire wear. Extremely worn tires are very susceptible to punctures and are especially dangerous in wet weather conditions. In the UK it is illegal to use tires with any bald patches, or with less than 0.04 inch (1 mm) of tread.

6   The tire tread pattern can give a good indication of problems in the maintenance or adjustment of tires and suspension components. The accompanying illustration shows some common examples of tire wear patterns and their usual causes. If a tire exhibits a wear pattern caused by incorrect suspension alignment, refer to Section 3.

7   Wheels must be replaced if they are bent, rusted or corroded, buckled, leak air, have elongated bolt holes or if the lug nuts won't stay tight. Damaged wheels should be replaced with new ones rather than repaired. Aluminum wheels are especially prone to corrosion and are easily scratched. When washing aluminum wheels use a soft cloth and a mild, non-abrasive detergent. If salty or alkaline water gets on aluminum wheels, they should be washed as soon as possible as salt and alkali can damage them.

8   Tire and wheel balance is important in the overall handling, braking and performance of the car. Unbalanced wheels can adversely affect handling and ride characteristics as well as tire life. Whenever a tire is installed on a wheel, the tire and wheel should be balanced by a qualified shop with the proper equipment.

9   US models are equipped with a compact spare tire which is designed to save space in the trunk as well as being easier to handle due to its lighter weight. The spare tire pressure should be checked at least once a month, and maintained at 60 psi (415 kPa).

10   The compact spare tire and wheel are designed for use with each other only, and neither the tire nor the wheel should be coupled with other types or size of wheels and tires.

11   Because the compact spare is designed as a temporary replacement for an out-of-service standard wheel and tire, the compact spare should be used on the car only until the standard wheel and tire can be repaired or replaced. Continuous use of the compact spare at speeds of over 50 mph (80 kph) is not recommended. In addition, the expected tread life of the compact spare is only about 3000 miles (4800 kilometers).

12   The spare is designed for your particular vehicle and should not be used on any other vehicle. Also, the diameter is smaller than a regular tire and the ground clearance is reduced by approximately one inch (25 mm).

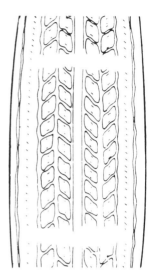

Fig. 10.1 Tread wear indicators appear as bands across the tread (Sec 1)

2 Wheel and tire — removal and installation

1   With the car on a level surface, the parking brake on and the car in gear (manual transaxles should be in Reverse, automatic transaxles should be in Park) remove the wheel cover (if equipped) and loosen, but do not remove, the wheel lug nuts. Block the wheel diagonally opposite the one which is to be removed.

2   Using a jack positioned in the proper location on the car, raise the car just enough so that the tire clears the ground.

3   Remove the lug nuts.

4   Remove the wheel and tire.

5   If a flat tire is being replaced, ensure that there is adequate ground clearance for the new inflated tire, then mount the wheel and tire on the wheel studs.

6   Apply a light coat of spray lubricant or light oil to the wheel stud threads and install the lug nuts snugly with the cone shaped end facing the wheel.

7   Lower the car until the tire contacts the ground and the wheel studs are centered in their wheel holes.

8   Tighten the lug nuts evenly and in a cross pattern, and torque to specs.

9   Lower the car completely and remove the jack.

10   Replace the wheel cover.

3 Suspension alignment — general information

1   Suspension alignment refers to the adjustments made to the front and rear wheels so that they are in proper angular relationship to the suspension and the ground. Wheels that are out of proper alignment not only affect steering control but also increase tire wear. The front end adjustments required on these models are toe-in, caster and camber, while the rear wheels are adjustable for toe-in only.

2   Because of the special equipment and techniques required, it is recommended that you take the vehicle to a properly equipped shop to have the suspension alignment checked and adjusted.

3   The following is a description of front end alignment to give a basic understanding of the purpose of these adjustments.

4   Toe-in is the turning in of the front or rear wheels. The purpose of a toe specification is to ensure parallel rolling of the front wheels. In a car with zero toe-in, the distance between the front edges of the wheels will be the same as the distance between the rear edges of the wheels.

5   The actual amount of toe in is normally only a fraction of an inch. A vehicle with a static toe in of 2.5 mm per wheel for example, would have a distance between the front edges of the wheels of 5 mm less than the distance of the rear edges of the wheels when the car is standing. This is because even when the wheels are set to toe in slightly when the vehicle is standing still, they tend to roll parallel on the road when the car is moving.

6   Toe-in adjustment is controlled by the tie rod end position on the tie rod on the front wheels and a star wheel adjuster at the inner ends of the trailing links on the rear wheels. Incorrect toe-in will cause the tires to wear improperly by making them scrub against the road surface. Proprietary instruments for measuring toe-in are available at auto accessory stores. If using such an instrument, follow its maker's instructions.

7   Caster is the tilting of the steering axis (the point around which the wheels rotate when turning) forward or rearward when viewed from

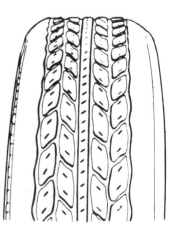

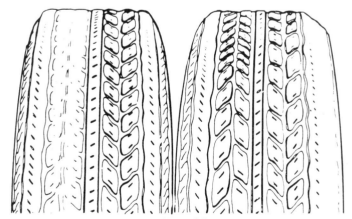

- Hard Cornering
- Under Inflation
- Lack of Rotation

- Incorrect Wheel Alignment
- Tire Construction Non-Uniformity

**Fig. 10.2 Typical abnormal tire wear patterns
(Secs 1 and 3)**

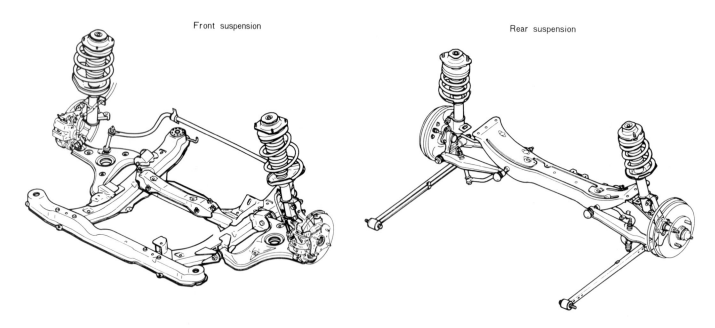

Front suspension

Rear suspension

Fig. 10.3 Front and rear suspension component layout (Sec 4)

above. Camber is the tilting of the front wheels from the vertical when viewed from the front of the vehicle. When the steering axis is tilted forward, the caster is said to be positive (+). Similarly, when the wheels tilt outward at the top, the camber is said to be positive (+). When the steering axis is tilted rearward the caster is negative (–) and when the wheels tilt inward at the top the camber is negative (–). The amount of tilt is measured in degrees from the vertical and this measurement is called the caster or camber angle. Positive caster allows the vehicle to track easily in straight line while negative caster makes it less stable. Camber angle affects the amount of tire tread which contacts the road and compensates for changes in the suspension geometry when the car is cornering or travelling over undulating surface.

4 Suspension system — general information

1   These models are equipped with independent front and rear strut-type suspension. This design uses a combination spring and shock absorber assembly which is mounted directly to the knuckle. A lower control arm which pivots on the chassis is also attached to the knuckle. At the rear, trailing links are used to locate the knuckle. In addition, stabilizer bars are used at the front and rear on some models.
2   Some models are also equipped with a three way damping system which adjusts the damping of the shock absorbers, either manually or automatically. This is accomplished by actuators mounted at the top of the struts which rotate the control rod approximately 60° to vary damping action. These models use gas shock absorbers, while non-adjustable models use conventional sealed hydraulic units.
3   Never attempt to heat or straighten any suspension part, as this can weaken the metal or in other ways damage the part.

5 Suspension system — inspection

1   The suspension components should normally last a long time, except in cases where damage has occurred due to an accident. The suspension parts, however, should be checked from time to time for signs of wear which will result in a loss of precision handling and riding comfort.
2   Check that the suspension components have not sagged due to wear. Do this by parking the car on a level surface and visually checking that the car sits level. This will normally occur only after many miles and will usually appear more on the driver's side of the vehicle.
3   Put the car in gear and take off the hand brake. Grip the steering

Actuator

Control rod

A–A' Cross section

Normal   Sport

Control rod

Selector valve

Fig. 10.4 The optional three way damping system operates the strut control rod to change the damping action (Sec 4)

wheel at the top with both hands and rock it back and forth. Listen for any squeaks or metallic noises. Feel for free play. If any of these conditions is found, have an assistant do the rocking while the source of the trouble is located.
4   Check the shock absorbers, as these are the parts of the suspension system most likely to wear out first. If there is any evidence of fluid leakage, they will need replacing. Bounce the car up and down vigorously. It should feel stiff and well damped by the shock absorbers. As soon as the bouncing is stopped the car should return to its normal position without excessive up and down movement. Do not replace the shock absorbers as single units, but rather in pairs unless failure has occurred at low mileage.

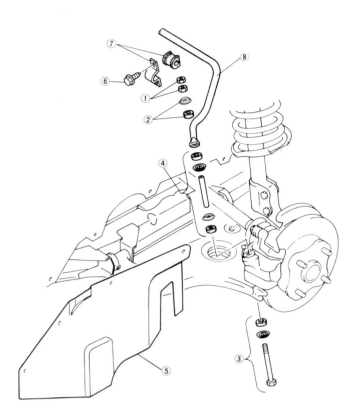

Fig. 10.5 Front stabilizer bar component layout (Sec 6)

1 *Nuts*
2 *Retainer and bushing*
3 *Bolt, retainer and bushing*
4 *Bushings, retainers and
   spacers*

5 *Splash shields*
6 *Bolts*
7 *Bushing and bracket*
8 *Stabilizer bar*

5   Check all rubber bushings for signs of deterioration and cracking. If necessary, replace the rubber portions of the suspension arm.

6   Stabilizer bar — removal and installation

1   Raise the vehicle and support it securely on jackstands.
2   On the front stabilizer bar, remove the front wheels and splash shields.
3   Remove the stabilizer bar-to-suspension arm bolts.
4   Remove the bushing and bracket bolts.
5   Remove the rear stabilizer bar from the vehicle.
6   On the front stabilizer bar, remove the rack and pinion assembly retaining bolts, pry the assembly up and then remove the bar by carefully working it past the rack and pinion and out through the left wheel well. (On RHD vehicles it may not be necessary to remove the rack and pinion retaining bolts.)
7   Inspect the bushings to be sure they are not hardened, cracked or excessively worn, and replace if necessary.
8   Place the stabilizer bar in position. Make sure the bar is inserted with the bushing alignment mark on the left side of the vehicle (photo).
9   Install the front stabilizer bar left side bushing with the edge aligned with the mark and the notch facing the rear of the vehicle.
10   After installing the the bushing bracket bolts, tighten them to the specified torque.
11   Install the end bolts and nuts and tighten them securely with one inch of thread exposed after tightening on the front stabilizer bar, and 0.6 inch of thread exposed on the rear stabilizer bar.
12   If the rack and pinion retaining bolts were removed, do not forget to tighten them to the specified torque.

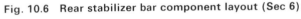

Fig. 10.6 Rear stabilizer bar component layout (Sec 6)

1 *Nuts*
2 *Bushing and retainer*
3 *Retainer, bushing and bolt*
4 *Retainers, bushings and
   spacer*

5 *Bolts*
6 *Bushings and brackets*
7 *Stabilizer bar*

6.8   Front stabilizer bar bushing alignment mark (arrow)

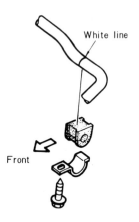

Fig. 10.7 The white line on the stabilizer bar must line up with the edge of the left bushing during installation (Sec 6)

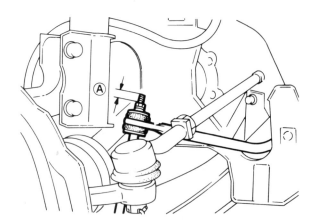

Fig. 10.8 After tightening, the front stabilizer bar link bolt must have one inch of thread exposed (Sec 6)

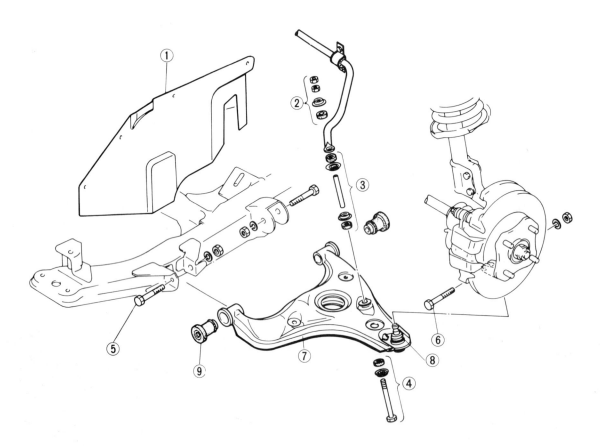

Fig. 10.9 Front lower control arm installation details (Sec 7)

1 Splash shield
2 Nuts, retainer and bushing
3 Bushings, retainers and spacer
4 Bolt, retainer and bushing
5 Lower arm bolts and nuts
6 Balljoint bolt and nut
7 Lower arm
8 Balljoint dust boot
9 Rubber bushing

7 Front lower control arm — removal, overhaul and installation

1 Raise the front of the car and support it on jackstands.
2 If only one lower control arm is being removed, disconnect only that end of the stabilizer bar. If both lower control arms are being removed, remove the stabilizer bar completely. Refer to Section 6.

3 Remove the wheel(s) and splash shield(s).
4 Remove the control arm bushing bolts that secure the control arm to the engine cradle.
5 Remove the balljoint-to-steering knuckle nut and then disconnect the balljoint from the steering knuckle, using a pry bar if necessary.
6 Lower the control arm from the vehicle.
7 Inspect the control arm bushings for hardening, cracking or exces-

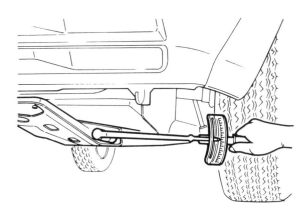

Fig. 10.10 The control arm bolts should be tightened to the specified torque after the vehicle weight has been lowered onto the suspension (Sec 7)

sive wear and the balljoint and dust boot for damage and wear. Replacing the dust boot requires special tools and techniques, so the control arm assembly should be taken to a dealer or properly equipped shop to have the procedure performed. The balljoint cannot be replaced without replacing the arm as well. New bushings can be installed using a vise and suitable sized tubes or sockets to press the old bushings out and the new ones in. Use soapy water as a lubricant when fitting the bushings.

8   Installation of the lower control arm is the reverse of the removal procedure. **Note:** *Do not tighten the lower control arm-to-engine cradle bushing bolts to their specified torque until the car has been lowered to the ground and its full weight is on the suspension.*

---

8   Front strut damper assembly — removal and installation

1   Raise the front of the vehicle and support it securely on jackstands.
2   Remove the clip and disconnect the brake hose from the strut.
3   Remove the strut-to-knuckle nuts and then remove one of the nut and bolt assemblies.
4   In the engine compartment, remove the upper strut cover (photo).
5   Remove the three way damper control switch (if equipped) (Section 11).
6   Remove the four strut damper-to-chassis stud nuts. Make alignment marks between the top of the strut and the mounting on the body, so that it can be installed in the same position.
7   If the strut is to be dismantled, slacken the piston rod nut one or two turns. Grip the piston rod if necessary so that it does not turn. **Do not** remove the nut completely.
8   Remove the remaining strut-to-knuckle nut and bolt and lower the strut damper assembly from the vehicle.
9   Inspect the assembly for oil leakage, damage to the dust boot and rust or damage to the spring. Further disassembly of the strut is described in Section 21.
10   Installation is the reverse of removal, taking care to tighten all fasteners to the specified torque. Observe the alignment marks made during removal.

---

9   Rear strut assembly — removal, inspection and installation

1   In the rear compartment of the car remove the rear panel for access. On three-way damping control equipped models, disconnect the adjuster switch. Remove the two upper strut-to-chassis stud nuts.
2   If the strut is to be dismantled, slacken the piston rod nut one or two turns (not possible yet on three-way damping models). Grip the piston rod if necessary so that it does not turn. **Do not** remove the nut completely.
3   Make alignment marks between the top of the strut and the mounting on the body, so that it can be installed in the same position.
4   Raise the rear of the vehicle and support it securely with jackstands.
5   Remove the clip and disconnect the brake hose from the strut.

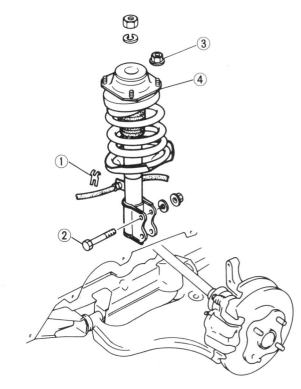

Fig. 10.11 Front strut damper assembly installation details (Sec 8)

1 Hose clip
2 Steering knuckle bolts
   and nuts
3 Nuts
4 Strut damper assembly

8.4   The front strut cover can be removed by pulling it off the studs

6   Remove the two strut-to-stub axle nuts and bolts and lower the strut assembly from the vehicle.
7   Inspect the strut for oil leaks, tears or damage to the dust boot and rust or damage of the spring. Further disassembly of the strut is described in Section 21.
8   Installation is the reverse of removal, taking care to tighten all fasteners to the specified torque. Observe the alignment marks made during removal.

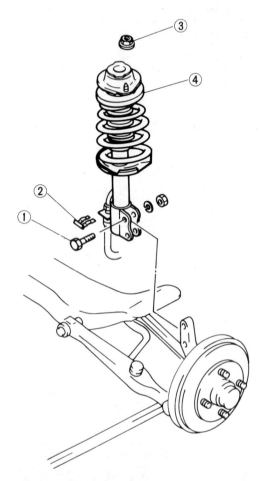

Fig. 10.12   Rear strut damper assembly component layout (Sec 9)

1 *Lower mounting bolt*   3 *Upper mounting nut*
2 *Hose clip*   4 *Strut damper assembly*

10   Rear suspension lateral and trailing links — removal and installation

1   Raise the rear of the vehicle and support it securely on jackstands.
2   Remove the fuel tank (Chapter 4).
3   Mark the position of the adjustment star wheel and nut for reinstallation to the same position. Moving the nut and star wheel will affect the rear wheel toe-in, so this is important.
4   Remove the lateral link-to-chassis crossmember retaining bolts, nuts and bushings and disconnect the stabilizer bar link (if equipped).
5   Unbolt the lateral links from the stub axle carrier, then remove them from the vehicle.
6   Remove the parking brake bracket bolt.
7   Remove the through bolts and lower the trailing link from the vehicle.
8   Installation is the reverse of removal. Install all bolts temporarily and then lower the vehicle weight onto the wheels before tightening to the specified torque.
9   Have the rear wheel toe-in checked by a dealer or properly equipped shop.

11   Three way damping control switches — checking, removal and installation

Note: *Electrical testing of the damping control 'switches' (actuators) is considered in Chapter 12, Section 5. A functional check may be made as follows.*

1   Open the hood and remove the rubber strut cover to gain access to the front suspension switches or open the trunk or hatch and remove the rear inner panel for access to the rear suspension switches.
2   Block the rear wheels and set the parking brake. Raise the front of the vehicle so that the wheels are clear of the ground and support it securely on jackstands.
3   Start the engine (ensure adequate ventilation) and engage a gear so that the speedometer indicates 9 mph or more. **Warning:** *If the vehicle falls off the jackstands, damage and/or injury may result.*
4   Have an assistant operate the damping control switches (on the control panel). With the 'AUTO' switch off, the switches (actuator) should be seen or felt to rotate the damper piston rods through approximately 60° when the SPORT/NORMAL switch is operated.
5   If none of the switches (actuator) behave as described, check for a blown fuse or disconnected wires, then have a Mazda dealer check

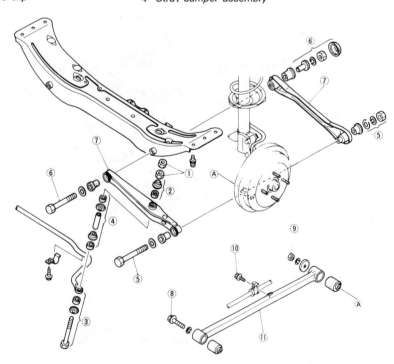

Fig. 10.13   Rear suspension lateral and trailing link installation details (Sec 10)

1 *Nuts*
2 *Bushing and retainer*
3 *Retainer, bushing and bolt*
4 *Retainers, bushing and spacer*
5 *Bolt and nut*
6 *Through-bolt, nut and spacer*
7 *Lateral links*
8 *Bolt*
9 *Nut*
10 *Bolt*
11 *Trailing link*

out the control unit. If only one of the switches is defective, check its wiring, and if that is OK, replace the switch.
6   When checking is complete, stop the engine and lower the vehicle.

Removal and installation

7   To remove a rear switch, first remove the rear suspension strut (Section 9). (This is recommended by the makers, but may not in fact be essential.)
8   To remove a front switch, first unplug the electrical connector.
9   Remove the retaining screws and lift the switch from the top of the strut.
10   Installation is the reverse of removal.

12   Steering system — general information

All models are equipped with rack and pinion steering. The components making up this system are the steering wheel, steering column, intermediate shaft, rack and pinion assembly, tie rods and steering knuckles. In addition, the power steering system also uses a belt driven pump to provide hydraulic pressure.

In a manual system, the motion of turning the steering wheel is transferred through the column and intermediate shaft to the pinion shaft in the rack and pinion assembly. Teeth on the pinion shaft are meshed with teeth on the rack, so when the shaft is turned, the rack is moved left or right in the rack and pinion housing. Attached to each end of the rack are tie rods which, in turn are attached to the steering knuckles on the front wheels. This left and right movement of the rack is the direct force which turns the wheels.

The power steering system operates in essentially the same way as the manual system, except that the power rack and pinion system uses hydraulic pressure to boost the manual steering force. A rotary control valve in the rack and pinion assembly directs hydraulic fluid from the power steering pump to either side of the integral rack piston, which is attached to the rack. Depending on which side of the piston this hydraulic pressure is applied to, the rack will be forced either left or right, which moves the tie rods, etc.

If the power steering system loses its hydraulic pressure it will still function manually, though with increased effort.

The steering column is of the collapsible, energy absorbing type, designed to compress in the event of a front end collision to minimize injury to the driver. The column also houses the ignition switch lock, key warning buzzer, turn signal controls, headlight dimmer control and

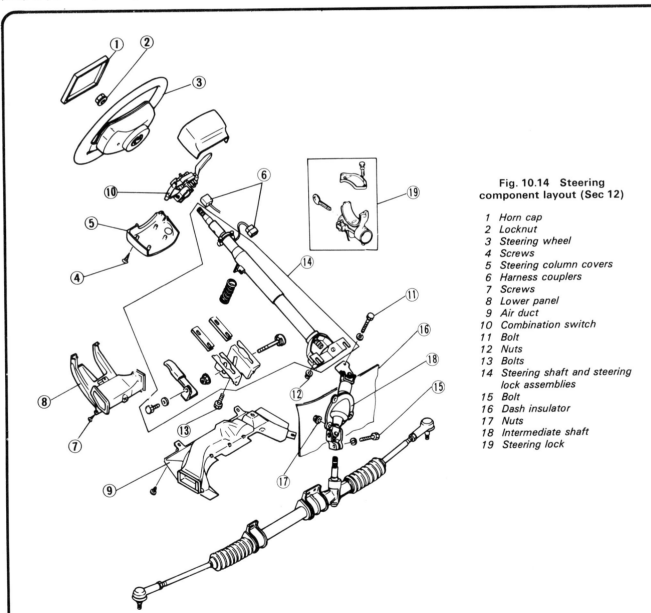

Fig. 10.14 Steering component layout (Sec 12)

1   Horn cap
2   Locknut
3   Steering wheel
4   Screws
5   Steering column covers
6   Harness couplers
7   Screws
8   Lower panel
9   Air duct
10   Combination switch
11   Bolt
12   Nuts
13   Bolts
14   Steering shaft and steering
     lock assemblies
15   Bolt
16   Dash insulator
17   Nuts
18   Intermediate shaft
19   Steering lock

windshield wiper controls. The ignition and steering wheel can both be locked while the car is parked to inhibit theft.

Due to the column's collapsible design, it is important that only specified screws, bolts and nuts can be used as designated and that they be tightened to the specified torque. Other precautions particular to this design are noted in appropriate Sections.

In addition to the standard steering column, an optional tilt version is also offered.

Because disassembly of the steering column is more often performed to repair a switch or other electrical part than to correct a problem in the steering functioning, some steering column disassembly and reassembly procedures are included in Chapter 12.

13   Steering wheel — removal and installation

1   Disconnect the negative battery cable.
2   Remove the horn cap and ornament and disconnect the horn wire (photo).
3   Be sure the steering wheel is unlocked, then remove the lock nut.
4   Mark the position of the steering wheel in relation to the steering shaft.
5   Using a steering wheel puller, remove the steering wheel (photo).
Caution: *Under no circumstances should the end of the shaft be hammered on.*
6   Installation is the reverse of the removal procedure with the following notes: Prior to installation, lightly coat the horn contact surfaces on the steering wheel hub with a moly-base grease. When installing the steering wheel on the shaft be sure the alignment marks on the steering wheel and shaft match.

14   Steering column — removal and installation

1   Disconnect the negative battery terminal.
2   Remove the steering wheel (Section 13).
3   Remove the steering column covers and unplug the harness connectors.
4   Remove the blower air duct.
5   Remove the combination switch (Chapter 12).
6   Remove the steering column retaining nuts and bolts and the intermediate shaft pinch-bolt.
7   Disengage the column from the intermediate shaft and lift the column carefully from the vehicle.
8   Because of its collapsible design, the steering column is very susceptible to damage when removed from the vehicle. Be careful not to lean on or drop the column, as this could weaken the column structure and impair its performance.
9   If the car has been in an accident which resulted in frame damage, major body damage or in which the steering column was impacted, the column could be damaged or misaligned and should be checked by a qualified mechanic.
10   To remove the ignition switch/steering lock, refer to Chapter 12.
11   The steering column is installed by reversing the sequence of the removal operation. Tighten the various fastenings to their specified torques (when known).

15   Steering knuckle and hub — removal and installation

1   Raise the front of the vehicle, support it securely on jackstands and remove the front wheel.
2   Lock the hub from turning by inserting a screwdriver or similar tool through the brake caliper into the rotor. Relieve the staking and remove the front hub locknut. This nut is very tight. Obtain a new nut for installation.
3   Unbolt the brake caliper and hang it out of the way.
4   Remove the strut-to-steering knuckle mounting bolts and nuts.
5   Remove the nut that secures the tie rod to the steering knuckle.
6   Disengage the tie rod from the steering knuckle (Section 16).
7   Remove the retaining nut and bolt and disengage the balljoint from the steering knuckle.
8   Remove the steering knuckle/hub assembly from the driveaxle, using a puller tool to disengage it from the driveaxle splines if necessary, and lift it from the vehicle.

13.2   Pry out the ornament for access to the steering wheel cover screws

13.5   A steering wheel puller can be used to remove the steering wheel

9   Inspect the knuckle for damage and corrosion and the bearings for looseness, rough turning or leaking grease. Disassembly of the hub requires a press and special techniques and this must be left to your dealer or a properly equipped shop.
10   Install the steering knuckle in position on the driveaxle and lower control arm and strut, install the strut and balljoint nuts and bolts and tighten them to the specified torque.
11   Install a new hub (driveaxle) locknut and tighten it by hand only.
12   Attach a spring scale to a front wheel stud and measure the force needed to start the hub turning. Note the scale reading.
13   Temporarily install the brake caliper. Lock the hub and tighten the hub (driveaxle) locknut to the specified torque, then remove the brake caliper. Measure the hub turning force again. If the force exceeds that measured previously (Step 12) by more than 4.4 lb, attention to the bearings is required.
14   If all is well, stake the locknut collar into the groove on the driveaxle, using a blunt chisel or punch (photo).
15   Install the tie rod and tighten the nut to the specified torque.
16   Install the brake caliper and the wheel. Lower the vehicle and tighten the lug nuts.

15.14   Peening the hub locknut into the driveaxle groove with a chisel

16.4   Using a "pickle fork" tool and hammer to disengage the tie rod from the steering knuckle

16   Tie rod end — removal and installation

1   Raise the front of the vehicle and support it with jackstands.
2   Remove the front wheel.
3   Remove the cotter pin and the tie rod nut that secures the outer tie rod to the steering knuckle.
4   Using a suitable tool, such as a "pickle fork", disengage the tie rod from the steering knuckle (photo).
5   Mark the relationship of the jam nut to the inner tie rod threads so similar front end alignment can be maintained upon installation as shown in the accompanying illustration.
6   Back off the jam nut from the outer tie rod.
7   Unscrew the tie rod end from the tie rod.

8   Inspect the tie rod end boot for tears or leakage of grease. To replace the boot, place the rod end securely in a vise and carefully tap around the outer circumference using a chisel and hammer as shown in the accompanying illustration, taking care not to damage the sealing surface. Insert a small amount lithium base chassis grease into the new boot and place the boot in position on the tie rod end. Press the boot securely onto the tie rod end using a vise and a suitable size socket or a press and Mazda tool 491243785.
9   To install, position the jam nut at its mark on the threads. Screw the outer tie rod onto the inner tie rod until it is snug against the jam nut.
10   Install the tie rod into the steering knuckle.
11   Install the tie rod nut, tighten it to the specified torque and install a new cotter pin.
12   Tighten the jam nut.

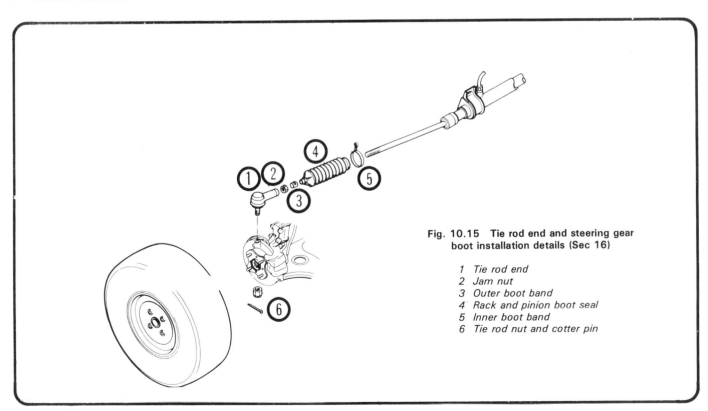

Fig. 10.15   Tie rod end and steering gear boot installation details (Sec 16)

1   Tie rod end
2   Jam nut
3   Outer boot band
4   Rack and pinion boot seal
5   Inner boot band
6   Tie rod nut and cotter pin

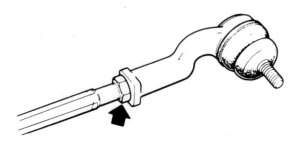

**Fig. 10.16   Mark the tie rod end jam nut position (arrow)
before removal (Sec 16)**

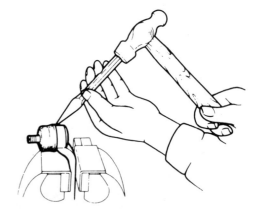

Fig. 10.17   Removing the tie rod end boot (Sec 16)

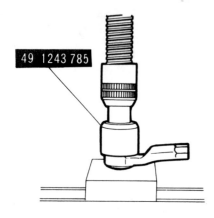

**Fig. 10.18   Installing the tie rod end boot using a press
and factory tool (Sec 16)**

13 Mount the front wheel and lower the vehicle. Tighten the lug nuts.
14 Have the front end alignment checked before driving the vehicle
any distance (Section 3).

---

17   Rack and pinion boot seals — replacement

1   The rack and pinion boot seals protect this assembly's internals
from dirt and water and should be checked periodically for holes, cracking and other damage or deterioration. Damaged boots should be replaced immediately to prevent expensive damage to the rack and pinion
assembly.
2   Remove the outer tie rod end (Section 16).
3   Remove the jam nut from the inner tie rod.
4   Use pliers to spread the outer boot clamp and remove it from the
inner tie rod.
5   Untwist the wire inner boot clamp and slide it off the boot and
onto the rack and pinion housing.
6   Remove the boot seal from the inner tie rod and the vehicle.
7   Clean any dirt from the exposed portion of the rack. Smear the
rack with grease and place a little grease inside the new boot seal.
8   Install the new boot seal so the large end is over the rack and pinion
housing lip.
9   Install the wire inner boot clamp over the large end of the boot
and tighten by twisting it with pliers.
10 Install the outer boot clamp over the small end of the boot.
11 Install the jam nut and tie rod end.

---

18   Rack and pinion steering assembly — removal and installation

1   Remove the pinch bolt that attaches the intermediate shaft to the
rack and pinion stub shaft.

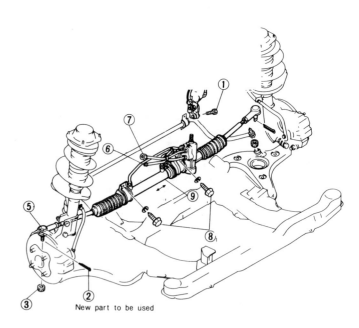

New part to be used

**Fig. 10.19   Rack and pinion steering gear installation
details (Sec 18)**

1 Pinch bolt   6 Power steering return hose
2 Cotter pins   7 Power steering pressure hose
3 Nuts   8 Bolts
4 Splash shield   9 Steering gear and linkage
5 Steering knuckle and
   tie rod connections

2   Raise the front of the car, support it with jackstands and remove
both front wheels.
3   Remove the cotter pins and nuts and separate the tie rod ends from
the steering knuckles (Section 16).
4   On power steering equipped models, unplug the switch, disconnect
the fluid lines and wrap rags around the lines to catch the fluid in the
lines (photo).
5   Remove the retaining bolts and remove the rack and pinion
assembly through the left wheel well (photo).
6   If the rack and pinion is in need of repair, there are several options
open to you. A new rack and pinion assembly can be bought as a unit
and installed. This, however, is the costliest route. If there is a shop
in your area that rebuilds rack and pinion assemblies, taking it to them
will be much cheaper than buying a new unit. Rack and pinions in good

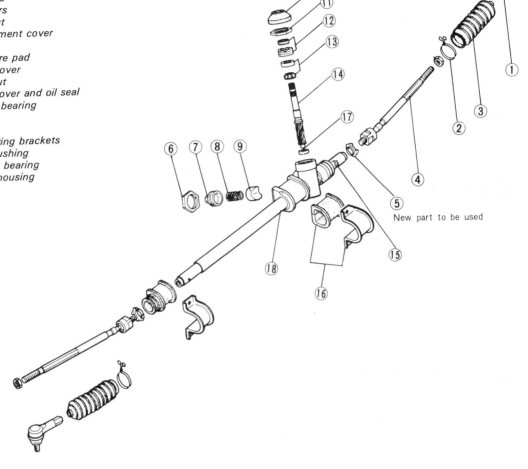

Fig. 10.20 Manual rack and pinion steering component layout (Sec 18)

1 Tie rod ends
2 Boot wires
3 Boot seals
4 Tie rods
5 Washers
6 Locknut
7 Adjustment cover
8 Spring
9 Pressure pad
10 Dust cover
11 Locknut
12 Rear cover and oil seal
13 Upper bearing
14 Pinion
15 Rack
16 Mounting brackets and bushing
17 Lower bearing
18 Gear housing

New part to be used

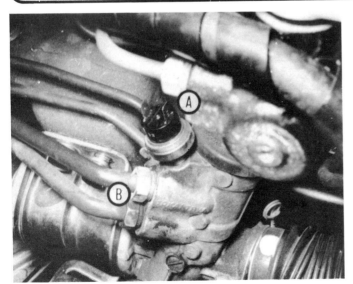

18.4 The power steering switch (A) and fluid line connections (B)

18.5 Withdraw the rack and pinion steering assembly carefully through the left wheel well

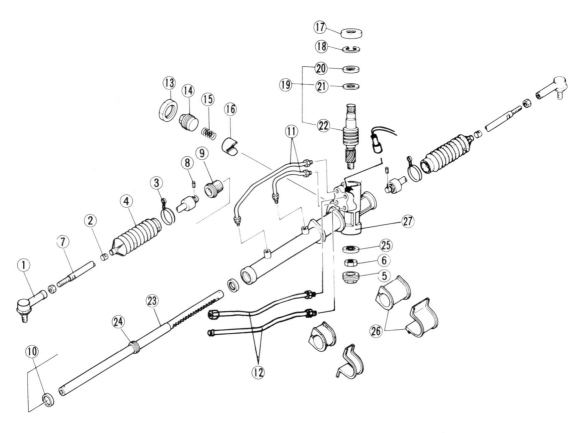

Fig. 10.21   Power rack and pinion steering component layout (Sec 18)

1 Tie rod ends	9 Rack bushing assembly	16 Rack support	22 Control valve assembly
2 Boot bands	10 Oil seal	17 Dust cover	23 Rack assembly
3 Boot wires	11 Fluid pipes	18 Snap ring	24 Seal ring
4 Boot seals	12 Fluid pipes and O-rings	19 Control valve, oil seal and	25 Bearing
5 Pinion plug	13 Locknut	bearing assembly	26 Mounting brackets and
6 Lock nuts	14 Yoke plug	20 Oil seal	mounts
7 Tie rods	15 Spring	21 Bearing	27 Gear housing
8 Spring pins			

condition can be also be found in wrecking yards. The final option is to rebuild the assembly yourself, though it is a somewhat difficult operation requiring the use of a press. Due to space limitations we are unable to give you a step by step procedure, but an exploded view of both racks has been included.

7   Installation is the reverse of the removal procedure. If equipped with power steering, following installation add the specified fluid to the reservoir and bleed any air from the system (Section 20).

8   On all models, following installation have the toe-in checked, and if necessary, adjusted.

19   Power steering pump — removal and installation

1   Disconnect the negative battery cable.

2   Raise the front of the vehicle, support it securely on jackstands and remove the right front wheel and splash shield.

3   Remove the power steering pump pulley nut.

4   Remove the alternator and drivebelt (Chapter 5). On models with air conditioning, also remove the compressor drivebelt.

5   Remove the pulley from the pump.

6   Disconnect and plug the power steering fluid lines.

7   Remove the four alternator/power steering pump bracket retaining bolts and remove the pump along with the bracket assembly from the engine.

8   Installation is the reverse of the removal procedure.

9   After installation, adjust the drivebelt tension (Chapter 1), fill the

pump reservoir with the specified fluid and bleed the system (Section 20).

20   Bleeding the power steering system

1   Following any operation in which the power steering fluid lines have been disconnected, the power steering system must be bled of air to obtain proper steering performance.

2   Raise the front of the vehicle and support it on jackstands.

3   Turn the front wheels all the way to the left and right several times. Check the power steering fluid level and, if it has dropped, add fluid. Repeat this procedure until the fluid level on the dipstick does not drop.

4   Start the engine and allow it to run at fast idle. Recheck the fluid level and add more if necessary.

5   Bleed the system by turning the wheels from side to side without hitting the stops. This will work the air out of the system. Be careful that the reservoir does not run empty of fluid.

6   When the air is worked out of the system, return the wheels to the straight ahead position and leave the car running for several more minutes before shutting it off.

7   Road test the car to be sure the steering system is functioning normally and is free from noise.

8   Recheck the fluid level to be sure it is up to the top arrow mark on the dipstick while the engine is at normal operating temperature and add fluid if necessary.

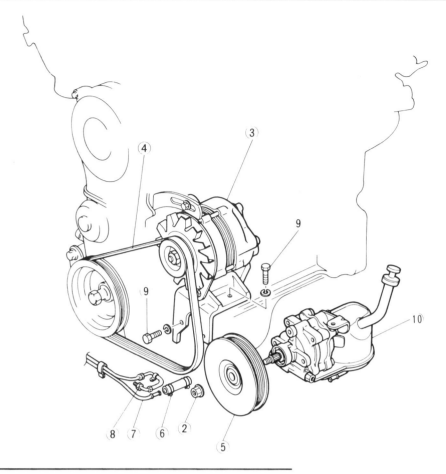

Fig. 10.22 Power steering
pump installation details
(Sec 19)

2 Pulley nut
3 Alternator
4 Drivebelt
5 Pulley
6 Hose band
7 Return hose
8 Pressure hose
9 Bracket bolts
10 Power steering pump

21 Suspension strut/damper assembly — dismantling and reassembly

Warning: *This procedure should only be attempted if spring compressing equipment of adequate rating is available. The use of makeshift or inadequate spring compressors may result in damage and/or personal injury.*

1   Remove the strut/damper assembly as described in Section 8 or 9. When applicable, remove the three-way damping control switch (actuator) also.

2   Clamp the assembly in a vise with protected jaws. Install the spring compressor and compress the spring until the pressure is off the spring seats.
3   Make quite sure that the compressor is secure, then unscrew and remove the piston rod nut and washer.
4   Lift off the mounting block, bearing (on the front strut) and spring upper seat (photos).
5   Carefully lift off the compressed spring. Set it down without jarring it.

21.4a   Removing the suspension strut mounting block

21.4b   Front suspension strut bearing

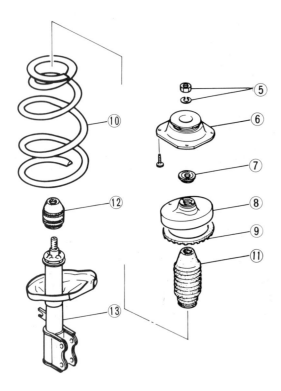

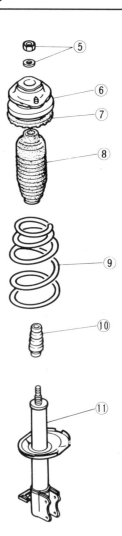

Fig. 10.23   Front suspension strut/damper components
(Sec 21)

5 *Piston rod nut and washer*   10 *Spring*
6 *Mounting block*   11 *Dust boot*
7 *Bearing*   12 *Rebound stopper*
8 *Spring upper seat*   13 *Damper*
9 *Spring seat*

6   The dust boot and rebound stopper can now be removed from the damper (photos).
7   If a new spring is to be installed, carefully release the compressor from the old spring and then compress the new one.
8   Reassemble in the reverse order to dismantling. It is easiest to tighten the piston rod nut to its specified torque after the strut/damper assembly has been installed on the vehicle.

Fig. 10.24   Rear suspension strut/damper components
(Sec 21)

5 *Piston rod nut and washer*   9 *Spring*
6 *Mounting block*   10 *Rebound stopper*
7 *Spring upper seat*   11 *Damper*
8 *Dust boot*

21.6a   Suspension strut dust boot

21.6b   Suspension strut rebound stopper

22 Rear hub bearings — replacement

1   Remove the hub, bearings and oil seal as described in Chapter 1, Section 27.
2   Drive out the bearing races from the hub, using a blunt chisel or punch. Work from the centre of the hub outwards, using the cut-outs provided for the passage of the drift (photo).
3   Clean out the bearing race seats in the hub. Lightly grease the new races and then tap or press them into position, making sure they are the right way around. Ensure also that the races enter squarely — if they are allowed to tilt, they may be damaged (photo).
4   Lubricate and install the bearings and oil seal, then install and adjust the hub — see Chapter 1, Section 27.

23 Rear stub axle carrier — removal and installation

1   Remove the brake drum/hub assembly (Chapter 1, Section 27).
2   Disconnect the brake hydraulic pipe from the wheel cylinder. Be prepared for fluid spillage.
3   Remove the four bolts which hold the brake backplate to the stub axle carrier. Withdraw the brake backplate and place it to one side, within the limit of movement allowed by the parking brake cable.
4   Unbolt the lateral links, trailing link and strut/damper from the axle carrier. The stub axle carrier can now be removed.
5   Installation is a reversal of the removal operations. Additionally, the brake hydraulic system will have to be bled, the hub bearings and the parking brake adjusted, and the various fasteners tightened to their specified torques (when known).

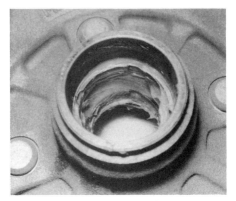

22.2   Rear hub with one bearing race removed

22.3a   Installing a rear hub bearing race

22.3b   Seating the bearing race with a hammer and a blunt punch

Chapter 11   Body

Contents

1   General information

These models are of unitized construction. The body is designed to provide vehicle rigidity so that a separate frame is not necessary. Front and rear frame side rails integral with the body support the front end sheet metal, front and rear suspension systems and other mechanical components. Due to this type of construction, it is very important that, in the event of collision damage, the underbody be thoroughly checked by a facility with the proper equipment.

Component replacement and repairs possible for the home mechanic are included in this Chapter.

2   Body — maintenance

1   The condition of your vehicle's body is very important, because it is on this that the second hand value will mainly depend. It is much more difficult to repair a neglected or damaged body than it is to repair mechanical components. The hidden areas of the body, such as the fender wells, the frame, and the engine compartment, are equally important, although obviously do not require as frequent attention as the rest of the body.
2   Once a year, or every 12,000 miles, it is a good idea to have the underside of the body and the frame steam cleaned. All traces of dirt and oil will be removed and the underside can then be inspected carefully for rust, damaged brake lines, frayed electrical wiring, damaged cables, and other problems.
3   At the same time, clean the engine and the engine compartment using either a steam cleaner or a water soluble degreaser.
4   The fender wells should be given particular attention, as undercoating can peel away and stones and dirt thrown up by the tires can

cause the paint to chip and flake, allowing rust to set in. If rust is found, clean down to the bare metal and apply an anti-rust paint.
5   The body should be washed once a week (or when dirty). Wet the vehicle thoroughly to soften the dirt, then wash it down with a soft sponge and plenty of clean soapy water. If the surplus dirt is not washed off very carefully, it will in time wear down the paint.
6   Spots of tar or asphalt coating thrown up from the road should be removed with a cloth soaked in solvent.
7   Once every six months, give the body and chrome trim a thorough waxing. If a chrome cleaner is used to remove rust from any of the vehicle's plated parts, remember that the cleaner also removes part of the chrome, so use it sparingly.

3   Upholstery and carpets — maintenance

1   Every three months remove the carpets or mats and clean the interior of the vehicle (more frequently if necessary). Vacuum the upholstery and carpets to remove loose dirt and dust.
2   If the upholstery is soiled, apply upholstery cleaner with a damp sponge and wipe it off with a clean, dry cloth.

4   Vinyl trim — maintenance

Vinyl trim should not be cleaned with detergents, caustic soaps or petroleum-based cleaners. Plain soap and water or a mild vinyl cleaner is best for stains. Test a small area for color fastness. Bubbles under the vinyl can be corrected by piercing them with a pin and then working the air out.

5 Hinges and locks — maintenance

Every 3000 miles or three months, the door, hood and rear hatch hinges and locks should be lubricated with a few drops of oil. The door and rear hatch striker plates should also be given a thin coat of white lithium base grease to reduce wear and ensure free movement.

6 Body repair — minor damage

See color photo sequence on pages 222 and 223

Repair of minor scratches

1   If the scratch is superficial and does not penetrate to the metal of the body, repair is very simple. Lightly rub the scratched area with a fine rubbing compound to remove loose paint and built up wax. Rinse the area with clean water.

2   Apply touch-up paint to the scratch, using a small brush. Continue to apply thin layers of paint until the surface of the paint in the scratch is level with the surrounding paint. Allow the new paint at least two weeks to harden, then blend it into the surrounding paint by rubbing with a very fine rubbing compound. Finally, apply a coat of wax to the scratch area.

3   If the scratch has penetrated the paint and exposed the metal of the body, causing the metal to rust, a different repair technique is required. Remove all loose rust from the bottom of the scratch with a pocket knife, then apply rust inhibiting paint to prevent the formation of rust in the future. Using a rubber or nylon applicator, coat the scratched area with glaze-type filler. If required, the filler can be mixed with thinner to provide a very thin paste, which is ideal for filling narrow scratches. Before the glaze filler in the scratch hardens, wrap a piece of smooth cotton cloth around the tip of a finger. Dip the cloth in thinner and then quickly wipe it along the surface of the scratch. This will ensure that the surface of the filler is slightly hollow. The scratch can now be painted over as described earlier in this section.

Repair of dents

4   When repairing dents, the first job is to pull the dent out until the affected area is as close as possible to its original shape. There is no point in trying to restore the original shape completely as the metal in the damaged area will have stretched on impact and cannot be restored to its original contours. It is better to bring the level of the dent up to a point which is about 1/8-inch below the level of the surrounding metal. In cases where the dent is very shallow, it is not worth trying to pull it out at all.

5   If the back side of the dent is accessible, it can be hammered out gently from behind using a soft-face hammer. While doing this, hold a block of wood firmly against the opposite side of the metal to absorb the hammer blows and prevent the metal from being stretched.

6   If the dent is in a section of the body which has double layers, or some other factor makes it inaccessible from behind, a different technique is required. Drill several small holes through the metal inside the damaged area, particularly in the deeper sections. Screw long, self tapping screws into the holes just enough for them to get a good grip in the metal. Now the dent can be pulled out by pulling on the protruding heads of the screws with locking pliers.

7   The next stage of repair is the removal of paint from the damaged area and from an inch or so of the surrounding metal. This is easily done with a wire brush or sanding disk in a drill motor, although it can be done just as effectively by hand with sandpaper. To complete the preparation for filling, score the surface of the bare metal with a screwdriver or the tang of a file or drill small holes in the affected area. This will provide a good grip for the filler material. To complete the repair, see the Section on filling and painting.

Repair of rust holes or gashes

8   Remove all paint from the affected area and from an inch or so of the surrounding metal using a sanding disk or wire brush mounted in a drill motor. If these are not available, a few sheets of sandpaper will do the job just as effectively.

9   With the paint removed, you will be able to determine the severity of the corrosion and decide whether to replace the whole panel, if possible, or repair the affected area. New body panels are not as expensive as most people think and it is often quicker to install a new panel than to repair large areas of rust.

10   Remove all trim pieces from the affected area except those which will act as a guide to the original shape of the damaged body, such as headlight shells, etc. Using metal snips or a hacksaw blade, remove all loose metal and any other metal that is badly affected by rust. Hammer the edges of the hole inward to create a slight depression for the filler material.

11   Wire brush the affected area to remove the powdery rust from the surface of the metal. If the back of the rusted area is accessible, treat it with rust-inhibiting paint.

12   Before filling is done, block the hole in some way. This can be done with sheet metal riveted or screwed into place, or by stuffing the hole with wire mesh.

13   Once the hole is blocked off, the affected area can be filled and painted. See the following sub-section on filling and painting.

Filling and painting

14   Many types of body fillers are available, but generally speaking, body repair kits which contain filler paste and a tube of resin hardener are best for this type of repair work. A wide, flexible plastic or nylon applicator will be necessary for imparting a smooth and contoured finish to the surface of the filler material. Mix up a small amount of filler on a clean piece of wood or cardboard (use the hardener sparingly). Follow the manufacturer's instructions on the package, otherwise the filler will set incorrectly.

15   Using the applicator, apply the filler paste to the prepared area. Draw the applicator across the surface of the filler to achieve the desired contour and to level the filler surface. As soon as a contour that approximates the original one is achieved, stop working the paste. If you continue, the paste will begin to stick to the applicator. Continue to add thin layers of paste at 20-minute intervals until the level of the filler is just above the surrounding metal.

16   Once the filler has hardened, the excess can be removed with a body file. From then on, progressively finer grades of sandpaper should be used, starting with a 180-grit paper and finishing with 600-grit wet-or-dry paper. Always wrap the sandpaper around a flat rubber or wooden block, otherwise the surface of the filler will not be completely flat. During the sanding of the filler surface, the wet-or-dry paper should be periodically rinsed in water. This will ensure that a very smooth finish is produced in the final stage.

17   At this point, the repair area should be surrounded by a ring of bare metal, which in turn should be encircled by the finely feathered edge of good paint. Rinse the repair area with clean water until all of the dust produced by the sanding operation is gone.

18   Spray the entire area with a light coat of primer. This will reveal any imperfections in the surface of the filler. Repair the imperfections with fresh filler paste or glaze filler and once more smooth the surface with sandpaper. Repeat this spray-and-repair procedure until you are satisfied that the surface of the filler and the feathered edge of the paint are perfect. Rinse the area with clean water and allow it to dry completely.

19   The repair area is now ready for painting. Spray painting must be carried out in a warm, dry, windless and dust free atmosphere. These conditions can be created if you have access to a large indoor work area, but if you are forced to work in the open, you will have to pick the day very carefully. If you are working indoors, dousing the floor in the work area with water will help settle the dust which would otherwise be in the air. If the repair area is confined to one body panel, mask off the surrounding panels. This will help minimize the effects of a slight mismatch in paint color. Trim pieces such as chrome strips, door handles, etc., will also need to be masked off or removed. Use masking tape and several thicknesses of newspaper for the masking operations.

20   Before spraying, shake the paint can thoroughly, then spray a test area until the spray painting technique is mastered. Cover the repair area with a thick coat of primer. The thickness should be built up using several thin layers of primer rather than one thick one. Using 600-grit wet-or-dry sandpaper, rub down the surface of the primer until it is very smooth. While doing this, the work area should be thoroughly rinsed with water and the wet-or-dry sandpaper periodically rinsed as well. Allow the primer to dry before spraying additional coats.

21   Spray on the top coat, again building up the thickness by using several thin layers of paint. Begin spraying in the center of the repair area and then, using a circular motion, work out until the whole repair area and about two inches of the surrounding original paint is covered.

Remove all masking material 10 to 15 minutes after spraying on the final coat of paint. Allow the new paint at least two weeks to harden, then use a very fine rubbing compound to blend the edges of the new paint into the existing paint. Finally, apply a coat of wax.

7 Body repair — major damage

1   Major damage must be repaired by an auto body shop specifically equipped to perform unibody repairs. These shops have available the specialized equipment required to do the job properly.
2   If the damage is extensive, the underbody must be checked for proper alignment or the vehicle's handling characteristics may be adversely affected and other components may wear at an accelerated rate.
3   Due to the fact that all of the major body components (hood, fenders, etc.) are separate and replaceable units, any seriously damaged components should be replaced rather than repaired. Sometimes these components can be found in a wrecking yard that specializes in used vehicle components, often at considerable savings over the cost of new parts.

8 Hood — removal and installation

1   Raise the hood.
2   Place protective pads along the edges of the engine compartment to prevent damage to the painted surfaces.
3   Scribe or paint lines around the mounting bracket, so the hood can be aligned quickly and accurately in the same position during installation (photo).
4   With an assistant supporting the weight, remove the bracket bolts and remove the hood from the vehicle.
5   Installation is the reverse of removal, taking care to align the brackets and bolts with the markings made prior to removal.

9 Hood lock mechanism and release cable — removal and installation

1   Remove the front grille cover.
2   If the same hood lock mechanism is to be reinstalled, scribe or paint around the outside edge of the mechanism so that it can be quickly and easily aligned.
3   Remove the retaining nuts and bolt, disengage the release cable and remove the lock mechanism from the vehicle.
4   In the passenger compartment, loosen the release cable nut and disengage the cable from the bracket.
5   Connect string or thin wire to the end of the cable and remove it by pulling it through into the passenger compartment.
6   Installation is the reverse of removal after connecting the string or wire to the new release cable and pulling it into position.
7   If the old release cable is broken, the hood can be opened by raising the front of the vehicle and operating the hood lock from below, using a long thin screwdriver.

10 Rear hatch damper — removal and installation

1   Support the hatch in the fully open position.
2   Unscrew the nut retaining the damper to the hatch (photo).
3   Remove the lower damper-to-body bolts (photo) and lift the damper from the vehicle.
4   Installation is the reverse of removal.

11 Rear hatch — removal, installation and adjustment

Removal

1   Disconnect the battery negative lead. Open the rear hatch and support it with a prop.

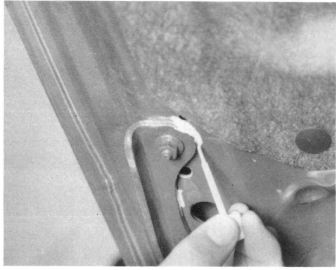

8.3   Mark the hood hinge position with paint

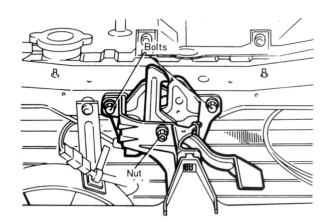

Fig. 11.1   Hood lock mechanism retaining bolt and nut
locations (Sec 9)

10.2   Use a wrench to unscrew the damper nut

10.3   The lower damper retaining bolts (arrows)

2   Place protective pads along the edges of the hatch opening to prevent damage to the painted surfaces while work is being performed.
3   Mark the locations of the hinges by scribing or marking with paint so they can be easily reinstalled in their original positions.
4   Unbolt the damper struts from the hatch (Section 10).
5   Disconnect any wiring harnesses which would interfere with hatch removal.
6   Remove the hinge retaining bolts and lift the hatch from the vehicle with the help of an assistant.

Installation

7   Place the hatch in position, aligning the hinges with the marks made during removal.
8   Install the hinge and damper retaining bolts, tightening them securely. Connect the wiring harness.

Adjustment

9   The positions of the hinge and striker can be adjusted as shown in the accompanying illustrations after loosening the striker bolts and hinge nuts on the body. It will be necessary to carefully pry back the trim panel and headliner to gain access to the hinge nuts.

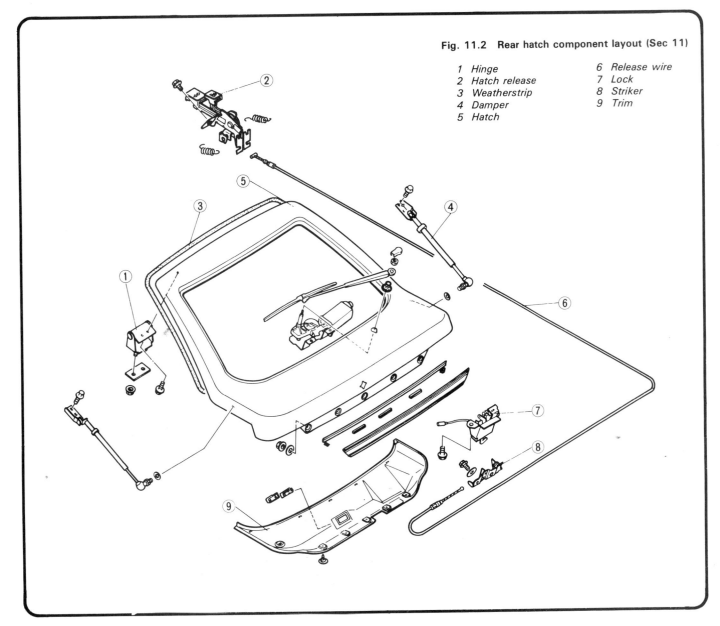

Fig. 11.2   Rear hatch component layout (Sec 11)

1   Hinge
2   Hatch release
3   Weatherstrip
4   Damper
5   Hatch
6   Release wire
7   Lock
8   Striker
9   Trim

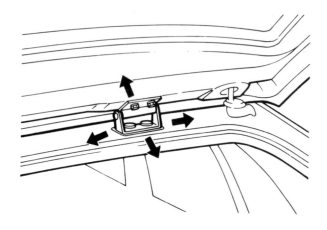

Fig. 11.3   Hatch hinge adjustment (Sec 11)

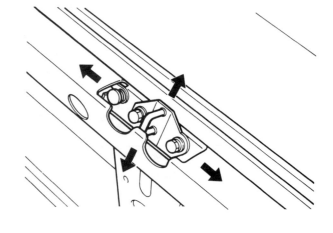

Fig. 11.4   Hatch striker adjustment (Sec 11)

12   Trunk lid — removal and installation

1   Open the lid and mark the location of the nut heads by scribing around them for reinstallation to the same position.
2   With an assistant supporting the weight, remove the retaining nuts and lift the lid from the vehicle.
3   Place the lid in position, install the nuts and tighten them provisionally. Check the fit of the trunk lid and adjust if necessary, then finally tighten the nuts.

13   Rear compartment lid lock assembly — removal and installation

1   Remove the trim panel for access.
2   Remove the protector (sedan and coupe).
3   Remove the retaining bolts and pull the lock out for access to the release wire and rod.
4   Disconnect the release wire and rod and lift the lock from the vehicle.
5   Installation is the reverse of removal.

14   Rear compartment lid striker — removal and installation

1   Remove the trim panel for access, if necessary.
2   Mark the bolt locations.
3   Remove the bolts and lift the striker from the vehicle.
4   When installing it may be necessary to adjust the position of the striker by loosening and tightening the bolts until the proper closing of the compartment lid is achieved.

15   Fuel filler/rear compartment remote release — removal and installation

1   In the passenger compartment, remove the kick plate, pull out the staples and peel back the carpeting for access to the release lever retaining bolt.
2   Remove the bolt and disconnect the wires from the lever assembly.
3   In the rear compartment, remove the trim panels for access.
4   Disconnect the wire from the rear compartment lock.
5   Disconnect the fuel filler wire from the bracket and pull on the wire to open the filler lid. Remove the nut and disconnect the wire.
6   Attach a string or thin wire to the rear compartment and/or fuel filler wire and pull the wire(s) through into the passenger compartment.
7   Installation is the reverse of removal after pulling the wires into place with the string or wire.

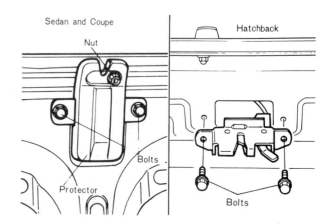

Fig. 11.5   Rear compartment lock installation details (Sec 13)

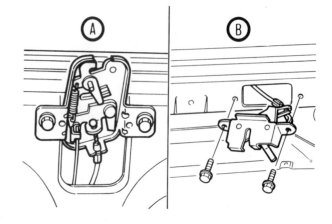

Fig. 11.6   Rear compartment lock and release wire installation details (Sec 15)

A   Sedan and coupe   *B   Hatchback*

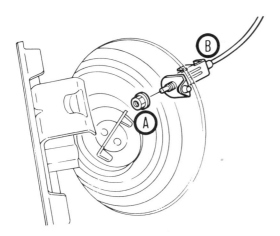

Fig. 11.7 Fuel filler lid wire attachment points (Sec 15)

A Nut   B Bracket

16 Door trim panel — removal and installation

1 Remove the window regulator crank or power window switch cover (photo). (The snap ring which secures the regulator crank can be released by inserting a strip of rag between the crank and the trim panel, and pulling it back and forth.)
2 Remove the inside door handle cover (photo).
3 Remove the arm rest retaining screws (photo).
4 Pry the trim panel loose along the bottom using a large screwdriver or pry bar to disengage the retainers. These retainers fit very tightly and care must be taken not to destroy them during removal (photo).
5 Remove the panel by pushing up and disengaging the lock handle at the top of the door (photo).
6 Carefully peel back the water deflector for access to the inner door panel (photo).
7 Installation is the reverse of removal, noting the following.
8 Place the water shield carefully back in position.
9 When attaching the door trim panel to the door, locate the top of the panel over the lock handle and press down on the trim panel to engage it.

16.1 Pry off the power window switch escutcheon with a screwdriver

16.2 The inner door handle retaining screw (arrow)

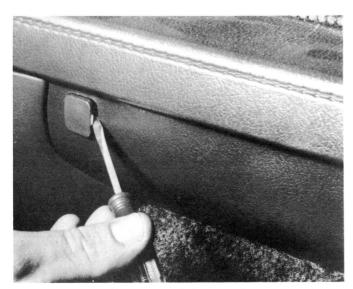

16.3 Use a screwdriver to pry off the cover for access to the arm rest retaining screw

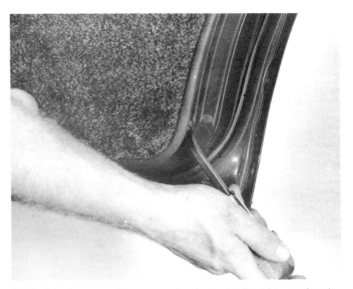

16.4 Insert a screwdriver or pry bar between the trim panel and the door and carefully disengage each clip

16.5   Remove the trim panel by pushing up (arrow) after disengaging from the door lock

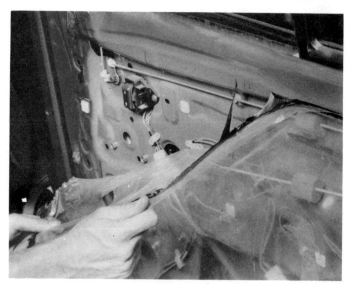

16.6   Take care when peeling the water shield off so that it is not stretched or torn

10 Position the trim panel on the inner door panel so that the panel retainers are aligned with the holes in the door panel and tap the retainers into the holes with the heel of your hand or a rubber mallet.

17   Trim fasteners — removal and installation

1   A plastic screw-type fastener is used extensively on these models. While this fastener appears to be a screw, it is actually a combination screw and clip. The base expands when the screw is threaded into it (photos).
2   To remove, hold the base with the fingers and remove the screw from the base with a Phillips screwdriver and then pry the base out with a flat bladed screwdriver.
3   To install, snap the fastener base into position and thread the screw in with the screwdriver.

18   Door glass and window regulator — removal and installation

1   Lower the door glass and remove the door trim panel and water shield (Section 16).
2   On power window models, disconnect the negative battery cable.
3   On rear doors, remove the belt line molding.
4   On power window equipped models, unplug the motor connector.
5   Move the regulator position if necessary so the glass installation bolts are accessible through the service holes.
6   On front doors, remove the bolts and lift the glass up and out of the door window opening.
7   On rear doors, remove the screw and bolt and lift the center channel out. Face the rear of the door glass downward, remove the lift bracket from the roller and then lift the glass up and out of the door. Remove the rear quarter glass.
8   On both front and rear doors, remove the installation bolt and lift the regulator through the service hole in the door.

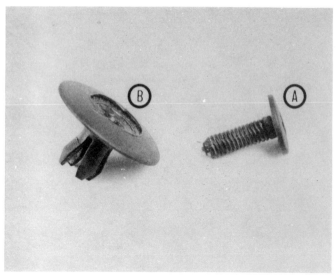

17.1a The plastic trim fastener consists of the base (B) and screw (A)

17.1b   Threading the screw into the base expands and locks the base in place

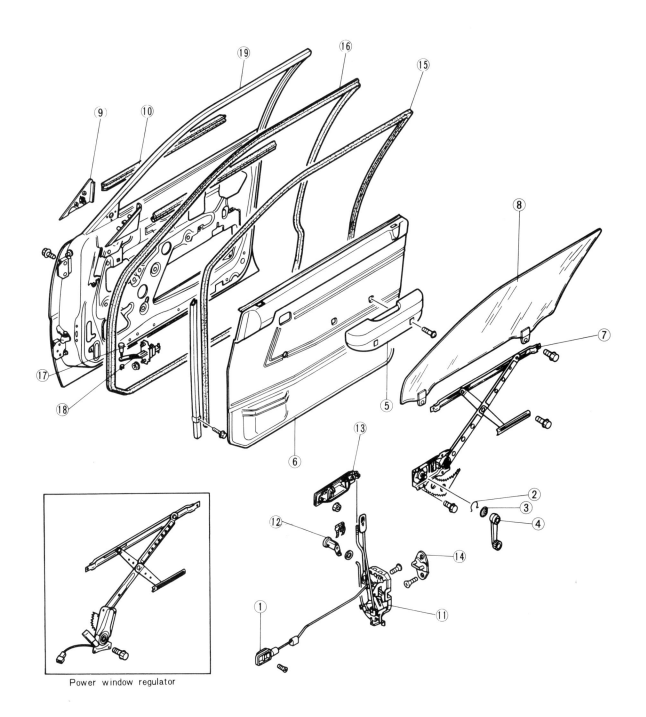

Power window regulator

Fig. 11.8 Front door glass and window regulator installation details (Sec 18)

1	Inner door handle cover	6 Door trim panel	11 Door lock	16 Weatherstrip
2	Snap ring	7 Regulator	12 Key cylinder	17 Checker pin
3	Escutcheon	8 Glass	13 Outer handle	18 Door checker
4	Regulator handle	9 Outer trim garnish	14 Striker	19 Door
5	Arm rest	10 Belt line molding	15 Glass channel	

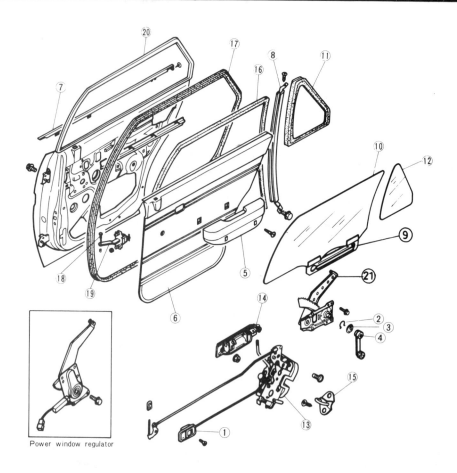

Fig. 11.9 Rear door glass and regulator details (Sec 18)

1 Inner handle cover	8 Center channel	15 Striker
2 Snap ring	9 Lift bracket	16 Glass channel
3 Escutcheon	10 Glass	17 Weatherstrip
4 Regulator	11 Quarter window weatherstrip	18 Checker pin
5 Arm rest	12 Quarter window	19 Door checker
6 Trim panel	13 Door lock	20 Door
7 Belt line molding	14 Outer handle	21 Regulator

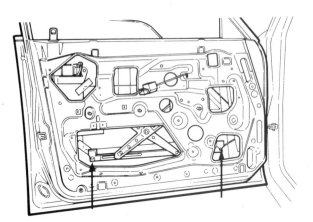

Fig. 11.10 Front door glass installation bolts (arrows)
(Sec 18)

Fig. 11.11 Rear door quarter window center channel
removal (Sec 18)

9   On power windows, unbolt the motor and remove it from the regulator. **Warning:** *Be very careful when removing the motor as the spring will be released, letting the regulator gear snap back to the Up position.*

10 Installation is the reverse of removal, paying attention to the following points.

11 Apply soapy water to the quarter window channel to ease installation.

12 On power window models, connect the battery negative cable and run the regulator to the Down position before installation of the motor.

13 After installation, run the glass up and down several times to make sure it operates lightly and smoothly, adjusting the regulator bolts as necessary.

19   Quarter window glass (coupe models) — removal and installation

1   Pry off the seat belt cover and unbolt the belt from the center pillar.

2   Remove the center pillar garnish.

3   Remove the glass installation nut, the lock installation tapping screw and then lift the glass from the vehicle.

4   Installation is the reverse of removal.

20   Console — removal and installation

1   Remove the shift knob.

2   Remove the parking brake covers, the rear seat ash tray and the rear console.

3   Remove the console side walls.

4   Remove the front console and shift boot assembly (photo).

5   Installation is the reverse of removal.

21   Instrument panel — removal and installation

1   Disconnect the negative battery cable.

2   Remove the instrument panel meter cover and hood (photo).

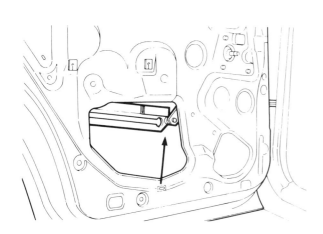

Fig. 11.12   Rear door glass lift bracket and roller (Sec 18)

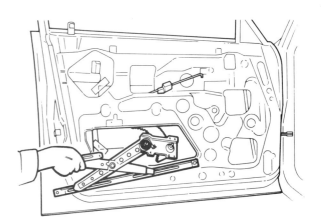

Fig. 11.13   Front door window glass regulator assembly removal (Sec 18)

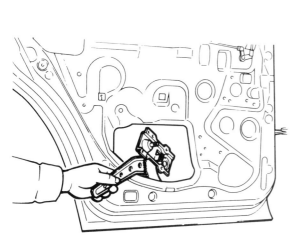

Fig. 11.14   Rear door window glass regulator assembly removal (Sec 18)

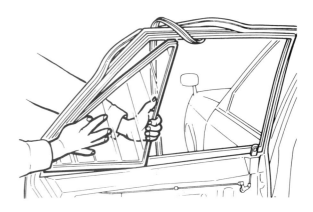

Fig. 11.15   Install the rear door quarter window into the channel using soapy water (Sec 18)

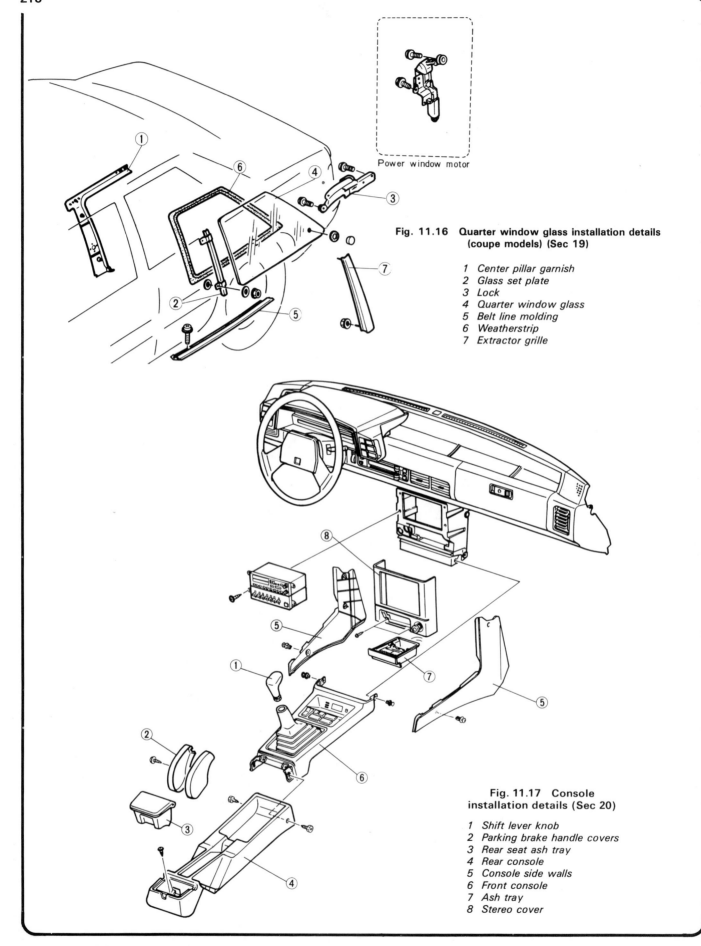

Power window motor

Fig. 11.16 Quarter window glass installation details (coupe models) (Sec 19)

1 Center pillar garnish
2 Glass set plate
3 Lock
4 Quarter window glass
5 Belt line molding
6 Weatherstrip
7 Extractor grille

Fig. 11.17 Console installation details (Sec 20)

1 Shift lever knob
2 Parking brake handle covers
3 Rear seat ash tray
4 Rear console
5 Console side walls
6 Front console
7 Ash tray
8 Stereo cover

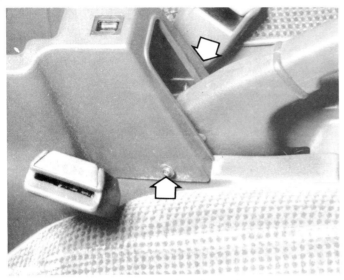

20.4 The front console bolt locations (arrows)

Fig. 11.18 Instrument panel component layout (Sec 21)

1 Upper meter cover
2 Meter hood
3 Meter
4 Steering wheel
5 Column covers
6 Lower air duct
7 Lower panel
8 Hood release knob
9 Dashboard undercover
10 Glove compartment
11 Heater wire
12 Side wall
13 Radio cover screws
14 Retainers
15 Console screws
16 Ash tray screws
17 Stereo cover
18 Speaker covers
19 Front pillar trim cover
20 Instrument panel retaining bolts (5)
21 Instrument panel cover and bolt
22 Instrument panel nuts (2)
23 Instrument panel inner bolts (2)
24 Steering column bolts (4)
25 Instrument panel

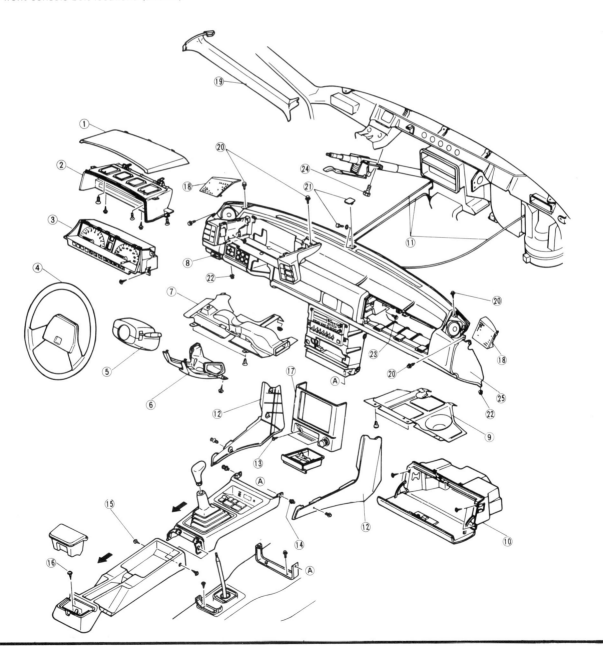

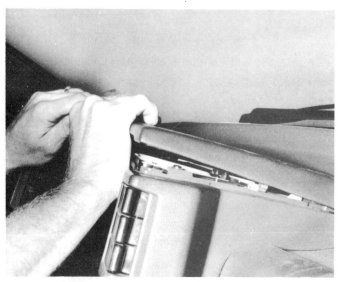

21.2   Grasp the meter top cover with both hands and snap it up to remove

21.4   Steering column cover screw location (arrow)

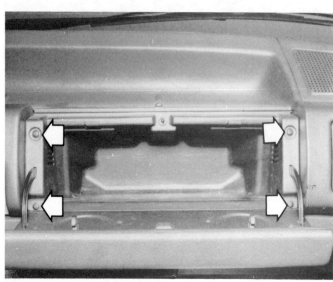

21.7   Glove compartment retaining screws (arrows)

3   Remove the meter (Chapter 12).
4   Remove the steering wheel (Chapter 10) and the upper and lower column covers (photo).
5   Remove the lower air duct, followed by the lower panel.
6   Remove the hood release knob and dashboard undercover.
7   Remove the glove compartment (photo).
8   Disconnect the heater control wire.
9   Remove the console side walls.
10 Remove the speaker and stereo covers (if equipped).
11 Remove the two front pillar trim panels.
12 Remove the retaining bolts and nuts and lift the instrument panel from the vehicle.
13 Installation is the reverse of removal.

22   Radiator grille — removal and installation

1   Open the six radiator grille retaining clips by pushing down on them, using a flat bladed screwdriver as shown in the accompanying illustration.
2   After disengaging all of the clips, lift the grille from the vehicle.
3   Place the grille in position, aligning it with the installation holes and then pressing into place.

23   Radiator grille cover — removal and installation

1   Open the hood.
2   Remove the retainers and lift the cover from the vehicle.
3   Installation is the reverse of removal.

24   Cowl plate — removal and installation

1   Remove the windshield wiper arms.
2   Remove the retaining screws, pry out the rubber seal retainers and remove the cowl plate.
3   Installation is the reverse of removal.

25   Front skirt panel — removal and installation

1   Remove the front bumper (Section 26).
2   Remove the six retaining screws and lower the skirt from the vehicle.
3   To install, place the skirt in position and install the screws finger tight.
4   Align the skirt end with the fender and tighten the screws securely, starting at the fender line.

26   Bumpers — removal and installation

1   Remove the bumper reinforcement bracket bolts and nuts and remove the bumper assembly from the vehicle.

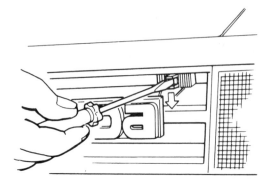

Fig. 11.19   Using a screwdriver to disengage the radiator grille clips (Sec 22)

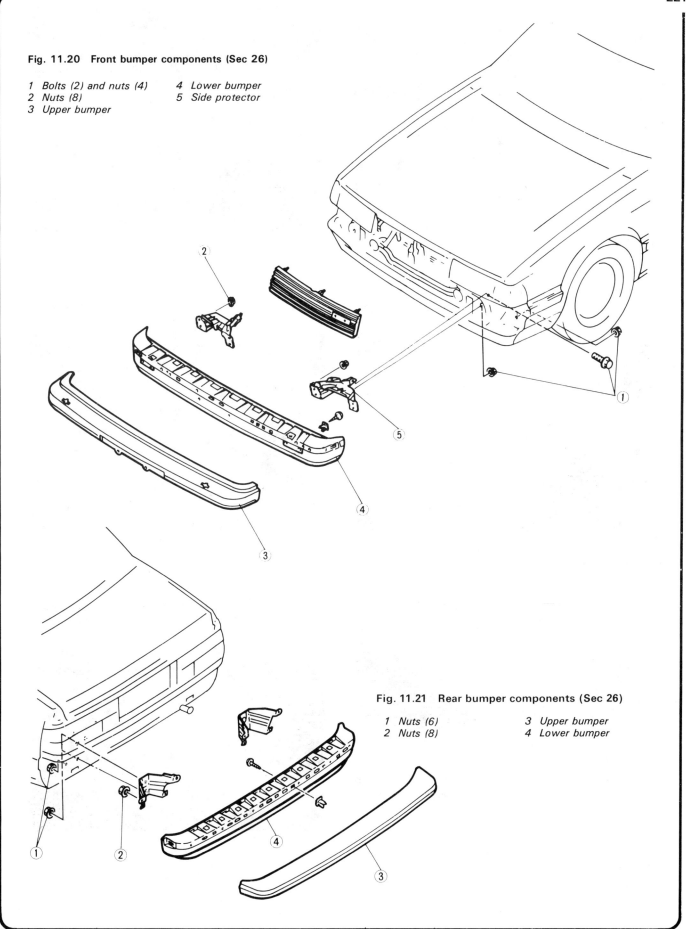

Fig. 11.20 Front bumper components (Sec 26)

1 Bolts (2) and nuts (4) 4 Lower bumper
2 Nuts (8) 5 Side protector
3 Upper bumper

Fig. 11.21 Rear bumper components (Sec 26)

1 Nuts (6) 3 Upper bumper
2 Nuts (8) 4 Lower bumper

This sequence of photographs deals with the repair of the dent and paintwork damage shown in this photo. The procedure will be similar for the repair of a hole. It should be noted that the procedures given here are simplified — more explicit instructions will be found in the text

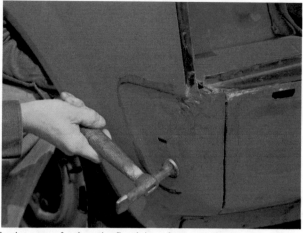

In the case of a dent the first job — after removing surrounding trim — is to hammer out the dent where access is possible. This will minimise filling. Here, the large dent having been hammered out, the damaged area is being made slightly concave

Now all paint must be removed from the damaged area, by rubbing with coarse abrasive paper. Alternatively, a wire brush or abrasive pad can be used in a power drill. Where the repair area meets good paintwork, the edge of the paintwork should be 'feathered', using a finer grade of abrasive paper

In the case of a hole caused by rusting, all damaged sheet-metal should be cut away before proceeding to this stage. Here, the damaged area is being treated with rust remover and inhibitor before being filled

Mix the body filler according to its manufacturer's instructions. In the case of corrosion damage, it will be necessary to block off any large holes before filling — this can be done with aluminium or plastic mesh, or aluminium tape. Make sure the area is absolutely clean before ...

... applying the filler. Filler should be applied with a flexible applicator, as shown, for best results; the wooden spatula being used for confined areas. Apply thin layers of filler at 20-minute intervals, until the surface of the filler is slightly proud of the surrounding bodywork

Initial shaping can be done with a Surform plane or
Dreadnought file. Then, using progressively finer grades of wet-
and-dry paper, wrapped around a sanding block, and copious
amounts of clean water, rub down the filler until really smooth
and flat. Again, feather the edges of adjoining paintwork

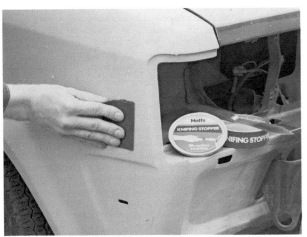

Again, using plenty of water, rub down the primer with a fine
grade wet-and-dry paper (400 grade is probably best) until it is
really smooth and well blended into the surrounding paintwork.
Any remaining imperfections can now be filled by carefully
applied knifing stopper paste

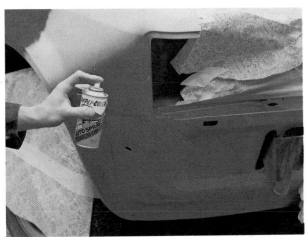

The top coat can now be applied. When working out of doors,
pick a dry, warm and wind-free day. Ensure surrounding areas
are protected from over-spray. Agitate the aerosol thoroughly,
then spray the centre of the repair area, working outwards with
a circular motion. Apply the paint as several thin coats

The whole repair area can now be sprayed or brush-painted
with primer. If spraying, ensure adjoining areas are protected
from over-spray. Note that at least one inch of the surrounding
sound paintwork should be coated with primer. Primer has a
'thick' consistency, so will find small imperfections

When the stopper has hardened, rub down the repair area again
before applying the final coat of primer. Before rubbing down
this last coat of primer, ensure the repair area is blemish-free –
use more stopper if necessary. To ensure that the surface of the
primer is really smooth use some finishing compound

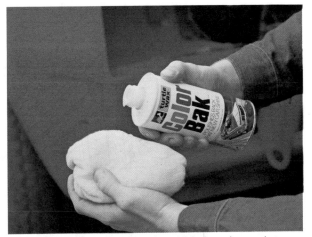

After a period of about two weeks, which the paint needs to
harden fully, the surface of the repaired area can be 'cut' with
a mild cutting compound prior to wax polishing. When carrying
out bodywork repairs, remember that the quality of the finished
job is proportional to the time and effort expended

2   Refer to the accompanying illustrations for bumper disassembly details.
3   Installation is the reverse of removal.

27   Fixed glass replacement

Due to the requirements for special handling techniques, the fixed glass such as the windshield, rear and side glass should be replaced by a dealer or auto glass shop.

28   Door outer handle — removal and installation

1   Raise the window to the full up position.
2   Remove the trim panel and peel back the water shield (Section 16).
3   Disconnect the control rod using a flat blade screwdriver as shown in the accompanying illustration.
4   Loosen the mounting bolts and remove the outer door handle from the vehicle. Disconnect the door handle switch (when so equipped).
5   Installation is the reverse of removal.

29   Exterior mirror — removal and installation

1   On power mirror models, disconnect the negative battery cable.
2   Pry off the trim cover.
3   On power mirror models, unplug the connector.
4   Remove the retaining screws and lift the mirror from the vehicle.
5   Installation is the reverse of removal.

30   Central locking system — general information

1   On models so equipped, the central locking system causes all the passenger door locks to follow the position of the driver's door lock. The components of the system are the driver's door lock switch, solenoid actuator for the passenger doors, a control unit and the associated wiring.
2   If the system malfunctions, the doors can still be locked and unlocked by hand. Check the appropriate fuse and fusible link if the system does not work at all.

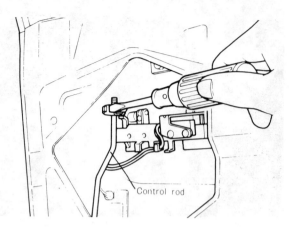

Fig. 11.22   Disconnecting the outer door handle control rod (Sec 28)

3   Access to the door-mounted components is achieved by removing the door trim panel and water shield (Section 16). Testing is by substitution of known good units; no repair is possible. Check for correct operation before installing the door trim.
4   The control unit (sometimes called a timer) is located behind a trim panel in the passenger footwell.

31   Doors — removal, installation, an adjustment

1   On models with power windows, central locking etc., disconnect the battery negative lead. Also disconnect the door wiring harness connector. It may be necessary to remove the door trim panel (Section 16) or adjacent body trim panels for access to the connector.
2   Mark around the hinge bolt positions on the door and on the door pillar. Remove the check strap pin.
3   Have an assistant support the door. Remove the hinge bolts from the door or pillar and lift away the door.
4   Installation is the reverse of the removal procedure. Observe the hinge bolt alignment marks if the original door is being installed.

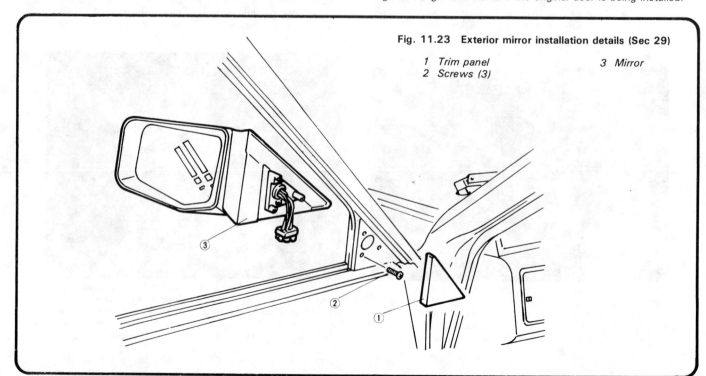

Fig. 11.23   Exterior mirror installation details (Sec 29)

1 Trim panel   3 Mirror
2 Screws (3)

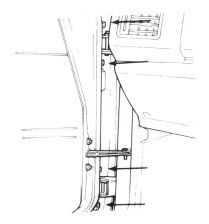

Fig. 11.24 Door hinge bolts (arrowed) (Sec 31)

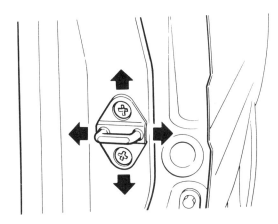

Fig. 11.25 Door lock striker adjustment — move striker in any direction (arrows) (Sec 31)

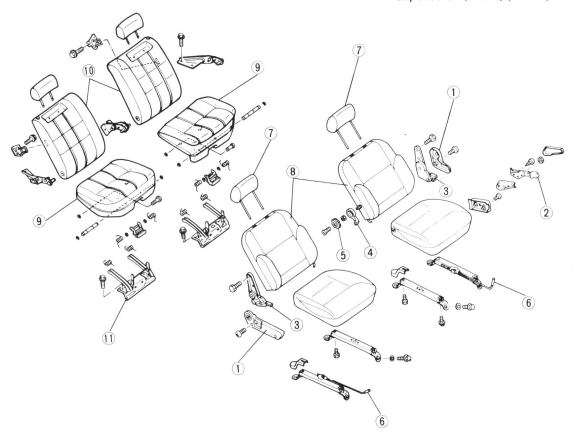

Fig. 11.26 Seats and fittings — Liftback (Sec 32)

1 Covers	6 Slide adjusters
2 Height adjuster	7 Head restraints
3 Reclining adjuster	8 Front seat backs
4 Lumbar support adjuster	9 Rear seat cushions
5 Lateral support adjuster	10 Rear seat backs

5   Check the fit of the door in its aperture. Adjust if necessary by slackening the hinge bolts, repositioning the door and tightening the bolts.
6   Adjust the position of the door lock striker if necessary so that the door closes easily and has no play when shut. Slacken the striker screws to adjust and tighten the screws when the correct position has been found.

32 Seats — removal and installation

Front seats

1   If heated seats are installed, disconnect the battery negative lead.
2   Move the seat as far back as possible and remove the screws which hold the front ends of the seat runners to the floor.
3   Move the seat as far forward as possible and remove the two rear securing screws.
4   Remove any side trim which may impede seat removal. Unplug the wiring harness connector from the seat heater (when equipped) and remove the seat.
5   Installation is the reverse of removal. Apply a little grease to the runners.

Rear seats

6   The fixed type rear seat cushion can be released by pressing it down and rearwards, then lifting it out. The hinged type cushion can be

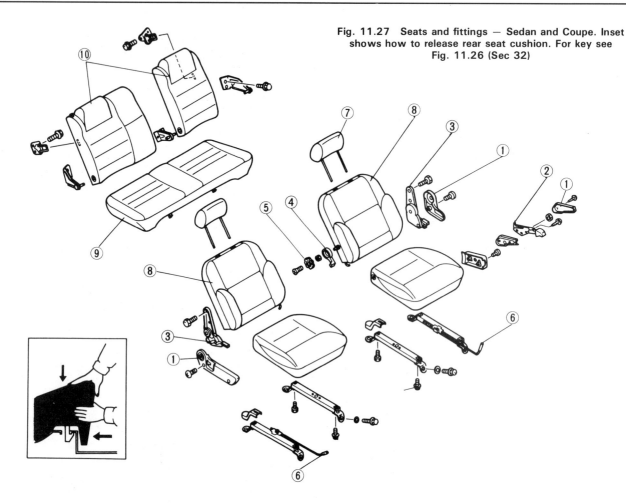

Fig. 11.27 Seats and fittings — Sedan and Coupe. Inset shows how to release rear seat cushion. For key see Fig. 11.26 (Sec 32)

pivoted forward, after which the hinge pins can be unclipped or the hinges themselves unbolted.

7 The seat back supports or hinges can now be unbolted and the seat back removed.

8 Installation is the reverse of removal.

33 Seat heaters — inspection and element replacement

1 Some European models are equipped with electric heating elements in the front seats. In the event of malfunction, first check the fuses and fusible links.

2 Disconnect the seat heater switch and check for continuity across the switch terminals. With the switch ON, there should be continuity between terminals 'b' (green wire) and 'c' (blue wire). Replace the switch if not.

3 Separate the wiring harness connectors under the seat. Check the cushion connectors for continuity. There should be continuity between the 'W' terminals on the 2-pole and 4-pole connector and between the 'B' terminals. If not, the cushion heater (or its wiring) is defective.

4 Check the seat back heater connector. There should be continuity between the 'Y' terminal on the single-pole connector and the 'B' terminal on the four-pole connector. If not, the seat back heater (or its wiring) is defective.

5 The heating elements can only be replaced complete with cushion or seat back, as applicable.

34 Sunroof — general information

1 An electrically-operated sunroof is available on some models. It is controlled by two switches in the overhead light unit.

2 Considerable expertise is needed to repair or replace sunroof components successfully. Any problems should be referred to your Mazda dealer or other specialist.

3 Keep the sunroof guide rails free of dirt.

4 If the sunroof motor does not operate at all, check the appropriate fuse and fusible link. The sunroof can be opened and closed manually using a hex head wrench as shown in the accompanying illustration. A suitable wrench was supplied with the vehicle and should be found in the glove compartment.

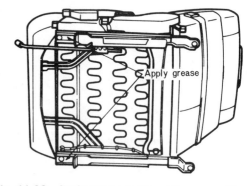

Fig. 11.28 Apply grease to the seat runners (Sec 32)

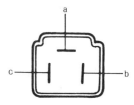

Fig. 11.29 Identification of seat heater switch terminals (Sec 33)

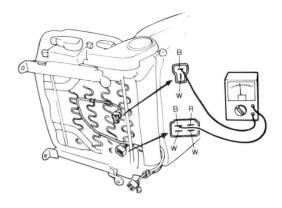

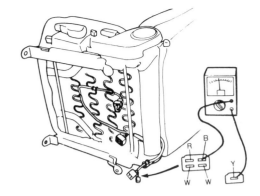

Fig. 11.30 Checking the seat cushion heater connectors for continuity (Sec 33)

Fig. 11.31 Checking the seat back heater connectors for continuity (Sec 33)

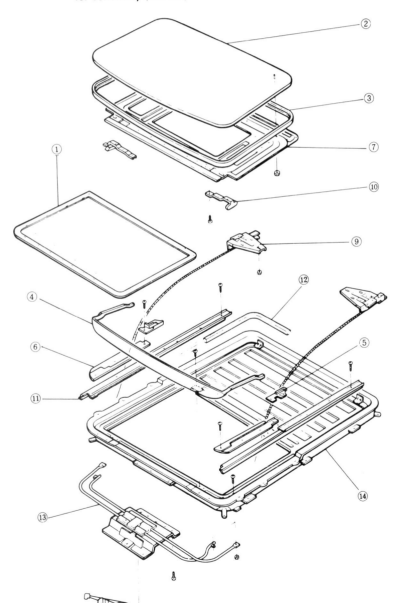

Fig. 11.32 Exploded view of the sunroof (Sec 34)

1 Inner trim
2 Outer panel
3 Weatherstrip
4 Wind deflector
5 Stopper
6 Rail
7 Lower panel
8 Motor
9 Rear guide bracket
10 Front guide bracket
11 Rail
12 Packing piece
13 Tube assembly
14 Frame

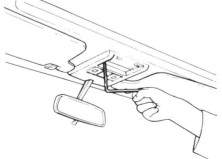

Insert and turn wrench as desired.

Fig. 11.33 Manual operation of the sunroof (Sec 34)

Chapter 12   Chassis electrical system

Contents

Specifications

Bulb

Bulb	Wattage	
	North America	U.K.
Front		
Headlight		
Inner.	50	—
Outer	35	65/60
Parking light.	5/8	5
Front turn signal light	27	21
Front side marker light	3.8	5
Interior		
Dome light.	10	10
Map light	5	6
Indicator lights		
Turn signal, hazard and fuel lights.	3.4	3.4
High beam, oil pressure, alternator, stop lights, brake, parking brake, fuel, washer level, tail and seat belt lights....	1.4	1.4
Illumination lights		
Automatic transaxle selector lever	3.4	3.4
Heater.	3.4	3.4
Meter.	1.4 and 3.4	1.4 and 3.4
Cigarette lighter	3.4	3.4
Radio.	3.4	3.4
Rear window defroster	1.4	1.4
Rear		
Turn signal light	27	21
Stop and tail light.	27/8	21/5
Back-up light.	27	21
Side marker light	5	5
License plate light		
5-door models.	6	5
All others	5	4
Luggage compartment	5 or 6	5

Torque specifications

	Ft-lbs	M-kg
Windshield wiper and rear wiper arm nuts	7 to 10	0.9 to 1.3

1 General information

The electrical system is a 12-volt, negative ground type. Power for the lights and all electrical accessories is supplied by a lead/acid battery which is charged by the alternator.

This Chapter covers repair and service procedures for the various electrical components not associated with the engine. Information on the battery, alternator, distributor and starter motor can be found in Chapter 5.

It should be noted that whenever portions of the electrical system are worked on, the negative battery cable should be disconnected to prevent electrical shorts and/or fires. **Note:** *Information concerning digital instrumentation and dash related accessories is not included in this manual. Problems involving these components should be referred to your dealer.*

2 Electrical troubleshooting — general information

A typical electrical circuit consists of an electrical component, any switches, relays, motors, etc. related to that component and the wiring and connectors that connect the component to both the battery and the chassis. To aid in locating a problem in any electrical circuit, wiring diagrams are included at the end of this book.

Before tackling any troublesome electrical circuit, first study the appropriate diagrams to get a complete understanding of what makes up that individual circuit. Trouble spots, for instance, can often be narrowed down by noting if other components related to that circuit are operating properly or not. If several components or circuits fail at one time, chances are the problem lies in the fuse or ground connection, as several circuits often are routed through the same fuse and ground connections.

Electrical problems often stem from simple causes, such as loose or corroded connections, or a blown fuse. Prior to any electrical troubleshooting, always visually check the condition of the fuse, wires and connections in the problem circuit.

If testing instruments are going to be utilized, use the diagrams to plan ahead of time where you will make the necessary connections in order to accurately pinpoint the trouble spot.

The basic tools needed for electrical troubleshooting include a circuit tester or voltmeter (a 12-volt bulb with a set of test leads can also be used), a continuity tester, which includes a bulb, battery and set of test leads, and a jumper wire, preferably with a circuit breaker incorporated, which can be used to bypass electrical components.

Voltage checks should be performed if a circuit is not functioning properly. Connect one lead of a circuit tester to either the negative battery terminal or a known good ground. Connect the other lead to a connector in the circuit being tested, preferably nearest to the battery or fuse. If the bulb of the tester goes on, voltage is reaching that point, which means the part of the circuit between that connector and the battery is problem free. Continue checking along the entire circuit in the same fashion. When you reach a point where no voltage is present, the problem lies between there and the last good test point. Most of the time the problem is due to a loose connection. **Note:** *Keep in mind that some circuits receive voltage only when the ignition key is in the Accessory or Run position.*

A method of finding shorts in a circuit is to remove the fuse and connect a test light or voltmeter in its place to the fuse terminals. There should be no load in the circuit. Move the wiring harness from side-to-side while watching the test light. If the bulb goes on, there is a short to ground somewhere in that area, probably where insulation has rubbed off of a wire. The same test can be performed on other components of the circuit, including the switch.

A ground check should be done to see if a component is grounded properly. Disconnect the battery and connect one lead of a self powered test light such as a continuity tester to a known good ground. Connect the other lead to the wire or ground connection being tested. If the bulb goes on, the ground is good. If the bulb does not go on, the ground is not good.

A continuity check is performed to see if a circuit, section of circuit or individual component is passing electricity properly. Disconnect the battery and connect one lead of a self powered test light such as a continuity tester to one end of the circuit, and the other lead to the other end of the circuit. If the bulb goes on, there is continuity, which means the circuit is passing electricity properly. Switches can be checked in the same way.

Remember that all electrical circuits are composed of electricity running from the battery, through the wires, switches, relays, etc. to the electrical component (light bulb, motor, etc.). From there it is run to the body (ground) where it is passed back to the battery. Any electrical problem is an interruption in the flow of electricity to and from the battery.

3 Fuses — general information

The electrical circuits of the vehicle are protected by a combination of fuses, circuit breakers and fusible links. The fuse box unit combines the fuse box, harnesses and their connectors and is located on the kick panel under the dash on the driver's side (photo).

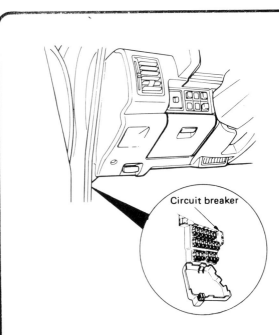

Fig. 12.1 Fuse box and circuit breaker location (Sec 3)

3.1 Fuse box location

3.2   The fuse location and type information can be found on the fuse box cover

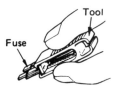

Fig. 12.2   Fuse type and replacement procedure (Sec 3)

Each of the fuses is designed to protect a specific circuit and the various circuits are identified on the fuse panel itself (photo). Miniaturized fuses of blade terminal design are employed in the fuse block.

If an electrical component fails, your first check should be the fuse. A fuse which has blown is easily identified by inspecting the element inside the clear plastic body. Also, the blade terminal tips are exposed in the fuse body, allowing for continuity checks.

It is important that the correct fuse be installed. The different electrical circuits need varying amounts of protection, indicated by the amperage rating molded in bold, color coded numbers on the fuse body and marked on the fuse box cover. **Caution:** *At no time should the fuse be bypassed with pieces of metal or foil. Serious damage to the electrical system could result.*

If the replacement fuse immediately fails, do not replace it again until the cause of the problem is isolated and corrected. In most cases, this will be a short circuit in the wiring caused by a broken or deteriorated wire.

The heater and air conditioner consume a lot of power and the fuse box contains a circuit breaker to protect their circuits. If the circuit is broken by the circuit breaker, turn off the air conditioner and heater before pushing the circuit breaker reset button.

4   Fusible links — general information

In addition to fuses, the wiring is protected by fusible links. These links are used in circuits which are not ordinarily fused, such as the ignition circuit.

The fusible links used on these models consist of special wires which plug into a fusible link block located on the inner fender panel adjacent to the battery. The location of other fusible links on your particular vehicle may be determined by referring to the wiring diagrams at the end of this book. The fusible links cannot be repaired, but a new link of the same size wire (available at your dealer) can be put in its place. The procedure is as follows:
   a)   Correct the fault which caused the link to melt.
   b)   Disconnect the battery negative lead.
   c)   Pull the fusible link straight out of the block.
   d)   Push a new fusible link securely into the block (photo).

5   Three-way adjustable suspension damper actuator — testing

1   Remove the damper actuator cover and unplug the connector (Chapter 10).
2   Use an ohmmeter to measure the resistance across the Sport

4.2   Fusible link replacement

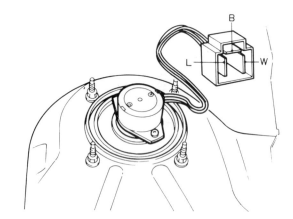

Fig. 12.3   Three-way adjustable suspension actuator connector (Sec 5)

(L to B) and Normal (W to B) terminals. The resistance should be between 2.8 and 3.3 ohms.

6   Combination switch — removal and installation

1   Disconnect the battery negative cable.
2   Remove the steering wheel (Chapter 10).

6.3   Removing the steering column trim halves

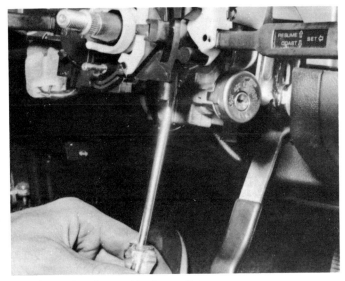

6.6   Loosening the combination switch screw

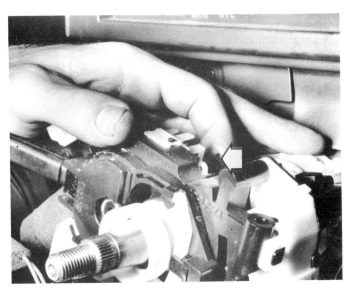

6.7   Press up on the combination switch locating tab (arrow) to release it, then slide the switch out of the column

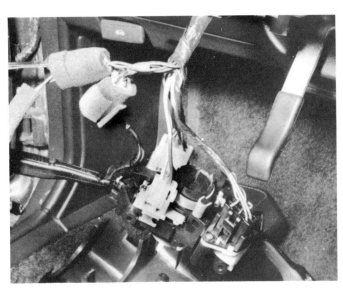

6.8   With the switch removed from the column, the connectors can be easily unplugged

3   Remove the screws and separate the column trim halves (photo).
4   Pull the ignition switch lock ring off.
5   Remove the ignition switch illumination bulb and (if equipped) lower the column tilt lever.
6   Loosen the switch clamp screw (photo).
7   Lift up on the locating tab and slide the switch off the column (photo).
8   Remove the combination switch from the column and unplug the connectors (photo).
9   Installation is the reverse of removal.

7   Ignition switch/steering lock — removal and installation

1   Remove the steering wheel (Chapter 10) and the combination switch (Section 6) to provide access to the ignition switch.
2   Drill out the ignition switch retaining bolts (photo), or unscrew them by driving their heads around with a chisel or punch. New shear head bolts will be needed for installation.
3   Remove the switch from the steering column and unplug the connector.

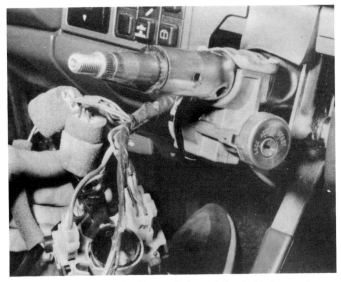

7.2   The heads of the ignition switch retaining bolts (arrows) can be drilled out to remove the switch

4   To install, place the switch in position, install the bolts and tighten them provisionally. Reconnect the ignition switch and check the switch and steering lock for correct operation. When satisfied, tighten the bolts until the heads break off.

5   Install the combination switch and steering wheel.

8   Headlight — removal and installation

1   Remove the radiator grille cover (if equipped) and grille assembly (Chapter 11).

2   Disconnect the negative battery cable.

Sealed beam-type

3   Remove the headlight bezel and combination light assembly.

4   Remove the four screws which secure the retaining ring and withdraw the ring. Support the sealed beam unit as this is done, unplug the connector and remove it from the vehicle (photo).

5   Position the new unit close enough to connect the wires and install the retaining ring and mounting screws.

6   Install the bezel and check for proper operation. If the adjusting screws were not turned, the headlight should not require adjustment.

8.4   Support the headlight while unplugging the connector

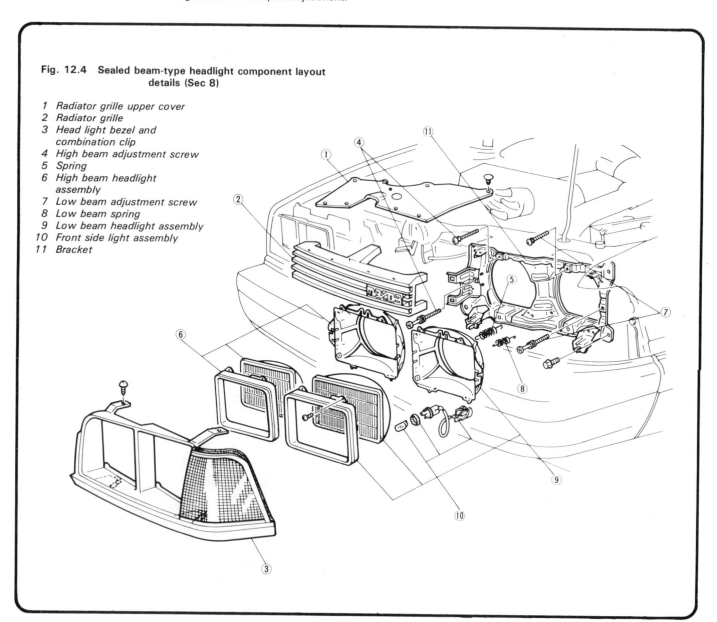

Fig. 12.4   Sealed beam-type headlight component layout details (Sec 8)

1   Radiator grille upper cover
2   Radiator grille
3   Head light bezel and combination clip
4   High beam adjustment screw
5   Spring
6   High beam headlight assembly
7   Low beam adjustment screw
8   Low beam spring
9   Low beam headlight assembly
10   Front side light assembly
11   Bracket

Fig. 12.5 Bulb-type headlight installation details (Sec 8)

1 Radiator grille
2 Front side light assembly
3 Bolts
4 Inner spring
5 Outer spring
6 Headlight adjustment screw
7 Bracket
8 Bolts
9 Bracket
10 Headlight assembly (cover,
   spring, lens, bulb and holder)

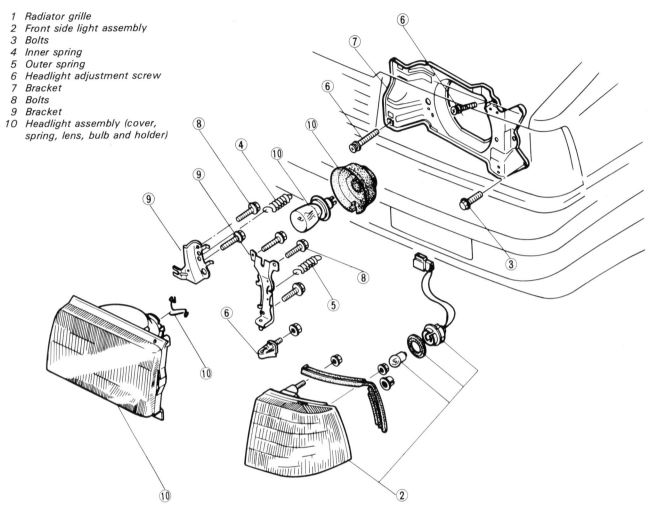

Bulb-type

7 Remove the front side light assembly.
8 Remove the bolts and release the springs which secure the headlight assembly. Disconnect the bulb wiring connector and remove the headlight assembly from the brackets.
9 For bulb replacement, see Section 10.
10 Installation is the reverse of removal.

---

9 Headlight adjustment

It is important that the headlights are aimed correctly. If adjusted incorrectly they could blind an oncoming car and cause a serious accident or seriously reduce the your ability to see the road.

Headlights have two spring loaded adjusting screws, one on the top affecting up and down movement and one on the side affecting left and right movement.

There are several methods of adjusting the headlights, the simplest method uses a screen or empty wall 10 feet in front of the vehicle and a level floor.

Preparation

1 Park the vehicle on a level floor 10 feet from the screen or light colored wall.
2 Position masking tape vertically on the screen in reference to the vehicle center line and the center lines of both headlights. **Note:** *If the vehicle has a four headlight system then four vertical lines plus the vehicle center line will be used.*

Fig. 12.6 The vehicle should be placed ten feet from a vertical screen or light colored blank wall (Sec 9)

3 Position a horizontal tape line in reference to the center line of all the headlights. **Note:** *It may be easier to position the tape on the screen with the vehicle parked only a few inches away.*

Adjustment

4 Adjustment should be made with the vehicle sitting level and the gas tank half full and someone sitting in the driver's seat.
5 Starting with the low beam adjustment, position the *high intensity* zone so it is just below the horizontal line and two inches to the right (LHD) or left (RHD) of the headlight vertical line. Adjustment is made by turning the adjusting screws.
6 With the high beams on, the *high intensity* zone should be vertically centered with the exact center two inches below the horizontal line. **Note:** *It may not be possible to position the headlight aim exactly for both high and low beams. If a compromise must be used, keep in mind that the low beams are the most used and have the greatest effect on driver safety.*
7 As an alternative to the procedure just described, the lights can be adjusted by a service station using optical alignment equipment.

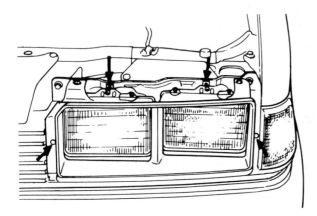

Fig. 12.7 Sealed beam-type headlight adjustment screw
locations (Sec 9)

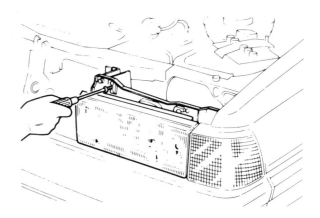

Fig. 12.8 Bulb-type headlight adjustment (Sec 9)

10 Bulb replacement

Front end

Turn signal and side marker lights

1   The turn signal and side marker light bulb can be replaced after removing the screws and lenses. Grasp the bulb and pull it from the socket (side marker) or press in and rotate the bulb counterclockwise (turn signal) (photos).

2   Install the new bulb, check for correct operation, then install the lens.

Headlight (bulb type)

3   Raise the hood. Unplug the wiring connector and remove the rubber boot (photo).

4   Release the spring clip and withdraw the bulb (photo). **Warning:** *If the bulb has just been in use it may be extremely hot.*

5   Do not touch the bulb glass with the fingers, since contamination from natural oils present in skin can blacken the bulb and cause premature failure. If the glass is accidentally touched, clean it with tissue and rubbing alcohol.

6   Install the new bulb, engaging the tabs on the bulb base with the recesses in the reflector, and secure it with the spring clip.

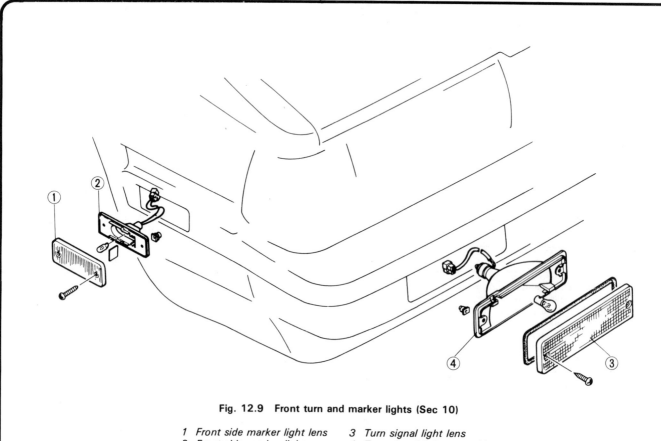

Fig. 12.9 Front turn and marker lights (Sec 10)

1 Front side marker light lens
2 Front side marker light
   assembly
3 Turn signal light lens
4 Turn signal light assembly

10.1a   The side marker bulbs insert straight into the socket

10.1b   The turn signal bulb is installed or removed by pushing in and rotating

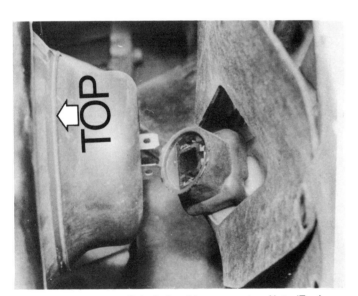

10.3   Unplug the headlight bulb wiring connector. Note 'Top' marking on boot

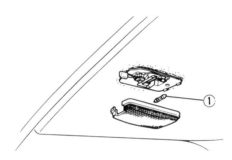

Fig. 12.10   Dome light bulb replacement (Sec 10)

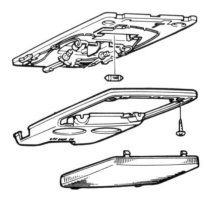

Fig. 12.11   Dome/map light bulb replacement (Sec 10)

10.4   Release the spring clip and withdraw the bulb

7   Install the rubber boot, observing the 'TOP' marking, and plug in the wiring connector. Check for correct operation, then lower the hood.

Interior

Ignition switch light

8   Remove the steering column cover for access. Pull the bulb from the socket and press the new one into place. Install the cover.

Sedan & Coupe

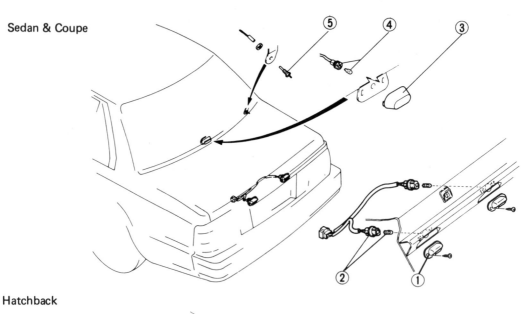

Hatchback

Fig. 12.12 License plate and tail light component layout (Sec 10)

1 License plate light lens
2 License plate bulb
3 Luggage compartment light lens
4 Luggage compartment light bulb and holder
5 Switch

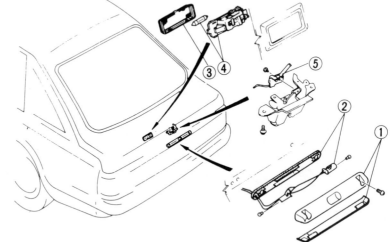

Dome/map light
9   Grasp the lens and pull down to remove it. Remove the bulb by pulling it straight down. Press the new bulb into place, check for correct operation and install the lens.

Optional overhead map light
10 Pry the light lens/button off with a small screwdriver. Remove the bulb by grasping it and pulling it out of the socket. Install the new bulb, check for correct operation and install the lens.

Instrument panel lights
11 The instrument panel bulbs can be replaced after removal of the instrument cluster (Section 12) (photo).
12 Rotate the holder, withdraw it from the panel and remove the bulb from the holder (photo). Some types of bulb are integral with their holder, and bulb and holder must be replaced as a unit.
13 Installation is the reverse of removal.

Radio illumination
14 The radio illumination bulb is located in a twist-in holder and is accessible after removing the radio (Section 11).

Heater control illumination
15 Withdraw the heater control panel as described in Section 15. It will be necessary to disconnect some of the cables until the panel can be withdrawn far enough for access to the bulb (photo).
16 Pull out the old bulb and install the new one. Check for correct operation, then install the heater control panel.

Glove compartment light
17 Remove the glove compartment, which is secured by four screws, for access to the bulb (photo).

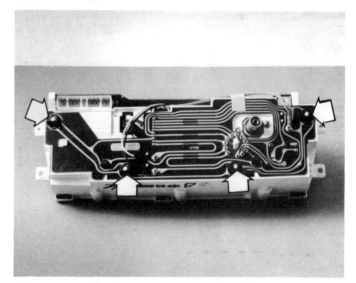

10.11   Instrument cluster bulb locations (arrows)

18 Pull out the old bulb and install the new one. Check for correct operation, then install the glove compartment.

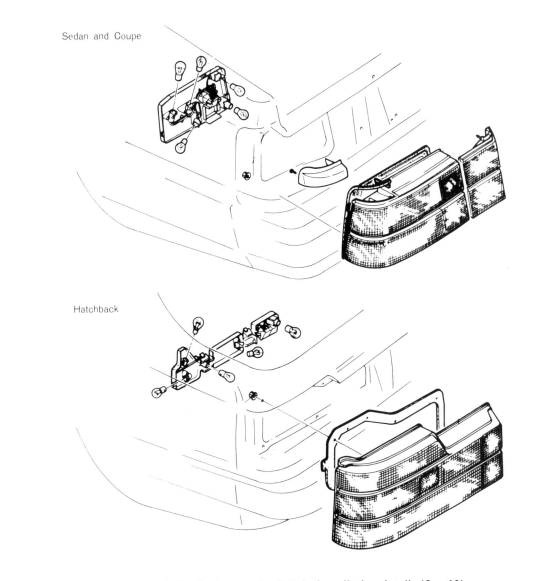

Sedan and Coupe

Hatchback

Fig. 12.13 Back-up and tail light installation details (Sec 10)

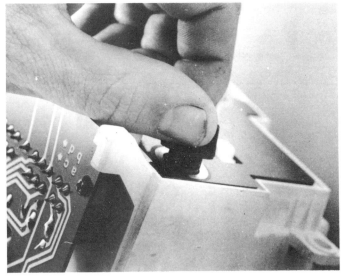

10.12 Turn the holder and remove it for access to the bulb

10.15 Heater control illumination bulb

10.17   Glove compartment light bulb

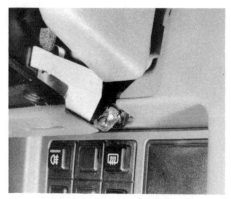

10.19   Instrument panel switch illumination bulb

10.21   Removing the footwell light

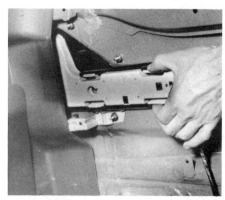

10.27a   Depress the tabs and lift off the housing

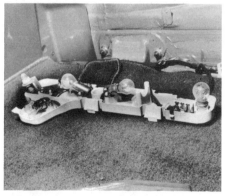

10.27b   With the housing removed, the bulbs can be easily replaced

Instrument panel switch illumination.
19 Remove the instrument panel trim from beside the illumination lens and hook out the bulb and holder (photo).
20 Replace the bulb, check it for correct operation, then relocate the bulb holder and install the trim.

Footwell light
21 Remove the trim from below the instrument panel and extract the bulb and holder from the trim (photo).
22 Replace the bulb and check it for correct operation. Install the bulb holder into the trim, then install the trim.

Rear end

Luggage compartment light
23   Pry off the lens, grasp the bulb and pull it from the socket.
24 Install the new bulb, check it for correct operation, then install the lens.

License plate light
25 Remove the license plate housing screws and housing for access to the bulb.

Rear lights
26 Remove the inner trim panel.
27 Depress the tabs and remove the light housing for access to the tail, back up, rear marker and parking light bulbs (photos). When installing, make sure the tabs snap into position when the housing is pressed into place.
28 Check for correct operation, then install the inner trim panel.

---

11   Radio and speakers — removal and installation

Radio
1   Disconnect the negative battery cable.
2   Remove the console side walls.

3   Remove the radio retaining screws (photo).
4   Pull the radio out and unplug the electrical connectors (photo).
5   Lift the radio from the dash.
6   Installation is the reverse of removal.

Speakers
7   Locate the speaker, referring to the accompanying illustration.
8   Rear speakers are accessible after opening the trunk or hatch. On front speakers it will be necessary to pry off the speaker cover.

11.3   Radio retaining screws (arrows)

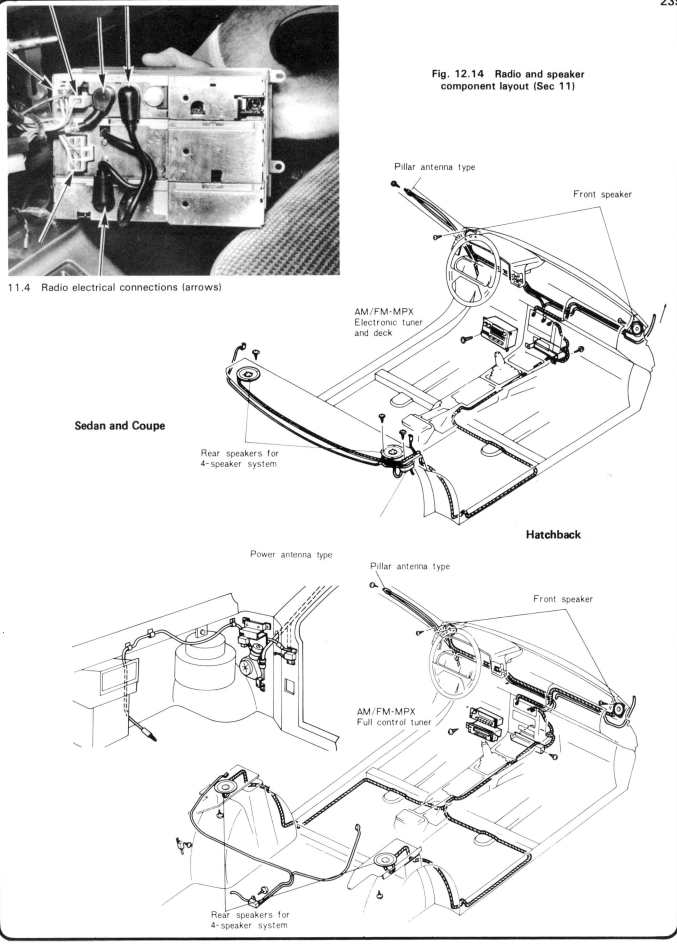

11.4 Radio electrical connections (arrows)

Fig. 12.14 Radio and speaker component layout (Sec 11)

Pillar antenna type

Front speaker

AM/FM-MPX
Electronic tuner
and deck

Sedan and Coupe

Rear speakers for
4-speaker system

Hatchback

Power antenna type

Pillar antenna type

Front speaker

AM/FM-MPX
Full control tuner

Rear speakers for
4-speaker system

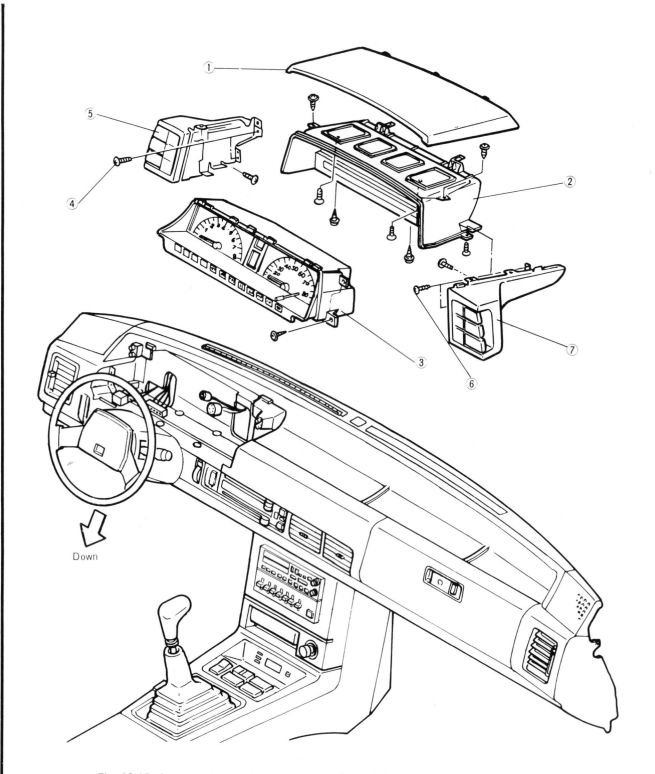

Fig. 12.15 Instrument panel cluster component layout (cluster switch equipped models) (Sec 12)

1 Upper meter cover
2 Meter hood
3 Cluster instruments
4 Cluster switch screws

5 Left cluster switch assembly
6 Cluster switch screws
7 Right cluster switch assembly

9 Remove the retaining screws, withdraw the speaker sufficiently to allow the connector to be unplugged and remove the speaker from the vehicle.
10 Installation is the reverse of removal.

12 Instrument panel cluster — removal and installation

1 Disconnect the battery negative cable and lower the adjustable (if equipped) steering wheel.
2 Remove the cluster upper cover screws and meter hood.
3 Remove the cluster retaining screws (photo).
4 Disconnect the speedometer cable.
5 Pull the cluster out, disconnect the wiring and remove the cluster and (if equipped) switch assemblies from the instrument panel.
6 Installation is the reverse of removal.

13 Instrument panel cluster instruments — removal and installation

1 Disconnect the battery negative cable.
2 Remove the instrument panel cluster (Section 12).

12.3   Instrument cluster left side retaining screws (arrows)

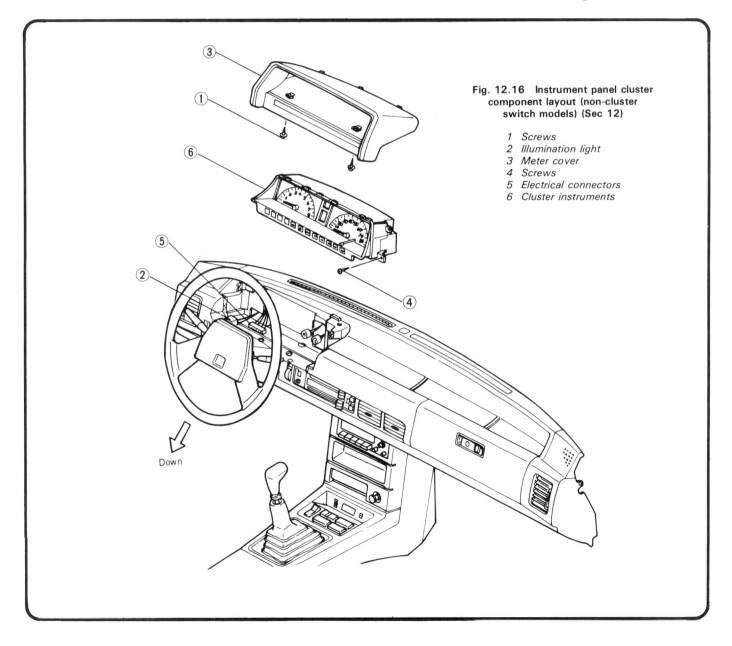

Fig. 12.16 Instrument panel cluster component layout (non-cluster switch models) (Sec 12)

1 Screws
2 Illumination light
3 Meter cover
4 Screws
5 Electrical connectors
6 Cluster instruments

Down

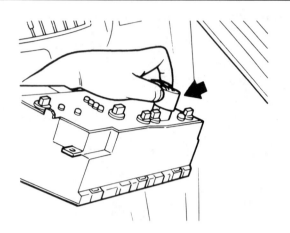

Analog (needle-type gauges) instrument cluster

3   Remove the front lens, printed circuit and plate.
4   Remove the retaining bolts and lift the instruments from the cluster.
5   Installation is the reverse of removal.

Electronic instrument panel

6   Remove the bulbs and sockets and retaining screws to remove the printed circuit boards from the meter case.
7   Remove the retaining screws and lift off the front lens plate.
8   Remove the tachometer and printed circuit assembly.
9   Remove the display switch assembly.
10 Remove the illumination control and knob assembly.
11 Remove the retaining screws and unplug the speedometer, fuel and temperature meters from the case.
12 Installation is the reverse of removal.

Fig. 12.17   Disconnect the cluster meter connector (arrow) by pressing the retaining clip (Sec 12)

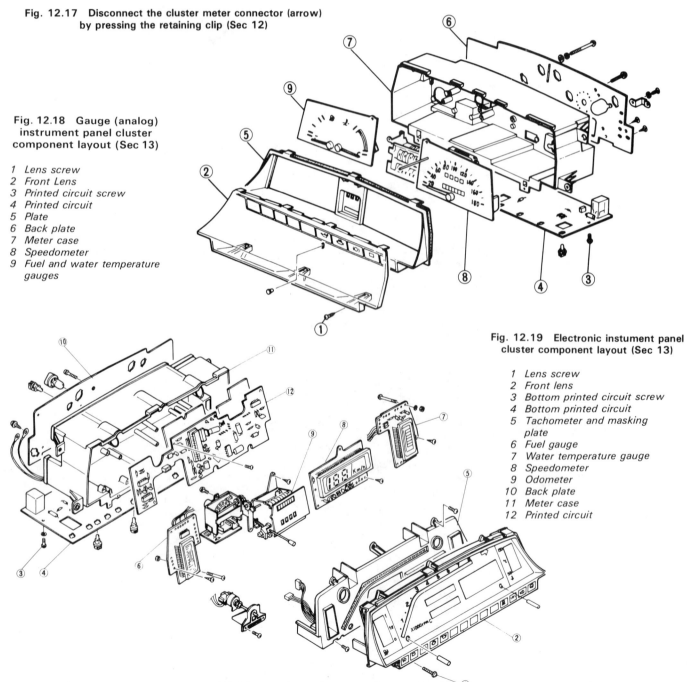

Fig. 12.18   Gauge (analog) instrument panel cluster component layout (Sec 13)

1   Lens screw
2   Front Lens
3   Printed circuit screw
4   Printed circuit
5   Plate
6   Back plate
7   Meter case
8   Speedometer
9   Fuel and water temperature gauges

Fig. 12.19   Electronic instument panel cluster component layout (Sec 13)

1   Lens screw
2   Front lens
3   Bottom printed circuit screw
4   Bottom printed circuit
5   Tachometer and masking plate
6   Fuel gauge
7   Water temperature gauge
8   Speedometer
9   Odometer
10 Back plate
11 Meter case
12 Printed circuit

14 Instrument panel switches — removal and installation

1   Disconnect the battery negative cable.

Cluster switches

2   Remove the instrument cluster panel (Section 12).

3   Remove the retaining screws, disconnect the wiring connector and lift the appropriate switch assembly off the cluster meter housing.
4   Installation is the reversal of removal.

Non-cluster switches

5   Carefully pry the switch from its location, unplug the wiring harness connector and remove the switch.
6   Installation is the reversal of removal.

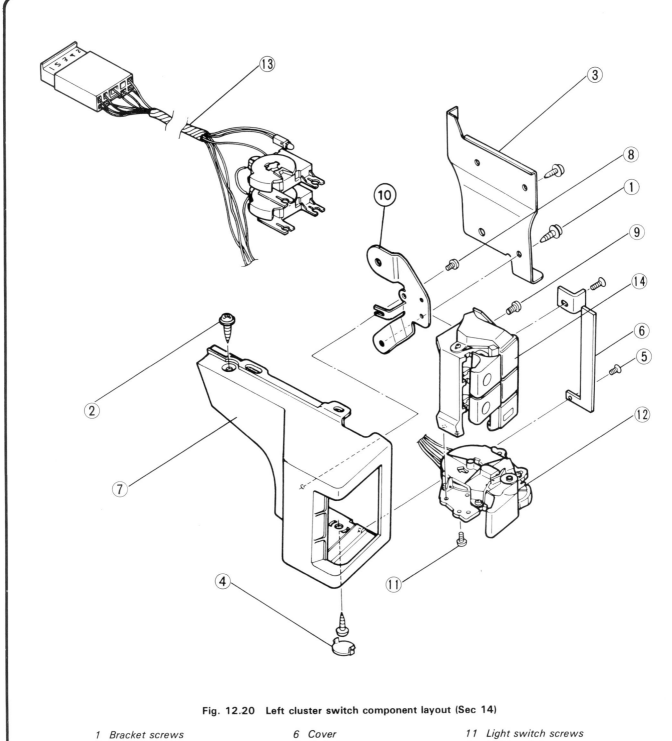

Fig. 12.20 Left cluster switch component layout (Sec 14)

1 Bracket screws	6 Cover	11 Light switch screws
2 Cover screw	7 Switch cover	12 Light switch
3 Bracket	8 Screw	13 Wiring harness
4 Screws and cover	9 Switch screw	14 Hazard lights and rear
5 Cover screws	10 Bracket	window defogger switch

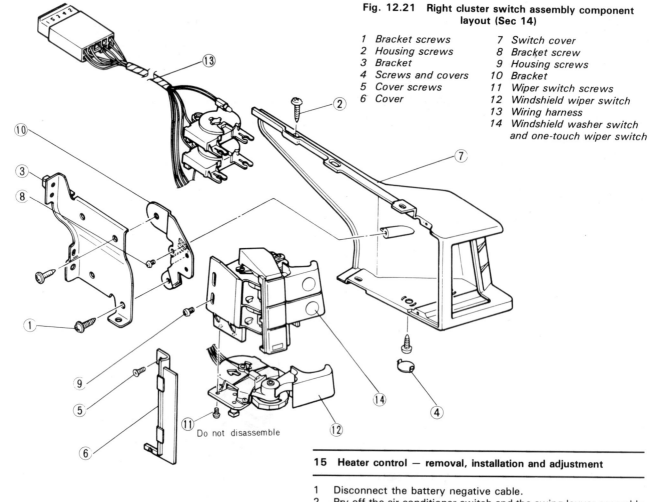

Fig. 12.21 Right cluster switch assembly component layout (Sec 14)

1 Bracket screws
2 Housing screws
3 Bracket
4 Screws and covers
5 Cover screws
6 Cover
7 Switch cover
8 Bracket screw
9 Housing screws
10 Bracket
11 Wiper switch screws
12 Windshield wiper switch
13 Wiring harness
14 Windshield washer switch and one-touch wiper switch

Do not disassemble

Fig. 12.22 Disconnect the cluster switch wiring harness by pressing in the direction shown with a flat blade screwdriver (Sec 14)

15 Heater control — removal, installation and adjustment

1 Disconnect the battery negative cable.
2 Pry off the air conditioner switch and the swing louver assembly and disconnect them for access to the control assembly retaining screws (photos).
3 Remove the control assembly retaining screws and remove it from the instrument panel (photo).
4 Unplug the electrical connector from the control unit.
5 Disconnect the control wires (photo).
6 Installation is the reverse of removal except for connection and adjustment of the control wires described below.

Mode wire

7 With the control knob set to Defrost and the mode lever pushed all the way forward, connect the wire and install the clamp.

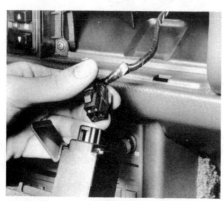

15.2a Pry the air conditioner switch off with a screwdriver for access to the screws

15.2b Squeeze the connector and unplug it from the swing louver

15.3 Heater control retaining screw locations (arrows)

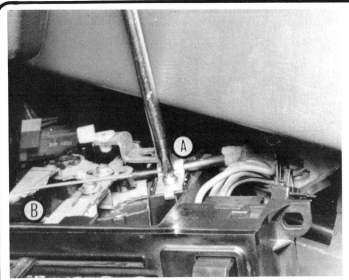

15.5 Disconnect the heater control wires by removing the clamp (A) and unhooking the end (B)

Fig. 12.23 Heater assembly component layout (Sec 15)

1 Heater unit
2 Air duct
3 Blower unit
4 Defroster duct
5 Defroster nozzle
6 Defroster nozzle grille
7 Center duct
8 Duct No. 1
9 Duct No. 2
10 Left side louver assembly
11 Duct No.3
12 Blower duct
13 Duct No. 4
14 Right side louver assembly
15 Duct No. 5
16 Louver panel assembly
17 Assist side duct
18 Front rear heater duct
19 Right rear heater duct
20 Left rear heater duct
21 Center louver assembly
22 Swing louver
23 Control assembly

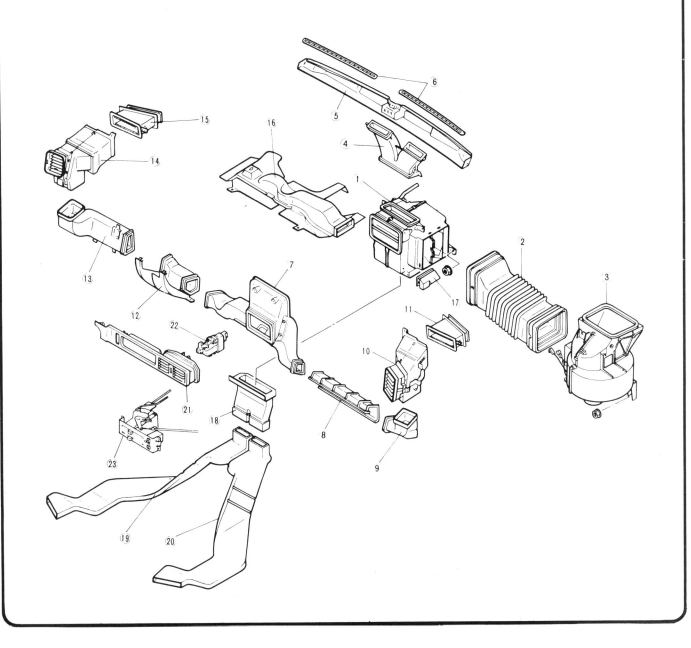

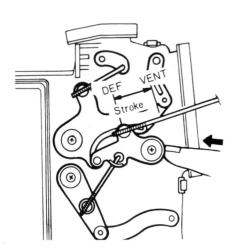

Fig. 12.24 Heater control mode wire adjustment (Sec 15)

15.9 The heater temperature control wire correctly connected to the selector lever

8 Connect the battery cable, turn the blower switch to the 4 position and make sure there are no air leaks from the center and floor area outlets.

Temperature control wire

9 Set the temperature control knob to Cold and push the heat/cool selection lever all the way up to the Cold position and connect the wire and clamp (photo).
10 The selection lever must move all the way from Cold to Hot as shown in the accompanying illustration.

Recirculated/fresh air selection wire

11 Pull the mode control knob fully outward.
12 With the recirculated/fresh air selection wire pulled out all the way to the Rec position, connect the wire and install the clamp.
13 Check for proper operation by pulling the control knob in and out several times.

16 Windshield wiper motor and linkage assembly — removal and installation

1 Disconnect the negative battery cable.
2 Remove the wiper arms by undoing the nuts and pulling the arms off their splines.
3 Remove the cowl and service hole cover.
4 Remove the linkage and motor retaining bolts, unplug the electrical connector and disengage the motor from the linkage as shown in the accompanying illustrations.
5 Withdraw the linkage from the vehicle through the body access hole.
6 Installation is the reverse of the removal procedure, making sure that the arm height is adjusted as shown in the accompanying illustration.

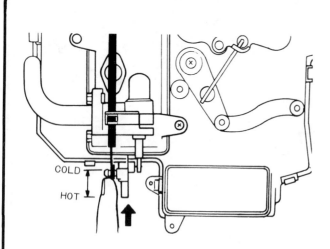

Fig. 12.25 Heater temperature control wire adjustment
(Sec 15)

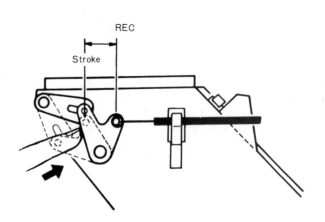

Fig. 12.26 Recirculation/fresh air selection wire
adjustment (Sec 15)

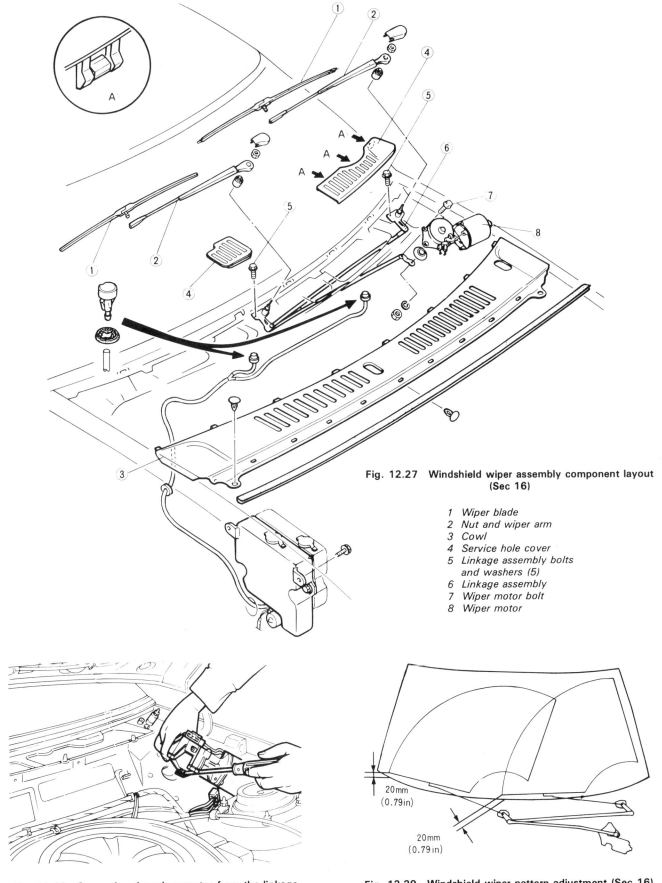

Fig. 12.27 Windshield wiper assembly component layout
(Sec 16)

1 Wiper blade
2 Nut and wiper arm
3 Cowl
4 Service hole cover
5 Linkage assembly bolts
  and washers (5)
6 Linkage assembly
7 Wiper motor bolt
8 Wiper motor

Fig. 12.28 Separating the wiper motor from the linkage
with a screwdriver (Sec 16)

Fig. 12.29 Windshield wiper pattern adjustment (Sec 16)

20mm
(0.79 in)

20mm
(0.79 in)

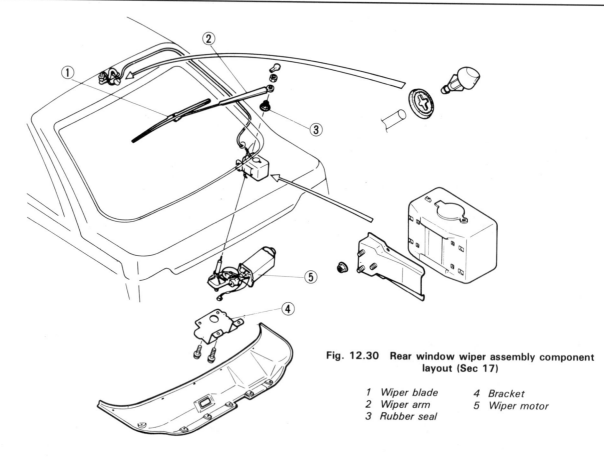

Fig. 12.30   Rear window wiper assembly component layout (Sec 17)

1 *Wiper blade*	4 *Bracket*
2 *Wiper arm*	5 *Wiper motor*
3 *Rubber seal*	

17   Rear window wiper assembly — removal and installation

1   Disconnect the battery negative cable.
2   Remove the wiper blade and arm assembly and the rubber seal.
3   Open the rear hatch and remove trim panel.
4   Remove the retaining bolts, bracket and wiper motor.
5   Installation is the reverse of removal, making sure to check the wiper arm height adjustment as shown in the illustration.

18   Power radio antenna — removal and installation

1   Remove the dash under panel, glove compartment, and the heater air duct and blower unit.
2   Remove the side trim and disconnect the antenna feed, but not the power.
3   Remove the antenna motor bracket with the motor and antenna pole.

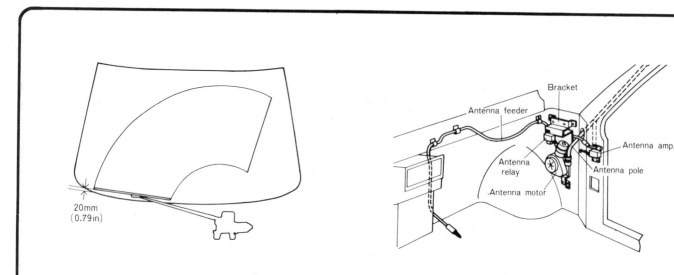

Fig. 12.31   Rear window wiper pattern (Sec 17)

Fig. 12.32   Power radio antenna installation detail (Sec 18)

4   To remove the antenna, first insert a flat blade screwdriver into the slot in the antenna pole and pull the antenna out approximately 1/2-inch as shown in the accompanying illustration.

5   Apply battery power to the B and BG terminals of the connector and pull the antenna out of the motor as shown in the accompanying illustration (Fig. 12.34).

6   Loosen the two antenna-to-pillar screws and remove the antenna pole from the body.

7   Install the antenna to the body and insert the toothed end of the antenna rope into the motor. Apply battery power as shown in the accompanying illustration (Fig. 12.35) to draw the antenna into the motor and push the antenna pole into the motor until it locks.

8   Install the motor and bracket assembly.

9   If the antenna does not extend fully, operate the motor several times to automatically adjust out any slack in the antenna rope.

19   Rear defogger (electric grid type) — check and repair

1   This option consists of a rear window with a number of horizontal elements that are baked into the glass surface during the glass forming operation.

2   Small breaks in the element can be repaired without removing the rear window.

3   To test the grids for proper operation, start the engine and turn on the system.

4   Ground one lead of a test light and carefully touch the other lead to each element line.

5   The brilliance of the test light should increase as the lead is moved across the element from right to left. If the test light glows brightly at both ends of the lines, check for a loose ground wire. All of the lines should be checked in at least two places.

6   To repair a break in a line, it is recommended that a repair kit specifically for this purpose be purchased from a dealer.

7   To repair a break, first turn off the system and allow it to de-energize for a few minutes.

8   Clean the area thoroughly with alcohol or paint thinner.

9   Apply strips of electrical tape to both sides of the area to be repaired. The space between the pieces of tape should be the same width as the existing lines. This can be checked from outside the vehicle.

Press the tape tightly against the glass to prevent seepage.

10 Using small brush or a marking pen, apply the silver paint mixture between the pieces of tape, overlapping the undamaged area slightly on either end.

11 Allow the repair to set for 24 hours or apply a constant stream of hot air directly to the repaired area. At 140°F the paint will dry in 30 minutes.

12 Although the defogger is now fully operational, the repaired area should not be disturbed for at least 24 hours.

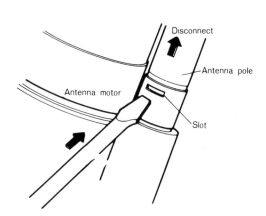

Fig. 12.33   Insert a screwdriver into the antenna pole and pull up on the antenna to remove (Sec 18)

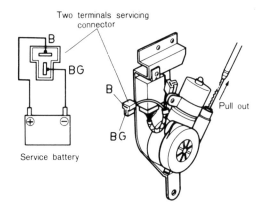

Fig. 12.34   Apply battery power to the connector as shown to release the antenna from the motor (Sec 18)

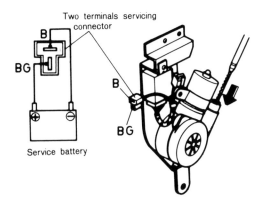

Fig. 12.35   Insert the antenna toothed rope and apply power to draw it into the motor (Sec 18)

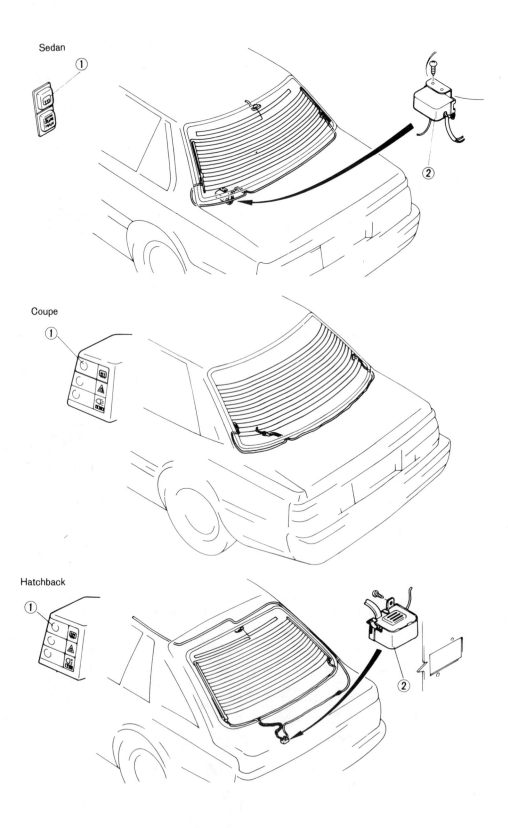

Sedan

Coupe

Hatchback

Fig. 12.36 Rear window defogger component layout (Sec 19)

1 *Defogger switch*   2 *Noise filter*

20 Sound warning system — general information

1   On models so equipped, the sound warning system alerts the driver to various malfunctions and operator errors by means of four different 'chimes'.

2   System and functions monitored are as follows:

Key left in ignition — Chime A
Door ajar — Chime C
Low fluid level/low oil pressure/no charge/rear light bulb
   blown — Chime D
Lights left on — Chime E

3   The warning unit is located behind the instrument panel on the driver's side. Any malfunction should be referred to a Mazda dealer or auto electrical specialist.

4   Do not disconnect the warning unit as a means of silencing it, since the function of some of the warning lights will also be upset.

21 Bulb checker system — precautions

1   The bulb checker system (when equipped) monitors the stop and tail lights. The system uses a special relay (the Stop and Tail Light Checker) which senses the current drawn by the right-hand and left-hand rear light circuits. An imbalance in the current drawn by the two sides, such as occurs when one bulb has blown, trips the relay and operates a warning light and/or chime.

2   From the above it will be obvious that any imbalance between the two lighting circuits can trip the relay. Such imbalance can be caused by installing bulbs of incorrect wattage. Sometimes two bulbs of different manufacture, although nominally of the same wattage, are sufficiently dissimilar to trip the relay and give a false alarm.

3   Wiring for a trailer socket must be arranged so that the current for the trailer lights does not pass through the checker relay, which could otherwise be damaged by the additional current drawn. Obtain a Mazda wiring kit designed for your vehicle, or consult an auto electrician.

22 Cruise control — general information

1   On models so equipped, the cruise control enables a steady speed to be maintained, regardless of gradients or other factors, without the driver touching the throttle. The main components of the system are shown in Fig. 12.37.

2   In the event of malfunction, check that the appropriate fuse is intact; that the actuator vacuum hose is attached at both ends and in good condition; and that the actuator control cable is adjusted so that there is 0.04 to 0.12 inch free play in the resting position.

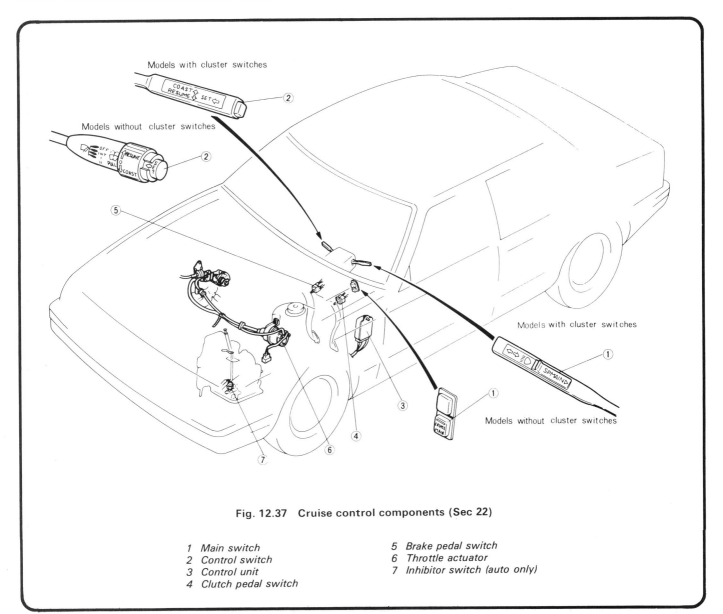

Fig. 12.37 Cruise control components (Sec 22)

1   Main switch
2   Control switch
3   Control unit
4   Clutch pedal switch
5   Brake pedal switch
6   Throttle actuator
7   Inhibitor switch (auto only)

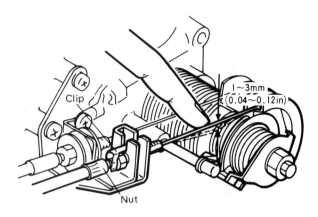

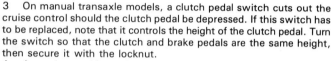

Fig. 12.38 Actuator cable adjustment (Sec 22)

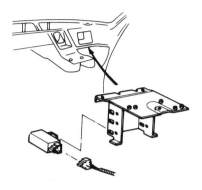

Fig. 12.39 Flasher unit location (Sec 23)

3   On manual transaxle models, a clutch pedal switch cuts out the cruise control should the clutch pedal be depressed. If this switch has to be replaced, note that it controls the height of the clutch pedal. Turn the switch so that the clutch and brake pedals are the same height, then secure it with the locknut.
4   Any other problem with the cruise control should be referred to a Mazda dealer or other specialist.

23 Flasher unit — removal and installation

1   A common flasher unit serves both the direction indicator and the hazard warning flasher systems. It is located on a bracket to the left of the steering column.
2   Disconnect the battery negative lead.
3   Remove the trim from below the instrument panel on the driver's side.
4   Slide the flasher unit out of its bracket, unplug the electrical connector and remove it.
5   Installation is a reversal of removal.

24 Fuel and temperature gauges — testing

1   If the fuel or temperature gauges give inaccurate readings, the problem may lie in the gauge or in the sender unit. With some simple equip-

ment (a multi-meter and some resistors) it is possible to test the gauges and senders.

Fuel gauge

2   Gain access to the fuel gauge sender unit by removing the rear seat and the inspection cover. Unplug the wiring connector.
3   Connect a resistor, of known value between 8 and 96 ohms, between the wiring connector 'Y' terminal and ground (vehicle metal). Make sure that no live wires are touching ground, then switch on the ignition.
4   Allow two minutes for the gauge reading to stabilize, then refer to Fig. 12.41 or 12.42 and compare the expected gauge reading with that actually obtained.
5   Repeat the test if possible with other values of resistor within the stated range. Switch off the ignition before changing resistors.
6   If the gauge reads 'full' or 'empty' regardless of the value of resistor, it may be that the wiring to the gauge is short-circuited or broken respectively. Otherwise, inaccurate readings are due to a fault in the gauge.

Fuel gauge sender

7   Remove the securing screws and withdraw the sender unit. **Warning:** *Take appropriate precautions against fire and fume intoxication.* Remove the sender unit from the vehicle.
8   Connect a multi-meter, set to measure resistance, across the sender unit terminals. Move the float up and down and compare the resistance at various positions with the values in Fig. 12.44.
9   If the resistance does not vary as specified, the sender unit must be replaced. Install the sender unit on completion.

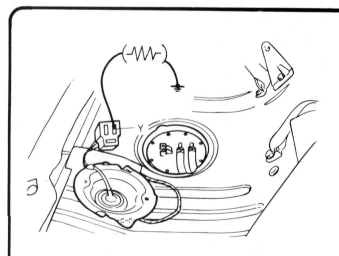

Fig. 12.40 Testing the fuel gauge (Sec 24)

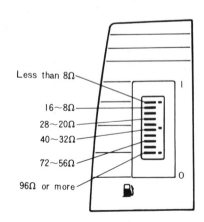

Fig. 12.41 Electronic fuel gauge readings for various resistances (Sec 24)

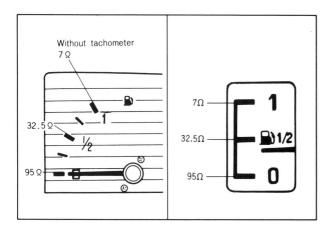

Fig. 12.42   Analog fuel gauge readings for various resistances (Sec 24)

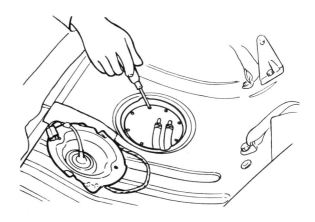

Fig. 12.43   Removing the fuel gauge sender unit (Sec 24)

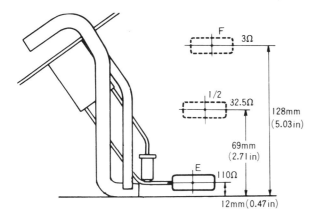

Fig. 12.44   Fuel gauge sender resistance values (Sec 24)

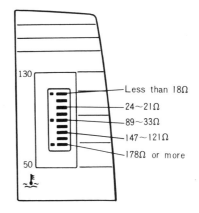

Fig. 12.45   Electronic temperature gauge readings for various resistances (Sec 24)

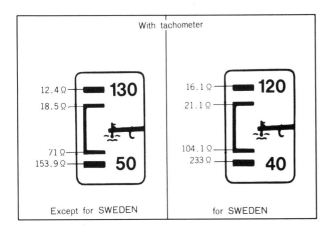

Fig. 12.46   Analog temperature gauge readings for various resistances — models with tachometer (Sec 24)

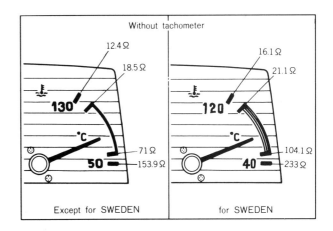

Fig. 12.47   Analog temperature gauge readings for various resistances — models without tachometer (Sec 24)

Temperature gauge

10   Unplug the electrical connector from the temperature gauge sender (located in the rear section of the thermostat housing).

11   Connect a resistor, of known value and within the limits shown in Fig. 12.45, 12.46, or 12.47, between the sender lead connector and ground.

12   Make sure that no live wires are touching ground, then switch on the ignition. Allow two minutes for the gauge reading to stabilize, then compare the expected reading with that actually obtained. Repeat if possible with other resistors.

13   If the gauge reads maximum or minimum regardless of resistor value, it may be that the wiring is short-circuited or broken respectively. Otherwise, inaccurate readings are due to a fault in the gauge.

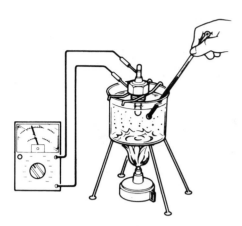

Fig. 12.48   Testing the temperature gauge sender unit (Sec 24)

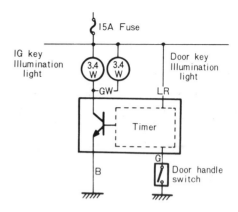

Fig. 12.49   Lock illumination system circuit diagram (Sec 25)

Temperature gauge sender

14   Drain the cooling system to below the level of the sender unit. Unscrew the sender unit and remove it.

15   Suspend the sender unit over a pan of water so that its bulb is immersed. Connect a multi-meter, set to measure resistance, to the body and the terminal of the unit. Heat the water to 176 °F (80 °C): the resistance at this temperature should be 53.5 ± 4.2 ohms.

16   If the resistance is out of limits, replace the sender unit.

17   Install the sender unit and refill the cooling system.

25   Lock illumination system — general information

1   On models so equipped, the lock illumination system lights up the driver's door lock and the ignition switch for approximately 20 seconds after the door handle is raised.

2   Apart from the lights themselves, the components of the system are a timer unit, located on a bracket beside the steering column, and a door handle switch.

3   Replacement of the ignition switch light bulb is included in Section 10.

4   Both the lock illumination light and the door handle switch are accessed by removing the door trim panel (Chapter 11). The door exterior handle must be removed in order to replace the switch.

26   Rear light cluster — lens replacement

1   Remove the bulb housing unit as described in Section 10.

2   Remove the nuts which secure the lens assembly (four nuts on Sedan and Coupe models, seven nuts on the Liftback). Withdraw the lens and seal.

3   Individual lenses can be removed after softening the glue which holds them in place, using a hair dryer or hot air gun.

4   Install the new lens, if possible re-using the old glue by heating it and pressing the lens into position. If insufficient glue is left for re-use, apply fresh glue to the grooves in the lens housing.

5   Check the assembled lens unit for leaks by floating it in a water bath.

6   Installation is the reversal of removal.

27   Relays — identification and replacement

1   The number and function of relays fitted will vary according to model and equipment. Typical installations are shown in Fig. 12.54.

2   If an electrical system incorporating a relay develops a fault, remember that it could be a bad relay causing the problem. Test if possible by substituting a known good relay.

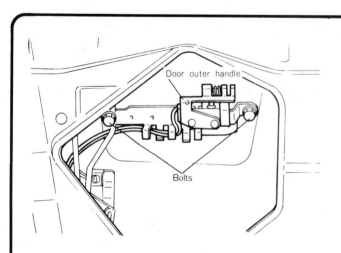

Fig. 12.50   Door handle switch secured to door outer handle (Sec 25)

Fig. 12.51   Softening the glue with a hot air gun (Sec 26)

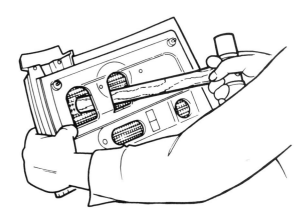

Fig. 12.52 Pushing out the old lens with a hammer handle
(Sec 26)

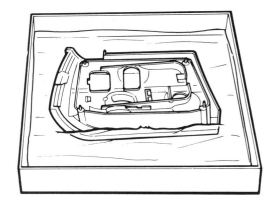

Fig. 12.53 Floating the lens unit in a water bath to check
for leaks (Sec 26)

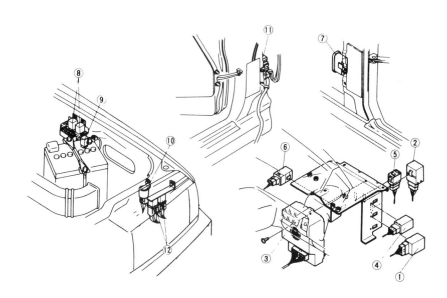

Fig. 12.54 Relay locations and functions (Sec 27)

1 Wiper delay	5 PTC heater relay (not UK)	9 Ignition relay
2 Stop/tail light checker	6 Flasher unit	10 Radiator fan relay
3 Audible warning unit	7 Horn relay	11 Central locking relay
4 Lock illumination timer	8 Headlight relay	12 Air conditioner relay

3   To replace a relay, release it from any securing clips or screws, then unplug it from its wiring connector.
4   Installation is the reversal of removal.

28 Speedometer cable — removal and installation

1   Remove the securing bolt and withdraw the speedometer cable and gear from the transaxle. See Chapter 1, Section 4.
2   Partly withdraw the instrument panel cluster (meter) as described in Section 12 until the rear of the speedometer is accessible. Unclip the cable from the speedometer.
3   Free the cable from the firewall and remove it from under the hood.
4   Transfer any grommets, and if necessary the driven gear, from the old cable to the new one.

5   Installation is a reversal of removal. Do not kink the new cable during installation, nor route it through tight bends.

29 Washer pumps — removal and installation

1   All models have a windshield washer pump. According to equipment, there may be additional pumps for the rear window and headlight washers.
2   Removal is similar in every case. First empty the reservoir as far as possible, or make arrangements to catch spilt washer fluid.
3   Disconnect the hoses and wiring connector from the pump. Remove the pump, either by pulling it out of the reservoir (when so mounted) or by releasing it from its securing clip.
4   Installation is a reversal of removal. Use new sealing grommets, hoses, etc. as necessary.

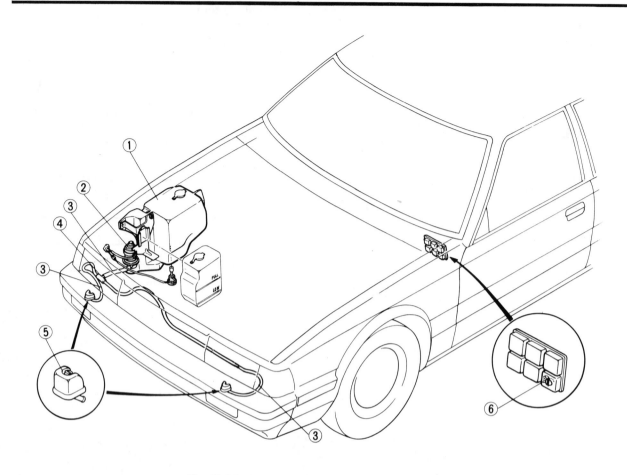

Fig. 12.55 Headlight washer components (Sec 29)

1 Reservoir	3 Hoses	5 Jets
2 Pump	4 Check valve	6 Control switch

Colour code

B	Black	Lb	Light blue	R	Red
Br	Brown	Lg	Light green	Y	Yellow
G	Green	O	Orange	W	White
L	Blue				

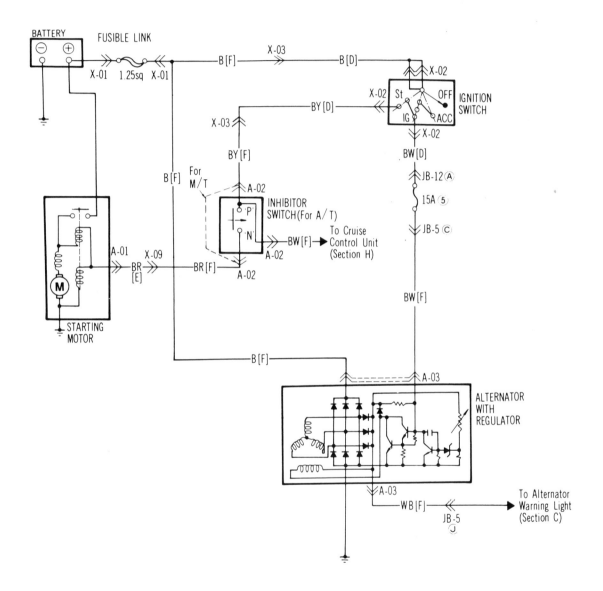

Charging and starting system wiring diagram (right hand drive models)

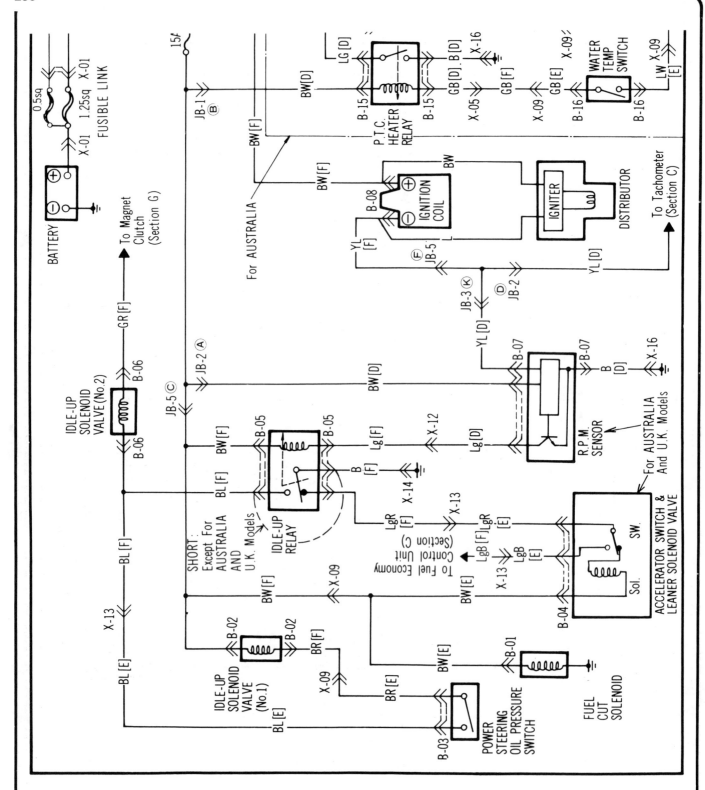

Engine control system wiring diagram (right hand drive models)

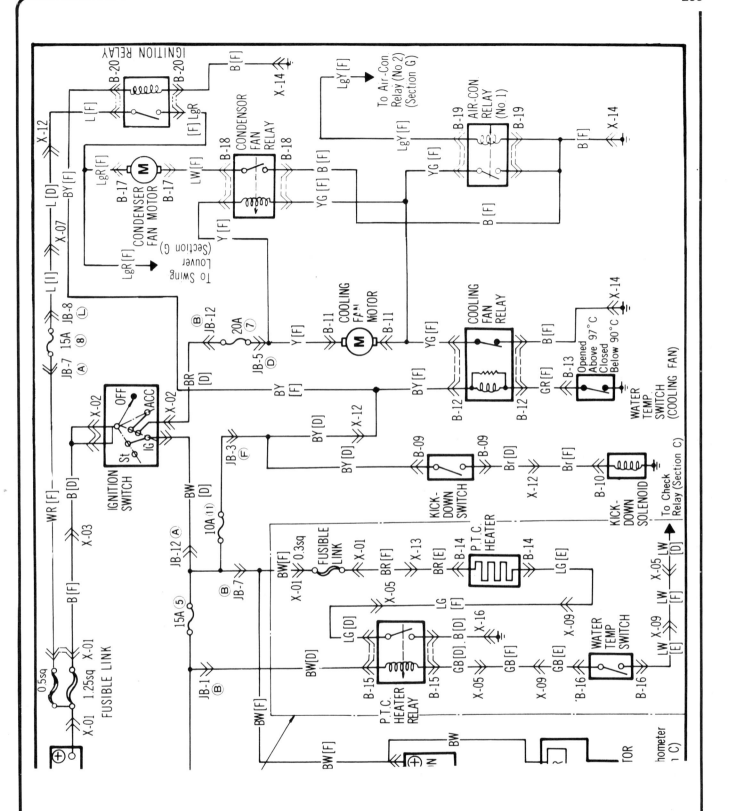

Engine control system wiring diagram (right hand drive models) (continued)

Instrument panel meters and warning lights and sound warning system wiring diagram (right hand drive models)

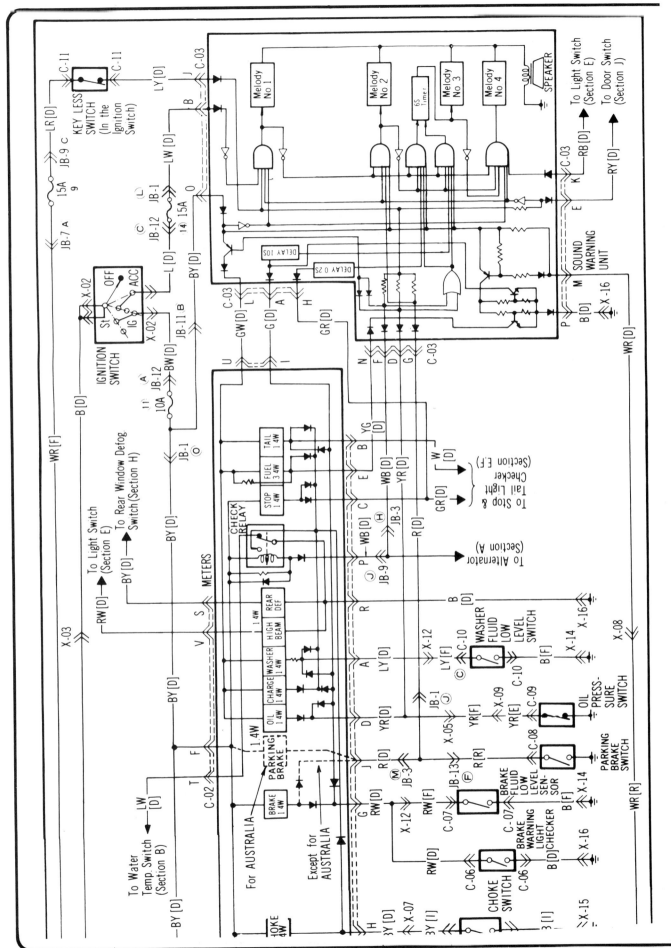

Instrument panel meters and warning lights and sound warning system wiring diagram (right hand models) (continued)

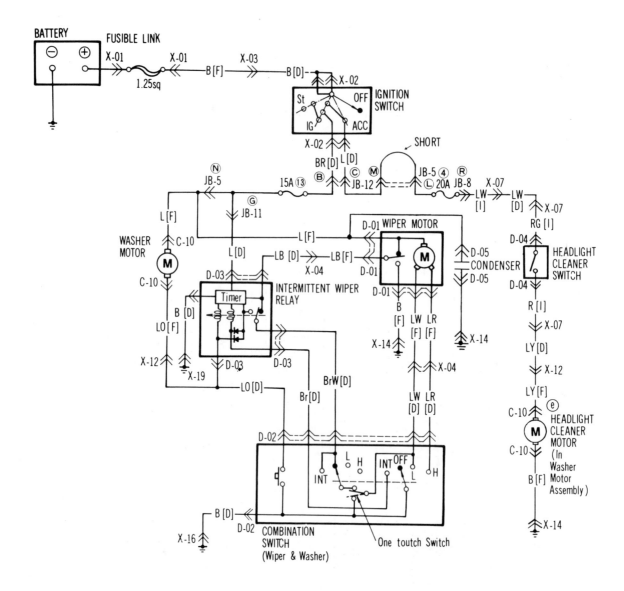

Wiper/washer and headlight washer (all except 5-door models) wiring diagram (right hand drive models)

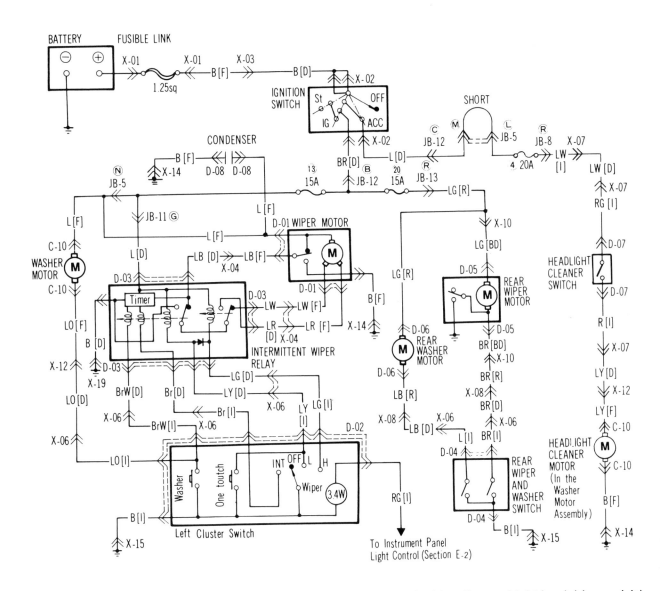

Wiper/washer, headlight cleaner and rear wiper/washer (5-door models) wiring diagram (right hand drive models)

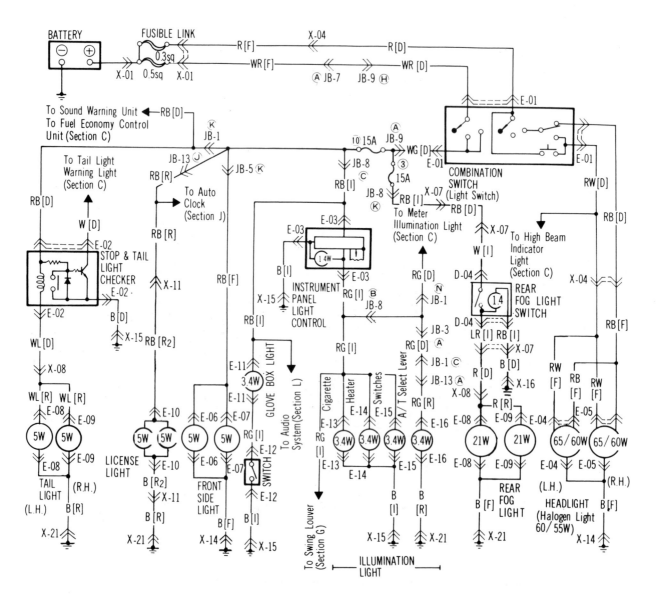

Headlight, tail, front side, front and rear marker, license and illumination lights wiring diagram (right hand drive models)

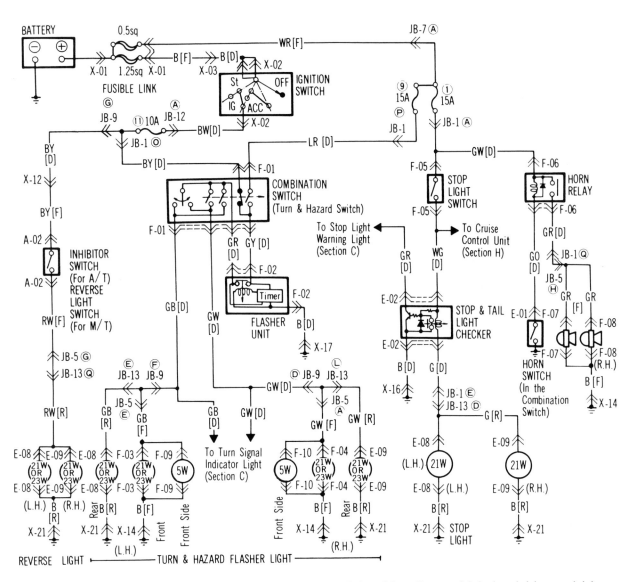

Turn and hazard flasher lights, horn, stop lights, backup, light wiring diagram (right hand drive models)

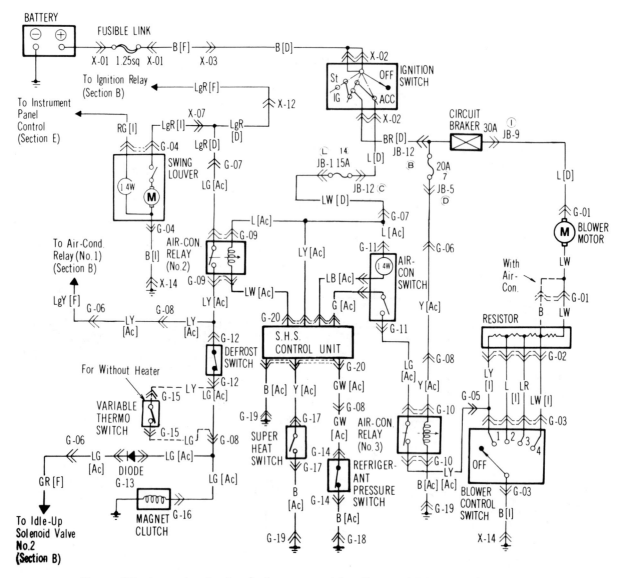

Air conditioning and swing louver fan motor wiring diagram (right hand drive models)

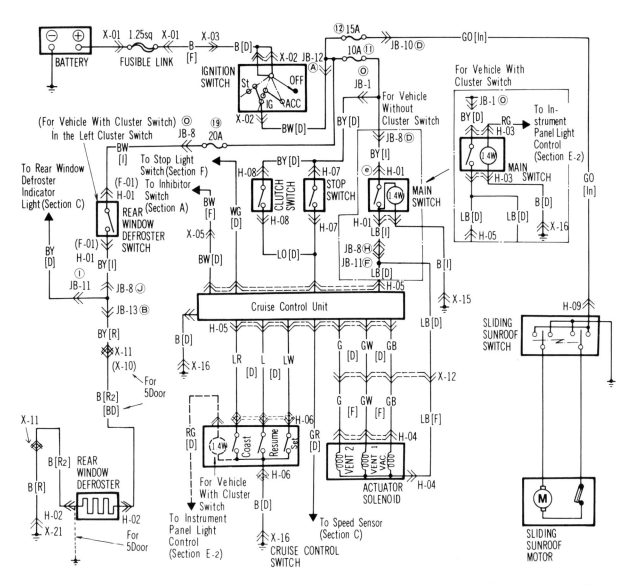

Rear window defroster, cruise control system and sliding sunroof wiring diagram (right hand drive models)

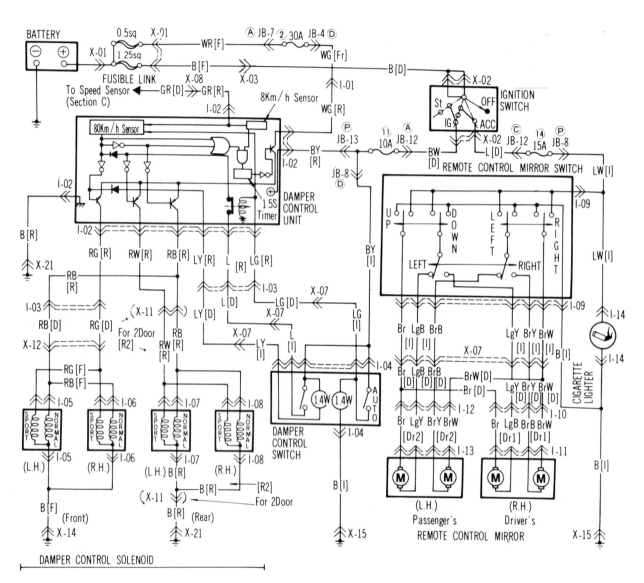

3-way adjustable damping system, power mirror and cigarette lighter wiring diagram (right hand drive models)

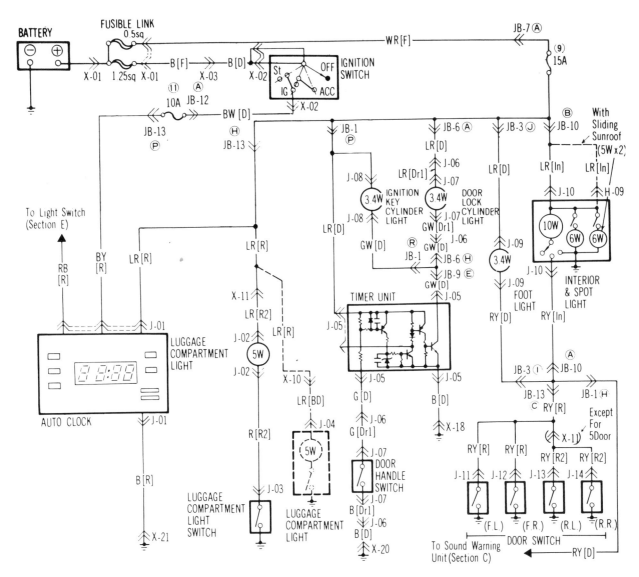

Digital clock, luggage compartment, ignition key, door lock, interior, spot and foot light wiring diagram (right hand drive models)

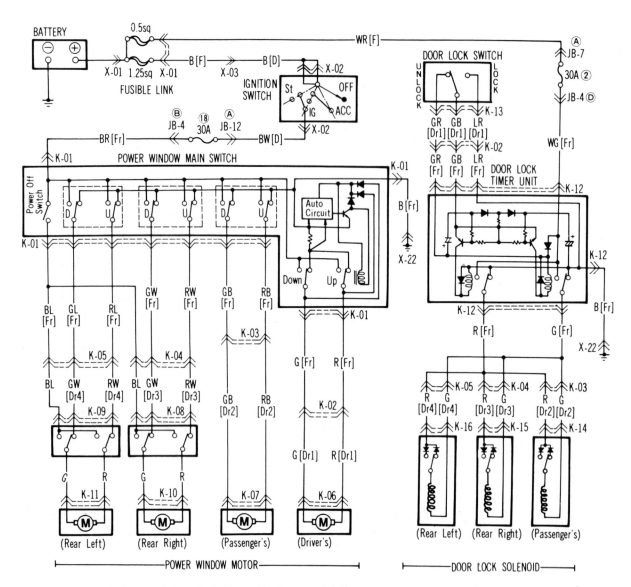

Power window and door lock (4- and 5-door models) wiring diagram (right hand drive models)

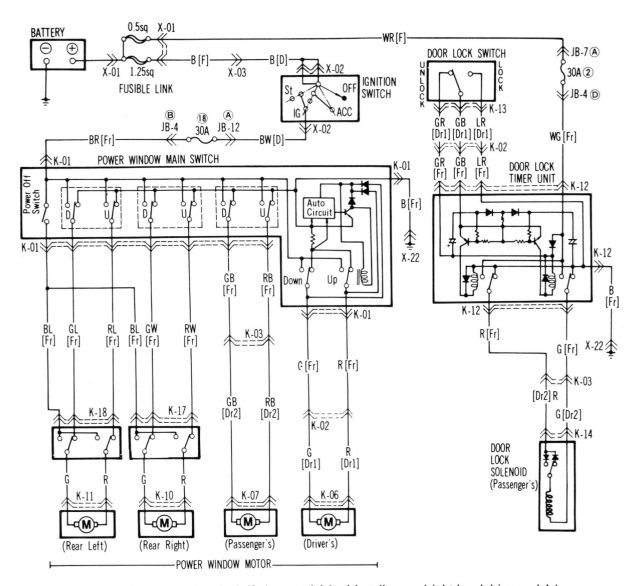

Power window and door lock (2-door models) wiring diagram (right hand drive models)

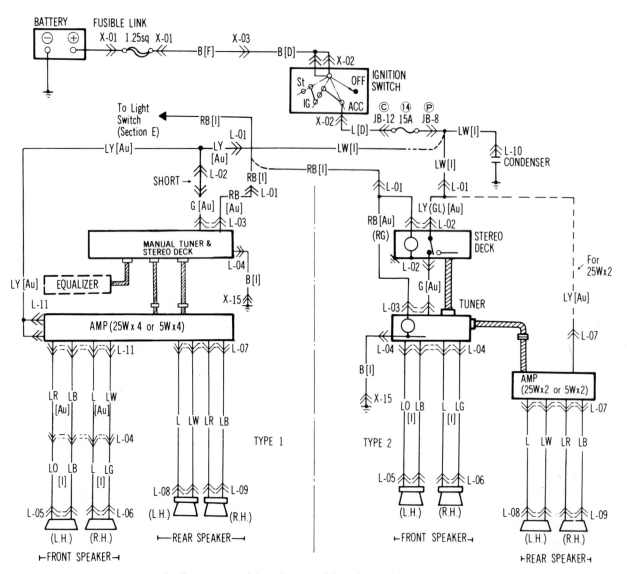

Audio system wiring diagram (right hand drive models)

Glossary

American	English	American	English
Antenna	Aerial	Muffler	Silencer
Axleshaft	Driveshaft, halfshaft	Natural gas	Gas (cooking or heating fuel)
Back-up (1)	Reverse (gear etc)	Oil pan	Sump
Back-up (2)	Counterhold (eg of locknut)	Panel wagon	Van
Barrel (of carburetor)	Choke, venturi	Parking brake	Handbrake
Blocked (of wheels)	Chocked	Parking light	Sidelight
Box and wrench	Ring spanner	Pinging (of engine)	Pinking
Bugs	Insects	Piston pin	Gudgeon pin
Coast	Freewheel	Primary shoe (of brakes)	Leading shoe
Cotter pin	Split pin	Prussian blue	Engineer's blue
Countershaft	Layshaft	Pry	Lever, prise
Damper (suspension)	Shock absorber	Quarter window	Quarterlight
Denatured alcohol	Methylated spirit	Recap	Retread
Dome lamp	Interior light	Regular	Normal, ordinary (grade)
Driveaxle	Driveshaft	Reinstall	Refit
Fender	Wing	Replace (1)	Renew
Fender well	Wheel arch	Replace (2 – rare)	Refit
Firewall	Bulkhead	Ring gear (of differential)	Crownwheel
Flashlight	Torch	Rocker panel	Sill (beneath door)
Float bowl	Float chamber	Rotor (brake)	Disc
Freeway	Motorway	Rubbing alcohol	Surgical spirit
Frozen	Seized	Secondary shoe (of brake)	Trailing shoe
Gas, gasoline	Petrol	Sedan	Saloon
Gas pedal	Accelerator	Shift	Gearchange
Ground (electrical)	Earth	Shop	Workshop
Header	Exhaust manifold	Side marker lights	Side indicator lights
Heat riser	Hot spot	Snap ring	Circlip
High (gear)	Top gear	Soft plugs	Core plugs
Hood	Bonnet (engine cover)	Stabilizer, sway bar	Anti-roll bar
Hot tank	Chemical cleaning/degreasing process	Standard (bolt etc)	Imperial (as opposed to metric)
		Station wagon	Estate
Install	Refit, fit	Store	Shop
Instrument cluster	Instrument panel	Tie-rod	Track rod
Instrument panel	Dashboard, facia	Throw-out bearing	Thrust bearing
Jackstands	Axle stands	Transaxle	Transmission (gearbox and differential)
Jam nut	Locknut		
Keepers (valve)	Split collets, cotters	Troubleshooting	Fault diagnosis
Kerosene	Paraffin	Trunk	Boot (luggage area)
Lash	Free play, clearance	Valve cover	Rocker cover
Latch	Catch (of door etc), lock	Valve lifter	Tapper, cam follower
License plate	Number plate	Vise	Vice (workshop tool)
Liftback	Hatchback	Vise-grip pliers	'Mole' wrench
Lineman's pliers	Electrical pliers	Windshield	Windscreen
Lug (engine)	Drive in too high a gear	Wrecking yard	Breaker's yard, scrapyard
Lug nuts	Wheel nuts	Wrench	Spanner
Meter	Instrument panel	Wrist pin	Gudgeon pin

Index